C000178359

Living Mobile

Integrated Solutions
On Wheels or On the Water

Living Mobile

Integrated Solutions
On Wheels or On the Water

Dave Jones

Ruinoll Impressions

Living Mobile

Any instruction and advice offered herein is made in good faith but is not intended to substitute for professional knowledge or consultation in the relevant areas. Be cautious and take care in all that you do.

References and links to other works and resources are intended as mere conveniences for the reader for the purpose of further edification. References and links offered by no means imply any relationship, affiliation, sponsorship, endorsement, or any sort of approval regarding the linked content or the operators of those resources linked. All sample prices given are from the website noted as of time of writing and may not reflect current prices.

Ruinoll Impressions

3916 N Potsdam Ave #1473
Sioux Falls, South Dakota 57104

Publisher's Cataloging-in-Publication Data

Names: Jones, Dave, author.
Title: Living Mobile: Integrated Solutions on Wheels or On the Water / Dave Jones
Description: Sioux Falls, SD : Ruinoll Impressions, [2020] | Includes references.
Identifiers: ISBN 9781735623306 (hardback) | ISBN 9781735623313 (paperback) | ISBN 9781735623320 (ebook)
Subjects: Travel | DIY | Boating | Camping | Cruising | Adventure | Electronics | Lifestyles

Copyright © 2020 by Dave Jones

All rights reserved. No part of this book may be reproduced or transmitted in any form or by any means, electronic or mechanical, including photocopying, recording, or by any information storage and retrieval system without the written permission of the publisher, except where permitted by law.

Contents

Part 2—Builds

Part 3—Extras

Introduction

This is an ideas book. The references and details on offer here are available elsewhere, sometimes in better or more complete form, though I have tried to make things as complete as possible given the scope of the work. My writing itself is in a particular style that I realize may be awkward for some people to read. But I think that the book was worth writing, and will be worth your time and effort to read, because of the ideas and insights that are included herein. These sparks, or seeds, are the distilled value at the heart of the book. Everything else, descriptions and details and extrapolations and references, is used to evoke and flesh out those ideas, to make them fully formed and explored instead of just half-baked. So read on, if you will, and share in my ideas and those of others.

Each section is encapsulated in itself and can be read as a stand-alone, though there are also many interconnected aspects of the work. So if all you care about is learning more about electric propulsion, for example, you might read the sections on Propulsion and Electricity and the Extras sections on Marine Electric Propulsion and On Batteries and on Protecting Electronics. Though if that is all that you read you will be missing out on many other ideas. Electric propulsion is a central theme in the book but by no means the only one. Given the way I have arranged things there is no need to read every section in order, though I sometimes refer to other sections either 'above' or 'below' a particular section and if you have the patience things may make more sense if read from front to back. In the Builds sections in particular I often assume that the reader has knowledge of the previous similar builds, either wheeled or marine.

Part One is about fulfilling needs. I have attempted to make this a go-to reference for any given need or problem that might come up for someone in a mobile living situation. Or indeed for anyone who might want to make their living solution a mobile one. I have arranged the sections in terms of the life needs or consequences that may confront the person living mobile. This book is a hub, a place to start before diving in further. Use it as such and I hope it will prove to be of value to you.

This book is not a detailed instruction manual for anything in particular. Instead, I have tried to broaden its scope sufficiently to encompass any need that might come up for you as you pursue the dream of living mobile. Each section offers further references by which you might find that detailed instruction manual, or at least further information. Nor is it geared toward the needs of static living solutions—specifically. I hope that there may be a great deal of overlap, or sufficient such to make this useful for off-grid static solutions. Neither have I devoted anything specifically to addressing the needs of the digital nomad that is not trying to take their home with them as they travel. But I hope such a person may find something herein for themselves as well.

There are many different types of mobile living. This book tries to provide solutions for those living mobile on wheels or on the water. Sadly, it does not seem feasible, as yet, to achieve a flying mobile home. So, whether you are part of the RV crowd or a cruising sailor, whether you are living in a converted tugboat or an old school bus, whether you are building your own camper or dreamily designing your own motor-yacht, this book will have something for you. Each needs section strives to include all important considerations for both wheeled and marine living. I have also noticed that some people like to trade off between them. If this is you then I am pleased to provide some consideration for all of your solutions in one book.

My object, in offering aid for you to solve each need, is in achieving and maintaining standards of civilization while living mobile. Most of us will not want to escape our real estate or apartment living only to forsake the standards and comforts which are an integral part of contemporary civilization. You need not feel that mobile living will mean you are on a permanent camping trip, sacrificing most convenience and standards in order to be free. I do not attempt to define for you what living a civilized life means; instead I attempt to offer a range of solutions for any given need for you to choose from, which may be anywhere from bare minimum up to quite luxurious. There will always be trade-offs, just as there are in static living, but by 'sacrificing' in areas that you consider less important you may achieve higher standards in other areas. Energy and communications technology has reached such a point that we are enabled to achieve civilized living without being tied down.

This is especially true because of the potential synergy attainable by integrating the disparate aspects of our living solutions. One way to so integrate is to have networked computer control of all electronic devices, ranging from a pump keeping your water system pressurized to your refrigerator interface to your GPS to your solar panels to your speaker setup...and so on. Everything electronic can be interfaced and networked for centralized control. But this is not the core of what I mean by integrated solutions. Instead, integrating is achieved by considering all aspects of your living situation, all needs that press upon you, as being solvable in conjunction rather than separately. The different systems are all inter-related and may work together to fulfill your life needs. The water system cannot be fully understood in isolation from the electric system or the waste system or the entertainment system—these are all subsystems of your home and should be designed and realized as such.

Hence my verbal focus on mobile living solutions rather than other ways of phrasing what you are trying to achieve. Your marine or wheeled home is an ongoing solution because the problems will also be ongoing. You will have to meet your needs every day and those needs must be met as part of an integrated solution rather than considered in isolation. This mindset may be more or less valuable for static living as well, but is critical for mobile living. Space is too tight and safety margins are too thin for you to...solve a problem with your propulsion system without also considering what impact that solution will have on the rest of the boat, for example. Or you may discover that you can solve two problems, or three or four, by changing one thing rather than all of them. Know your subsystems and how they inter-relate. You may never be an expert in the various fields that they represent, but you can be an expert in your own home, your own particular solutions, regardless of how complex the individual components may be. Your mobile living solution is your vehicle to achieving your dreams, your integrated solution—think of it as such.

Part Two of this book is dedicated to offering sample integrated solutions for your consideration. I have tried to include samples which do not fit the norms but nonetheless provide viable integrated living solutions. It is my hope that these sample solutions, which may not be perfect for any of you, will help to stimulate your own process as you seek out your own solutions. Attention has been paid to options for converting existing platforms as well as to new builds. This book tries to be about achievable goals, but we must never cease to dream about better things.

I do not ask that you rely on the advice that I give in the various sections of the book. I hope that such may prove valuable for you, but also strive to provide multiple types of resource in each section so that you may easily chart your own course. I wrote this book in order to share the fruits of my own passion for learning about alternative living solutions; it is my hope that you will benefit from the extensive research I have put in as well as from my occasional insights. Explore the further research avenues I offer as a complement to and realization of your goals in reading this book. I consider the selective inclusion of other information sources to be a large part of the value of the work. We live in an information age which can be overwhelming; I have worked through thousands of different sources so that you do not have to. Please consider all links, videos, and books that I cite in each section as good places to go for further information (in one way or another). Where I have been brief, they may be detailed. Where I have offered conclusions and advice, they may better take you through the steps to arrive at those judgments.

I will close this introduction with a charge to you: strive to make the world better wherever you may go. As we journey we are also intruding, imposing a bit of our own lives onto each new place. We should keep this in mind and also try to give back, to swing the balance the other way and so make each new place better for our having been there. Many people tend to disapprove of those trying to live mobile lives, for various reasons both real and imagined. It is incumbent upon each of us to support the mobile community as we journey by living responsibly and so assert our rights to continue to do so.

Here are some select video links to help inspire ideas about mobile living options.
youtu.be/mQPBZZ0Xelk
Living on a big trimaran sailboat with low impact systems (SailOceans).
youtu.be/hRHskbdRFFs
Self-sufficient life on a budget sailboat (Sailing Project Atticus).
youtu.be/AlqYKrQXh1o
Young couple living on a narrowboat (Charlie Pauly).
youtu.be/tuaFGqN_UFE
Nice RV coach as a long term home (LivinLite.net).
youtu.be/xdhXBYUa1UI
Full conversion of a Ram Promaster van into a mobile apartment (Civ Div).
youtu.be/Cy4erT5I6dQ
Low-cost van as stealth home (Different Media).
youtu.be/Lg37Cbx-kak
An interesting documentary on intentional wheeled living (Michael Tubbs).

youtu.be/UzyWyH9r-To
More of an upper-scale look at RV living. Good links into the intentional nomad community (RV Nomads).
youtu.be/1QRxbPSqOME
A short documentary on the motoring boat life in the Pacific Northwest (Different Media).
youtu.be/ibP5IQxId34
Longer documentary about moving from a van into a sailboat. Around the world on a shoestring. The sad ending makes for a bit of a cautionary tale (Chasing Bubbles).

Part One—Needs

1.

Planning

Always begin by forming at least some idea of what you want to do and why you want to do it. Funds, space, and capabilities will be limited. This requires that trade-offs and compromises be made in order that you may accomplish some of what you want and, hopefully, everything that you actually need. Whether you are buying, building, converting, or just tweaking a few things, have a clear purpose in mind and devote sufficient time and resources to planning things out. Careful planning in particular will save you funds, space, and capabilities—enabling you to get more from less. So stop, take some time, and evaluate your goal of living mobile. Make a new beginning, right now, and start planning out the fulfillment of the goals you have right now.

For every need you fill, your solution should have a definite purpose which encompasses more than just satisfying that particular need. You will be integrating a specific system into your living solution and so must account for its own needs and value to you over time. Is this a short-term or long-term solution? What is the expected system run-time or number of uses? What will the appropriate maintenance cycle be? How will it impact the resale value of the mobile platform? How will it interact with my other systems? Unless you are going for the cheapest solution you can find and will just use it until it breaks, all of these questions and more will need answered. Sometimes such a quick-and-dirty method is appropriate—I have used such myself on occasion. Even when you do choose the expedient solution, however, spending some time on planning what you will do when it does break can be helpful.

Deciding on definite purposes and planning out their fulfillment becomes even more important in regards to the mobile living solution as a whole, with the need to integrate your various systems into a coherent platform. This book is intended to serve as an aid to your planning, as much as possible, but it cannot substitute for the power of your own thought applied to your own particular solutions.

Records and planning can be accomplished solely in the mind, in electronic form, or written out on paper. I tend to utilize a mixture of all three, depending on what I am doing. Paper records take up more space and can be less durable, but also do not rely on a somewhat expensive and potentially fragile electronic platform that has its own definite requirements. Loose sheets, folders, note cards, notebooks, pens, pencils, and other such materials are widely available and do not require electricity to work. Electronic records have their own drawbacks, but can be easily copied, moved, manipulated, and can be kept in vast amounts on a small device. Do whatever you find appropriate—but please try to keep some records. Planning a complex project is greatly aided by the reminders for the memory and solidified insights that records provide.

I know that I need not harp upon the importance of research, as here you are reading this book to help research your project, but do try to keep in mind the various types of research that may be open to you. The internet offers an enormous amount of information for our perusal, but there is so much that mental saturation is reached and some forms of discrimination become desirable. Curated knowledge resources, such as libraries and journals and books, help to organize our preponderance of information. Librarians in particular have become information retrieval specialists and can be very helpful for targeted research efforts. Also, much of what can be found on the internet is there for commercial reasons—the information offered is there for a specific purpose which may not align with your own. This is fine as long as it is kept in context, of course. Much of the research for this book was done online and I have made every effort to direct you to good online sources to help you continue your own research, but viewing the information on a particular web page will be much more fulfilling in conjunction with an awareness of other knowledge sources. I will want to keep in mind my understanding of fluid dynamics when viewing retail offerings of boat propellers, for instance, and may also want to have open a secondary resource such as Gerr's *Propeller Handbook*.

Fulfillment Levels

Low: Don't do any formal planning at all, or just a bit in your head. Do not articulate your overall purpose except to yourself. Let your dreams and desires come together organically and propel you toward a solution. Research only as required.

This sounds somewhat romantic and of course requires little extra effort on your part, but will likely prove to be both inefficient and ineffective for larger projects or over longer periods of time.

Medium: Spend time thinking and planning in an organized fashion. Perhaps you keep a notebook to record your thoughts and efforts. Lay out for yourself your overall purpose and also relevant sub-purposes. Plan out a path to reach these goals. Research specific ways that each goal can be fulfilled.

This is a good approach and will be sufficient as long as you are not building your own living platform or other complex systems from scratch. If more detailed efforts or extensive travel is intended then more planning will be called for.

High: Fully chart out your purpose and all related aspects. Carefully plan out every possible effort that will be called for to fulfill your purpose. Engage in ongoing research to expand your understanding of how your goals can be fulfilled. Meticulously record and organize these preliminary and ongoing efforts in either electronic or paper format—and preferably both.

Though none of this extensive effort will accomplish anything physical toward fulfilling your goals, it may make the difference between success and failure in a complex project. Or lead to your aborting an unrealistic project. Knowing what to do and how to do it are at least as important as the actual doing. Your planning efforts will have a direct impact on your final results.

2.

Propulsion

A mobile living solution must have some sort of propulsion in order to remain mobile. This section will look at the various motor options available to keep your wheeled or marine solution moving. Please keep in mind that the structure of your living solution (which will be considered more fully in the next section) will be directly influenced by your mode of propulsion. Which is not to say that you cannot switch between diesel or gasoline engines or instead all electric, but a motor-yacht cannot be turned into a sailboat without more effort and money than the conversion would be worth (though it is possible). The basic hull structure is simply not in place.

The structure of a motor-driven conveyance, wheeled or marine, will be very similar for the different motor types, but the different operating capabilities of various motors will lead to certain structural load and mounting differences in the vehicle. Different motor types are also best suited to particular applications, in accordance with the properties of the motor.

Propulsion may be differentiated by the energy source which is used to drive it. I will consider electric, hybrids, diesel, gasoline, alcohol, natural gas, LPG, hydrogen, and wind (sailing) to be the feasible options worth looking at for now. Some more so than others. Perhaps one day soon we will all be using fusion bottles for our power needs and the debate will be resolved, but for now there are both benefits and drawbacks for each possibility.

Electric

Electrical propulsion will operate on the same principles covered in the Electricity need section below. Electricity, from a battery bank or a generator or both, is used to power a motor which turns the propeller or the driveshaft or the wheels. This may be all electric, in which power is drawn only from a battery bank, or hybrid, in which power is being generated during propulsion in addition to drawing on the battery bank (or instead also charging the battery bank).

A serial hybrid system will generate electricity with a generator which is then cabled to the motors which drive the propulsion. If you have any sort of generator installation for producing electricity on the move then your setup will be considered serial hybrid. This may be wired directly to the electric motors or instead run through a battery bank.

A parallel hybrid system will insert an electric motor somewhere in the existing drive train of a fuel burning engine. Propulsion may then be achieved via the electric motor or the fuel burning engine or even both in conjunction. This would seem to provide the benefits of both systems, but it will also entail the drawbacks of both as well. This sort of arrangement might be utilized when modifying an existing fuel-burning emplacement that still works fine and thus would not be cost effective to replace. By inserting an electric motor for parallel hybrid drive, one can gain the benefits of having electric propulsion sometimes while also retaining the benefits of a fuel-burning mechanical drive engine at others. Some will also consider this more reliable than complete dependence on an electrical system.

You can have an all-electric car or boat, with the power only coming from the battery bank and no generator. This means you will have to stop to recharge somewhere when running low or be able to get by on just what you can generate with renewables like solar or wind power. In this case the energy reservoir of your battery bank will determine how far and how fast you can go before recharge is required. There are many all-electric cars on the roads these days and also a number of short-range electric boats. Battery technology has advanced to the point that a pure electric build is a feasible alternative, especially when used in conjunction with multiple renewable charge sources.

There are various electric car retail offerings out there, or you could convert an existing wheeled vehicle to electric power. Most boats will need to be converted as there are very few offerings, new or used, with electric drive. Though they are out there and electric-drive yacht market offerings are increasing. For conversions, you can contract the work out, do it all yourself, or instead opt for one of the kit options available to save money but still have professional tailoring. Going all electric may reduce your overall range and speed but it will also eliminate fuel use—saving money, weight, and space by eliminating the engine and fuel tanks. A wheeled solution will be able to mount limited solar or wind renewable sources (if any) so frequent recharging will be required. It is possible for a marine solution to mount sufficient renewable power sources, especially solar, to derive propulsion energy needs from those sources alone. Even for extended cruising. This will require a custom build to maximize both energy collection and efficiency of propulsion. As detailed in the section below on Electric Marine Propulsion, electric drive boats can take advantage of efficiency options that are not available to combustion drive boats—provided that they have been designed for that purpose.

I have included a few general links here to get you started. Resources are much more widely available for the ever-growing wheeled electric community, so I have not devoted a section specifically to that. Though there are various useful bits here and there, especially in the wheeled builds of Part Two.

vanclan.co
Some interesting things to say about electric van living and other topics.
evsource.com
A selection of wheeled conversion kits.
ddmotorsystems.com
One place to start looking at electric boat conversions.
www.elcomotoryachts.com
Offers inboard and outboard electric marine motors.
www.electricmotorwholesale.com
An interesting site with discounted prices for industrial AC induction type motors.

www.sailinguma.com/the-motor
Tells how it is possible to have an electric propulsion setup for very little money, with a used brushed DC motor (PMDC).

Motors and Controllers

Every variable speed electric motor, which will be the type required in order to be useful for propulsion, will also require a motor controller. These controllers may be as expensive as the motor itself and must be factored into cost considerations. The way the setup will work is that power flows will be routed into the controller and from there into the motor. The controller produces speed variation in the motor by altering the power flow into it, in a specific method determined by the motor construction. Modern controllers using solid state electronics are very high efficiency devices and afford much better motor control than previously available options. This is one of the primary reasons that widespread electric propulsion is coming into vogue. Motors themselves are all very old designs (though with some newer wrinkles). Better controllers are making almost as big a difference in electric propulsion as are better batteries. Regen must be a specific feature of the controller. Indeed, controllers themselves must be very closely tailored to a specific motor and use. Sometimes controllers are re-programmable to allow for different applications, but usually programming is done only be the manufacturer or reseller according to the initial dictates of the buyer.

The main electric propulsion motor types are DC brushed, AC induction, and the frictionless permanent magnet motors, BLDC (brush-less DC) and PMAC (permanent magnet AC). These latter two will be very similar in motor design, with slightly different windings. The main difference will be the specific type of electrical flow that is fed to them by the controller, but in both cases the controller itself may be supplied with DC power from batteries. The vast majority of marine and wheeled electric propulsion motors are one of the permanent magnet motor types, though I think the Elco motors use AC induction and there are one or two suppliers out there that use brushed DC.

Brushed DC (somewhat confusingly also called PMDC, permanent magnet DC) motors are the least expensive and also require simpler control methods, further reducing costs. They will be heavier for a given power rating than the frictionless permanent magnet types. Efficiency tends to be lower than other types. The brushes themselves will produce sparks so these motors must be carefully shielded, and cannot be installed in locations that may have combustible fumes unless the motor is completely sealed from air exchange. Also, this motor type will have the highest maintenance needs as those brushes will wear out over time.

Induction AC motors (three-phase asynchronous, for propulsion purposes) are more expensive, sometimes much more so, and will also require a more complex controller. They tend to be very heavily built but also very durable. Most AC induction motors are manufactured for heavy industry use and some varieties are completely sealed from environmental contamination or damage. Their controller units are generally designed to receive AC grid power, but there are a few options out there for DC powered controllers which will themselves invert to the appropriate AC power for the motor feed. Overall power efficiency will be somewhat lower than the permanent magnet varieties, though this can vary depending on the controller. They can be built much larger and more powerful than will be practical for a permanent magnet motor, so this may be the best choice for very high powered solutions.

BLDC and PMAC motors are very similar to each other, though they are wound differently and the individual controllers must be specifically tailored to and programmed for the motor and use. For a given power rating, these motors will be smaller and thus more efficient in terms of weight than other types. Which is often very important for mobile applications. They will also be at least slightly more efficient than DC brushed and AC induction in terms of power draw for a given load output. They are vulnerable in extreme conditions to demagnetization and the lower overall mass will mean that better cooling systems will be required than for other types. But if carefully installed and well-maintained these make for some of the best mobile propulsion motors. PMAC types will be slightly more efficient and have better torque characteristics than BLDC types, but will also require better controllers and so may be somewhat more expensive. For most DIY marine electric propulsion applications I consider PMAC to be the motor of choice, though care must be taken not to over-speed the motor during regen. As mentioned, both of these types can be fed with DC power from batteries through their controller units.

For most motors, extended use below 50% continuous rating is inadvisable, as efficiency will be very low and larger amounts of heat will be generated. So motors must be sized so that any long duration use is at power levels above that 50% motor capacity. In addition to the links above, consider the following when sourcing electric motors and other parts.

www.cloudelectric.com
www.thunderstruck-ev.com
motenergy.com
www.hpevs.com
evolveelectrics.com
www.electricmotorsport.com

And here are some specific places to look at controller units.

www.kellycontroller.com
www.curtisinstruments.com
www.sevcon.com
www.cafeelectric.com

Gearing or Reducing

Electric motors will all have a specific rotational speed designed into the build structure. Speed control is possible at levels below this nominal speed but should never exceed that rate as damage to the motor may ensue. If you need to reach a higher rotational speed then you may gear up through either a belt and pulley arrangement or an actual gearbox. The electric motor output shaft will then be spinning slower than the working shaft that it is turning. Gearing up will reduce torque (rotational force) at the same time that it increases working shaft speed.

Gearing down will be more common. This is the application of mechanical assistance to reduce final output speed which also has the effect of increasing torque. If your motor has a higher RPM rating than you require for your application a reduction will decrease that speed in your working shaft while increasing rotational force. So acceleration might be increased for a wheeled application or a larger propeller could be turned in a marine application.

Moderate gearing can be accomplished by use of belts or chains and pulleys. One pulley will be mounted to the electric motor shaft while another will be mounted to the working shaft. If the pulley on the working shaft is smaller then speeds will be increased and torque decreased and if the pulley on the working shaft is larger then speeds will be reduced and torque increased. This is a direct relationship, such that if the pulley on the working shaft is twice as large (in diameter) than the pulley on the motor output shaft then speed will be cut in half and torque will be doubled. Pulleys can be used to gear up or down to perhaps a four or five to one maximum ratio (4:1, 5:1), but beyond that a more durable system will be required. Two or three to one ratios (2:1, 3:1) are more common with pulleys.

More aggressive gearing can be accomplished with mechanical reducers. These are more expensive and might cost as much as the motor itself but are the only lasting way to accomplish gearing ratios of 9:1, 15:1, or as high as 30:1. So if for instance you have a large propeller that only needs a maximum rotational speed of 200 RPM for your desired thrust output but is very heavy and thus will require a significant torque rating to move, you can use a 6000 RPM electric motor combined with a 30:1 gear reducer. Horsepower (overall power input) will be constant but torque will be greatly amplified. Though that is an extreme example.

Gearing for electric motors is a different application than a transmission that might be used with a combustion engine. A transmission might have multiple different forward gear ratios or only one, but it will also have a reverse gear for changing the output direction. Reverse gears are unnecessary with electric motors as the output direction can be changed via electrical manipulation from the controller and a reversal in motor turning direction. Consider the following links for gear reducer samples.

www.worldwideelectric.net/product-category/gear-reducers
www.surpluscenter.com/Gear-Reducers

Hybrids

You can utilize a serial hybrid setup, which is the same as all-electric except you will have a generator...and have to deal with an engine and its fuel again. This does permit considerably more leeway in where you place your engine (generator) and also in type of fuel used. So you could have an LPG (propane) generator placed somewhere other than your drive-train which provides enough electrical power to run your electric drive motors. Or just to increase the range of your battery bank. There will be efficiency losses at every step of the way, of course. In converting LPG to electricity, maybe storing it in the batteries for a while, and drawing from the batteries to run a motor, you will be losing some potential power at each conversion. This should be considered when planning your solutions.

Parallel hybrid setups are a bit different. The idea is that you can gain most of the advantages of electric drive without actually losing the different capabilities of a fuel-burning mechanical drive engine.

www.evalbum.com/304

This links to a story about someone with an electric car but also an optional trailer with only a diesel engine on it to push the car around when the battery runs down. I seems to me that any wheeled living solution with a trailer could utilize some variation of this model.

If your setup involves a truck and camper, you could equip the camper with electric drive motors and a battery bank. Given adequate bracing and system interlinks, the trailer drive could be used to supplement the power of the truck engine or even push the truck forward by itself.

betamarine.co.uk/resources/Sales_Brochures/Hybrid-HE-SB/#page=1

This links to a sales brochure for a UK-based company that offers a parallel hybrid marine drive. This type of installation is not very popular—most boaters who switch seem to go serial hybrid if not all electric instead. Though the vast majority of boats out there still utilize a conventional diesel or gasoline engine.

Electric propulsion, pure or hybrid, is by no means free power. There is always an energy cost, in terms of money and other impacts. That being said, there are many ways to generate electricity. The world is moving, slowly but inexorably, toward continual reduction in pollution and waste from non-renewable materials and fuel use. Having electric propulsion in place becomes more attractive every year as technological applications advance and costs become lower. If not making the switch now, then at least consider that you may be changing to electric propulsion somewhere down the road. Fossil fuels in particular will eventually run out and costs can be expected to rise continually until they do.

Electric Propulsion Sample Options

$13,995; EP-40 Electric Inboard

Drop in electric propulsion motor. Elco motors have a good reputation and long history. From www.elcomotoryachts.com

$15,995; QuietTorque 45.0 LC

Another full-install option with a similar power output. From electricmarina.com

$3357; HPEVS AC35 with Curtis 1236SE-5621 Controller

This is a DIY kit for sailboat or wheeled conversion. Note that the motor is less powerful than the two options above and the system is not designed as sealed against the marine environment—though you can do that yourself also. From thunderstruck-ev.com

Diesel

Diesel engines operate on compression principles. The diesel engine will compress the fuel sufficiently that it will spontaneously combust without any spark required (though in cold weather glow plugs are used to add heat), but in order to do so reliably it must be heavily built to withstand the high pressures involved. The heavy build of a diesel engine adds weight, which is not desirable for mobility. The very high tolerances and fine engineering of a diesel engine also increase both initial cost and costs for maintenance.

Diesel fuel itself is oily and not very volatile, but when highly compressed will burn well and provide steady power. The smell is distinctive. It is a petroleum product and thus cost is a factor of market forces, but it will always be slightly more expensive to produce than gasoline. There are also ongoing advances in bio-diesel, but as yet it has less desirable attributes than petroleum sourced diesel. Most current engines can only tolerate a small amount of bio-diesel mixed in. Some regions are beginning to mandate a certain mix of bio-diesel in commercial diesel fuel, with levels to increase over time.

A diesel engine may be converted to run on vegetable oil, providing another renewable fuel option. It will not run quite as well, however, and will need somewhat more maintenance. Even with extensive filtering vegetable oils do not burn as well or as cleanly as diesel or bio-diesel, leading to soot buildup and other engine problems. Energy density is also lower, reducing range for a given fuel tank size.

The power that is generated by a diesel engine offers more torque (rotational force) than a comparable gasoline engine but less top-end horsepower. So, diesel propulsion is reliable and good for high torque requirements, but is also more expensive for both initial purchase and for maintenance, heavier, and provides less in the way of horsepower (top speed).

Diesel propulsion is often used in applications that require more torque or expect heavy use. Thus commercial transport on the highways is almost exclusively diesel powered. The heavy loads and long hours are borne more easily by diesel power. Cruising boats are almost all diesel powered as well. Displacement hulls do not need to move very fast and the extended durability of diesel engines and higher safety of diesel fuel are important considerations. If you expect extended motoring on your boat or will have a heavy wheeled solution as your home you should seriously consider the advantages of diesel propulsion.

Note that there are many newer types of diesel engine which branch into designs focusing on reducing weight and increasing available power. These are the turbo-diesels being put into new passenger vehicles or on high-speed boats. They do save in weight and increase horsepower, but at the cost of longevity and more expensive components. Expect them to have increased costs over time and require more frequent repair. To their credit, they will run more smoothly and with significantly reduced emissions in comparison to conventional diesel engines.

Wheeled Diesel Sample Options

~$50,000; Dodge Ram 2500 w/Turbo Diesel; 370 horsepower, 850 lb-ft of torque; 19780 lb towing
A new pickup truck with excellent towing capacity for wheeled living.
From www.ramtrucks.com

~$38,000; Chevy Express Cargo w/Turbo Diesel; 181 horsepower, 369 lb-ft of torque; 6800 lb towing
A new van with good interior space but still powerful enough to tow a trailer. Very possible as a wheeled living solution. Note that the gasoline and gaseous versions below have even more towing capacity (with higher powered engines but more fuel use to get there).
From www.chevrolet.com

Gasoline, Alcohol, LPG, Natural Gas

A gasoline or gaseous type engine, in contrast, will operate through controlled explosion of its fuel source. Compression is involved, but at much lower levels and with looser tolerances than a diesel engine. An ignition spark is generated at a specific point of compression and with a particular air-fuel ratio, which together provide the chemical mixture for the controlled explosion which moves the mechanical drive. A gasoline engine is thus inherently more complex than a diesel engine, but may also be built more lightly and to lower tolerances.

Gasoline is a volatile fluid and gives off noxious fumes when exposed to air. It can be much more dangerous than diesel fuel and when spilled may ignite from any spark or even static electricity. The power that is generated tends to be higher horsepower but lower torque. So, gasoline propulsion is lighter than diesel, provides better top end horsepower by weight, and tends to be less expensive both for initial emplacement and for maintenance. It is also less durable and provides less torque at a given power level. The fuel is not as safe to use or to store.

Wheeled Gasoline Sample Options

~$40,000; Dodge Ram 2500 w/V8 gasoline; 410 horsepower, 429 lb-ft of torque; 17580 lb towing
From www.ramtrucks.com

~$35,000; Chevy Express Cargo w/V8 gasoline; 341 horsepower, 373 lb-ft of torque; 10000 lb towing
From www.chevrolet.com

An explosion type (gasoline) engine may also use other fuels such as alcohol, natural gas, or LPG. As a liquid fuel, alcohol will share many of the characteristics of gasoline. It burns cleaner but is more volatile. It also burns hotter and will increase engine wear. Most gasoline now has some alcohol (ethanol) mixed in. Gasoline and alcohol (when used as fuels and kept in tanks that may attract water) will both become less usable with long storage and thus less suitable as a fuel source over time, though they may be stabilized with additives to increase this shelf-life.

Natural gas has a fairly low energy density as a fuel source and in addition is difficult to compress for easy storage. It can however be generated by renewable means such as biomass methane production and thus will still be used when petroleum production is too expensive or gone completely. It can be compressed but this requires very high pressures and thus thicker tanks and more safety requirements. In future this hurdle may be overcome as early research into adsorbed natural gas has shown that storage at lower pressures is possible if the gas is adsorbed into another material such as carbon fibers. At this present time natural gas propulsion seems less feasible than using LPG or some liquid fuel. However, a gasoline or especially an LPG engine may be converted to natural gas use at some later point without much difficulty.
bluegasmarine.com
This is an interesting look at natural gas fuel for marine use.

LPG (liquefied petroleum gas—propane or butane or both) has higher energy density than natural gas and is much more easily stored. It is less safe in certain applications—LPG is heavier than air and may get trapped in spaces when spilled (like gasoline but even more explosive), whereas natural gas is lighter than air and will float up. It has the distinct advantage, especially over gasoline, of nearly indefinite storage life. LPG and natural gas both tend to produce less engine wear over time when compared to gasoline or alcohol (cleaner burning so less soot). Many gasoline engines may be converted to LPG use. Any LPG engine may be converted to natural gas use, and vice versa. Please note that I write convertible. The fuels are not interchangeable without conversion, but the conversion requirements may be fairly simple.

Gaseous Wheeled Sample Option

~$35,000; Chevy Express Cargo w/CNG/LPG/gasoline capable engine; 341 horsepower, 373 lb-ft of torque; 10000 lb towing
From www.chevrolet.com

Hydrogen

Hydrogen is an explosive gas and thus may be used to drive an engine, but its properties are distinct and so it requires a dedicated build. This may or may not be more efficient than using the hydrogen to directly generate electricity to run an electrical motor—that will depend upon a number of factors. But almost no-one is currently using hydrogen for fuel-burning engines and a number of people are experimenting with serial hybrid drives using hydrogen fuel cells to produce electricity. Hydrogen is the cleanest burning fuel there is. It will produce only pure water as 'waste', which may in turn be used for other purposes. Hydrogen is an energy storage medium, a fuel. It may at some point become possible to easily generate hydrogen on a mass scale and then transport it anywhere for use, but not yet. There are still many hurdles to overcome both in production and storage. At this time it is possible to utilize hydrogen, directly or indirectly, for propulsion, but still difficult and very expensive. See the Electricity section for further information.

Sailing

As technology advances the all-solar (or coupled with wind generators) electric vehicle will become feasible for more and more applications, but at this time the sailboat remains the best option for fuel-less propulsion. This will still be limited by available winds. You will never be able to sail directly upwind. But you can still sail around the world without any fuel use at all.

Sailing utilizes the same forces of air pressure as do electric fans. The sails are arranged in such a way that air pressure is higher in back of them than it is in front, which creates force in the forward direction and a corresponding motion. Straight downwind this will only be a push, as most people imagine when thinking of sailing. Upwind sailing, not directly but still against the direction the wind is blowing, is only possible because one can also harness a pull on the sails by manipulating their shapes and angles. Most boats will actually sail faster somewhat upwind then they do straight downwind, because they can harness both pull and push forces instead of push alone.

Many sailboats large enough to be considered a mobile living situation will in fact be motor-sailors. That is, they will have sails which will sometimes be in use but will also have a propeller which may be engine driven or electric motor driven. This is because such an arrangement, while more costly, greatly enhances both convenience and versatility in terms of propulsion.

Note that sail propulsion saves you fuel costs, but your initial setup will easily set you back the price of an engine. Mast, rigging, boom, and furler might set you back $5k to $20k or more. Sails and running rigging will be more on top, possibly $4k to $10k. Prices will rise and fall dramatically depending on the size of the boat, of course, and if you can acquire the materials and do the work yourself you can have substantial cost savings. When buying used, remember that all of these components are under constant wear when sailing and must be maintained and replaced at intervals. The standing rigging, for example, might be expected to last for ten years of moderate use but should then be replaced.

www.cruisersforum.com/forums/f48/cost-of-new-mast-and-rigging-138113.html
A discussion regarding costs for sailing setups.

improvesailing.com/questions/cost-of-new-sails
A detailed posting on sails costs and alternatives to new sails.

References and Further Research:

Mathys, Charles. *My Electric Boats.*

Leitman, Seth and Bob Brant. *Build Your Own Electric Vehicle.*

Doane, Charles. *The Modern Cruising Sailboat*

Calder, Nigel. *Marine Diesel Engines*

Marino, Emiliano. *The Sailmaker's Apprentice.*

Toss, Brian. *The Complete Rigger's Apprentice*

www.parkermotion.com/whitepages/Comparing_AC_and_PM_motors.pdf

evmc2.wordpress.com/2014/12/04/basic-motor-types-pmdc-bldc-ac-induction-and-synchronous-and-series-dc

plugboats.com/electric-inboard-boat-motors-guide-over-150-motors

www.trailerlife.com/towing/tow-vehicles/diesel-versus-gas

www.alternative-energies.net/pros-and-cons-of-biodiesel

www.enginebuildermag.com/2015/05/cng-and-propane-engine-builds

www.boats.com/reviews/blue-gas-marine-natural-gas-outboard-first-look-video

www.sailmagazine.com/diy/fuel-consumption-tug-vs-cruiser

www.vicprop.com/displacement_size.php?action=calculate

youtu.be/bMXR1UYSMa4
Interesting presentation on needs and costs for electric sailboat propulsion.

youtu.be/1Y1_TSdR2j4

Actual demonstration and testing for electric conversion for a sailboat. Note that those Firefly batteries can be replaced with LiFePO4 later on to greatly enhance the system.

youtu.be/pcj2lQwH7N4

All solar van living, including propulsion. A good look at what will be required (at the current state of technology).

youtu.be/DQr4RS50v4Y

Time-lapse video for a weekly maintenance cycle on a larger marine diesel. All marine diesels should have some maintenance or at least inspection on a regular basis. Even though many of them do not get this proper care.

youtu.be/aZv4IXFPMqg

A good look at the heat exchange mechanism on this very well maintained and clean small-boat diesel.

youtu.be/9hzP133RIoE

Extended presentation comparison video for vanlife (between gasoline and diesel).

youtu.be/dRTSftUqQ9U

Demonstration of an older outboard motor that has been converted from gasoline to LPG fuel.

youtu.be/qB7h7ftdsQA

Professional walk-through for converting a vehicle to LPG.

youtu.be/pgdXbe1in64

Video about a demonstration boat using hydrogen power. Note that the boat itself uses electric propulsion. The hydrogen is only used as an energy storage medium and is converted to electricity to generate power. The boat design is interesting and a bit of a showcase for the versatility of electric propulsion. I find it most interesting that the onboard hydrogen is being generated directly from seawater.

Fulfillment Levels

Low: Just stick with whatever is already included in your living platform, or drop in whatever you think will work or is easy to get. Follow required maintenance, but do not give overmuch care or thought to it. Run it until it quits.

If your propulsion solution is short term then you need not put overmuch effort or money into it. You can also get by with cheaper or ad-hock solutions if you expect to always be in range of getting help. There is a point, with older engines, where they will hold together OK and give moderate service, but if you try to fix their numerous minor issues or to take them apart you may not get them going again without a total rebuild. If that. At that point they should be used until they quit running or until you are ready to put something better in. Just don't expect reliability—engines at that point may keep running for quite a while and they may decide to quit the next day.

Medium: Know and understand your propulsion solution, whether existing to the platform or sourced elsewhere. Take care with system maintenance and have some idea of what is going on with the system otherwise. Keep records.

For serious cruising or other longer term solutions, you will want a propulsion system in much better shape and much better maintained. This is your lifeline to mobility, which in some extreme cases may turn out to be the difference between living and dying. Regardless of circumstance, however, propulsion is arguably the most important system within your mobile living solution. Do not neglect it and always have at least some awareness of what is going on with it. This does not mean you should worry over it all the time. Just be aware and ready to take necessary action.

High: Design and build, or have designed and built, your own custom propulsion system. Pay rigorous attention to system maintenance and system feedback. Keep meticulous records.

If you are good enough, or those that you hire are good enough, a custom solution will always be better than a stock option. Lavishing care on that custom solution thereafter will not hurt, and most likely will help gain you an enduring and reliable system.

3.

Structure

After propulsion, we must choose a structure for the vehicle which both integrates our desired type of propulsion and permits us to incorporate all of our chosen integrated solutions. The structure must be strong enough to remain stable in form despite all normal forces which will act upon it, along with some built in redundancy. If, however, it is made much stronger than required there will be an unwarranted increase in cost or weight or both and expenses will increase or mobility will suffer. And so there must be a balance in terms of materials chosen and structure formed. A trade-off.

Sail propulsion does have an impact on required hull form. There must be one or more masts to support the sails, which will require a certain amount of bracing in the hull against strain. In addition to this, a monohull sailboat will need to have some resistance against being turned over by the force of the wind on the sails, as transmitted to the hull by the masts. This is accomplished by some form of ballast low in the hull, such as a weighted keel. This ballast may be a significant proportion of the weight of the vessel, slowing speed while sailing and increasing fuel costs while motoring because of the added mass. Multihull sailing vessels do not require added ballast, as they are kept stable (upright) by the hull form itself. Each hull is buoyant and resists being pushed down in the water. The spacing between the hulls means that the vessel itself will stay reasonably level side to side despite any sideways wind force upon the masts. Both types of hull form are stable front to back because of inherent hull buoyancy and by being longer than they are wide.

Other boats will have different requirements, though generally fewer. The propeller must be securely fastened to the hull in order to transmit its thrust to the whole boat. The shape of the hull will differ depending on whether it is designed to ideally plane above the water (at higher speeds), remain in the water which is displaced as it moves forward, or instead some compromise between the two.

Wheeled vehicles will need to account for wind resistance alone, rather than wind and water both, and size restrictions will be determined by road standards. Beyond these considerations, all vehicles will become more expensive the larger the structure is, in terms of construction, maintenance and repair, and propulsion costs. The cost of a sailboat, for instance, is said to double for every ten feet in added length.

Materials

The materials chosen for vehicle structure will be as important as the form. Generally the materials chosen will be some compromise between strength, weight, availability, workability, and cost. Other considerations will also come into play that impact these basic calculations. Wood requires more labor and may rot, but if you are doing the labor yourself it is free and if kept encapsulated in epoxy the wood will be protected from rot. And so forth.

Steel is a common building material for many types of vehicles. On the positive side, is is strong, resists impact, is somewhat cheap, and is relatively easy to work with and repair. Against this we must consider that steel is heavy, can be more expensive than other materials, and will constantly corrode to a greater or lesser extent depending on conditions. If you can weld it yourself or with friends or family, and you can get decent steel at a reasonable price, this may be your best option. The cost of the metal has gone up steadily over time, however, and looks to continue to do so. It is still the most common structural material used for vehicles for commercial purposes. Note that stainless steel is much more expensive and can be weaker and thus is generally not used as a structural material.

Aluminum is lighter than steel for a given strength and in many cases will resist corrosion much better than steel. It is also more expensive (thus far and in most places) and requires special welding equipment and greater skill to work with properly. If you can absorb the higher cost it is to be preferred over steel because of the weight reduction and corrosion resistance.

Laminates

Laminate construction (or 'fiberglass') is very common for recreational vehicles, both marine and wheeled. Some type of hardening resin (plastic) is combined with a structural component (which usually is some type of fiberglass) to produce a solid laminate with better properties than any individual component. Epoxy/carbon fiber laminates are high strength for very little weight and are now common in performance racing. The greatest advantage of laminate construction is its versatility. There are various materials on offer at various price points, but you can mix and match to achieve the specific properties you desire. Laminates may also be molded into almost any shape desired and thus provide great flexibility of form. Coring materials, put into the middle of laminate layers, can add increased stiffness and other properties depending on the material used.

Epoxy resins are the best and strongest available but also the most expensive. There are various types of epoxy, distinguished by their curing process and properties when fully cured. The epoxy used should be suited to its application. Marine structural epoxies tend to be of the amine-cured variety and these are suitable for wheeled use as well. Epoxy will bond to many substances (though not all) and is commonly used to repair laminate construction even if another resin was used for the initial layup. Epoxy mixed with wood flour (very fine sawdust) and other fillers is used in wood bonding and can actually be stronger than the wood itself in certain respects. Materials encapsulated in epoxy are preserved from environment and deterioration. Epoxy prices vary widely, but I will include some distributor examples here for your perusal.

Epoxy Sample Options

$150; 105 Resin w/205 Hardener; 1.2 gal

West System epoxies are the standard for marine use—though many consider their prices to be somewhat inflated.

From www.westsystem.com

$128; Basic No Blush; 1.5 gal

An alternative vendor of quality epoxy.

From www.epoxyusa.com

$98; Kit with Any combo of resin and hardener; 1.5 gal

Another alternative. Raka epoxies are good quality and have very attractive pricing.

From raka.com

$4510; 105 Resin w/205 Hardener; 63.3 gal

Bulk option.

From www.westsystem.com

$2390; Basic No Blush; 30 gal

Bulk option; this is the same vendor as epoxyusa.com.

From www.epoxyproducts.com

$1395; Kit with Any combo of resin and hardener; 30 gal

Bulk option for Raka. Notice the much lower price. The attributes for each of these epoxies listed will be somewhat different and thus suited to different uses, but Raka does offer a variety of tailored formulations for different applications.

From raka.com

$3394; Resin Research 2000/2100; 78 gal

Another vendor option.

From fiberglassflorida.com

Ester Resins

Vinylester and polyester are the other two resins most common in marine use and elsewhere. Polyester resin is much weaker than epoxy and will tend to pass some moisture over time (osmotic blistering), but is also much cheaper. Vinylester falls somewhere in between the properties of the other two and is priced accordingly. Despite their drawbacks in comparison to epoxy, these resins are widely used to save on costs or when weight is less of a factor, though often there will be a top-seal of epoxy as well, at least in marine use, to prevent blistering.

Note that these two also have limited shelf lives. Epoxy hardens in response to a specific reaction when the two parts are combined, but the ester resins are very slowly hardening from the point of production. They are hardened in use for laminate construction by adding a catalyst that greatly speeds up the hardening process, so you can slow or speed up the layup by adding less or more catalyst.

Ester Resin Sample Options

$70; Evercoat Boat Yard Resin (polyester); 1 gal

From westmarine.com

$38; Polynt General Purpose Polyester Resin; 1 gal

From fiberglassflorida.com

$178; Evercoat Vinyl-Ester Resin; 1 gal

From www.westmarine.com

$58; T-40 Vinyl-ester Resin; 1 gal
From fiberglassflorida.com

Structural

The structural component of a laminate may be any number of things, but the most common are e-glass, s-glass, aramid, and carbon-fiber.

E-glass is also known just as fiberglass. It was originally produced for electronic components (thus the 'e'), but has become the most common structural component in use for composite construction. It consists of thin glass strands that have been joined or woven together in some manner to produce a material somewhat like fabric. That fabric is brittle in and of itself, being made of glass, but when laid up into a multi-layer laminate can be very strong. E-glass is cheap to produce and widely available, but is weaker in almost all respects compared to other materials.

S-glass is also fiberglass, but is manufactured in a different way. It is perhaps half again as strong as e-glass by weight and tends to have a price to match. S-glass is used in some applications where it is desirable to save weight or volume or both. A stronger material such as s-glass can make for a laminate which is just as strong but requires fewer layers. Alternatively, s-glass can be used as extra support for specific areas of a composite structure, without having to increase layers or build up 'stringers' that break up the smoothness of the structure.

Aramid fibers are more commonly known as Kevlar or Twaron, which are two of the trade name aramid fabrics. They are not necessarily as strong as fiberglass in all respects, but are very much better in certain areas. In particular, they are very resistant to abrasion and impact and so add these qualities to a laminate when placed in the layers of the structure. They are more expensive than e-glass though less so than carbon-fiber.

Carbon-fiber materials have a very high strength to weight ratio and so tend to be used when it is desirable to save structural weight. They are very expensive (thus far) when compared to these other structural components and so tend to be in use only for specialty purposes or when cost is less of a factor.

Fabrics

Structural materials for laminate construction may also be differentiated by how they are joined together in themselves—the shape and weave of the 'fabric' of the material. Matting or chopped strand mat (CSM) consists of short pieces, usually e-glass, which are all struck together and into a roll of fabric by a binder. CSM provides strength in all directions, because the strand orientations are random, but the overall strength is low because the strands are so short. It is often used as a filler or backing between laminate layers.

Woven roving consists of rovings, or bundles of long fiber strands, which are woven somewhat loosely into and over each other to form a continuous sheet. It makes a heavy, coarse fabric. Woven roving will be the main strength element in most laminate construction, but takes more resin to wet and shows a heavy print if used in outer layers. It is common for the center of the laminate to be alternating layers of roving and CSM, with the outer laminate to be cloth instead for smoothness.

Cloth is woven as well, but from finer strands of material and much more tightly. This makes for a much smoother laminate layer. Cloth may be placed as the outer layer of a laminate build or instead as the only layer when sheathing a wooden build for encapsulation. There are many different weaves and weights of cloth to choose from.

Axial fabrics are not woven, but instead consist of layers of strands which all lie in a single directional orientation and are joined together by little pieces of non-useful material. This is desirable because it avoids the micro-fracturing that occurs in the individual strands when they are woven back and forth into roving or cloth. The end result is that axial fabrics are much stronger than other types of layout, but only along the direction that the fibers are oriented. Axial fabrics in multiple layers, such as bi-axial or tri-axial, will have a different axis or orientation for each layer so as to provide strength in different directions.

Laminate Structural Sample Options

$285; Fiberglass CSM 1.5oz x 50in; 83 yard roll; 95 lbs
From www.fiberglasswarehouse.com

$210; Fiberglass Woven Roving; 18oz per sq. yard; 50in wide; BEH roll 89 yards
From www.fgci.com

$330; Fiberglass cloth; 4oz per sq. yard; 50in wide; 60 yard roll
From fiberglasssite.com

$472; Fiberglass Bi-axial 45 x 45; 17oz per sq. yard; 50in wide; 60 yards
From store.raka.com

$1290; Kevlar style 5285; 5oz per sq. yard; 60in wide; 60 yard roll
From www.uscomposites.com

$1590; Carbon Fiber Fabric Roll; 5oz per sq. yard; 50in wide; 100 yard roll
From www.carbonfiberglass.com

Wood

Wood has a range of properties depending on the species and individual tree that it came from, with varying hardness, durability, strength, and appeal. It may also be anywhere from free to quite expensive. It is easy to work with and there are any number of tool options available to do so with. If encapsulated with epoxy it may last forever. It is well worth considering wood as a coring material for laminate construction. It is also the most appealing building material psychologically for many people.

Wood Sourcing Sample Options

Wood/lumber is usually too heavy to ship far, but there should be a supplier in whatever area you are. This site lists lumber suppliers by state in the USA.
www.glen-l.com/resources/lumber-suppliers.html

$2675; White Oak, quarter sawn, kiln dried; 500 board feet of 15/16in thickness
This is an example of a wood order from a mill in Ohio. White oak is suitable for boat building as it is strong and rot resistant. Quarter sawn boards offer greater longitudinal strength than plain sawn boards.
From www.homesteadhardwoods.com

Conversion

Any boat, RV, camper, or trailer can be modified or converted, if you keep your goals within what is possible. A fiberglass or wooden structure can be reinforced or braced with epoxy laminate 'stringers' to increase or change load bearing characteristics in a given area. Epoxy will bond to most existing fiberglass and many other materials, though you will want a sample test to be certain. A steel or aluminum structure can be altered by cutting and/or welding. As long as you take responsibility for all components required for the final structure, you can modify your living solution in many different ways.

There are any number of older boats, RVs and trailers out there. Even if stripped down to bare hull or the equivalent, if the basic structure is sound then rebuild or conversion may be better options than trying to build something new.

References and Further Research

Hankinson, Ken. *Fiberglass Boatbuilding for Amateurs.*

Brown, Russell. *Epoxy Basics.*

Devlin, Samuel. *Devlin's Boatbuilding.*

Brewer, Ted. *Understanding Boat Design, 4th edition.*

Gerr, Dave. *The Elements of Boat Strength for Builders, Designers and Owners.*

Steward, Robert M. and Carl Cramer. *Boatbuilding Manual, 5th edition.*

Rossel, Greg. *The Boatbuilder's Apprentice.*

Casey, Don. *This Old Boat, 2nd ed: Completely Revised and Expanded.*

www.rvingplanet.com/blog/the-ultimate-guide-to-rv-construction-what-you-need-to-know-before-the-rv-is-yours

www.jrconsumer.com/FreeRVReport.pdf

enrg.io/dont-buy-build-high-end-diy-rv

www.synthx.com/articles/trailer-strength.html

www.boats.com/resources/boat-building-construction-resin-fiberglass-cores

building-strip-planked-boats.com/content/introduction

youtu.be/dLdmd-Pqs84
A demonstration video for commercial RV construction.

youtu.be/1G62JHALM5Q
Tour of an RV converted from a large box truck.

youtu.be/ezDWPijo0xU
Interesting discussion of structural matters for a professional van conversion.

youtu.be/iDVao9ZgGd8
Collage video showing the build of a camper trailer from scratch.

youtu.be/ImYd5UYukv0

Good demonstration video showing commercial boat building methods.

youtu.be/MrQoIqZDoOI

First in a series of videos documenting an Australian building a catamaran sailboat.

www.youtube.com/user/boatworkstoday

This is a link to a channel instead of a specific video. Provides a number of demonstrations and instructionals for working with epoxy, wood, and/or fiberglass.

youtu.be/7HlhSZWqkKk

Extensive series of videos on the backyard build of a steel sailboat. Thought provoking.

youtu.be/Y-MWardh9K8

Picture sequence of an aluminum boat build from a kit. Note that it is not strictly necessary to paint an aluminum boat and that doing so can lead to corrosion issues.

Fulfillment Levels

Low: Find a pre-built structure, new or used, and rely on it to hold together on its own. Just use what is already there.

This is what most people do, but is really only a minimal level of fulfillment. Learning about an existing vehicle can be difficult, as inner layers become a mystery once they are covered over. For most applications it will be fine to rely on a structure as manufactured, but only if you stay within the initial design parameters of the build.

Medium: Buy and possibly modify an existing structure that fits your requirements. Have a good knowledge of the strengths and weaknesses of the particular design. Understand requirements for repair or modification. Keep records.

Simply learning about your vehicle structure, even if you do not intend to alter or repair it yourself, is a big step up. This means that you will know what does need repaired in case of a failure or what will need to be altered for an upgrade, instead of relying on others. This level of knowledge may also enable you to do these things yourself, depending on structural material and design aspects.

High: Design and build your own platform structure (or have done). Have intimate knowledge of every aspect of the vehicle build. Keep meticulous records.

If you are able to do the work yourself (or with helpers), and you are sufficiently versed in what you are doing to do it properly, then you can achieve solutions that would not otherwise be possible. Be wary, however, and plan things out very carefully. For every successful build story you come across there might be ten abandoned projects that you don't hear about.

4.

Electricity

We need harnessed power to charge our devices, light the dark, provide motive force, and reduce our labors. Electricity can do all of these things, though many of them can be done by other means as well. With electricity, unlike any other source, we have a unified means to store, transmit, and use power. Electricity is the wonder power. It has become ever-present in our lives and we cannot do without it and remain part of the civilized world. Your electrical setup will not keep the rain off, but it will still be the core of your mobile living solution.

An integrated electrical system has become both desirable and necessary for living in contemporary civilization, whether in a static or mobile system. The versatility of electricity harnessed as a power source permits the fulfillment of many needs. Mobile living solutions have become much more viable recently with the advent, widespread availability, and low cost of such vital components as energy dense rechargeable batteries and versatile mobile computing, coupled with the opportunities for remote income generation, socializing, and indeed many aspects of living permitted by the burgeoning internet. We can work online now, at least some of us, and make a viable living while doing so. We can live anywhere and still keep in touch with family and friends. We can pick up our (properly designed and integrated) homes and shift to a new base point. And we can do all of these things through the use of a reliable electrical power system integrated into our living solutions to leverage that power into helping provide for our needs.

This begins with electrical generation or transmission and also requires storage and conversion of electrical potential. This section will explore all of these aspects of electricity, starting with basic principles and proceeding down to specific hardware options for mobile solutions. I know of no other up to date published guide for all of these matters and will strive to give you the most current technical solutions. However, these matters are changing rapidly and my own guide cannot expect to remain fully up to date for very long. For this reason I will attempt to give you a sufficient basis for understanding, within this section, that will allow you to adapt to changing technology options.

Basics

Electromagnetism has been identified as one of the fundamental forces of this reality. It is all pervasive and ever-present. Chemical interactions, which all life processes and more rely upon, may be said to be nothing more (or less) than the electrical interactions of the component atoms involved. Electricity and magnetism are never truly separate, though we often speak solely in terms of one or the other as being most relevant, and any integrated system must consider both the magnetic potential within electrical runs and the electrical potential in magnetic devices.

Do not attempt to interact with electrical installations without utilizing proper care and safety procedures. The same power which we harness to our needs can act harmfully upon the human body, even to the point of death. Take great care and always know what you are doing. Redundant safety is critical for any electrical installation. Do not be satisfied with insufficient grounding or circuit interrupt points. Whenever possible, work on unpowered systems and components—and know what to do to power or de-power these things.

Basically, an electrical system is comprised of a series of insulated cables and/or wires which transmit electrical potential from one point to another. We then tap into this system with various devices, whether directly wired in or through the use of an outlet and plug, which draw upon that potential to power the use of the device. Further complexities in a system are to insure redundancy and safety, such as the use of fuses or breakers to isolate sections of an electrical system in the event of failure, or to provide control access.

AC

All residential standard electricity uses AC (alternating current) power, in which the current potential, which may be understood as direction of flow, continuously flips back and forth from negative to positive. This is transmitted at a certain standardized voltage, which may be understood as the line pressure of the electrical potential as it is transmitted. Residential voltage standards vary globally anywhere from 110 V to 240 V AC. Also, the rate (frequency) at which the power potential flips back and forth varies in different countries between two main standards. In most of the Americas and elsewhere the frequency standard is 60 Hz (Hertz, number of flips back and forth per second, or cycles per second), while in Europe, China, and elsewhere the frequency standard is 50 Hz.

In addition to voltage and frequency variations, the outlet plugs which are used to tap into this potential are of different shape and design in many different places, sometimes from one country to the next. An American appliance will not (and should never) plug directly into a Danish outlet; a Danish appliance will not (and should never) plug directly into a Thai outlet, and so on. There are adapters which permit you to convert between plugs, but you should be very aware of the voltage and frequency of electricity you are tapping into and whether your appliance will safely operate with that input. This can be dangerous for more than your single appliance. Some places, such as parts of Great Britain, mandate that each appliance itself have an integrated fuse or breaker—because the electrical systems that you tap into there may not have this safety feature. In such case using an appliance without integrated protection may cause damage to the wiring or even a fire.

Each electrical appliance or device is designed to operate at a certain power potential (at a certain voltage and frequency) and will operate poorly or not at all (and possibly cause a safety hazard) if connected to an improper source. Any mobile living solution must be aware of these differences and plan accordingly for the proper electrical conversions.

DC

DC (direct current) is the other main type of electrical power that we utilize. Many devices, even those we plug into an outlet (including all computers), actually run on DC power. In the case of computers, cell chargers, etc, the AC current from the outlet is converted into the appropriate DC current by an integrated device in the plug or within the appliance itself. All batteries discharge and recharge on DC power. Given the importance of stored (battery) power to mobile solutions, it is incumbent to have at least a DC electrical system but likely also an AC system as well. These sub-systems will interact at certain points but must be kept separate otherwise. DC and AC power may be converted from one to the other as appropriate but they do not mix otherwise.

DC current, unlike AC current which flips back and forth, has a consistent positive and negative direction of flow. Somewhat counter-intuitively, current flows out of a battery from its negative terminal and into it through its positive terminal (so always disconnect the negative cable first when doing battery work). In order for the flow to happen, however, there must be a continuous circuit of potential, so many people think of the 'potential flow' as coming from the (entirely necessary and thus ever-present) positive side.

Current

Amperage (Amps) is another major aspect of electrical power. This may be understood as how much power potential flows. Your system will operate at a certain voltage continuously, but the number of amps that are drawn will show how much power potential has been utilized. Total power then is often expressed in Watts (or Kilowatts), which is nothing other than how many amps were used at a given voltage (Watts are equal to volts multiplied by amps; $W=VA$). Tracking amperage is especially important for battery use, as amp draws are limited by battery technology. That is, you can only draw so many amps at a time from a given battery. For some battery chemistries, the more amps you draw at once (higher rate of amp draw) the less total power (in watts) can be draw from the battery before recharge. Higher amp draws will also require thicker wiring. It is the amp flow through the conductive wires that generates heat. Try to draw too many amps through too small a wire and it will melt or burn.

Other Concerns

Computerization will be discussed further below, but electrical systems may be (and increasingly are) linked into a computerized (networked) control and monitoring system for centralized feedback and control. 'Smart' systems, houses, cars, etc. are often linked to the internet for third party access, but any mobile living solution can be so integrated and so monitored and controlled (whichever devices or system aspects are so integrated and allow such) from a workstation, a laptop or tablet, or even remotely from a smartphone or other net interface. Whether wheeled or marine, your entire mobile living solution, when linked to a continuous power supply, can be 'smart'-ified through the use of judicious computerization and networking.

Above all, however, we must keep in mind that mobile electrical power is limited. A static grid is designed to provide continuous reliable power, but every mobile system will rely upon either tapping into stored power, such as batteries, or instantaneously generating power, such as with a solar panel or a generator. Or else tapping into static 'shore power'. Because of this, all power use for a mobile solution must be calculated and monitored. These tasks can largely be computerized as well, but you must still have some way to generate every bit of power that you use.

There is always a cost for power. That cost goes up when it is stored for later use and also goes up according to the inefficiency of generation. Batteries store a finite amount of power and will do so for a finite number of discharge cycles. And so the cost of the batteries must be accounted for in the total cost of power calculations. Efficient use of power is key. It is only through the efficient use of limited power that civilized mobile living solutions are possible at all. Always consider power efficiency when planning your living solution—and also where and when it is better not to use power. Each use of power has a cost. You may have more power by spending more for it, but you may also save power by using less.

Generation of Electricity

All electricity use requires a source from which the electrical current flows. You may run your setup strictly on batteries but will still need to charge them, and so will require some source of power. That source may be a static utility grid at times, but this subsection will focus on methods for generating electricity while your living solution is mobile or off-grid.

Electricity is primarily generated by use of rotating magnetic fields to excite the movement of electrons; rotate (or revolve) a magnet around a conductor and electricity will flow. This automatically generates AC current as the rotation occurs. All magnets have polarity and as the position of the north pole and south pole reverse in reference to the conductor, so too does the direction of the current flow. Devices such as alternators produce DC current by using components known as diodes which only permit electrical current to flow in one direction. So the generator (alternator) will only pass current in one direction and that potential will flow directly (as DC) down a single wire to a battery, rather than flipping its direction back and forth. The diodes rectify the generated AC power into a steady DC current.

The current which is thus produced, whether AC or DC, will not yet be voltage (or frequency, for AC) regulated, and so will not yet be usable as power. There are exceptions to this: AC generators which have an internal voltage output regulator and only operate at a certain speed will produce a specified current type (the speed of rotation determines Hz). A solar installation may produce current at a static voltage, though varying amperage, according to the specific design and number of panels. Newer AC generators are even able to use solid state electronics to give a specified output frequency regardless of the rotation speed of the generator. However it is achieved, there must be some conformity or rectification of voltage and/or frequency before actual use. The specific method for this varies according to type of generation and needs, but may involve inverters (converting DC to AC power or vice versa), transformers (stepping from one AC voltage to another), battery chargers (taking AC or DC power and charging a battery bank according to specific parameters), and others. We will look more at these types of devices below.

You need not limit yourself to tapping into static grid power to charge or run your devices. Mobile electrical generation is still limited by size and expense, but there are many options which may be used both in conjunction or separately to source power. These include solar collection, wind generation, engine-driven generation, motor-based regeneration, hydrogen exchange, and even muscle-powered generation.

Solar

Solar panels are popular even though the amount of power they can generate is limited, as they represent a fixed initial expense in exchange for unending power generation through the life of the product. This is the ideal, of course, and realization of that unending power flow must pass several barriers. They only generate electricity when exposed to sunlight, so never at night. The rating of the panels, angle of the sunlight, the presence of any shade on the panels, intensity of the sunlight at a given frequency range, and the specific technology of the cells themselves (which operate at various, though never ideal, efficiencies) all impact how much actual current flow is achieved. Also, physical damage to an installation may lead, at worst, to a total loss of the product and thus the power flow from it.

Solar panels themselves will always generate DC current, unlike standard magnetic generators. The impact of solar radiation on the panels will consistently displace electrons and so will generate a consistent voltage and an amperage flow in accordance with the amount and intensity of solar radiation impacting the panels at any given time. There is no alternation of magnetic poles and thus no alternation of current flow. Because of this, more of the electricity generated from a solar panel will be usable power (at least for charging a battery), as it will not need to be inverted (a process which always involves at least some power loss).

Technology in the field of solar cells is constantly changing and efficiencies seem to go up and prices down almost every year. Solar cells are not limited to rigid formats (though as yet those are the most efficient) but may also be moderately flexible to be fitted on curved surfaces or even consistently flexible for use in novel areas. It is possible to replace the trampolines on a catamaran with solar fabric, for example, or an entire sail on a sailboat. There is even experimentation ongoing to utilize the exterior body of an automobile, which now will be just painted surface, as a solar power collection surface instead.

Because of this flexibility of application, solar cells are appropriate for every mobile living solution. The installation may be small or large, uniform or varied, but every mobile living situation will have at least one battery which will benefit from this continuous (daily) free (after initial costs) source. It is not advisable at this time to attempt to construct your own solar cells, as the industrial processes of formulation are beyond the scope of the layperson. It is entirely possible to design and install your own solar installation from bought components, however. There is very little standardization in the solar industry as yet and almost all installations are designed locally and installed ad-hock according to local conditions and availability and cost of necessary components. It requires some intensive learning and research but little or no personal experience to purchase and install the components of your own solar power installation.

Average solar panel prices are running somewhere around $100 US for a 100-Watt Monocrystalline panel, as of this writing. Larger panels are more cost efficient. Expect to pay 50% more for a flexible panel and a bit less for a polycrystalline panel, but prices do vary widely. Quality varies as well, but product demand and brand recognition seem to be the more important factors in pricing. So you can get better prices and still good quality if you look at different brands and their reviews. Polycrystalline panels are somewhat less efficient, but they have lower prices because they do not sell as well and thus may be worthwhile. They do tend to take up more space than monocrystalline panels for a given power rating, though not always and if you have the room there is nothing wrong with using them. Polycrystalline panels will not be effected as much by shading losses, so they might be the better choice in applications that have constant shading, such as with many sailboats.

Because space will be limited, you should look at the highest power output rated cells first. Cells are rated after manufacturing and testing for output so there may be multiple ratings for panels which are the same size. You should emplace flat panels on what flat surfaces you have, but also consider adding flexible panels for curved surfaces. If the different types you choose are not suitable for wiring together that is fine, as you can use multiple solar chargers for separate panel sub-systems.

It is best to avoid buying kits that include inverters or chargers, at least for those kits which seem to offer a discount. The included electronics will be of low quality in order to keep the kit price down and will be unlikely to meet all of your long term needs. I will discuss electricity conversion further below, but for now will say that it is much better to invest in core electronics that will do everything you need and do so reliably. Kits will also include brackets and fasteners and wiring, but all of these things are bulk products and may be easily acquired from many different sources.

Solar panel output ratings are for the ideal output. Meaning direct sunlight at a certain temperature range and no shading on the panel at all. You will never reach the ideal output. That 100-Watt panel might provide you with 500 watt-hours in a full day...and it might not. Grid power where I am now runs about 12 cents per kilowatt-hour (kWh). So a 100-Watt panel that cost you 100 USD to buy might provide you with 6 cents of grid electricity per day, before factoring in line and conversion losses.

As the point is to be free of the grid this low return may be acceptable. Space is limited for solar emplacement on mobile living solutions and you will almost never be able to emplace sufficient panels to meet more than modest electrical needs, but if you only have modest needs or you have other power generation sources then having at least some solar is still desirable. Those panels will produce electricity whenever the sun is out, with no input or further work on your part. The ease of use, provided that installation is done right and safety requirements are considered, makes this option well worthwhile.

Solar Panel Sample Options
$239; Heliene 300W; 65.5 × 39.4 × 1.6 in; 48.5 lbs; monocrystalline
$242; Astronergy 345W; 77.17 × 39.06 × 1.57 in; 48.28 lbs; polycrystalline
$225; SunPower SPR-E-Flex-110W; 46.0 × 23.0 × 1.0 in; 8 lbs; flexible (up to 30 degrees)
From www.wholesalesolar.com

Wind

Wind power generation is another renewable option. Indirectly, it is still solar driven, as wind moves in accordance with the heating and cooling of the atmosphere driven by the solar cycle. As with solar panels, wind power is derived from a device and system that requires an initial expense and no further cost outlays thereafter. Barring damaged or failed components.

Wind generators harness the force of the wind on the moving surfaces of the device to spin an electrical generator and thus produce electrical current. This is generally an alternator-type setup that produces DC current, which is then fed into a charge controller which charges the batteries as possible. In areas of steady wind, which is often the case in marine settings at least, a wind generator setup may well generate more power than a comparable solar setup and sometimes much more. It will work day and night, but is highly variable as generation is directly dependent upon the wind blowing. It will also only work in a certain range of wind force, depending upon the specific design and control of the unit in question. So, for example, you may need to have at least six MPH winds but no more than fifteen MPH.

There are a number of commercial offerings available tailored to both the RV/camper and cruising boater markets. These are not necessarily interchangeable as products for the boating market are required to withstand more challenging conditions. Prices, quality, durability, and power generation potential vary widely. Most seem to be more expensive than they should be, given the components, but nothing significant has happened as yet in the (ever-growing) market to incentivize much cost efficiency and force prices down. Until that happens, it may be advisable to consider a custom installation of your own. The basic electrical setup itself may be as simple as a given mounting and wiring of the alternator in a car. I would however urge you to consider the available market options first, as the output of a wind generator installation is, after the wind, predominantly dependent upon the aerodynamics of the turning body, particularly that of the individual blades and of the fan in conjunction. The design and construction of efficient blade shapes as fit into a fan and turning body, that will not break with use, may be difficult to achieve—though also rewarding both in personal satisfaction and in potentially thousands of dollars saved.

As with solar, wind power generation is variable and you will never get as much output as you might think based on the marketing campaigns. Some units will not provide power at all until there is a good steady breeze. Most areas do not have sustained winds that will provide power for hour after hour. Even the best wind generators will rarely, if ever, get up to their full rated power. Details on the Raptor G5 Freedom were included here for comparison purposes. It is possible to use one in a mobile situation but they are meant for fixed locations—they are relatively heavy and bulky. At the 60 MPH winds to achieve full power most of us will be seeking shelter out of the wind, for ourselves and our home. The Superwind 350 provides max output at a more realistic 28 MPH, but even those conditions will be rare—unless you spend time offshore in a cruising boat, which is the market that this model caters to.

As I hope you can see from my included examples, there are a number of places to seek out a wind turbine for your particular solution. The market is constantly changing.

Small wind turbine companies have been going in and out of business repeatedly over the past decades. My best advice for you at this time is to look at reviews and comparisons for boating or sailing wind generators, whether your living solution is wheeled or marine. This is a fairly stable market with good competition. The products on offer will tend to be more expensive, but are durably constructed and sealed against the environment.

Wind and solar power generation are good complements for each other. Both are subject to variable conditions but often one will still work when the other does not. Neither of them are suitable for continuous heavy power use, but both together can easily meet power needs that are intermittent or moderate. As you can see from my included price samples, though there are cheaper options, a durable wind generator will be more expensive than a comparable solar setup. It will also require more care and maintenance due to the moving parts. Do not jump into wind power unless your setup and conditions warrant it, but if they do warrant it then this renewable free power source is very worthwhile.

Wind Turbine Sample Options

$140; Happybuy Wind Turbine Generator; startup at 5.6 MPH, 400W output at 12V in 27 MPH winds
Inexpensive but not very durable.
From www.amazon.com

$549; Rutland 504; startup at 6 MPH, 12W output at 12V in 17 MPH winds, up to 80W; 7.7 lbs
Rather low output and expensive for that, but it is lightweight and should be durable.
From www.emarineinc.com

$530; Raptor G5 Freedom; 200W at 12V at 19 MPH winds, up to 1200W at 60 MPH winds; 43 lbs
Impressive specs at a good price, but may not last long in a marine or similar high corrosion environment. I think most of us will not be spending much time in 60 mph wind conditions.
From mwands.com and www.enniswindandsolar.com

$1190; Primus Wind Power 1-ARBM-15-12 Air Breeze; 200W output at 12V above 9 MPH winds; 13 lbs
Good option for wheeled platforms. Peak power will be generated at the lower wind speeds common inland.
From www.solar-electric.com

$1759; Silentwind Pro; 400W max output at 12V at 31 MPH winds; 15 lbs
Good marine option.
From www.silentwindgenerator.com and www.emarineinc.com

$2650; Superwind 350; 350W max output at 12V at 28 MPH winds; 25.3 lbs
Another good marine option.
From www.superwind.com and marinewarehouse.net

Engine

Engine-driven generators rely upon a fuel source, generally gasoline, diesel, LPG (liquefied petroleum gas—propane or butane or a mixture), or natural gas to rotate an electrical generator system, which may be designed to produce AC or DC power as its final output. Because of fuel storage, cost, and safety requirements, fuel used is always the first consideration in generator selection. These generators may be designed to provide continuous or intermittent power—continuous models are better built and will always be more expensive but running an intermittent model continuously will lead to greatly reduced product life.

For wheeled living solutions, gasoline generators have been the norm. More recently, dual-fuel models that will run on both gasoline and LPG have become more available. In addition, these and also plain gasoline generators can be relatively easily converted to run on natural gas via a kit. So, even with a generator designed for gasoline only, you can have a tri-fuel option with appropriate modifications. This is because even liquid fuel models will convert that liquid to a fuel-air mixture (using a carburetor or injectors) before combustion. Conversion kits only need to account for the proper mixture of LPG or natural gas with air to match the designed combustion product of the carburetor or injectors. All of these are open motor setups and tend to be very noisy, even with a muffler in place on the exhaust. This noise can be reduced by placing the generator in an enclosure of some sort, that may account for sound reduction, cooling, air intake and exhaust, etc.

LPG fuel has several attractive qualities. It may be stored almost indefinitely, while gasoline has a much shorter storage life unless stabilized. It is less messy. The cost is comparable and may be lower than gasoline. The tanks tend to be more versatile and portable without the risk of spills. It may be used for cooking as well as power generation, avoiding the efficiency losses involved in converting to electricity and then back to heat for electric cooking.

Against these positive qualities we must balance the main reason that LPG has at times been more or less popular: safety. It is a potentially explosive gas that is heavier than air. In a boat, designed to keep air inside the hull and water out, spilled vapors may become trapped indefinitely and could lead to a fire or explosion at any spark (such as the bilge pump kicking on). Safety will be less of a concern in a wheeled situation but it will still be very important to guard against any leaks. Note however that gasoline shares many of the same safety concerns.

Even so, provided that care is taken in checks and maintenance and even more-so that redundant safety measures are put in place during design and installation, LPG driven electrical generation may well be the best option (currently) for both wheeled and marine living solutions, insofar as power generation on demand is required. It will be more suited to wheeled applications because there tend not to be places for vapors to get trapped. For marine use, monohulls will have fewer safety options with LPG than multihulls, as a multihull will more easily be able to site storage tanks and generator such that spilled vapors will not be trapped in the hulls themselves. For example, they could be emplaced in drain equipped compartments on the bridgedeck of a catamaran.

In the long term solar or wind will be more cost effective because no fuel is required, but an engine generator can provide a lot more power in a compact space and a shorter amount of time. The cheap example I include here (though still durable for intermittent use) is gasoline powered, but there are comparable LPG or dual fuel models that will allow long storage of fuel. Even an inexpensive portable generator can be built into a permanent installation. You will need to account for air intake and exhaust, cooling, soundproofing, and fuel safety, but all of that can be done with off-the-shelf components and a bit of research.

Gas Generator Sample Options (AC output)

$399; Predator 4375W Extra Long Life (gasoline); 4375W starting and 3500W running; 108 lbs
From www.harborfreight.com

$999; Champion 100165 (gasoline or LPG); 9375W surge and 7500W rated; 215 lbs
From www.electricgeneratorsdirect.com

$2699; (Honda) Propane/Natural Gas Generator; 10.5kW max and 9.5kW continuous; 195 lbs
From www.centralmainediesel.com

$7499; Propane/Natural Gas Generator; 22kW max and 21kW continuous; 1295 lbs
From www.centralmainediesel.com

$9999; Kohler Marine Generator 5EKD (gasoline); 5kW; 290 lbs
From www.colburnpower.com

Diesel generators are very durable, but cost more to purchase and maintain. They are widely used in the boating world in addition to a main propulsion engine that also runs on diesel. This dual engine setup, one for propulsion and one for electrical generation, has been common because propulsion engine alternators are not suited to the demands of charging a large battery bank.

Recently it has become more possible to emplace a secondary high output alternator on the propulsion engine and so do away with the dedicated power generator entirely. Integrel Solutions is one company offering this type of setup, with a system arrangement using reactive control that does not limit propulsion power, mostly drawing off excess energy that would otherwise be wasted. Those seeking to convert a boat with diesel propulsion into their living arrangement may wish to consider such an arrangement in place of a dedicated generator unit.

As you can see below, diesel options are both heavier and more expensive than gasoline or LPG or natural gas options. They are also much more durable and reliable if properly maintained. Still, the main difference will be in the fuel characteristics unless you must keep costs down. If diesel is best with your setup, go that way; if LPG will work better, consider that option.

Diesel Generator Sample Options

$4255; Yanmar Portable YDG5500W-6EI; 5500W surge and 5000W continuous; 249 lbs
From www.absolutegenerators.com

$9989; Kubota Lowboy Pro GL 14000; 14kW surge and 12kW continuous; 904 lbs
From www.absolutegenerators.com

$16235; Kohler Marine Generator 14EOZD; 14kW; 770 lbs
From www.colburnpower.com

$18922; Cummins Onan CM20-3; 20kW prime; 1145 lbs
From www.absolutegenerators.com

We can tap into any propulsion engine to charge batteries or run electronics. All propulsion engines are already equipped to do this, in that each of them will have a starter battery which is charged by a belt driven alternator which taps into excess engine capacity to charge that battery and also power the DC electrical system while the engine is running. Capacity for this stock alternator will be limited, however, and it should not be expected to meet heavy electrical loads. It is quite possible to replace a stock alternator with a higher capacity or more efficient model, which will enable higher power draws. In some cases it may also be possible to emplace a secondary alternator in order to increase electrical generation without removing the existing starter battery/alternator arrangement. That is the method used by Integrel Solutions. This can actually be a better solution than attempting to upgrade an existing alternator. Larger capacity alternators will have much larger form factors in order to handle the higher heat from the increased power output.

Regen

Motor based regeneration is a type of power generation that is particular to mobile platforms such as marine or wheeled living situations. Many electrical propulsion motor types will also generate electricity if mechanical force is applied and the motor turned with that, rather than being powered to turn with an electrical current—the same device may be a motor or a generator depending on direction of electrical flow. It can be so arranged that usable power is fed back into a battery bank whenever mechanical force can be used to turn your motor.

So, an electric or hybrid car that is braking can start with the motors in regen, drawing force off of the wheel rotation as the car slows because of the motor resistance, producing electricity, with any excess motion before the desired stopping point being braked mechanically in the traditional manner. This will work with any arrangement in which electrical motors are used to move a wheeled vehicle, provided that the type of motor permits it and that whatever control arrangement is in place provides for the possibility.

One interesting potential with regen and wheeled electric propulsion in general is that any vehicle trailer may also be mounted with axle or hub motors. This will reduce power requirements on the vehicle being used to tow and will also provide the possibility of regen from those motors while braking, increasing range and efficiency of propulsion. The Dethleffs e.Home Coco trailer is a concept example of this in practice, which is equipped with a battery pack and is also covered in solar panels for passive recharge.

Marine (sailing) regen is somewhat different in use but operates on the same principles. If the propeller is driven by an emplaced electric motor for propulsion then that motor can also be turned into an electric generator from the motion of the propeller when the craft is under sail. This will reduce sailing speed accordingly because of increased resistance to the propeller turning, but every propeller will produce some drag anyway when the boat is under sail and at least in this case that drag will be harnessed for electrical generation. Reports are that multihulls, with their faster sailing speeds, are able to better take advantage of regen for power generation—useful amounts of regen power require higher sustained speeds.

In converse, a trickle of power run through an electric boat motor while sailing (instead of using regen) can eliminate that endemic propeller drag effect and this practice may be used without overall power loss if solar or wind generation sources are in play. So, the propeller will turn under (slight) power input as the craft moves under sail, eliminating drag because it will be in motion and passing water. In this way sailing speed may be increased without significant power draw. Sailing speed can be increased even more, of course, with a larger power input to the motor which will add direct thrust to the boat-speed (motor sailing). This is one aspect of electric propulsion that is often overlooked because the marine world is conditioned to think in terms of propeller drag with combustion motors—with electrical motors even larger propellers can have very little drag under sail. And with no overall power loss if alternated with short periods of regen.

I have no ready options for you to consider in the case of regen. It will be highly dependent on motor and controller setup and must be designed for. AC type motors themselves will automatically be capable of regen but the return power routing can be tricky—so the motor controller must be designed for it. Regen will not work at all with certain DC type motors.

However, here is an example of a hydro generator which is to be lowered in the water from a sailboat while sailing in order to generate power from the water flow. This will increase drag while being used and will take up extra room in your boat, but provides another power generation option for boats that do not have an electric propulsion motor.

$5378; Watt and Sea 600W 12V Cruising 24" Hydrogenerator
From www.emarineinc.com

Hydrogen

Hydrogen fuel cells, which produce electricity directly rather than driving an engine, are another potential source of electricity, though at this time they are expensive and not widely used. More properly, the hydrogen is an energy storage medium and the fuel cell uses the hydrogen to (directly) produce electricity, so there would still be tanks and a generator though operating on different principles.

The purchase of hydrogen is both costly and not widely available, as yet. In addition, fuel cells themselves tend to be rather expensive. Until these problems of cost and availability are solved hydrogen fuel cells will not be in widespread use. There are some significant safety concerns as well. Hydrogen is highly corrosive and so requires special tanks and lines and also any leak may lead to an explosion.

Still, the theory is sound and there have also been practical demonstrations of the viability of the arrangement both in wheeled and marine applications. In practice, hydrogen may be stored in some sort of tank arrangement. It is then fed into the fuel cell, which combines the hydrogen with oxygen to produce water and electricity and a little waste heat.

Simple, elegant, and clean. I look forward to the time when this has become more feasible than engine-driven generation. It may well also become more popular than solar or wind generation, as being more reliable and potentially more cost effective. As an energy storage medium it is superior to batteries in many, though not all, ways. At least on cruising boats, it could help to shrink down larger battery banks.

It is possible even now to use excess electricity from wind or solar or alternator to generate hydrogen to store for later use. You will need an electrolyzer, a tubing and storage arrangement, and a fuel cell to turn it back into electricity. There are serious safety considerations. Hydrogen can be very corrosive if not handled properly and may explode (as in the Hindenburg). Overall it is much more expensive and dangerous (currently) than other options...but you can still produce your own fuel in this way.

Hydrogen Gas Generator Sample Option

$3999; HOGEN GC; will produce up to 600 ml/min; runs on AC; 20.5 x 9 x 14.5 in; 60 lbs

From www.cheshirenterprise.com

Fuel Cell Sample Option

$12269; Greenhub 2 – 1000; up to 900W output (DC or AC versions); 16 x 24 x 10 in; 95 lbs

From www.fuelcellstore.com

Muscle

Simple muscle power is another possibility for electrical energy generation—and one that seems to be generally overlooked or glossed over. And yet, mobile living solutions are mostly limited in space and tend to reduce potential exercise opportunities. Why not produce electricity while maintaining fitness? Exercise bikes, rowing machines, ellipticals, and stair climbers all operate around rotating hubs that may be equipped with simple generators. Indeed, most commercial units are already self-powering by this very method.

Press and lift type workout arrangements can be made to operate a pulley to turn a generator or instead a pump to raise water into a tank (which can then be drained to turn a generator by gravity power). Storage space may be an issue but custom arrangements should be able to fit some sort of muscle powered workout generator into any mobile living solution. Collapsible units are not outside of the realm of possibility. The SportsArt company is currently marketing dedicated exercise units for power generation. The Eco Gym health clubs claim to obtain their business power needs from both muscle and solar power.

This will not be feasible as a main power source for most—you might expect to generate 100W with continuous moderate exercise. Still, for emergency use or light power needs it is a viable alternative. You could run a small laptop for a couple of hours on 100W. I have provided some links to ready-made solutions for this, but such will always be more expensive. It is entirely possible to cobble together a muscle power generator out of scrap parts. For a longer term solution you might consider buying the electronics new to fit into used exercise equipment.

www.gosportsart.com/status-cardio/eco-powr-line
windstreampower.com
www.thegreenmicrogym.com

Storage of Electricity

A mobile living system needs to be able to store energy for later use and also have the capacity to draw upon that energy immediately and continuously. This sub-section will consider battery options, as the best way to store and keep electrical energy on hand, and capacitors, as having several niche applications that batteries are less suited for. Also see On Batteries in Part Three for further information.

Batteries

Every mobile living situation will need a battery bank. Even if you are living in a converted vehicle with no power other than the propulsion engine you will still need a battery to start that engine and will likely use it for other things as well. Most setups will need a house bank in addition to any starting batteries, composed of deep cycle batteries joined together to increase storage capacity. Such a battery bank (equipped with appropriate charging devices) can act as an important filter for disparate voltages and frequencies of generated electricity which all charge into the battery bank, with a single DC voltage then able to be drawn off the bank for DC power and AC power to be inverted from that DC source as needed.

Batteries are electrochemical devices which are a collection of one or more battery cells. The individual cells will produce electricity at a specific voltage (depending on the chemistry involved) and may be coupled together inside the battery pack to produce the nominal voltage of the battery itself. This nominal voltage is standardized to be 12 Volts in most cases. As such, appliances which are rated to run at 12V DC may be run by directly connecting them in circuit to such a battery. If higher voltages are required, batteries may be linked together in series to combine their voltages together or a DC-DC converter may be used to increase voltage.

If the DC system negative is connected to one battery's negative terminal, and that battery's positive terminal is linked to the negative terminal of a second battery, and the second battery's positive terminal is then linked to the system positive, then those batteries are in series and, provided that both batteries are the standard 12V, the system voltage will be 24V DC. Batteries in series provide additive voltage. The system capacity (amperage potential or amp-hours) will remain unchanged, though the available power (W or kW) will have doubled due to the doubling of the voltage. To increase amperage capacity, batteries may be linked together in parallel instead.

To parallel, simply link together all negative terminals to the system negative and all positive terminals to the system positive. In this configuration, given 12V batteries, the system will be at 12V but the system capacity will increase along with the capacity of each new battery. So, two 100 amp-hour batteries in parallel will provide 200 amp-hours, and so on.

Large storage batteries of the type that are needed will mostly likely be either lead-acid based or lithium based. Lead acid batteries may be wet-cell, gel-cell, AGM (absorbed glass mat), TPPL (thin plate pure lead), or carbon enhanced. Lithium based possibilities are changing fast, but currently the most important chemistry, which overcomes or ameliorates many of the limitations of previous formulations for mobile living, is LiFePO4 (Lithium Iron Phosphate). LiFePO4 batteries are superior in many ways to all of the lead-acid forms, with one notable exception: initial cost. In addition to the cost of the batteries, accessories which are designed for lead-acid batteries may not be appropriate for use with LiFePO4 batteries, which may lead to an even higher conversion cost from a previous system in that more components will need to be replaced.

Wet-cell: Also known as flooded batteries, they are still the most common type because of low initial cost. May off-gas hydrogen when over-charged. Low charge and discharge rates, but if well constructed will still have higher cycle life than gel-cell or most AGM.

AGM: Alternative formulation that permits a higher charge rate. They tend to be vibration resistant, but also permit fewer charge cycles than wet-cell.

Gel-cell: Lower charge rates than AGM but good for slow deep discharge and provide more cycles than AGM.

TPPL: Variant of AGM, designed to permit higher charge and discharge rates without cycle loss. More expensive than the previous three but also better characteristics under many conditions.

Carbon-enhanced: Also known as Lead-Carbon. A further enhancement of AGM batteries. Best available lead-acid batteries for deep cycle. Increased amount of usable power, higher charge and discharge rates, and much higher potential cycle life.

LiFePO4: Completely different technology. Perhaps twice the price of carbon-enhanced, as yet, but provides superior performance in every respect.

Each of these battery technologies may be designed for different applications and to varying quality standards. The best alternative at this time for mobile living is to use LiFePO4 batteries. As noted, initial cost is higher. In spite of that, cost over time promises to be substantially lower. 'Promises' to be because careful installation and maintenance are required to sustain longevity for any type of battery—please consider battery longevity requirements when designing your installation and regulating use. LiFePO4 batteries are also much lighter in weight. They can charge and recharge faster. They have greater usable capacity.

A Battle Born 100 amp-hour LiFePO4 battery retails at just under a thousand US dollars. You might find a deep cycle flooded lead-acid battery at two hundred US dollars, which will provide the same voltage and is rated for the same (nominal) power capacity. But the LiFePO4 option will offer twice the usable power capacity between charges, be half the weight, and may well last ten times as long (or more) for a given usage.

Carbon-enhanced lead acid batteries, such as the Firefly, are about the closest you can get currently to LiFePO4. Retail is about half the cost of a Battle Born. Performance characteristics for carbon-enhanced are much better than wet-cell lead acid but still lower than LiFePO4 and longevity is still projected to make the latter be the clear cost winner over time. For an existing installation designed for lead-acid, it may still be better to opt for something like the Firefly than to also replace various other charging and power regulation equipment.

Battery Sample Options

$182; AutoCraft Gold 65, 850 CCA; 45 lbs; wet-cell; 12V

This is a starting battery and not suitable for deep cycle applications. It is included for comparison purposes—will provide approximately 100Ah at 12V, but only to full discharge which will damage the battery. Perhaps 50Ah will be normally usable.

From shop.advanceautoparts.com

$130; Duracell SLI31MDC; 59 lbs; wet-cell; 105Ah at 20hr; 12V

Capacity is over a 20 hour discharge period—you will get 1.26 kWh from this deep cycle battery if you pull it out over a 20 hour period. So that is a continuous discharge of only 5.25 amps at 12V. You will get less power from it the more you draw at once. Standard practice is to only discharge these to 50% capacity, which means it can only store half of its rated power reliably and even less with higher discharge rates—you will need more batteries, taking up space and weight, to do the required work.

From www.batteriesplus.com

$279; West Marine Deep Cycle 105; 60 lbs; wet-cell; 105Ah at 20hr; 12V

A more realistic price for a durable deep cycle wet-cell battery; it will have more discharge cycles over time. Still has all the drawbacks of the previous option.

From www.westmarine.com

$358; Lifeline AGM GPL-31T; 64 lbs; AGM; 105Ah at 20hr; Capacity 195 minutes at 25A, 340 minutes at 15A, 688 minutes at 8A; 12V

Notice similar specs to above. Main difference is the somewhat faster charge and discharge rate. Will be expected to provide fewer discharge cycles than the West Marine Deep Cycle.

From www.batterystuff.com

$300; Deka Dominator Gel-8G-31; 76 lbs; gel-cell; 98Ah at 20hr; Capacity 190 minutes at 25A, 335 minutes at 15A, 690 minutes at 8A; 12V

Similar specs to the AGM above, but will accept lower charge rates and likely have more discharge cycles.

From www.batterymart.com and eastcoastmarinebattery.com

$387; Northstar NSB-AGM31A; 76 lbs; TPPL; 103 Ah at 20hr; Capacity 220 minutes at 25A; 12V

Notice the longer reserve discharge time as compared to the Lifeline above. This translates into higher acceptable charge and discharge rates, though as you can see the difference is not great.

From www.impactbattery.com

$512; Firefly G31; 75 lbs; Carbon-enhanced; 110 Ah at 20hr, 110 Ah at 10hr, 101 Ah at 5hr; 12V

There are several differences with this type. As you can see from the available specs the discharge rate may be increased to over 20A without much reducing potential energy draw. It will also permit deeper discharge levels, to 70% or even 90% discharged, without loss of capacity between cycles. On top of those very significant improvements, expected number of cycles before battery death may be four times higher than standard AGM or TPPL. The claim is 1000 cycles at 80% depth of discharge or 3000 cycles at 50% depth of discharge. A much superior battery at less than twice the price.

See fetchinketch.net/boat-projects/battery-upgrade for a real use update of these batteries. Even though these are the best lead-acid batteries out there they are still not widely used because everyone is jumping to lithium instead.

From fisheriessupply.com

$949; Battle Born BB10012; 31 lbs; LIFePO4; 100 Ah, 100A continuous current, 200A surge current; 3000-5000 cycles at 75-80% depth of discharge; 12V

The differences are rather enormous here. Permits 1200W to be drawn continuously with no capacity loss, as compared to 63W from the Duracell wet-cell above. Even the Firefly only specs at 242W according to available figures. Three to five times the cycle life of a Firefly, which itself is four times a normal AGM. Half the weight.

From battlebornbatteries.com

$863; Bioenno Power BLF-12100AS; 28 lbs; LIFePO4; 100Ah, 100A continuous current, 200A surge current; 12V

Option two. Warranty is for two years as opposed to 10 years for the Battle Born.

From www.bioennopower.com

$900; Renogy Smart RBT100LFP12S-G1; 26 lbs; LIFePO4; 100Ah, 100A continuous discharge, 50A continuous charge; 4000 cycles at 80% depth of discharge; 12V

Option three. Five year warranty. A number of sellers are coming out with LiFePO4 battery types now. As you will see below, they are not overly difficult to assemble, though the process is somewhat technical.

From www.renogy.com.

LiFePO4 Cells

As an alternative, and unlike with large lead-acid battery types, one can purchase LiFePO4 cells individually and construct a battery therefrom—at considerable cost savings though with the caveat that there will need to be an external battery management system in place. These management systems are included in most packaged lithium batteries, as the chemistry and characteristics are so different from lead-acid. However, in an integrated mobile living system that relies so much on electrical usage, there should already be external battery management in place regardless of whether the batteries have internal control. You will be so dependent upon the battery bank that redundancy is desirable. The following link is to an article (one of many on that excellent site) which discusses and demonstrates further information on LiFePO4 and building batteries from cells. Please note the warnings given in the article. The retail options given above are easy solutions for what might be a much more difficult and complex process if you assemble them yourself. marinehowto.com/lifepo4-batteries-on-boats

LiFePO4 cell sample options

$165; LiFeMnPO4 Prisimatic Module; 7lbs; 3.2V; 100Ah; 2000 cycles to 80% depth of discharge
From www.batteryspace.com

$129; CALB CA100Fl; 3.2V; 100Ah; 2000 cycles to 80% depth of discharge
From www.electriccarpartscompany.com

$124; Fortune ECPC; 3.2V; 100Ah; 3000 cycles to 80% depth of discharge
From www.electriccarpartscompany.com

$125; Winston WB-LYP100AHA; 3.2V; 100Ah
From shop.gwl.eu

Please note that these are 3.2V cells—you will need four of them for a (nominal) 12V battery. The variance in price between these suppliers seems to be partially a matter of how they handle shipping charges, which will be extra. As with all batteries, cycle life will vary and figures given for that will not be based on real-world usage—so take cycle claims with salt, both for these cells and for the sample batteries above.

Portable Power

There are also battery products which offer a compact solution to power needs, in that the enclosure incorporates ports to link into for power draw, much as a generator unit might have. These are the so-called portable power stations and power banks. A power bank is a smaller device which will fit into a pocket and hold multiple recharges for a cell phone. A portable power station is a larger device, perhaps the size of a counter-top microwave, which will charge bigger devices such as laptops or even power small appliances for a period of time.

Some portable power stations will include small solar panels and may be referred to instead as 'solar generators', which is not really a correct term but is what is used for marketing purposes. Larger solar generator products are offered as a ready-made solution to storing and using the power from a solar installation. These all-in-one solutions will include the battery, the solar charger, and an inverter, which will save you from having to source and plan and install these parts yourself. Because of this such offerings will be suitable for some people. However, there are a number of drawbacks to them—they cannot be expanded or repaired, they are very low capacity, they charge very slowly, and they are very expensive for what you actually receive.

If you have limited power needs, a portable power station may be all that you require in the way of expanded battery capacity. If you need more then just get another one. This will be easy and not overly expensive at first, but will never be as efficient as a tailored solution.

Portable Power Sample Options

$17; Iniu Power Bank; 10Ah; output up to 3A; USB output, USB C input.

$250; Jackery Portable Power Station; 240Wh; solar panel optional
$450; Rockpals Portable Power Station; 540Wh; solar panel optional
$1900; Maxoak Power Station; 2400Wh; portable solar generator
From www.amazon.com

Capacitors

Capacitors are another type of electrical storage device. They are limited in the amount of energy that can be stored (as yet) but are able to discharge and recharge very quickly and with little or no overall capacity loss. Some marine and automotive applications use capacitors for engine starting. Many home appliances are equipped with start capacitors to reduce inrush power draw requirements. They can be useful for absorbing overcharge states or power fluctuations. They may also be utilized to maintain system voltage, for a time, if battery power drops out. Research into using capacitors as a battery replacement is ongoing and may well prove viable for more applications in time.

Capacitor Sample Options

$345; Powersports SuperBANK SB150-975L; 4 lbs; Super Capacitor Bank; 12-15V; Max Amps 3000; CCA (cold cranking amps) 660; Max Power 1200W; Watt Hours 8.16
This could be used as a battery replacement for starting an engine. It holds very little potential power (8.16Wh) compared to a battery, but can discharge all of that power very quickly. You would need to be able to charge it from your house bank, as it will tend to lose charge over time. The price is several times higher than a conventional starter battery, but one key draw for supercaps as a starter battery is that they have over a million potential charge cycles. One of them may last a lifetime instead of just the few years of a conventional starter battery.
From 4xspower.com

$1079; KAPower Battery Booster KBI BCK112035; 29lbs; electrochemical capacitor; 4-16V; Pulse Cranking Amps (PCA) 1778; Capacitance 600 F; Max Power 17.5 kW; Cycle Life ~1,000,000
This is a capacitor solution that is marketed to the marine industry as an engine starting backup. Even if all of your batteries are too drained to start the engine, this capacitor will be able to take what low charges they can put out and pile it all together for an engine starting jolt—potentially many times, if needed. For larger engines, this is a better solution for engine starting than the option above.
From www.emarineinc.com

Electrical Power Conversion and Control

There are many different devices for the conversion and regulation of electricity. Your particular solution may have need of many or none of these devices, but most of us will need at least a few of them. I have mostly detailed these here separately, but keep in mind that there will be combined options available as well, such as an inverter/charger.

Battery Chargers

A battery is a collection of electrochemical cells that reconfigure themselves internally as they discharge or receive electrical current. The charging process itself tends to be highly voltage sensitive. A battery charger is a device that regulates the voltage and amperage (current) that is input into the battery so as to enable full charge as quickly as possible without damaging the battery or reducing useful life—ideally. More specifically, a battery charger will convert AC power into a particular DC charging current. DC charging sources, such as wind or solar, will need DC voltage and current regulation instead.

Battery charger usage will be highly dependent upon what specific type of battery is being charged. A charger that is only programmed for wet-cells will not work properly even with AGM or gel-cell. It might cause serious damage with lithium chemistries and dramatically shorten lithium battery life. This is because lead-acid batteries tend to have three distinct charging phases—bulk, absorb, and float. The bulk charge is faster and puts in the most current at the highest voltage, but lead-acid batteries will accept less charge the more full they get, so there is a shift at some point into absorb charging. The absorb charge may also be known as a 'trickle charge' and some types of battery chargers will only charge at this rate (slowly and carefully). Bulk charging is faster but can potentially damage a worn battery. Finally, though, after the absorb charge phase tops off the battery a charger will shift into float mode. The float charge is meant to keep a battery topped off. It may apply a steady or intermittent voltage over a long period of time. This is actually desirable for certain lead-acid batteries, but float charging kills lithium batteries (if over a certain voltage). Also, an absorb charge is unnecessary and undesirable with lithium chemistries because the entire charge cycle can be a bulk charge...and there are many reports of trickle-type charging having a damaging effect on lithium batteries.

So, your charger must be specific to your batteries. You should not charge your batteries without a specific charger or at least a battery management system that accounts for that specific battery chemistry. Many commercial chargers may have different modes for gel-cell or AGM and this should be fine, but do not pop in lithium batteries and expect them to last as long as they should with your old charger still in place. Many newer chargers are programmable for type and may even allow you to set your own voltage and charge rates—which is very desirable provided that you know what you want. If you have LiFePO4 batteries there must be some specific charging solution for them. For commercial offerings like the Battle Born there will be a BMS or battery management system included in the packaging. In that case just be careful to adhere to the manufacturer instructions for charging. A tailored LiFePO4 charger will still be preferred.

Battery Charger Sample Options

$225; Progressive Dynamics Inteli-Power RV Converter and Smart Battery Charger PD9245C; 12V; 45A

Basic solution for wheeled applications. Will take shore-power AC to charge batteries and also power the DC system. Claimed to work for wet-cell, AGM, gel-cell, deep cycle batteries. Not programmable. Not suitable for lithium.

From www.etrailer.com

**$240; Progressive Dynamics Inteli-Power RV Converter and Battery Charger –
Lithium PD9145ALV; 12V; 45A**

The same hardware without the 'smart' system and preprogrammed with a 'custom lithium charging profile'. Not programmable and may or may not be suitable for your specific batteries.

From www.etrailer.com

$148; Marinco MAR-28210; 12/24V; 10A

Basic marine solution. Low amperage and only suitable for wet-cell or AGM.

From www.wholesalemarine.com

$435; Mastervolt Chargemaster 12/25-3 10976181; 12V; 25A x 3

Higher quality option for marine use. Claims suitable for all battery types. Not programmable.

From www.westmarine.com

$1155; Victron Multiplus C CMP122200100; 12V; 80A; 2000W

Combination inverter/charger. Programmable to suit any battery. Suitable for marine or wheeled use.

From victronenergyusa.com

Battery Management Systems

A battery management system is a specific series of devices to monitor and generally control your battery bank. It will include sensors at the batteries, a monitor for output to you, and possibly also some sort of programmable or settings interface. This may include a number of components from various sources but I will put some samples for you here. An actual management system will be more important with lithium batteries, but any battery bank will need some sort of monitor.

Battery Management Sample Options

$140; Choice BMS ECPC; 12-24V; for lithium battery packs; includes 2 temperature sensors

Basic system for wheeled electric vehicles.

From www.electriccarpartscompany.com

$282; Pico Battery Monitor; 12-24V

Just a monitor, but a nice one. Multiple inputs, output to a fixed screen or an app.

From www.simarine.net

$440; Orion Jr 2 BMS; 12-48V; for lithium packs up to 16 cells in series

Quality BMS for smaller banks. Full featured and programmable.

From www.orionbms.com

$890-$1680; Orion BMS 2; 12-800V

Quality BMS for larger banks. Priced according to number of cells managed (4 – 180, or up to 340 cells with added remote modules).

From www.orionbms.com

Voltage Regulators

A voltage regulator is a device which produces a fixed output voltage from variable input voltage. For our purposes this will be a component of power generation from an alternator. Many alternators may have internal regulation as well, but it will be setup for a specific use. An external voltage regulator may be programmable and thus tailored for your specific use.

Voltage Regulator Sample Option

$340; Balmar 614H; 12V multistage external regulator; Customizable programming.
From shop.marinehowto.com

DC to AC Inverters

An inverter is a device which draws DC power, usually from a battery but also from DC charge sources such as solar, and inverts it into a specified type of AC power at a given voltage and frequency. Every mobile living solution should have some type of inverter in order to allow the use of standard AC appliances and devices. Most should consider an integrated inverter/charger such as the Victron Multiplus above or the Magnum Energy option below. As you can see, inverters become more expensive as their power rating increases. When sizing your inverter, consider all of your power draw needs and also add a 'cushion' on top for reserve capacity. You will still need to be aware of your usage and even juggle device use at times.

Inverter Sample Options

$30; Bestek MRI3011BU; 300W max 12V DC to 110V AC (60Hz)
Simple but effective. Only useful for powering one or two devices such as a laptop.
From www.amazon.com

$340; Naturepower 38320; 2000W max 12V DC to 110V AC (60Hz)
Designed for RV use. Not suitable for marine environments and not nearly as capable as the next option, though the power ratings match.
From www.campingworld.com

$1375; Magnum Energy MS2012 Inverter/Charger; 2000W
Fully capable, programmable inverter/charger solution comparable to the Victron Multiplus above.
From www.altestore.com

Galvanic Isolation

An isolation transformer is a device used in marine applications to isolate shore power from the boat AC power system in order to reduce the chance of galvanic corrosion. It may also be useful in some wheeled situations. A marine battery charger should have an isolation transformer built in, but many automotive battery chargers do not. A galvanic isolator is a similar device but not as effective in all situations. Common practice is to include a galvanic isolator on smaller vessels and an isolation transformer for larger vessels.

You might instead choose to draw all shore power to your platform through a marine battery charger, which should already be built around an isolation transformer and thus will insure protection from shore-based corrosion problems or stray current, instead of using a separate isolation transformer. All of your AC power needs would then be inverted from your DC system, which in turn would be powered from that battery charger. There will be some conversion losses, but if you are on shore power anyway then the losses will not matter much as long as you design in a bit of extra system capacity (which you should do anyway).

Galvanic Isolation Sample Options

$230; Newmar Galvanic Isolator NMR GI-30; 30A
From fisheriessupply.com

$659; Charles ISO-G2 Isolation Transformer 93-ISOG2/6-A; 30A
From www.wmjmarine.com

Charge Controllers

A charge controller will have a dual purpose. It is mostly a charging device for your batteries from the solar panels or other DC charging sources, but it also keeps the panels, etc, from drawing power from your batteries at night or when not producing. If you have solar panels then you must meet these purposes somehow, whether with a solar charge controller or as integrated functions in other devices. Still, a decent charge controller is not expensive and will help protect your solar panel (and battery) investment. Some such as the Xantrex example here will work for multiple types of DC charge sources and have user set control options.

Charge Controller Sample Options

$151; Xantrex C60
Charge controller for both wind and solar generators. Rated for 60 amps continuous load.
From www.amazon.com and www.xantrex.com

$157; Victron Smartsolar MPPT 100/20
Solar controller. Rated for 20 amps continuous load.
From victronenergyusa.com

DC to DC Converters

These are devices for the purpose of converting between 12/24/48/72V DC power. For some applications you will want to have devices which require a different voltage than that which your battery bank provides. In that case a DC converter will be needed. It may be desirable and has become much more common to configure a battery bank at 24V or even as high as 72V DC. In that case converters will be in use in order to allow DC subsystems at particular voltage levels.

DC DC Converter Sample Options

$209; Mastervolt Dc Master; 12V to 24V converter

Stepping up from 12V to 24V. Higher voltage permits smaller wiring and can be important for long cable runs.

From www.hodgesmarine.com

$319; Newmar 32-12-10; 20-50V to 13.6V DC converter

A convenient variable step-down inverter. Note that most 12V appliances will handle a bit of over-voltage very well and even perform better in some cases, which is why this 13.6V converter will mostly work for 12V electrical appliances.

From www.wmjmarine.com

AC to DC Power Supplies

These are similar to an inverter, but are more of a niche use. Otherwise known as benchtop power supplies, they will output a varied DC voltage from standard AC power. Very helpful when balancing out individual LiFePO4 cells or for battery maintenance in general. Also good for limited electroplating purposes.

Benchtop Power Supply Sample Options

$180; Volteq HY1520EX; 0-15V DC, 20A switching power supply
$430; Volteq HY3050EX; 0-30V DC, 50A switching power supply
From www.mastechpowersupply.com

Total Solutions

The following companies offer various suites of products that together will serve to meet almost all of your mobile living energy conversion and management needs, and are all geared toward the wheeled and marine markets. To some extent you may even mix and match the different product lines, though do inquire what impact that may have on your interface integration. I have tried to provide samples above from each of them. These are all quality sources and I urge you to check into each of these product lines for any given electrical power management need.

Magnum Energy www.magnum-dimensions.com
Mastervolt www.mastervolt.com
Victron Energy www.victronenergy.com
Xantrex www.xantrex.com

References and Further Research

Calder, Nigel. *Boatowner's Mechanical and Electrical Manual.*

The go to resource for any mobile electrical system design or installation or troubleshooting. Useful for both marine and wheeled solutions. Excellent manual on legacy equipment.

Gibilisco, Stan and Simon Monk. *Teach Yourself Electricity and Electronics.* 6th Edition.

Rivers, Collyn. *Caravan and Motorhome Electronics: the complete guide.*

Little known in the USA, but Rivers is experienced and very knowledgeable. This is an integrated electrical system guide for wheeled living similar to Calder's guide for boating. Tailored for the Australian market but still very useful for other regions.

Gerr, Dave. *The Nature of Boats.*

O'Connor, Joseph. *Off-Grid Solar.*

Bartmann, Dan and Dan Fink. *Homebrew Wind Power.*

Rozenblatt, Lazar. *Home Generator*

For those uncertain about choosing a generator and getting started. Not a DIY guide. Covers both portable and permanent installations.

Dempsey, Paul. *Home Generator Selection, Installation and Repair.*

Goes into further detail about home power generation, including DIY and personalized solutions.

Barre, Harold. *How to Upgrade, Operate, and Troubleshoot 12V Electrical Systems.*

Wing, Charlie. *Boatowner's Illustrated Electrical Handbook.*

rvshare.com/blog/rv-electrical

gnomadhome.com/van-build-solar-electrical-wiring

faroutride.com/electrical-system

marinehowto.com

newwiremarine.com/how-to/wiring-a-boat

www.westmarine.com/WestAdvisor/Marine-Wire-Terminal-Tech-Specs

www.wired2fish.com/boats-trucks-electronics/10-basic-rules-for-wiring-a-boat

www.marinesurvey.com/yacht/ElectricalSystems.htm

www.uscgboating.org/regulations/builders-handbook-downloads.php

youtu.be/tdur_Ln-9cE

An extended presentation on boat electrical system design and choices. Note that these system designs are tailored for a lead-acid battery bank (they recommend Firefly batteries). Check out the Pacific Yacht Systems channel for more of this type of presentation, including a series on marine electrical basics.

youtu.be/NImNGe_3TYk

A similar presentation in regards to wheeled electrical considerations. Talk is based around a particular van build.

youtu.be/_IgSWVoa2uE

Another van build electrical video which focuses a bit more on installation.

youtu.be/eA7O7y5e2r4

First part of a series that focuses on user level information for an established RV electrical system.

youtu.be/cX4s-bxn4fs

Good intro video for electrical concepts. This channel has a lot of good information, especially for DIY work, LiFePO4 battery/cell usage, and solar power.

youtu.be/xuZg4NasCVw

Video that focuses on the components needed for a wheeled solar power setup.

youtu.be/Ht1kl37pJ2E

Example solar setup for a DIY campervan.

youtu.be/QcxFB1sVEJI

A boat with a very heavy solar energy focus.

youtu.be/L4XeHDYpR_w

Shows a more typical boat solar setup, as well as the rest of the power system for this sailboat.

youtu.be/qhstBD0w2hg

Setup and portability considerations for wind power on a trailer.

youtu.be/0uArpuWHVTg

Review video that presents a good overview of the components of a boat wind generator setup.

youtu.be/MsxDvm71AVg

Shows an alternative type of wind power generation that takes advantage of the mast height on a sailboat.

youtu.be/UaBxY-Pr_vI

Just a showcase video for various portable generators. Nice in that it highlights some new features that are being offered.

youtu.be/9VVNFSH7Gjk

This is a sales pitch for a particular marine generator product line, but it also goes into detail on the various features of marine generators and why they are specifically suitable for the marine environment.

youtu.be/QWgbM9DoA7A

One couple discussing their electric boat motor setup, including regeneration results.

youtu.be/Lj-_WMdwJSg

Brief explanation and good shots of a homemade hydro generator for a boat.

Fulfillment Levels

Low: Use the stock options of your platform to meet your device power needs and add a portable power unit if you need a bit more. Keep the platform electrical systems separate and undisturbed. Hire out repairs for your electrical systems if something breaks down.

If you are insistently non-technical and you do not hire someone else to tailor your electrical systems, or if you are doing a 'no-build' solution, then this will work. Power capacity will be limited.

Medium: Plan out your electrical needs and extend and/or upgrade the electrical system of your platform accordingly. Source, emplace, and wire in parts yourself or hire others to do so. Keep records.

By understanding your electrical system and its capacities, you will be able to utilize or expand upon its capacities in order to meet your own required needs. You will be able to integrate systems together and achieve higher efficiencies. Note that this level of fulfillment need not be very expensive—everything will depend on system capacity and uses.

High: Design a complete electrical system for your platform and build it (or replace existing circuits). Keep meticulous records.

If you are building from scratch then you already have a good opportunity to achieve a high level of fulfillment for your electrical needs. Even if you are not, stock electrical systems for mobile platforms tend to be rather minimal and can always be improved upon.

5.

Networking

By networking, I am here referring to electronic networking of computer components. This will cover both internal networking between your own electronics and external networking between you or your electronics and some remote source, usually via an internet connection. So, every time you get online to check your email you are networking (externally). If you setup your boat speakers to both play music from your laptop and relay the bilge pump alarm, you have networked your internal electronics.

Internal

If you have any sort of electronics on board at all, you will need some way for those devices to communicate with you—and possibly among themselves. This subsection will consider various points regarding internal communications and networking for your mobile solution.

Networking simply means having an interface in place for the exchange of data from point to point. This can be as simple as stringing two cans together to make a primitive telephone. For our purposes though it will more specifically mean having an established electronic infrastructure in place to enable communication between computerized devices. This infrastructure can be wired cables, wireless, or even use your existed electrical wiring.

Wired

Wired cabling may be of a variety of types, but the standard is to have some type of ethernet cable system in place that enables digital communication either from point to point or through one or more central hubs. Wired networking is more reliable and provides faster stable data transfer, but the initial investment may be higher. The cables may be subject to corrosion over time and in certain environments, but this concern can be ameliorated with care of installation.

Wired Network Sample Options

$229; CAT-6A Ethernet cable; 1000ft
Required cabling for a wired network. You probably will not require this much of it, but will also need to consider plug ends and switches.
From www.cablewholesale.com

$16; TP-LINK TL-SG105; Unmanaged network switch, 5-port
Basic switch for wired networking.
From www.newegg.com

$150; Netgear Gigabit Smart Managed Pro Switch GS110TPv2; 8-port
Configurable switch for tailored networking.
From www.newegg.com

$93; Ubiquiti Networks ER-X-SFP; Wired ethernet router
Router for wired networks to connect to an internet access interface.
From www.amazon.com

Wireless

Wireless networking is having one or more wireless routers in place, that communicate with individual devices remotely via radio signals. More convenient in some ways, in that no cabling is necessary and the routers can be moved around as desired, but also has certain drawbacks. The radio signals may cause interference between various pieces of equipment. This system is also dependent upon having a wireless radio integrated into each device accessing the network. Also, data speeds tend to be lower than wired and the interlinks may drop in and out over time.

Wireless Network Sample Options

$56; Linksys WRT54GL Wireless Broadband Router
Entry level wireless router.
From www.newegg.com

$180; Asus RT-AX3000 Dual Band WiFi Router
Advanced wireless router. Faster and more secure.
From www.newegg.com

$10; TP-Link TL-WN725N
Small usb wireless adapter, for connecting devices that are not equipped with an internal radio.
From www.newegg.com

Powerline

Powerline networks are a third option. It is possible to emplace devices that send and receive data signals through existing power electrical wiring, without interfering with electrical draw. They can be made to work on AC or DC wiring but not both at once. There may be some RF noise that interferes with other types of radio communication. Does not require new cabling and may be faster, more secure, than more reliable than a wireless network. The devices themselves tend to be a bit more expensive than a wireless router but are still fairly low priced. Most devices do not allow pass-through power and so will take up an outlet space. Generally they only permit standard ethernet cables to hook in (and to connect your devices).

Powerline Network Sample Option

$55; D-Link Powerline DHP-601AV

A pair of basic powerline network adapters. Will permit network communication through existing AC electrical wiring. You may increase number of networked points with additional adapters.

From www.newegg.com

NMEA

The NMEA cabling system for boats is waterproof, rugged, and RF shielded, and many critical marine systems may be designed to communicate using this type of network. Given that, it is also somewhat expensive, requires special software protocols to interface, and is limited in data transmission speeds. It is fairly common for boaters to have ethernet cabling or a wireless router in place in addition to NMEA cabling. If you do plan on long-term cruising, you should emplace an NMEA network in order to securely link critical systems. This will insure durable, shielded communication between important devices like your onboard GPS, radar, depth sounder, chart plotter, autopilot, engine instruments, and more. Your NMEA network can also be interfaced to other (PC) computing devices with a network gateway.

NMEA Network Sample Options

$70; NMEA Network Starter Kit, Model 124-69

Small cabling package for something simple, like connecting your autopilot to your GPS.

From www.amazon.com

$295; USB100; NMEA 2000 USB gateway

For interfacing PC devices with NMEA networks.

From www.maretron.com

$695; IPG100; Internet protocol gateway

For permitting direct access and control of NMEA networks via IP enabled devices. Also links to a cloud service for global interface range.

From www.maretron.com

Integration

Once your network is in place, many things become possible. Any number of devices, through some type of interface, may be linked in to an existing digital network. With patience, care, and not a great deal of money, you may be able to enable remote feedback and even control for every electronic device or system within your mobile living solution. Remote start for engines and generators. Adjust your freezer temperature. Receive a warning when your bilge pump kicks on. Or that an exterior motion sensor at your campsite was tripped. Access your nanny-cam from your phone. The possibilities are nearly endless.

Having such a system in place also permits programmable outcomes, whether or not the individual devices you have linked are already able to operate on a programmed schedule. You could set up a central computer, which need not be very capable or expensive, to receive continuous monitor signals from every linked device. It would then be fairly simple to program the computer to warn you if certain conditions arise or even to send certain commands out if other conditions arise. Such as notifying you if the batteries drop below a certain level of charge, or starting a generator to top them up.

DIY networking would seem to require a certain level of technical competency—more than most people have. Fear not, as there will always be tech savvy people who are willing to help you out for a fee. This will become part of the cost equation but the potential benefits from having such a system in place may still outweigh that drawback. And of course it is always possible for you to expand your knowledge of electronics and computing. Such knowledge is becoming almost as important as basic literacy for navigating our civilization.

Wheeled networking help can be obtained from Silverleaf Electronics, Coretronics Inc, and Lippert Components, among other venues. Most if not all new marine systems are being designed with networking as a core feature. Networked boating help can be found at almost any marine electronics installer.

External

Our home is an island, our sanctuary...but we all need to stay in touch with the outside world. This section will consider options for the mobile living solution to stay networked externally, mostly via internet.

External communications may also refer to making a phone call or using the audio band radio, but here the focus will be on internet connectivity. We all need to get online sometimes and most of us may need to be online more often than not, or at least to have that connection in place at need. I will consider the four main methods of achieving internet access: cable/DSL, cellular, Wi-Fi, and satellite.

Cable/DSL is the fastest and most reliable method—but requires a fixed location. There may be no data caps at all. Rates are usually on a monthly basis and are quite reasonable. If you have a static situation for more than a month at a time this may be a good option for you while you are there. While mobile you will need to look elsewhere.

Cellular

Cellular band internet is on the rise and very many people are using it now. There are many options out there which are highly variable in terms of rates and speed and data. This will change country to country and with different places in the same country. It is the most flexible option for mobile connectivity, but will be limited to places that there is a cell tower in range. Which means this will be much more reliable when near a major road or close to shore but less so offshore or for remote camping. Data plans with cellular networks and distributed providers are always changing and new plans are coming out all the time. Shop around and check out recent reviews. Try not to make long term commitments to a given plan unless it is a really good deal.

Cellular Internet Sample Options

This site provides a good overview of external networking systems for a boat along with some product recommendations.

seabits.com/best-lte-antenna-booster-boat

$200; weBoost 4G Maine Antenna 304420
Cell network signal boosting antenna, omnidirectional. Sealed against marine environments.
From www.weboost.com

$1090; Axxess Marine AX100AL Global Antenna; 9-10 dBi gain
Very high quality multi-band omnidirectional cell network signal booster antenna. Rated for marine environments. Hand made.
From www.frontiercomputercorp.com

$45; WiFix AO 1LW727V8; 698-2700Mhz, 6-8 dBi gain, 4G Omni-directional antenna
Effective cell network booster antenna. Will work anywhere, but not sealed against marine environment.
From ltefix.com

$1500; Max Transit 2XLTE; Multi-LTE router/modem.
This device will act as a combined internet router for both wifi and cellular signals. External antenna will need to be emplaced, though are not strictly required. Industrial-grade.
From www.peplinkworks.com

$350; Winegard Connect 2.0
This is a signal booster/router for both wifi and 4G LTE cell signals. Geared for RV market. Wireless but encryption secured.
From www.campingworld.com

$500; weBoost Drive 4G-X OTR
Complete kit for boosting cell signal while on the road. Up to 50 dB of gain.
From www.waveform.com

$130; Netgear 4G LTE Broadband Modem
May be used as a mobile internet hotspot from cellular signal. Will accept an external antenna. Unlocked, so may switch out SIM cards from multiple carriers.
From www.amazon.com

$120; Skyroam Solis Lite
Catered hotspot device. Works in over 130 countries globally. No physical SIM cards required. Skyroam offers their own flexible data plans. This is a simple solution for those who need streamlined cellular internet without hassles or much thought required.
From www.skyroam.com

Wi-Fi

Wifi internet is more of a distribution method, in that it relies on someone else having an internet connection, usually cable or DSL. Mostly this will mean accessing local wifi at free hotspots or for a nominal fee, but can also include mobile hotspots and network providers with multi-point access. Local wifi will be available on an ad-hock basis and relies tapping into the established connection of some business or friend as you travel. Can be free, at least in terms of cash, but there are often hidden costs (like data hijacking) or some obligation incurred. A mobile hotspot is a device that will tap into cellular networks specifically to provide you with an internet connection. This may be a better option than using a phone or voice included plan, but is still limited to working within cell tower range. Some internet providers offer the option to tap into local wifi within its own distribution network as you travel. Some vehicle manufacturers offer mobile wifi access, also through the cell network, so if your vehicle is new or not very old you may consider contacting the dealer to see if you can get wifi through them.

Wifi Internet Sample Options

$129; Parabolic Grid Antenna

A directional range extender antenna for wifi. Will increase signal range up to eight miles away, but must be pointed at network source. Can be swivel mounted to enable turning.
From www.simplewifi.com

$99; Omni Antenna

This option is omnidirectional for signal boost, but the range extension is only up to one mile.
From www.simplewifi.com

Satellite Internet

Satellite internet relies on a direct line of sight connection with a constellation of satellites in earth orbit. This is the only option that can offer a truly global range—at least if you can see the southern sky and the current weather is not too bad. More expensive and can be very expensive, especially for ocean crossings or remote land locations. Data speed tends to be low. The receiver/transmitter might cost thousands of dollars. That is, these points apply to traditional geostationary satellite networks.

The Starlink project by SpaceX already has over 500 satellites in orbit and plans to emplace up to 40,000 or so in total. These objects are emplaced in a lower orbit than traditional communication satellites, so they will require more of them for coverage, but this is already the largest commercial satellite constellation in existence. New launches are ongoing. The greater number of platforms will permit higher data processing rates. With a sufficiently large constellation in place they plan to offer cheaper, broadband speed internet access with a global range. Keep updated, as this may become a better option for mobile living than cellular or wifi. At worst it should still be a better option for most than traditional satellite. Service is scheduled to begin in North America in 2020 and elsewhere as early as 2021. As of this writing no paid service is being offered but Starlink is getting into beta testing of the network.

Amazon is working on a rival network called Project Kuiper. As yet, they have no satellites in space, but they are competing for federal funding and in a few years this could become a reality as well...which would be a good thing as it would likely drive down prices.

Oneweb is another possible future satellite internet option, also using low Earth orbit modules. They do have over seventy satellites in orbit and initially planned over six hundred in total, but declared bankruptcy in early 2020. As of this writing, a consortium of partners including the UK government and an Indian-based multinational conglomerate have purchased the Oneweb assets and are working on continuing operations, though possibly under a different name branding.

Google has a scheme for internet for remote areas also, but their Project Loon uses high-flying balloons to increase connectivity. This is meant for the expansion of cellular network connections and is not designed as a separate satellite type system. It will probably be used as a semi-temporary measure to increase cell coverage range, mostly for impoverished areas of the globe or during times of disaster.

Geostationary Satellite Internet Sample Options

$6995; RVDataSat 840 system
Complete hardware package for wheeled satellite internet. Data plans range from $80 - $410 monthly.

From www.rvdatasat.com

$74995; KVH TracPhone V11-IP
Hardware cost for this top-end global marine satellite internet antenna and modem. Data plans range from $995-$7995 per month or $200 per gigabyte.

From satellitephonestore.com and www.mobilesat.com

$13995; KVH Tracphone V3-IP
Low-end hardware from same provider, also for marine use.

From satellitephonestore.com

$1080; Iridium 9555 Satellite Phone
Cost for Iridium satphone—limited data use. The Iridium Go! plan is $135 per month plus $1+ per minute.

From www.globalmarinenet.com

Summary

At this current time for mobile living, wifi is nice when it is in range and satellite has extreme range and can be useful for keeping in touch, but cellular data transfer remains the best internet option in terms of price and versatility. Your setup can be hybrid. Some wireless modems are able to tap into cell signals in multiple bands and also utilize wifi when available. Options are always changing as new tech and applications emerge and people shift to whatever system works best at the moment.

References and Further Research

Dunphy, Chris. *The Mobile Internet Handbook - For US Based RVers, Cruisers, and Nomads, 5th edition.*

bareboat-necessities.github.io

www.thegpsstore.com/Marine-Networking-101.aspx

boatprojects.blogspot.com/2012/12/beginners-guide-to-nmea-2000-nmea-0183.html

seabits.com/best-lte-antenna-booster-boat

faroutride.com/internet-vanlife

citimarinestore.com/citiguide/how-to-get-internet-on-your-boat-your-best-options

www.rvmobileinternet.com/overview

www.technomadia.com/2019/02/our-mobile-internet-setup-for-rv-and-boat-how-weve-kept-online-for-13-years-of-technomadic-travel

youtu.be/bHWrRG_kdn8

Demonstration that you don't need to buy all of your electronic gadgets—a homemade signal booster.

youtu.be/jYdfH0vhBuc

Discussion on NMEA boat networking considerations.

youtu.be/g25yQwdtu-w

Good visual breakdown of boat internet issues.

youtu.be/BmNTJrdLHMc

Story about installing a Viasat satellite internet system on a popular sailboat YouTube channel.

youtu.be/3bsqVPwsPwQ

Considerations for increasing range and connection for van dwelling internet.

youtu.be/L1EzZ6aFxPU

Good discussion of wheeled internet solutions.

youtu.be/JYhsQSQOEbM

Design and use of a DIY chart plotter.

Fulfillment Levels

Low: Do not have any internal networking at all; access each of your devices manually. Use your cell phone for internet and maybe use it as a hotspot for your laptop.

This level will work fine if your needs are few. Complex electronics and networking solutions are expensive and you can get by without them...though having them is much nicer and increases your life options.

Medium: If wheeled, have a wireless network to connect compatible devices. Have the capability to use wifi when in range, maybe with a signal booster, and also have a mobile cell hotspot.

If marine, have your critical systems linked via NMEA and also have wired or wireless networking in place. Get internet when near shore using wifi and cellular data. You might also keep a satphone for backup communications when away from shore. Usually you will be able to get by with wireless networking, unless you are on a boat in which case critical systems must have solid reliable wired connections. Wifi is good when you can get a good connection and may be free or at least cheaper. Cellular internet has much better range.

High: If wheeled, link all electronics together with a protected wired network. Also have a wireless modem connected for convenience. Have range and signal boosting options for both wifi and wireless, which are both piped into a dual modem. Consider satellite internet as well.

If marine, link all of possible systems into your NMEA network and all other electronics into a wired network. Also have a wireless modem for convenience. Have range and signal boosting options for both wifi and wireless, which are both piped into a dual modem. Have full satellite internet for when out of range of shore. A wired network will always be more reliable than wireless networking, just as wireless networking, when it works, will always be more convenient. So the high end option is to have both, but routed through the wired network. Better antennae for wifi and cellular will improve data speeds and increase range. For wheeled solutions, satellite internet will mostly be a luxury, unless frequently boondocking in remote areas. For marine solutions, satellite internet may be the only way to free you from the shore if you need to be online. I am carefully monitoring the Starlink project and similar options.

6.

Applications

This section is about those things we do while living that are on a bit higher tier than basic systems. While living mobile, we need to solve such needs as how to continue learning or how to make money or how to just chill out and relax for a while, all within the same limited space that we do everything else. Or by moving our platform to where we can fill these needs. This section is about ways that we can integrate solutions for these needs into our mobile living solution. I have been brief herein, but please consider following my suggestions toward further research.

Education

Stop learning, start dying. Continual learning is an even more pressing need for those living mobile. We have to react and adapt to changing situations much more often than most people living static lives.

Learning is difficult and uncomfortable. It can be very frustrating and is often expensive. It also seems to be a key component to living a healthy fulfilling life. When we stop learning for long periods of time our mental abilities atrophy and tend to erode. Learning should be as much a part of our routine as physical exercise.

There are many ways to go about stretching the mind. This can be achieved through computer use and there are continually emerging educational resources to be found online. This is a very useful and versatile method and should not be ignored, but we can also learn in many other ways.

We can read, in electronic format or print. Watch videos or demonstrations or just the world as it goes by. Hands-on learning is also important—we learn many things by doing, by practicing, by trying, that we cannot learn otherwise. We learn by imitating other people or things.

We can also learn by simple contemplation, a method not often utilized by westerners, who tend to want to immediately engage the senses when learning. But just sitting still and reviewing the past in your mind is a good way to cement the learning process.

There need be nothing special in place to make your living solution suitable for learning, but it is a vital human need and should never be ignored. Also, you can tailor your systems or your activities to be conducive to learning, for adults or especially for children. An integrated digital audio-visual system will be further discussed in regards to entertainment, but such can equally well be used for learning or productivity.

Productivity

We all need to do some sort of work. It may be merely a creative outlet or just for money or even (if we are lucky) for both purposes at once. Regardless, whether you are productive and to what extent will be influenced by the ways in which you plan out and approach your working solutions.

This will be highly dependent upon the type of work you do. Your solution may be as simple as having a laptop and an occasional internet connection. Even for this simple setup though we can consider the differences in relative productivity that a dedicated arrangement or space can offer.

Do you work better when you can separate work-time from downtime? Most people keep these things divided in their mind based on their spatial location—whether they are at work or at home. If this is more comfortable for you, then even for mobile living you can separate workspace from other spaces. What about a flip-desk that you fold down during work-time? Or a curtain that you put up just for when you work?

You may also consider changes in ambiance such as a specific lighting arrangement or sound system that signal to you when to be productive. If you record audio, it is quite possible to construct a closet-sized or smaller insulated sound booth. For video, a blue-screen or green-screen can be put on a roller system to go down or up as needed.

Entertainment

Though it may be argued that we can get by without, every human who has ever lived has felt the need to be entertained. It is the balm for our active minds. It is the expansion that complements the contraction from when we have to concentrate. It is ease and pleasure.

Entertainment may take passive or active form. The difference is in the level of interaction that the person being entertained has with the medium of entertainment. To be passively entertained means watching or listening or both with no need to provide feedback. Active entertainment requires the input of the person being entertained as a participant. Passive entertainment is important and tends to be an easier way to pass the time, but active entertainment is much more stimulating and engages more of the mind.

Non-electronic forms of entertainment are going out of vogue as the digital age looms forth to swallow us all, but I think there is also something lost if we let go of them entirely. Playing cards with a group in person can be stimulating in ways that doing so through an electronic interface never will be. Sending the kids out to play, when safe, may be more valuable to them than any number of hours on a computer or in front of a tv.

That being said, electronic entertainment is convenient and extremely versatile. It can enrich our lives in ways that may never happen without it. We cannot all take a trip down to the ocean floor or up into space, but if those who do make recordings then we can all gain some benefit therefrom. Or if coders make simulations then we can have at least part of the experience of being there.

Consider all options when planning how to integrate your entertainment options into your own living situation. That which we do to entertain ourselves touches upon many other aspects of our lives.

Just as static living situations can have a tv in every room and speakers emplaced anywhere, so too can mobile living solutions provide for having audio and visual output (and even input) in many different locations—provided that special considerations are accounted for. Emplacements must account for the potential for vibration and movement, as kinetic shock can be very damaging to electronics. Weather and corrosion concerns must also be accounted for.

Screens and speakers both may be wired or wireless in terms of the communication interface, but wireless options will be more expensive and less robust. Power supply must also be accounted for regardless. A portable device with a battery can be put anywhere for a time but must be charged or the batteries replaced to continue use. Most permanent or semi-permanent installations will need to be wired for both power and data.

Consider that you may integrate any audio-visual devices into a combined system for internal networking and control, entertainment, education, and productivity purposes. A wall mounted screen (or two or three) in your main salon can be the visual output for a PC build that also connects you to all of your networked devices. Running one program would let you watch a movie. Run another to turn lights on or off, and so on. Your control interface could be a wired or wireless keyboard and mouse, but it could also be any number of options that meet your needs, such as a separate touch screen or a linked tablet or laptop. Home networking has made many advances in the last several decades and most, if not all, of these can be made to apply to a mobile living solution.

References and Further Research

Taylor, Kathleen and Catherine Marienau. *Facilitating Learning with the Adult Brain in Mind*

Barret, Robin. *Work From Home While You Roam.*

Myers, William. *Road Cash*

Fodor's. *The Complete Guide to the National Parks of the West.*

Drake, David. *The Legions of Fire*

Modesitt, L. E., Jr. *Empire and Ecolitan*

Bryant, Jefferson. *How to Design and Install In-Car Entertainment Systems.*

www.mentalfloss.com/article/585137/6-benefits-reading-every-day

www.artofmanliness.com/articles/how-and-why-to-become-a-lifelong-learner

liveyourlegend.net/self-guided-education-manifesto-teach-yourself-anything

lifehacker.com/top-10-highly-desired-skills-you-can-teach-yourself-5905835

www.freecodecamp.org/news/a-guide-to-teaching-yourself-to-code-and-getting-a-job-db7908dfb12e

lifehackmethod.com/2020/04/05/how-to-be-productive-work-at-home

thisanxiousmum.com/how-to-be-productive-at-home

outboundliving.com/working-making-money

careerkarma.com/blog/remote-working-guide

youtu.be/QzcdeFD42vU

Taking mobile education from a different angle, this is the story of a university student that lives in her van.

youtu.be/oE62OZ5QAww

Good examples for establishing productivity areas in your platform.

youtu.be/akyxfzs22hE

Detailed breakdown of how one van dweller has escaped the office.

youtu.be/caZmZs4JpxI

Discussion of various methods to make money while boating.

youtu.be/iieCJk2E7dw

A UK couple discusses entertainment options for their van.

youtu.be/CLuESTDVZyk

How one family manages entertainment while living aboard.

Fulfillment Levels

Low: Make no special provisions, beyond what you can do with the devices you have or with what you gather or order at need.

These higher needs can often be fulfilled in a variety of ways. If you approach the matter haphazardly you should still be fine, but your solutions may prove to be less effective than otherwise.

Medium: Make some effort to design your systems and living space with these three purposes in mind. Improve your ongoing education by making a schedule or taking notes on your learning or arranging a particular ambiance suitable for studying. Improve your productivity by organizing your spaces for work. Enhance your entertainment by a similar effort.

Doing these things deliberately and incorporating their fulfillment into our whole living solution will help to save time and effort in the long run while also improving the efficacy of our efforts.

High: Do similar things, just more-so. You might put more work into a particular effort, or spend more money on better electronics components. You might even design your systems especially with a particular application in mind, such as permitting you to use electric or pneumatic tools for sculpting.

If you wish, you can design and devote much of the resources available for your living solution to a particular effort, a particular application. If your work requires it, if your education demands it, or if your entertainment wants it, it can probably be managed, though perhaps with extraordinary effort or expense.

7.

Water

We need water to live and every mobile living solution must account for its acquisition, treatment, and storage in some manner or another. This section will attempt to explore various ways that these needs can be accomplished, in order that you may have potable (clean, drinking use) water on hand when you need it or just want it, to drink, to wash, to cook, to clean, or for any of the other uses that this rather miraculous substance is good for.

In its pure form water is simply a collection of molecules, each comprised of two hydrogen atoms and one oxygen atom. We will almost never encounter pure water, however, as the waters of earth are constantly being moved about and mixed with other things. Some of these mixtures are desirable for our purposes and some are not. Some will be desirable for some purposes but not for others. Three tablespoons of table salt (sodium chloride) dissolved into a quart of water will make a brine which cannot be drunk or used for most other things, but is well suited for pickling vegetables. Mineral water, with various earth elements dissolved in, tastes much better than pure water and is healthy to drink, but may lead to deposit buildup in systems which use water for other things. Water mixed with ethylene glycol (antifreeze) will be poisonous if drunk but has superior qualities when cooling an engine.

Potable Water

But all of the desirable mixtures can be accomplished later; our first consideration will be how to acquire potable water that is relatively pure. For most practical purposes this will mean that the water has undergone some type of treatment before it gets to you or that you apply that treatment yourself. Even 'pure' mountain brooks may have significant levels of bacteria buildup. An exception to this will be springs and wells in which there is a natural filtration process to make the water safe for use—be wary, however, as springs and wells used by local people who have become accustomed to that particular water mixture may not be safe for a traveler.

Rainwater will generally be safe to drink and use, though not always; if there are harmful atmospheric contaminants rainwater should not be drunk as it will pick up anything that is in the air. It may also be contaminated with biologics that are drawn up into the atmosphere along with the water cycle, though these are generally purified out (killed off) by sunlight or ozone.

Any water source, no matter how contaminated, can be made potable after sufficient treatment. Granted, it will always be better to start with as clean a source of water as possible. It is easier to put things into water than to take them out of it. With some exceptions, you should start with public or commercial water supplies (tap or bottled) whenever possible, as these sources have already been purified and treated in various ways that save you the effort.

This pre-treatment can be taken too far. Some processes, such as steam distillation, might remove desirable elements as well, that when present provide better taste or nutritional value. In which case you may consider adding desirable minerals back in via a mineralization system. Other practices, such as adding chlorine to inhibit bio-growth, may have both benefits and drawbacks. Chlorinated water has an excellent record for reducing the spread of parasites and disease, but will also dry out the skin and may be detrimental to digestion and at least slightly reduce overall health. Chlorine (and fluoride) can be filtered out or at least reduced, but there must be specific systems in place to accomplish this.

Tap and bottled water will be treated and delivered to different quality standards in different parts of the world or from different suppliers. Some bottled water is just packaged tap water. Some tap water may not be treated at all. Parasites which do not respond to standard treatment methods can colonize public water supplies. Know the local conditions and understand that for many places you may travel to having your own water treatment system in place will be essential.

Basic Filtration

The first step will always be filtration of particulates. This should really be in place for all water intake systems regardless of source. Even those drawing from reliable public water will want to remove any bits picked up from the lines themselves. A simple in-line wound string filter will suffice for most permanent installations. The filters themselves are inexpensive and should be replaced as needed. In extremis or for a more basic setup, filtering water through cloth like a t-shirt or a sock will remove the worst of it.

Basic Filtration Sample Options

$4; OMNIFilter 10" sediment filter (2 pack); for sand, dirt, rust particles; filter life 15000 gal
A basic wound cotton filter.

$13; OMNIFilter 10" Whole House Filter Housing
A housing for that filter, suitable for being plumbed into your water line.

From www.menards.com

Treatment

After that first step there are various methods in use which may or may not be appropriate for your situation:

Boiling: This will kill off living organisms in the water, but will not remove heavy metals, organics, most chemicals, or radiological contamination. Water should be boiled for at least one minute and for three minutes at higher altitudes than 6500 feet or 2000 meters.

Iodine, chlorine: May be added directly to water to kill off living organisms. Will not address other concerns. Should be added in appropriate amounts and you must also wait for a specified time before drinking. Carefully follow instructions or have a prepared method. For iodine add five to ten drops tincture of iodine per quart and wait thirty minutes. For chlorine bleach add eight drops per gallon and wait thirty minutes.

Filtration: With good enough filters in place all contaminants may be removed. There should still be at least two stages of filtration. There are various options available of the market, but carefully consider the specifics of your chosen product. Filters capable of removing bacteria and viruses may have a low flow rate and thus may only be suitable for drinking water. For several years I have used (black) Berkey water filters for this purpose, as being both effective and cost efficient, but the flow rate is only about one gallon per hour per two filters. Those two filters will purify about six thousand gallons before replacement, but must be cleaned periodically by scrubbing the exterior.

Reverse osmosis: this is a special type of filtration and usually involves multiple filters before the osmotic filter, but is characterized by forcing pressurized water at a thin film composite membrane which will only permit certain sized molecules to pass. Marine water-makers are a type of reverse osmosis filtration used to reclaim potable water from seawater. UV sterilization may also be included as a final step.

UV: May be included as a final step in water filtration to kill off (or render harmless) any remaining viruses or bacteria. Ultraviolet radiation at a specific wavelength and level of intensity saturates the water being treated in various ways according to system design. This is one of the ways that water is purified in the natural world, as it flows across the surface of this world in sight of the sun or drifts through the atmosphere.

Ozone: Widely uses in some parts of the world in place of or in addition to chlorination. Ozone is a reactive substance that will not only kill off viruses and bacteria but also break down organic compounds and improve both taste and smell. Forms naturally in the atmosphere as sunlight reacts with water vapor. May be dangerous to inhale in significant quantities but is considered safe in water treatment. More commonly used in mobile living in air filter systems which remove odors.

Distillation: Boil or evaporate water into vapor and recapture that vapor by condensing it back to water. Scale may be anywhere from a small solar still to an enormous industrial plant. If cross-contamination is avoided this will remove all significant contaminants. Will also remove desirable minerals.

Atmospheric collection: Pass air through either a cooled area to condense humidity to dew or through a desiccant to absorb humidity for reclamation. Effectiveness will vary based on humidity levels. Portable versions are possible but seem to require a high energy input for the results.

Various Water Treatment Sample Options
$2; Up&Up Concentrated Bleach; 64oz / 2qt
A bottle of bleach that may be used to sterilize water.
From www.target.com

$8; Potable Aqua Iodine Tablets; 50 tablets will treat 25 qts; 3 oz bottle
Iodine for the same purpose. Not as heavy as the bleach but will treat much less water overall.
From www.rei.com

$7; OMNIFilter Paper Carbon Filter; improves taste and reduces odor and sediment; 5 gal per minute flow; filter life 15000 gal or 3 months.
A secondary filter to improve water quality.
From www.menards.com

$107; OMNIFilter Carbon Block Filter; reduces lead and cysts; 5 gal per minute; filter life 20000 gal or 2 months.
A secondary filter to remove specific elements.
From www.menards.com

$280; Proseries RV Reverse Osmosis System; 4 stage
A full reverse osmosis water filtration system designed for RV use.
From reverseosmosis.com

$417; 3M 3MRO301 Reverse Osmosis Water System; 3 stage; 8.28 gal per day; 1500 gallons or 12 month life.
An under-sink reverse osmosis filtration system that may be suitable for mobile use.
From www.aquapurefilters.com

$490; Sterilight B5017; 12V DC UV system; filters extra; 5 gal per minute
A UV water treatment system.
From www.rvwaterfilterstore.com

$240; Aquamate Solar Still; 1-7.5 cups water per day; 48 oz weight
An emergency use solar still that will reclaim potable water from almost any source. This is a packaged and reusable solution, but a temporary solar still may be extemporized from any number of materials.
From www.landfallnavigation.com

Water System

To design your permanent use water treatment system you must account for the expected quality of your intake water. If you will only be operating in well-developed regions with good public water quality then you may not need any treatment at all, or only a basic filter to catch line particulates. If you expect to be able to operate off-grid or in places with poor water quality then you will need a more extensive system. If unpowered (except for water pressure) this could be a series of filters and perhaps added chemical sterilization when in jug or tank. If powered you could incorporate reverse osmosis or UV or ozone treatment. If you have access to plenty of fuel you could even boil all incoming water, before or after filtration.

Consider that all filters will have a specific flow rate and also a specific amount of water that they will be able to treat. If you will be operating in different areas with different intake water quality, you could section off different filter tiers in order to preserve your filters for when they are needed or to increase flow rate when intake water is of good quality. This is a simple matter of plumbing in bypasses and adding valves to be able to isolate or add in specific filters or filter groupings from the main water line. The actual setup will require planning and be somewhat tedious to accomplish, but if done carefully should make for a lasting and trouble-free subsystem. The extra cost for components will be more than offset by reduced filter use. You will of course want to ensure that your bypass valves are readily accessible.

Note that your water intake system may need to account for particulate filtration, removal of organic compounds, removal of chemical compounds, sterilization of biological contamination, removal of heavy metals, scrubbing for taste, adding in desirable elements, and other considerations. Some of this will be for health safety and some for increased desirability or taste. Tailor your system to your own requirements and desires.

Silver

It is possible to use physical silver, in some form or another, to disinfect and also to reduce or eliminate the growth of microorganisms. It used to be common practice, before refrigeration, to put a silver coin into a pitcher of milk so that it would keep for longer. So-called 'colloidal' silver has become popularized in recent years for a number of uses. For various reasons widespread use of silver for disinfectant purposes is discouraged, but there are still specific use-cases where it may be an appropriate solution. Burn victims are sometimes treated with a colloidal silver solution topically in order to reduce the chance of infection, for instance.

Colloidal silver can be purchased commercially, but most sources are not recognized by medical authorities and quality can be very difficult to ascertain. The best solution may be to make your own. I have been able to produce fairly high quality colloidal silver at home through a simple setup, requiring only a fish-tank bubbler, a power adapter, some clips, a container, and two pieces of pure silver. The bubbler should be as gentle as possible—its purpose is to agitate the water without losing any to spillage. Adding an aeration stone on the end of the air line can help with this. AC current should be supplied (from the power adapter only)—not DC. Both leads off of the power adapter must be silver as the current will be alternating back and forth. I have had good results from a power adapter supplying less than one amp at nine volts AC, but you can have some variation as long as you keep overall wattage fairly low—for safety, but also for quality reasons. A variety of used but still useful power adapters can usually be found at a thrift shop or similar source.

So, start with distilled water in a glass container. Put in your bubbler line. Wire the two lines of your power adapter (with alligator clips or some other method) to your silver pieces, and only the silver should extend into the water. Cover with plastic or some other non-conductive substance. Turn the power on, for both the bubbler and the adapter. Let run for twelve to twenty-four hours. This will produce a single batch, according to the size of your container, of water in which tiny bits of silver have been suspended by electrolysis. The silver bits will remain in suspension for a time, longer if the water is kept chilled and away from sunlight. The color of the finished product should be absolutely clear to the naked eye. Do not use colored colloidal silver for any potable purpose. You can check the efficacy of your production method by shining a laser light, red or green, through the finished product, as compared to a control sample of distilled water. The concentrated laser light will reflect off of the silver particulates, allowing you to get some idea of saturation levels. Note that these are very tiny pieces of silver and that your silver power leads should last through very many batches.

Finally, do not buy, produce, or use colloidal silver for any reason if you are at all unsure of what you are doing. I have included here, for educational purposes only, a method that has been useful for me in the past. The solution I produced could be drunk, in moderation, without apparent harm. I have preserved stored water by adding a bit into the jug before sealing (instead of adding chlorine or iodine). I have reduced spoilage (from mold and other growths) when pickling and canning by spraying a bit on top before closing the lid. Colloidal silver should not be used, except in extremis, as a substitute for professional medical care. It can be useful for certain medical purposes but not for others—a licensed doctor will be the best person to decide which. It is not a cure-all; it has specific properties and will interact with your body and with micro-organisms in specific ways.

Storage

After made potable, it will be desirable to store water for later use. This involves keeping it separate from the rest of the world beyond a water-tight and preferably air-tight barrier, which any sealed tank will provide. Depending on the tank material, there may be some leaching of chemicals over time that will effect taste or possibly render the water non-potable. This process will be accelerated by the presence of sunlight and heat—so it is always best to store water in a cool place away from the sun. For long storage, there must also be some method in place to inhibit the growth of bio-organisms, as there will always be some contamination from airborne sources even if treatment was perfect. Chlorine may be added or there are other water preservation products available. Adding baking soda may help with taste or odor concerns.

Most mobile living solutions will take on water directly from treated sources, pumped into tanks and possibly filtered, and then stored for use. Cruising boats might also have a water-maker (reverse osmosis) system onboard to extract potable water from seawater while passage-making or at convenience—at the cost of power use.

Water specifically for drinking may be kept to a higher standard by emplacing an additional filter before a small holding tank near or in the kitchen area. For example, a water line could be run overhead with a valve or faucet directly over a standard Berkey water tank which has been semi-permanently affixed in place, maybe with straps screwed into the wall/bulkhead. Other types of drinking water filters may be placed directly inline without the need for an additional holding tank, such as with under-sink arrangements.

Tank material will have an impact on water quality and also on the usefulness of the tank over time. Aluminum tanks have been widely used but have also widely suffered from corrosion issues over time, particularly from stray currents or galvanic corrosion in places where moisture is constantly in contact with the tanks. Stainless steel tanks may suffer from the same problems but less so, especially with higher quality alloys which are a better, though more expensive, alternative. Plain steel tanks will corrode, but may be built thick to increase time between replacement. Plastic tanks will not corrode but may leach chemicals into the water (depending on the type) and also become more brittle over time. Laminate (fiberglass) tanks will be stronger than plastic but will have some different chemical characteristics depending on the resin used.

Your choice of water tanks will be heavily influenced by your specific needs and setup, but also by your operating environment. Marine solutions will have more corrosion issues, depending on whether they operate salt or fresh or both. Wheeled solutions will also need to account for corrosion but to a lesser extent. Plastic tanks which have been specifically designed for potable water are readily available and may be the best overall solution for most people. If you are concerned with chemical leaching you will want to carefully research the type of plastic used. If you need a stronger tank material you may have to go with metal or laminate tanks instead. Laminate (fiberglass) tanks can be built-in to a platform that is being constructed out of laminate and can be used to get useful storage capacity out of curved spaces or dead space. If you are very careful you can also store your drinking water in glass jugs. Glass is fragile and heavy but does not otherwise suffer from any of the drawbacks that other tank materials do.

Water Tank Sample Options

$17; Coleman 5 Gallon Water Carrier, Blue
A basic portable water storage container. I would be concerned with chemical leaching over time or in high-heat environments.
From www.walmart.com

$200; 30 Gallon RV Fresh Water Tank; 40" x 20" x 10"
A water tank designed for RV use and suitable for wheeled purposes. Plastic, and thus subject to all of the plastic issues.
From www.plasticwatertanks.com

$279; 30 Gallon Marine Water Tank; 40" x 20" x 10"
A tank the same size and material and marketed for marine use. May or may not be the exact same tank as above—marine products are often sold at a premium, usually because marine products must meet higher standards because of the harsh operating environment, but sometimes just to take advantage of a captive market.
From www.plastic-mart.com

Pressure

Unless your water system is completely manual or instead fed only by gravity, you will need a pump of some sort to get it where you want it to go. This need not be electric; a manual pump arrangement can be workable, especially for smaller systems or subsystems. Many marine sinks are equipped with a manual pump to bring in raw water from a through-hull. This untreated water is generally ok to use for washing dishes or other secondary tasks, but that will depend on your location.

Electric pumps are much more convenient for general use, however. The arrangement is usually such that an electric pump is coupled to a pressure switch. The switch will kick on, powering the pump, if the water line drops below a certain pressure. If will then kick off again when once a certain pressure is reached. There should be at least a small range between the kick on point and the kick off point. There should also be some provision to stop the pump from running when dry or if there is a leak in the line. This is a safety concern as well as to save the pump from burnout and to save power—a runaway pump is a fire hazard.

Not much pressure is required for the small platforms of a mobile living solution. Somewhere between ten and twenty psi might be plenty, even though forty is more common. You will need to determine the amount of head in your line (how far up the water has to travel to the highest point) to determine how much pressure you actually require. Water pumps are not power hogs and do not require an extensive electrical system, but lower pressures will save you power nonetheless. A small pressure tank (accumulator tank) can ease the strain on your pump and also increase your water supply. Marine platforms will (of course) want to have redundant bilge pumps in case of water leaks, especially for a pressurized system.

References and Further Research

Calder, *Boatowner's,* Chapter 12

Casey, *This Old Boat*

Ludwig, *Water Storage*

www.cdc.gov/healthywater/drinking/travel/backcountry_water_treatment.html

www.msrgear.com/blog/complete-guide-to-water-treatment

www.ncbi.nlm.nih.gov/books/NBK310823

youtu.be/7gieUNuZan4
Detailed discussion of wheeled water system options by a gentleman in the UK.

youtu.be/9XEL-hj1F3w
Vanlife water system tour.

youtu.be/0kbKg3UbAXQ
Van build water system walk-through.

youtu.be/tETjcFKccjM
Discussion of water-makers for boats, including custom build option.

youtu.be/-Ov-24uJ8oE
Water system tips for a production motor-yacht.

youtu.be/Qq6mk2LjOzY
Rebuilding the water system on a sailboat.

Fulfillment Levels

Low: Buy bottled water or jugs and fill from a tap when available. Add disinfectant if necessary.

Cheap and convenient in the short term, but a poor long term solution for a number of reasons.

Medium: Emplace water tanks in your living solution along with permanently installed plumbing. Account for filtration and disinfectant needs, with specific filters and additives, according to your operating environment.

Not a lot more expensive, though more work will be required. Much more suitable for long term use and can be appropriate for those who do not venture far from civilization.

High: Emplace multiple water tanks in order to fully isolate portions of your water supply from cross-contamination. Install a carefully planned filtration and treatment system in-line to process all intake water before storage. Keep on hand alternative or emergency water options. Fully account for any long term storage concerns.

If you will be operating in primitive conditions for long a complex treatment installation will be very desirable in order to provide consistently clean water for use. If operating in remote locations, ensuring redundancy in water supply may be essential. Remember that you will only survive a few days without, so always have contingency plans for water needs.

8.

Air

We all want clean air to breathe. We also like to have that air at a comfortable humidity level and to move it around from time to time, or even harness it to do work. This section will consider systems that can be integrated into your living system to handle dust, smells, smoke, humidity, aerosol chemicals, motor exhaust, and even to do work for you.

Filtration and Purification

Any continuous air movement or vent system must account for dust and particle buildup in some way—even if that just means sweeping the floor periodically. Air filtration is a method used to remove particles or other contaminants that are suspended in the air, by moving the air through the controlled passage of the filter. Air filters tend to be just strands or tendrils or fibers which will pass gasses but snag at and hold all but the smallest of particulates. They may be used until full and discarded or flipped over and blown or washed out for reuse. Any passage where there is regular air movement may be suitable for filter emplacement. More expensive filters may remove secondhand smoke, allergens, chemicals, and more. These are commonly available in any number of sizes to suit your needs.

Air Filter Sample Options

$4; True Blue Basic FPR 5 Pleated Air Filter; 12in x 12in x 1in
Very basic air filter option. Good for large particles only.
From www.homedepot.com

$131; Honeywell Elite Allergen Pleated FPR 10 Air Filter; 12in x 12in x 1in
A much better filter which will remove most allergen sources, such as smoke, dander, and pollen.
From www.homedepot.com

Purification

Active (powered) air purification methods also exist which follow similar principles to some water purification methods, but tend to have potential drawbacks in addition to consuming electricity. The simplest and best home air purifier is the houseplant. All of them will take in your waste CO_2 and produce oxygen and different varieties will reduce various toxin sources that may be in the air. A kept aloe plant will produce oxygen, reduce airborne toxins, and offer a balm for damaged skin. In a confined space it will also reduce humidity, as will other succulents. Houseplants and people form a symbiotic relationship. There are also various powered options out there, but results will vary widely and you may not have the electrical energy to spare.

Air Purification Sample Options

$15; Aloe Vera Plant; 4 in pot
Natural air filtration. What you breathe out, it breathes in, and vice-versa.
From gardengoodsdirect.com

$400; G3 Series UV Ionic Air Purifier; 12V DC, 15W; up to 300 sq ft
A device which uses electricity to ionize air as it passes through, which will tend to break down particulates and also kill many microorganisms.
From www.airoasis.com

Movement

Air movement is caused by pressure variation. That's it. Wind moves from areas of high pressure to areas with lower pressure through the easiest path. Openings such as windows on either side of a structure that is otherwise blocking wind path will have air movement through them as the easiest way past. Fans move air by creating a higher pressure zone on the back side than on the front, causing air movement toward the front. Fans small and large may be emplaced throughout the living space to facilitate the movement of air. Smaller varieties do not require much electricity and all of them may be turned on or off at will.

Consider that computer case fans are designed to be long lasting with very low power draw and can be powered by any DC source—like the batteries in your mobile solution. These can be used alone or in series for custom built small-scale vent and/or filtration systems.

Fan Sample Options

$25; 12 Volt "Tornado Fan" with Removable Mounting Clip
A small mobile fan that will run on 12V DC power.
From www.12volt-travel.com

$60; Caframo Compact 2-speed 12V DC Fan
A marinized fan, somewhat larger, also for 12V DC systems.
From www.westmarine.com

$155; Fantastic Vent Model 4000 801250 Smoke
A roof vent fan designed for wheeled use. Reversible, 3-speed, standard 14 inch square.
From www.adventurerv.net

$17; APEVIA AF512S-BK; 120mm PC case fans, 5 pack; 12DV, .25A; 30000 hour life
A pack of five computer case fans with very low power draw and long usage life. Airflow from any one of these will be limited, but used in series they can be very useful for custom venting arrangements.
From www.newegg.com

Humidity

With open air movement through a structure from and to the outside humidity control is generally not feasible. If there is restricted or very little air movement then humidity may be raised with a humidifier device (requiring water input) or lowered by use of a dehumidifier (which reclaims water). A dehumidifier does not produce potable water but what it does produce may be treated to become potable. Atmosphere control for comfort will be dealt with further in the heating and cooling sections.

Powered Humidity Control Sample Options

$27; SmartDevil Personal Desk Humidifier; battery powered
A small humidifier device to increase the humidity of a workspace.

From www.amazon.com

$23; Eva Dry E-500 Renewable High Capacity Dehumidifier
A small dehumidifier device to reduce the humidity of a workspace or other small area.

From www.eva-dry.com

$47; Lonove Dehumidifier; battery powered; 185 sq ft
A larger capacity dehumidifier. Runs on standard residential AC power, and thus will be a larger draw on your battery bank than a DC model because of inverter conversion losses.

From www.amazon.com

To Do Work

Air may also be compressed and stored for controlled release to generate power or to blow things clean. Air compressors are simple machines and relatively energy efficient. Pneumatic systems and tools are widely available and should be at least considered for every living situation. For some uses, such as inflating a tire, a pneumatic system is required.

Tire pressure is a constant concern and so you should at least have on hand tire inflation sealer cans for emergencies. Ideally, you should have your own air compressor and fittings as well, provided you have the electrical power for it. Muscle-powered pumps, small or large, are also available and may substitute for an electric compressor.

Air Compression and Storage Sample Options

$13; Fix-a-Flat 16oz
Compressed air and puncture sealant combined together in a can.

From www.fixaflat.com

$10; Air Foot Pump; up to 45 psi
Designed mostly for bicycle tires, this pump will still work for larger vehicle tires in an emergency—though with much work from you and with greater wear on the pump.

From www.harborfreight.com

$21; Lifeline AAA 300 PSI 12 Volt DC Air Compressor
An emergency tire inflation device designed to be plugged into a lighter socket. Best to have your engine running during use or be able to tap into a house bank.

From www.amazon.com

$36; EPAuto 12V DC Portable Air Compressor Pump; up to 70 psi
A more durable 12V pump with digital functionality.
From www.amazon.com

$286; Puma 3/4-HP 3-Gallon 12-Volt Continuous Duty Air Compressor
A very durable utility air compressor designed for 12V systems.
From www.aircompressorsdirect.com

$380; 15 Gallon Air Tank Horizontal; 200 psi; 12in x 33in; 51 lbs
An even more capable utility compressor.
From www.compressorworld.com

Ventilation

Most boats have little or no active air control, but any marine vessel can benefit from an appropriate and properly designed system. For example, a fan and/or air filter may be mounted on fixed rails over a port (window), to be slid aside to open the port or as desired. This will provide you with a custom air intake or exhaust port. Two of these on opposite sides of the boat will create steady airflow even in still conditions. The filters may be designed to screen out insects and filter out undesirable elements in the exterior atmosphere.

All combustion engine compartments should have deliberate airflow, for heat dispersion if for no other reason. Filters may also be emplaced against dispersal of chemical or combustion smells. Baffles in the exhaust line may be considered to help reduce noise. For example, a custom air-duct may be run from an engine compartment to its own port outlet. It would require a fan to push air out and also a screening arrangement at the port and some way for water coming in to be drained. A baffle or muffler arrangement may be included to reduce noise outside the port. In addition, the air consumption needs of the engine must be allowed for. If the exhaust fan creates a low pressure zone in the compartment (or there is one anyway just from the engine sucking in air) and there is insufficient seepage from the rest of the boat then engine performance will suffer. Air intake can be routed from another port arrangement.

There should also be consideration regarding exhaust fumes from engines or generators for wheeled solutions. A window or inward blowing fan at the rear of a vehicle may suck in fumes, but an outward blowing fan will guard against this.

Engine Blower Fan Sample Option

$133; 3" DC Marine Blower – 125 CFM
A standard marine engine blower fan. Should be switched on prior to turning on engine in order to evacuate any combustible fumes. May also be used for exhaust or intake purposes, though direct exposure to exhaust fumes should be avoided in order to reduce corrosion.
From www.fisheriessupply.com

Diving

Air lines for close diving and dive compressors for scuba are also very useful for marine living solutions. There are commercial options available for both and custom arrangements may also be considered. All custom arrangements should be carefully researched and utilized. There are important safety considerations for any depth of water which commercial solutions will have accounted for. Sudden pressure loss beyond a certain depth may result in injury or death. Be very careful and know what you are doing.

Diving Sample Options

$1495; Air Line by J Sink; 12V160-3
A diving air line linked to a floating compressor motor, with safety arrangements to maintain air pressure.
From airlinebyjsink.com

$8983; Nuvair Nomad Two-Stage Low Pressure Diesel Compressor
A full scuba diving compressor system, for filling tanks. The diesel motor increases the expense but can simplify fuel needs and will be very dependable.
From www.americandivingsupply.com

$2980; Max Air 35 Scuba Tank Compressors; AC electric or gasoline
Electric or gasoline options for filling scuba tanks.
From www.scuba.com

Desiccants

Desiccant pouches for humidity control are an inexpensive way to guard against mold and mildew caused by condensation. These are widely used in marine environments but can also be placed in cracks and crevices of wheeled solutions to help reduce mold growth or as needed for leaks.

Desiccant Sample Options

$8; 100 Packets 2 Gram Silica Gel Desiccant Pack
Small desiccant pouches. Low price and will reduce humidity in small areas. May have limited re-usability if gently warmed in an oven or similar device.
From www.amazon.com

$13; Interteck Packaging 10 Gram Silica Gel Packets; 30 pack
Larger desiccant pouches specifically designed to be re-usable after warming the moisture out.
From www.amazon.com

$61; Container DRI II Desiccants; carton of 32 bags
Much larger desiccant pouches designed for use in ship containers. Will absorb a significant amount of moisture.
From www.uline.com

References and Further Research

Brylske, Alex. *The Complete Diver*

Silva, Carlos. *Build Your own Hookah and Shallow Water Diving Helmet.*

www.deeperblue.com/beginners-guide-scuba-diving

www.epa.gov/sites/production/files/2018-07/documents/guide_to_air_cleaners_in_the_home_2nd_edition.pdf

www.aircompressorsdirect.com/stories/156-How-to-Pick-the-Perfect-Air-Compressor.html

youtu.be/ikBuYB7S-fY

Nice video on a DIY vent fan for wheeled setups.

youtu.be/nODxIJeGGyw

Very basic but still safe arrangement for limited range underwater work (dive line).

youtu.be/guADtkWHRlM

Detailed video showing one boater's efforts at humidity control.

youtu.be/VidZMqmTgJQ

Discussion on the limitations and capabilities of air purifiers.

youtu.be/AiZmkcK4ufY

Discussion on ventilation and humidity for van living.

Fulfillment Levels

Low: Open a door or window when you want some airflow. Maybe keep a fan or two. Have some desiccant pouches on hand for marine living. Keep a can of fix-a-flat or a small compressor for wheeled living. Stick with stock venting and exhaust installations on all motors.

Basic steps are fine as long as you are satisfied with your air quality and usage.

Medium: Arrange air filtration options for your living space. Emplace vents and fans to control airflow. Attempt some humidity control, depending on climate environment. Keep a utility compressor for general use and maybe a diving line arrangement as well. Keep houseplants.

Stepping up your air control game a bit will not be very expensive over time and can greatly improve quality of life.

High: Beef up your filtration methods, possibly with both powered and unpowered solutions. Attempt to fully control airflow with a ventilation and filtration system, with humidity control either built in or separate or both. Use both vent fans and space and/or portable fans for air movement. Keep a utility compressor on hand and maybe a dive compressor as well. Keep houseplants. Consider custom venting arrangements for engine and electrical spaces.

Filtration and air control can be significantly improved if desired, though at rising cost. If you are doing a centralized heating/cooling arrangement then full vent systems may be a necessary step. Most steps at this level of fulfillment will be some incremental increase over the medium level.

9.

Food

Fulfilling the need for food while living mobile can be more of a challenge than for those living sedentary, but it can also be more rewarding. Included here are thoughts that may or may not help you, but the main idea I hope to get across is that there are many, many ways to get adequate nutrition. Or a thriving level of nutrition. And to store food for later use. And to prepare your food for consumption.

Acquisition and Generation

For most the acquisition of food will involve some sort of shopping, but even here there are different aspects to consider. Shopping can be wholesale or retail, though to some extent online shopping is blurring this distinction, in which case we can think of the difference more as being in bulk or not. Retail outlets sell things in small quantities or packages but at a significant mark-up. These are more convenient and cheaper at any given moment, but more expensive over time. Wholesale or bulk shopping means purchasing larger amounts at a discount or with a lower markup, often with the need to repackage the purchase into usable quantities at home. Bulk shopping may require a large freezer or more storage space than you have, but consider your options carefully as it is a good way to save money.

We can also divide our shopping into whether we purchase prepackaged and already prepared foods or instead the basic ingredients needed to assemble and cook meals ourselves. Prepackaged foods are convenient and require less preparation, but often contain undesirable additives and may be lacking in nutrition. Cooking from ingredients permits healthier, more wholesome, and more satisfying meals and is often less expensive, but also requires more time and you must have the arrangements in place and the cookware necessary to enable you to do this. Mobile living solutions vary greatly in terms of available cooking setups and of course you should do what is best for your own situation, but, provided safety is considered, there are a number of arrangements that may permit controlled heating of food.

Micro-production of nutrition sources is possible in any living situation. Plants or gardens can be crammed in anywhere there is sunlight—just bring (carefully balanced) soil and keep them watered. Small animals require minimal enclosures and husbandry may be very simple. Consider that guinea pigs, which are very easy to raise and require almost no space, are a food animal for many people in South America. Certain types of insects or worms are even easier to produce and can provide a good source of protein and vital nutrients. Fish tanks are heavy for their size but are another possibility. These sources can also be combined and cycled—worms to feed the fish that feed you, which then makes fertilizer for the plants that feed the worms, and so on.

We may also hunt, trap, fish, or gather food sources from the natural world... provided that we account for local laws, respect property rights, and keep food safety in mind. This is a very broad area of its own that I will not dive into here. It is worth considering that human pollution of the environment consistently impacts wild animals more than it does domesticated animals. Wild creatures may be eating garbage or plastic or other undesirable human waste or agricultural products and their living environments may be polluted by chemicals or toxins. These and other factors will impact the quality of food harvested from wild creatures.

If hunting is your thing, you can move about to catch the different seasons for different areas. Depending where you are at any given time, fishing may be a much more viable option for you. Hand-line fishing in open water requires very simple equipment but can be easy and rewarding. Cast netting in shallow waters requires only a net and some patience. If you are in a semi-fixed location that has fairly clean water, a simple net or barrier system can enable you to raise your own fish without having to bring heavy tanks into your home.

A rack of herbal plants in a window can improve atmosphere and provide spices for food. Also consider that there are various you-pick options run by local farms as produce (especially fruit) comes into season. I have picked blueberries, strawberries, and cherries in this way, with great satisfaction. Look for information in your current or intended locale or even plan your movements around these.

These different options may be more or less appealing to you. You may also have ethical concerns that touch upon some of them. Always do the best you can within what you think is right. But also keep in mind that there are other options and many ways to keep yourself fed. Learning and increasing our knowledge about ways and methods that we do not consider normally acceptable may be distasteful but is not wrong in itself. Such knowledge, even for practices we do not normally utilize, may be very useful in extremis or if our situation changes.

Preservation

There are many ways to preserve food, whether just between shopping trips or after you raised it or found it yourself. Simply sticking most foods in the fridge will help them keep for longer, but here I will focus on drying, pickling, canning, vacuum sealing, and freezing. Your refrigerator space is likely to be somewhat limited.

Drying

Drying many foods to remove the water content will extend their shelf lives, sometimes almost indefinitely. Purchased foods that have been dried may keep for much longer. In addition to this, removing the water from many foods which can be eaten dry will intensify the flavor.

With sunlight and a bit of heat, many foods can be dried by setting them on a plate or sheet of plastic or clean rock. Think sun-dried tomatoes. I have seen Nepalese farmers drying grain on a plastic sheet at the side of the road. Stronger sun, hotter temperatures, and lower humidity levels will lead to better results.

A dehydrator appliance will draw very little power and enable the drying of many different foods. Slice up meat, season it, and make your own jerky at half the price or less. Turn those leftover grapes into raisins. Make applesauce into fruit snacks. Experiment and find out what you like—store-bought dried foods, like raisins, are only those things which are commercially viable, but you are not so limited and can find things that you like to dry but will never see in the store.

Smoked meat is also dehydrated, though the smoke both adds flavor and works as a preservative. I prefer a good flavored jerky myself, but smoking has its uses and some people find it to be very appealing.

Dehydrator Sample Options

$75; Nutrichef Electric Food Dehydrator; 5 trays; 250W
A smallish, low power option. Which may be best for most mobile platforms.

$230; Excalibur 2900ECB Dehydrator; 9 trays; 440W
Larger unit with a larger power draw, but can dry more food at once.

$349; Brod and Taylor Sahara; Folding unit for small spaces; 700W
Even higher power draw, but will fold away to save space when not in use.
All three found on www.amazon.com

Pickling

Pickling is a lost art for most people but one I consider to have critical importance for dietary balance. For thousands of years most of our ancestors were consuming pickled foods most of the time...until industrial canning came along. Pickled foods contain live cultures of specific types of beneficial bacteria, while canning attempts to sterilize the food to preserve it longer. These beneficial micro-organisms, especially lactobacillus, have been part of a symbiotic relationship with humans throughout the many generations that our ancestors were pickling their food. Digestive health suffers without them. This will not be noticed by everyone, but if you feel there might be something lacking in your diet then you may wish to look further into pickling. Pickling is the one preservation method here that may actually increase nutritional value, in that the process can make more nutrients bio-available.

Even putting the health considerations aside, pickling is a very useful way to extend the shelf life of certain foods. It enables us to get our vegetables without regular shopping and can provide a welcome change from dried or canned or frozen food. Most vegetables, some fruits, and some other foods can be pickled. Pickled eggs are convenient and can be very tasty. They can be chopped into a salad, sliced as a side dish, crumbled into a casserole, and have many other uses. Cabbage is cheap and can be kept for months as sauerkraut, which is very easy to make. I frequently make up a basic sauerkraut from cabbage, water, salt, and some caraway seeds. Away from the store for weeks or months at a time? Pickling is one way to still get your daily vegetables or to keep eggs on hand.

Storage Jar Sample Option

$11; Ball Smooth Glass Mason Jars

Just to point out that glass storage jars, which can be used for pickling, are inexpensive and readily available. They are fragile in regards to impact, but otherwise rather durable and with sufficient padding can be safely kept.

From www.walmart.com

Canning

Canning is not all bad. Canned foods will keep much longer even than pickled foods and still provide much of the nutritional value of the fresh produce. Home canning is very possible, but must be done correctly to be safe. Botulism, which can kill, may result from improper sterilization when home canning. Incidentally, botulism does not occur with live pickled foods as the organism which causes it is crowded out by lactobacillus.

Canning Sample Option

$82; Mirro 92116; Pressure cooker and canner combo; 16qt

A stove-top appliance that can be used for pressure cooking or canning if placed over heat. Versatile and no electricity required.

From www.amazon.com

Vacuum

Vacuum sealers help to preserve food by sealing it away from all air. The vacuum pump removes the air from a package and a heat strip seals the package tight by melting the plastic. This is often used in conjunction with freezing, but even by itself will help preserve all food types. These products are common and inexpensive and do not have large power requirements.

Vacuum Sealer Sample Option

$199; Foodsaver FM5460; 2-in-1 Vacuum food preserver

A good quality vacuum sealer unit. Want to avoid freezer burn on your meat? Here you go. Vacuum sealed foods will often keep for two or three times longer than they normally would.

From www.foodsaver.com

Freezing

Freezing is also a very useful method of food preservation, but uses much more power than a dehydrator and its use must be balanced against available power. A freezer utilizes the same compression/expansion technology as a refrigerator or air conditioner. It is a heat pump. When gasses or compressible liquids are first compressed and then allowed to expand, there is a transfer of heat. The compressor itself which is the main power draw for such a system may be run directly with electricity or instead with a fuel source such as propane. The power draw in either case is significant.

Frozen foods will lose nutritional value over time, but this loss can be controlled by temperature control and by restricting airflow to the food. Keep frozen food at zero degrees Fahrenheit (negative eighteen degrees Celsius) or below. 'Deep freezing' by cooling the food much more quickly will result in food keeping for longer, but has a commensurately larger power draw and is mostly used in industrial settings. At home, we can keep frozen food better for longer by sealing the food away from airflow and especially oxygen. Plastic, especially thin plastic, does not seem to be a firm oxygen barrier. This is one reason why freezer bags are thicker than storage bags (or should be). Using thicker plastic storage bags or even doubling the bag will increase time before nutrition loss. The same will be true of any container frozen food is kept in. Keep the air out especially, but also keep oxygen (which may move slowly through plastics) away. Glass containers that seal may work well but care must be taken not to break the glass which will be more brittle when cold and may shatter if warmed quickly. Metal containers or bags that seal are fine as well.

Storage

Food will keep for longer if kept dry, cool, and away from sunlight. Mostly. Some produce will do better if kept in a high humidity environment. This is why people with root cellars will have both dry and damp sections.

For storage of food, mason jars are inexpensive, may be re-used, and are very versatile. The only drawbacks are the durability of the glass and that the lids must occasionally be replaced. Durability in a mobile situation can be greatly improved by a custom storage build complete with padding. Lids (rings and seals) are sold separately and extras should be purchased when getting the jars as they wear out much faster than the jars do. You can also source alternatives to the stock lids or just make your own.

In some areas where the water is clean, seawater may be used in pickling, though more salt must still be added to make brine. Pickled herring, barreled in brined seawater, was a major European commodity for centuries. Salted (pickled) beef and pork and vegetables were staples for many ancient mariners. Seawater contains trace minerals which are rare elsewhere. In spite of these attractions, it may not be a good idea to use seawater for your pickling except in very clean waters for a bit of local flavor, and even then only after filtration. Human pollution of global waters is even worse than land pollution and seawater also contains heavy metals and other undesirables along with those trace minerals.

Dried food like rice and beans or pasta will keep for a very long time, can be stuffed into almost any unused storage space, and will provide a nice cushion against hunger in an emergency. Beans may be difficult to cook well, but lentils have a similar nutritional value and are much easier to prepare.

Preparation

Most foods still need to be cooked or prepared in some way. There are a variety of methods that can be used and many different appliances available. We could use an oven, a stove-top, a microwave, a blender, a toaster, a steamer, a slow-cooker, a food processor, a fryer, an air-fryer, a grill...the list goes on and on.

For mobile living solutions, energy commitment and safety will be the main concerns. Most electric appliances require AC current and the power needs may be steep. Fuel-burning cooking is more efficient of power use and appliances are available which burn most possible fuels. I am aware of those which burn LPG, alcohol, kerosene, or even diesel. A wood-burning or solid fuel stove or oven or grill is also possible.

Cooking Devices Sample Options

$43; Coleman Gas Burning Camp Stove; two burners, propane

A simple camp stove.

From www.amazon.com

$117; Camp Chef Everest 2 Burner Stove; propane

A better quality camp stove.

From www.amazon.com

$278; Furrion RV Cooktop - Triple Burner; propane

A cooking range to be installed in wheeled platforms.

From www.etrailer.com

$99; Origo 1100 Series 220V 1 Burner Boat Stove; electric

A small electric stove-top for marine use.

From www.greatlakesskipper.com

$1520; Force 10 3-Burner Gimbaled Electric Range; 1200W burners, 1300W oven; electric

A full electric stove and oven for marine use. Mounted on a swivel for cooking on monohull sailboats.

From www.defender.com

$2415; Bristol Diesel Cook Stove; diesel

A diesel burning stove and oven. Can also use kerosene or stove oil. Fully marinized for long use.

From dickinsonmarine.com

$132; Avanti MKB42B Multi-Function Oven; electric convection oven with 2 burner range on top

Interesting alternative. A toaster oven with two electric burners on top. Space-saving and inexpensive, though not marinized and so would need to be protected from salt air over time.

From www.compactappliance.com

Safety

Redundant safety measures must be in place regardless of the methods used. Keep a fire extinguishing method on hand. This may be a commercial fire extinguisher, but a jar of baking soda or even a bucket of sand will help in a pinch. It is usually best not to use water alone, as that will tend to spread the fuel source out over a wider area. Lines and fittings should be inspected regularly and replaced as necessary. This last is often neglected but remains of critical safety importance.

It is best not to eat food which has become stale or started to rot, not even with extra cooking or heavy spicing. Borderline food can often still be fed to any pets or livestock available (which both tend to have much hardier digestive processes) or composted.

Corrosion of fittings will be a much larger concern in marine environments. Also, most of the fuels mentioned above will tend to gather in the bilge with any spill and can become a major safety problem. Have measures in place to prevent this and also to address it if it ever does occur. Otherwise do not use these fuels anywhere that they may seep downward. Electric cooking may be much safer if done properly, though the power draw is not inconsequential.

For campers and RVs, lines and fittings which are not normally accessible should still be inspected, especially for older models. Corrosion can be almost as bad as for marine solutions in areas which use road salt in the winter or are near to the coast.

Kitchen Appliances Sample Options

$113; Contoure RV-780B RV Microwave; 0.7 cubic ft.
Small microwave cooker designed for RV use.
From www.rvupgradestore.com

$159; Muave' Small Microwave Oven; stainless steel, for boats or RVs; 0.7 cubic ft.
Same size microwave but designed to accommodate marine use as well.
From www.salvinco.com

$149; EdgeStar IP210RED Portable Ice Maker; 28lbs daily
A small-form ice maker.
From www.compactappliance.com

References and Further Research

Smith, Edward. *The Vegetable Gardener's Container Bible*

Lang, Elliot. *Eating Insects. Eating Insects as Food.*

Bannerot, Scott and Wendy Bannerot. *The Cruiser's Handbook of Fishing.*

MacKenzie, Jennifer, Jay Nutt, and Don Mercer. *The Dehydrator Bible*

Katz, Sandor Ellix. *The Art of Fermentation*

Kingry, Judi and Lauren Devine. *Ball Complete Book of Home Preserving.*

Accetta-Scott, Ann. *The Farm Girl's Guide to Preserving the Harvest*

Roberts, Lynn. *RV & Camping Cookbook — Healthy Living on a Budget*

Dabney, Silvia Williams. *The Boater's Cookbook*

theboatgalley.com/tag/boat-cooking/

www.propanesafetyfirst.com

www.ag.ndsu.edu/publications/food-nutrition/food-storage-guide-answers-the-question/fn579.pdf

youtu.be/gKcVxvhb0Zk
Well thought out videos covering food concerns for cruising boaters, but applicable for others as well. Just search the channel for 'food'.

youtu.be/DVwdb94G0yo
Video is a bit awkward, but has some great ideas for wheeled living food options. Also check out part 2.

Fulfillment Levels

Low: Keep in range of shops and stores and restaurants. Have only a few items of food convenience or snacks. Don't bother with preservation or storage. Maybe have a small camp stove or equivalent.

Especially for wheeled living this can be a viable option. Just drive to where the food is and eat there. Though I would suggest that having emergency supplies on hand is a good idea.

Medium: Keep dried foods and other long storage items. Actively engage in the food preservation methods of your choice to help with a varied and nutritional diet. Have established appliances and cookware. Grow at least a bit of your own food, such as herbs in a window box.

This sort of setup will enable you to go for much longer periods between shopping trips or restaurants. Home prepared food can be tailored to your own dietary needs and preferences and, once you have your setup in place, can be very inexpensive in comparison to eating at restaurants.

High: Be able to supplement purchased foods with those you grow or find yourself. Have a full range of preservation and storage options. Carefully plan out your food storage and consumption. Have multiple cooking/appliance options for preparation.

It is possible to provide for all of your own food needs on a mobile platform for months at a time, without any supplement from outside sources. Even if this is not necessary it can be very comforting to have the capability to go without shopping for an extended period whenever you please. Energy consumption may go up somewhat, but the increase need not be large and depends on what methods you utilize.

10.

Heating

Active heating for the entire platform may be optional if you only operate in warm climate zones or have other arrangements for the colder months. Even if this is the case for you, however, you will still want to have some heating options on hand in case of emergency or just for comfort. If you do operate in cold areas, then heating is essential and your system must be carefully designed and integrated in order to maximize efficiency. Generating heat over time is an energy intensive process. Water tanks must be kept from freezing. Structural materials must be kept somewhat warm when working so as not to become brittle. And the warm bodies of the living inhabitants must be kept that way.

Insulation

Heat energy is always radiating and dispersing. The basic elements (atoms) of this world are always trading heat energy with one another, more quickly the greater the disparity in heat energy between them, until some rough equilibrium is reached. When you are heating a space you want to slow down this process (it cannot be stopped completely) in order to retain the heat you have generated in the space you want to keep warm. This is where insulation comes in. Well, insulation and control over air (and water) circulation in and out of the living space.

Your living solution should have permanent insulation in place. This will greatly aid in temperature control, for both heating and cooling. Insulation itself is not expensive but must be sealed away from any living quarters to keep it both intact and away from people exposure. There are many different varieties, from free clay or dirt or straw to fiberglass to various foams and other thin-board types to spray-on types. Insulation is just a general term for any material which reduces heat flow. Fiberglass insulation is bulky and may mold or be damaged by water over time, but is cheap and effective. Mineral wool is similar in form to fiberglass but is more expensive and will not be affected as much by moisture. Rigid foam insulation will not insulate as well, but has a longer life span, is physically durable, and will resist moisture. Spray foam insulation can be smelly for quite a while, but it is cheap and lightweight and ignores moisture. There are also options such as Relectrix, which is a kind of quilted Mylar, or Armacell, which is a type of plastic foam.

Consider combining spray-foam and rigid foam insulation, or mineral wool and rigid foam. Spray foam can be sprayed into every crack and crevice and will actually form an airtight barrier (with closed-cell types). Mineral wool will not form that airtight barrier, but provides a significantly greater R-value than thin insulation and will not be greatly effected by trapped moisture. Placing rigid foam over top, in either case, will increase R-values and also create a flat and somewhat durable surface to facilitate the next building steps. If you want this layer to be breathable you can easily leave gaps and if you want it sealed you can add caulking and tapes as appropriate.

Radiant heat insulation is very useful for applications where you would like heat to go in a specific direction. So you might place some underneath of an underfloor water circulation line for radiant heat, to reflect that heat upward. Or inside of a vented engine compartment to better direct the waste heat elsewhere.

Insulation Sample Options

$19; Guardian R-13 Kraft Faced Fiberglass Insulation Roll 23in x 32in

A basic roll of fiberglass insulation. Notice that this alone will cover a fairly small area. It must also be kept moderately dry over time.

From www.menards.com

$24; Owens Corning R-15 Ultrabatt Mineral Wool Insulation 15in x 47in

A batt of mineral wool insulation.

From homedepot.com

$12; Johns Manville Foil Faced Polyiso Foam Board Insulation; 1/2in x 4ft x 8ft; R-2.7

A basic sheet of foam board insulation. It has also been faced with a layer of heat reflective foil to increase the R-value.

From www.menards.com

$15; Owens Corning Foamular Rigid Foam Board Insulation; 1/2in x 4ft x 8ft; R-3

This is XPS (extruded polystyrene) foam board, which is stronger and more durable than the polyiso above.

From homedepot.com

$15: Reflectrix R-3.7 Reflective Insulation 16in x 25ft

A piece of reflective-type insulation. Note that all reflective insulation will require an air gap on the reflective side in order to be effective. This will increase space requirements and also leave an area of potential condensation.

From www.menards.com

$302; FROTH-PAK 200 Foam Sealant Kit; covers 200 sq. ft at 1in thick; R value 5.5 per inch thickness

A DIY spray foam kit.

From www.menards.com

Body Heat

At its most basic level insulation will involve trapping body heat to keep you warm. Extra clothing or blankets will insulate to help us keep the heat we put off naturally. Materials such as wool or some synthetics will provide greater benefit than lighter fabrics like cotton and will also warm even when wet. Mylar (as in space blankets) is a thin film or sheet which has the property of reflecting heat (from the body or otherwise) and is very inexpensive. The camping and backpacking market is a good resource for this basic type of heating solution. Blankets and insulated clothing should really be the first way that you keep yourself warm regardless. Body heat is free (as long as you get enough to eat) and putting on some extra clothes will reduce overall heating requirements for the living space.

These are also good emergency heating options; Mylar in particular takes up very little space and is quite effective at warming up a body—though it does lack the comfort that fabrics offer. Also consider thermal underwear and stout socks.

Body Heat Sample Options

$35; Charcoal gray Classic Wool Blanket
A wool blanket. It will insulate and trap body heat even when wet.
From swisslink.com

$20; Army Style Wool Blanket
A military style wool blanket. Less comforting but with all the same characteristics otherwise.
From majorsurplus.com

$16; Science Purchase 73MYLARPK20; Mylar blankets; 54" x 84"; pack of 20
A pack of twenty Mylar blankets, each of which can enable a person to survive in freezing temperatures.
From www.amazon.com

Heating

Active heating may be considered in terms of central heating and zone heating. Air itself is a rather poor conductor of heat and so central heating will always be inherently less efficient, in energy terms, than zone heating—if the purpose is to warm a particular area or person within the living space. Even if you circulate your heat through water pipes you are still relying on the air to disperse that heat. If the purpose is instead to raise and maintain the temperature of the entire living space at a certain level, central heating may be more efficient, in energy terms, than zone heating. Especially if your platform is well insulated.

My impression is that most people do well with some combination of zone and central heating. The central heating can be kept at a moderate level, above freezing but below the range of human comfort, while zone heating arrangements can be used to supplement that heat in specific areas. The apparatus of dispersal for the central heating will really be for the purpose of general climate control—the same pipes used to circulate hot water can also circulate cold. The same vents used to circulate hot air can also circulate cold air and can also be used to control and filter air movement.

Note that something like heat tape (low power electric resistance heat taping) can be used to place zone heating at water tanks and along water lines. This can be used to supplement a low-power central heating system or replace it entirely in moderately cold weather.

We may generate heat by burning some sort of fuel or by using electricity. These may be point sources of heat or instead centralized generation which is then circulated out by air or by a water pipe arrangement. So, this could be a central air furnace or a boiler and radiator arrangement. It could be space heaters or a wood burning stove. We could be burning wood or pellets, LPG, diesel, or kerosene. We could be using an electric space heater or a heat pump (reverse cycle) arrangement. There are many different ways to generate heat but I will try to touch on the important ones for mobile solutions here.

Fuel burning heaters may use a number of different fuel types and may be found in a number of different arrangements. They must be monitored with care to avoid fire and will generate combustion gasses such as carbon dioxide and carbon monoxide that can cause injury or death if they build up in the living quarters. Detectors for these should be put in place if using combustion heat and careful venting arrangements will be required.

Wood: a wood burning heater can burn found and often free fuel and if the emplacement is carefully designed and maintained may be the best option for certain solutions, especially those which are tight on power use.

LPG: good choice for remote locations or if LPG is already being used for another purpose. Redundant safety measures should be in place.

Kerosene: a petroleum derivative. More available in some places than others. Clean burning and no excessive safety considerations.

Diesel: convenient as a heat source if already using diesel for propulsion. Possibly too much trouble otherwise, though a well-designed heater will be very fuel-efficient.

Electric resistance: this is the same principle as an electric stove, coupled with a fan for air movement. Electricity is passed through a resistance coil which then heats up. Much less efficient than fuel-burning to produce heat unless you have access to plenty of cheap electricity.

Heat pump/reverse cycle: uses a compression cycle to move heat from one location to another. May be used to either heat or cool a space depending on the direction of heat movement. Versatile, but not usable at more extreme temperature ranges so may also require that alternative systems be in place.

Heat once generated may be dispersed by open air movement or instead through a duct system which will permit the heating of selected spaces. It can also be circulated through dedicated water pipes and radiated out at chosen points. Centralized air duct systems may be used for both heating and cooling; water circulation systems are more suitable for just heating unless you do not mind the condensation buildup that will occur when circulating fluid colder than the air.

If you are already using one type of fuel for another purpose then it will be simplest, unless going with electric heat, to have a cabin heater which also burns the same fuel. Engine heat exchange heaters are also available that draw off waste heat from the engine in a similar manner to automobiles—though of course the engine must be running to produce heat.

Using electric, a heat pump will use less power than a comparable resistance heater. In marine applications heat pumps will use heat drawn from raw water and so will be dependent upon water temperatures being above about 50 degrees Fahrenheit or 10 degrees Celsius. Below this level another heat source must be used. Heat pumps using exterior air instead of water will have similar restrictions, though this will vary somewhat from model to model.

Vehicles, RV's, campers, and trailers tend not to be heavily insulated and so will lose heat quickly in cold weather. Some sort of constant heat source should be considered—though running the engine just for heat will be very wasteful. If already using diesel then a diesel heater should be considered, provided that professional standards are adhered to for installation and use. If not already using diesel then LPG may be your best option, unless you have a large battery bank and excess power.

Active Heating Sample Options

$626; Newport Solid Fuel Heater; flexible as to fuel type—wood, charcoal, coal, etc
A 'wood' burning heater. Fans, vents, or custom water piping can be used to better circulate heat from this zone source.
From dickinsonmarine.com

$240; Mr. Heater Vent-Free Propane Radiant Wall Heater
Does not account for intake or exhaust, so will consume oxygen and produce carbon dioxide when used. Includes a low-oxygen shut-off sensor.
From www.northerntool.com

$457; Sig / Dickenson Cozy Cabin Heater – Propane
A marinized (and much more durable) propane heater.
From www.go2marine.com

$132; Sengoku KeroHeat; kerosene heater, portable, radiant
Kerosene heating is widely used in Japan. This well-engineered product is durable and inexpensive.
From www.amazon.com

$896; Diesel Air Heater Planar 2D-HA-PU27
A diesel heater, with digital control, for marine or wheeled platforms.
From planarheaters.com

$2673; Wallas XC Duo Diesel RV Stove/Heater
A combination cooking stove and heater, diesel, for marine platforms.
From scanmarineusa.com

$3627; Wallas Spartan Diesel Heater (marine)
A very high output diesel marine heater.
From scanmarineusa.com

$33; Trustech Space Heater; 1500W
A basic electric space heater.
From www.amazon.com

$788; DAW Series Dial-A-Watt Marine Electric Forced Air Wall Heater
A marinized electric space heater suitable for heating a moderately large boat.
From www.fisheriessupply.com

$987; Domestic Heat Pump; heater and air conditioner combo system
An RV-style heat pump, for climate control when not in extreme temperatures.
From pplmotorhomes.com

Water Heating

If you use water lines and radiant heat then your entire central heating system can be based on your water heater. Even if you do not you may be able to get by without a separate heater depending on your needs—hot water can be piped to a small radiator setup with a blower to move the warmed air through vents or just into the cabin. Your water heater may be an on-demand heater or instead a tank kept at a constant temperature. Or one of each. The tank version will be more suitable for constant heating circulation while the on-demand water heater will be more suited for occasional use. Radiant heating will be more suitable for wheeled platforms, as most marine platforms will flex and work which can put a strain on piping. And water leaks when the system is damaged are somewhat more of a serious problem on a boat.

You can also manage without any water heater at all, provided that you do not mind taking cold showers or otherwise keeping your water supply at the ambient temperature of your platform.

Some boat heaters are designed to offer water heating capabilities in addition to space heating. This can be a good option if you only need or want hot water in the colder months when you will be running the boat heater anyway.

References and Further Research

Calder, *Boatowner's*, Chapter 15

rvshare.com/blog/rv-hvac

www.sailmagazine.com/diy/warm-and-snug

youtu.be/dxlXywAu1Cg
Radiant water heat installed in a camper-van.
youtu.be/ESVK57Fqi8U
Video overview of wheeled heating options.
youtu.be/Us5dThtk2BY
Central heating and hot water setup for a UK narrowboat.
youtu.be/qV3KsQe7VPI
Heavy duty diesel boat heating in sub-arctic conditions.
youtu.be/d1DA4G3zUL8
Presentation of the West Marine boat heater product line.

Fulfillment Levels

Low: Don't bother with normal heating. Keep some emergency heating supplies on hand. Pick up a space heater if you feel the need.

If you stay where the weather is warm this may work fine. Note however that this also means cold showers, unless you work out some separate water heating arrangement. Solar water warming is a good complement for an unpowered setup.

Medium: Insulate as possible. Integrate a modest central heating system with your existing air vent system. Possibly go with liquid radiant heat instead. Use space heater options for specific areas and consider zone heating of sensitive water tanks and lines. Keep yourself warmer by putting on heavier clothing and using heavier bedding in order to reduce the overall heating burden. Have a backup fuel-burning heating option on hand if going with all electric otherwise. Keep some emergency supplies.

This will insure that all of your bases are covered and will prepare your living solution for all but the most extreme conditions—which can be prepared for in turn with incremental additions to existing systems.

High: Fully insulate your platform. Integrate both air heating and radiant heating central systems (depending on platform suitability), with excess heating capacity for extreme conditions. Consider separate and redundant heaters for every significant space. Fully account for heating of utility spaces. Have cold weather indoor clothing and bedding on hand. Keep redundant emergency supplies.

A fully capable redundant system suitable for inhabiting the coldest of climates in comfort. At the cost of high energy use. Though this can be reduced somewhat with extra insulation.

11.

Cooling

Cooling, such as from air conditioning or refrigeration, is not really a survival need, but it can make a huge difference for comfort levels and general quality of life. It will almost always be energy intensive to get much below ambient temperatures, but sufficiently equipped off-grid mobile systems can still manage occasional A/C, a fridge and freezer, an ice-maker, and more.

General cooling may be achieved by passive airflow through openings, active airflow from fans, or active heat siphoning such as by a heat pump or air conditioner (or refrigerator), combined with fans for dispersal. Just using airflow has been covered already in a previous section, so I will focus on heat siphoning options.

A reverse cycle heat pump may also be used to cool. This is essentially an air conditioning unit that will pump heat out of a space during its cooling cycle and pump heat (as available) into a space during its heating cycle.

Compression and Expansion

Air conditioners, heat pumps, refrigerators, and freezers all work on compression and expansion principles. That is, a refrigerant (a liquid that boils/changes to gas at a fairly low temperature) will be put though a series of compression/expansion cycles. This involves altering the pressure on the refrigerant to force a phase change between liquid and gaseous states. That transition of the phase change naturally involves useful thermodynamic effects.

First, the refrigerant is compressed into liquid, which causes it to heat up in itself as the greater energy of the gaseous state transitions to a liquid state. The heat that was collected during the evaporation stage is much easier to radiate off from the liquid form. If you want the heat then this will be part of the heating cycle, but if you do not want this heat then this will be waste heat to be radiated off. In either case this heated fluid is run through a series of coils to allow the excess heat to radiate out of the closed system in which the refrigerant resides. On a fridge this will be done outside of the insulated box whereas a reverse cycle heater will run a fan through these coils to distribute the heat through the living space. The heat radiation process takes place within the condensing unit of the system, which starts at the compressor and moves through the heat coils. That compressor is the big power draw for the system.

Once run through the condenser coils (the hot side) the refrigerant is run through an expansion and evaporation cycle. The evaporator itself is also a set of coils. As the compressor increased the pressure upon the refrigerant to force it into liquid form, so the expansion valve will greatly reduce the pressure upon that liquid which will induce it back into gaseous form. And as the transition to liquid form involved a heating of the refrigerant so the transition to gaseous form will involve a cooling of the refrigerant (in itself). As the refrigerant is run through the evaporator coils (and it is evaporating into gas) the cooler gaseous form will absorb heat, which has a cooling effect on those coils. So the coils will be cooler than ambient for that location and will absorb heat from the immediate area.

The effect is such that heat or cold are not spontaneously generated, but instead heat is moved from one place to another simply by the compression and expansion of the refrigerant as it moves through the cycle which is mechanically designed into the system. During the cycle the refrigerant will collect heat from one location and disperse it at another. A reverse cycle (heat pump) system will be designed such that the direction of heat flow can be reversed without changing the physical layout.

Compressor Power

Refrigeration units will have electronic control of some sort, and fans mounted at the separate coils can increase system efficiency, but most of the power draw for refrigeration will be the compressor itself. A standard household refrigerator/freezer might draw over eight hundred watts during its cooling cycle, and much higher than that (briefly) for the inrush/starting current. Mobile refrigeration will thus be limited to smaller capacity units, unless your electrical system can handle surges well in excess of one hundred amps for a twelve volt system. Note however that some devices will have a startup capacitor in order to not draw excessive amounts of amps when first powering the motor.

Dedicated air conditioning or refrigeration units may be run only on electricity but may also be designed to run on natural gas or LPG along with a little electricity for control and fans. That is, a small internal combustion engine will be used to power the compressor instead of having an electric compressor. In either case the amount of space being cooled and the temperature difference with the exterior will have significant impacts on power or fuel usage. Trying to cool large spaces or getting them much colder than ambient temperatures are both energy intensive propositions.

Evaporation

Evaporative coolers, in contrast, function by intentionally evaporating water into hotter, dryer air in order to cool it down. So just using one part of the cycle completed by the refrigerant above. Air is taken in, water is evaporated into it, and the cooler, wetter air is expelled. Many people, especially those used to air conditioning that dries the air, will find the moist cool of evaporative cooling to be uncomfortable. However, this method does have the distinct advantage for a mobile living situation in that it uses much less electricity than compression-based air conditioning units. The method will work best in dryer climate situations, but if this applies to you then you may consider this a viable option. Marine environments tend to be much more humid, but what if you were to combine an evaporative cooler with a desiccant? This type of solution has been proven on larger scale, such as with the DEVAP system. For you, this might be cumbersome and still less effective than AC, but if power generation is the limiting factor then it still might be a possible cooling solution for you.

Mobile

Marine heat pumps may draw upon raw water as a heat sump and so will be useful in a wider temperature range than land-based units. This must also be monitored as another potential place for corrosion. All compressive air conditioning is power-hungry but with a sufficiently powerful electric setup, and especially when running a generator, it is very possible to have onboard a boat.

RV and camper refrigeration has previously been primarily accomplished by propane (LPG) driven units, but with larger (LiFePO4) battery banks and increasing solar use many are switching over to DC electric refrigeration and even air conditioning solutions. For air conditioning though, at least for now, most are still limited to grid power or when running a generator or just sticking with propane.

However, if your electrical system is equipped to handle air conditioning loads then you can still get some benefit, with much less power draw, by accepting temperatures only marginally below that of the exterior. The larger the temperature gap that you aim for the more your AC will need to run and the more power you will need to use. But if you aim for only a five or ten degree difference from the exterior then your power consumption will be greatly reduced. The benefit will be more significant than you might expect, as the AC will also reduce the humidity of the interior, which will enhance the natural cooling processes of the body.

Air Cooling Sample Options

$140; Hessaire MC18M Portable Evaporative Cooler
A basic evaporative cooling unit. Will increase humidity. Cooling for up to 500 square feet. Consumes 85W of power.

From www.amazon.com

$1026; Coleman Mach 10 Low Profile Heat Pump
RV style reverse cycle heat pump. Runs on AC power. Consumes 1600W for cooling and 1840W for heating.

From www.airxcel.com

$1259; 6000 Btu/h Self Contained Marine Air Conditioner and Heat pump
Marinized heat pump system. Runs on AC power. Consumes ~650W. Relies on using exterior water for heating/cooling cycles.

From www.marinaire.com

Making do with less

Do consider that you can get by quite well, even in hot weather, without air conditioning. There is a period of adjustment in which the body adapts, but after you let go of the attachment to that feeling of cool dry AC air you will find a new comfort level. Fans can help out a great deal and use much less power than AC. You may especially consider mounting fans to point at sleeping areas. Most of the natural cooling that the body uses will come from evaporating moisture (sweat) off of the skin. Increased airflow will accelerate this process.

Access to cold drinks and food will also improve your outlook when living without air conditioning. Fortunately a small refrigerator and even a freezer is within the energy budget for relatively modest electrical systems. Small container spaces and good insulation permit these devices to get by with smaller compressors that run only infrequently, translating into small(ish) power draws.

Refrigeration Sample Options

$146; Criterion 3.1 cu. ft. Black Double-Door Compact Refrigerator
A residential mini-fridge. Will have a smaller compressor than a full-size model and so draw less power.
From www.menards.com

$884; ARB Portable Fridge Freezer 50 Quarts
A low-power top-loading portable fridge. Runs on DC, around 50W. Includes an AC adapter.
From www.amazon.com

$842; Norcold NR751BB Refrigerator / Freezer
A small unit designed to run on 12/24V DC or AC power. Suitable for marine installations; uses integral venting.
From www.boatandrvaccessories.com

References and Further Research

Calder, Nigel. *Boatowner's,* Chapter 11.

Cunning, Terry. *Winterize Your RV: Inside and Out*

Wells, Robert. *How to Live in a Car, Van or RV*

www.marinetalk.com/best-marine-refrigerators/

www.sailmagazine.com/diy/beat-the-heat-retrofit-an-ac-system

www.gonewiththewynns.com/air-conditioning-sailboat

rvshare.com/blog/rv-air-conditioner/

youtu.be/XHPIEy9Ciac
Considerations for off grid AC use in an RV.

youtu.be/TEfbzXR1pPU
Close up look at a fridge installation on a boat.

Fulfillment Levels

Low: Go without air conditioning. Go without refrigeration, beyond a cooler or icebox. You might have a fan or two for airflow cooling.

Cooling is not really required, so in the short term or if you can handle it you can save a lot of power by going without.

Medium: Go without air conditioning, except possibly a very small unit. Keep a small fridge and maybe a separate freezer. Possibly an ice-maker. Space cooling will mostly be accomplished with low-power methods such as fans and evaporative cooling.

By limiting refrigeration cooling you may also limit the strain on your power reserves. So battery draw or generator run time will be greatly reduced. For those who become accustomed to the conditions this can be quite comfortable.

High: Full AC for interior spaces. Larger fridge and freezer capacity. An ice-maker. As many fans as you want.

At this level you are not concerned with power use. Maybe you have an onboard generator and ample fuel reserves, or are plugged into shore power. Luxurious and decadent.

12.

Sanitation

Sanitation is civilization, or at least a necessary element of it. We clean ourselves, our clothes, and our homes to feel better, to stay healthy, and to be more welcoming of others. Keeping clean while mobile can be something of a challenge at times, but there are still various options to address personal care, laundry, and general cleanliness.

Personal Care

This will take many forms, but they all involve maintaining a state of physical well being over time. The largest concern for your mobile living solution will be the energy and space required to go through a daily wash cycle. These concerns may be minimized with careful arrangements and, as with all things mobile, by becoming accustomed to frugal solutions.

Showers (may) take much less water than a bath and can be temporarily rigged almost anywhere, given the right materials. For comfort, we often want hot shower water and a permanent and private shower setup, but these are not really necessary. A hip bath can be used as an alternative to showering or to a full tub bath and will take up much less space, weight, and water per bath than a full tub.

With determination and a higher energy budget, you could also manage a sauna arrangement. This might be tricky to implement, but will require minimal water. There is no reason that a constructed shower stall cannot also be a sauna, even in the confined spaces of mobile living.

At the lower end of the fulfillment scale we can clean ourselves with a sponge or rag or wet-wipes. Some people do this anyway between showers in order not to bother as often with the excess moisture generation or just the inconvenience of their personal bathing solution. There are many solutions to the need to be clean—we can even make like the Romans, who used to rub oil into their skin and scrape it off, to get rid of excess dirt before bathing in water.

Portable showers that can be setup or taken down at need can be a good way to save space...or to still have a shower option when you just don't have the space for one otherwise. For something a little more permanent but still portable, you can use a raised pan and curtain arrangement. As long as the showerhead is set to spray straight down and the curtain is long enough to channel the water into the tub, then any materials which fit your situation will do. I have seen a fixed shower using an old wooden barrel as the tub. A plastic storage tote would work as well, as long as it held up. You could also just square off any piece of wall space and build a laminate enclosure down to a drain, at the cost of a bit of wood and some fiberglass and resin. Don't get caught up in traditional arrangements—mobile living means versatile living.

Personal Care Sample Options

$119; Ecotemp L-5 Portable Outdoor Tankless Propane Water Heater; LPG
Designed to be installed at a site temporarily, this product can provide hot water showers year round as long as your LPG tanks are kept full.
From www.hotcampshowers.com

$70; Outback Porta Privy; instant setup upright privacy tent
A simple pop-up tent that packs away small. Privacy for bathing or other needs.
From www.hotcampshowers.com

$100; Nemo Helio
A portable pressure tank with pump that can be warmed in the sun. A durable (with care) and simple shower solution.
From www.nemoequipment.com

$12; Simple Shower Portable Camping Shower
A much simpler camp shower arrangement. This is a showerhead designed to be affixed to the opening of a bottle or water bladder.
From www.amazon.com

$36; Summer Shower Solar Bag 5 Gallon
A reinforced water bladder with hose. Warm in the sun, hang, and shower off.
From www.hotcampshowers.com

Laundry

Laundry can be cleaned in several different ways as well. Machine washing is convenient, but if you cannot justify the expense or space or power draw then you can do the same thing with a bucket or two, some soap, and your hands. There are also various stages in between. Self (muscle) powered laundry machines are available which are more mobile and take up less space. Compact machine washers which require limited power draw and water are available, but are more costly to purchase.

Clothing dryers are a true mobile luxury because of the large power draw, but are becoming more efficient every year and may be suitable for your living solution. Otherwise a line to hang clothes and perhaps a fan will suffice. Hang dried clothes may tend to be wrinkled but this can be reduced with skill and care.

Laundry Sample Options

$20; Breathing Washer
A modified plunger type device for agitating clothes in your own bucket or basin.
From www.breathingwasher.com

$50; MyPortaWash Compact Portable Non-Electric Washing Machine
A simple plastic container-washer with a foot-pedal agitator/spinner.
From www.amazon.com

$59; The Wonder Wash
Portable compact manual clothes washing device. Several design differences from previous option.
From laundry-alternative.com

$85; Mini Countertop Spin Dryer 2; electric spinner to remove water from clothes; 82W
No heated dry; this is a centrifuge device that spins the clothes very fast. Low power and will get most of the water out.
From laundry-alternative.com

$300; Panda PAN56MGP3; 1.34 cubic foot portable electric clothes washer
Compact, fairly low power clothes washing machine. Requires AC power and pressurized water supply and drain.
From www.amazon.com

$1145; Splendide Washer/Dryer Combo; Single machine, 1560W max
A washer and dryer in one, this unit is marketed to the RV community for use when on-the-hook. So it assumes constant shore power and a pressurized water hookup. Otherwise the high power draw might be difficult to manage.
From www.pplmotorhomes.com

Other Considerations

The way we clean, how much effort it takes, and how often we need to do it all start at the design stage for the home itself. Do you like the idea of having lots of fancy wooden scroll-work to add character to your living space? Expect to spend more time and effort cleaning than you would with flat panels and minimal decoration. Do you want to avoid grout buildup in your shower stall? Consider smooth fiberglass instead of some sort of tile surface. Function and form are intertwined for all of the compact solutions required for mobile living. Aesthetics should always be tempered with practicality.

Norwex

There are a variety of cleaning chemicals out there to choose from, but there are also non-chemical options. There is at least one company (Norwex) which markets cleaning cloths which are to be used dry or wet down just with water. They are threaded with nano-silver which kills off micro-organisms. They are somewhat pricey, but are supposed to last quite a while and will save you the costs for cleaners.

Norwex Sample Option
$55; Norwex Household Package
Set of three microfiber, silver enhanced cloths.
From shopus.norwex.biz

Steam

If you have some excess power available, you could also consider a steamer for cleaning. Steam cleaning can be very effective for certain applications and is chemical free.

Steamer Sample Option

$20; PurSteam
Handheld steamer for surfaces, fabrics, barbecues, defrosting, etc.
From www.amazon.com

References and Further Research

Harless, Jesse; *Smash Your Comfort Zone with Cold Showers*

Ward, Jess. *The Intrepid Woman's Guide to Van Dwelling*

www.theroadisourhome.com/2018/06/18/shower-toilet-build-how-to-van-conversion

outboundliving.com/hygiene

www.sailorsforthesea.org/programs/green-boating-guide/non-toxic-cleaning-products

youtu.be/NXYPHasQHtk

Good demonstration of the two buckets method for laundry. This is on a sailboat, but will apply elsewhere as well.

youtu.be/_7c7kYkT5OA

Full water-maker and laundry room setup on a sailboat. Makes an interesting comparison to the above video.

youtu.be/VZkYE1K43cM

Compilation video for van living shower solutions. Be sure to check out the five channels linked in the description and used for the video.

Fulfillment Levels

Low: Shower elsewhere, such as at truck stops and gyms. Use wet-wipes in between. Wash clothes at a laundromat, or using the two bucket method. Clean the house with a rag and bucket.

Other than keeping your platform clean, sanitation can be taken care of elsewhere, provided that you stay close to those amenities. It can also be taken care of with little or no power use if you engage in manual cleaning methods. You will require potable water. Manual laundry can require even more potable water than efficient laundry machines.

Medium: Have some shower arrangement on hand. Have some laundry solution on hand. Work out more efficient ways to keep your home clean (and hopefully have it designed such that cleaning is easier).

Being able to wash inside (or near) your living solution is an important step up. At this level, you might still use outside services when available, as they might be easier and will not otherwise muck up your own spaces, but will also have your own working sanitation solutions. The cost might even be lower at this level, depending on what you might otherwise pay to do these things elsewhere.

$60; Square Single Bowl Marine / Boat Sink

A simple marine sink with drain.

From www.plumbingsupply.com

$122; LaSalle Bristol Double Sink

A double sink for wheeled applications.

From www.dyersonline.com

$67; 5 Gallon RV Holding Tank

A small holding tank suitable for graywater.

From www.ntotank.com

Garbage

Solid waste (or garbage) is a general category which includes everything else which we may want to dispose of, yet there are many different types that need not be lumped together. Organics can often be composted. Many things can be re-used or recycled. Other solid waste must be stored for legal disposal.

Composting is a viable option for mobile living solutions, provided that care is taken in design and operation to mitigate undesirable factors. Aeration is necessary, but the smell can be filtered or vented to a better location than the cabin, or otherwise kept outside. Periodic cleaning will be required. Composted waste may be used but otherwise need not be kept in limited storage spaces. 'Disposal' in this case is more a matter of giving back valuable nutrients to the natural world, provided that such disposal is legal and appropriate where it is done.

Because space is always limited, compacting garbage may be important. This can involve crushing cans or folding boxes or even using a compactor arrangement, powered or not, to reduce the volume of the waste.

Solid waste may legally be dumped overboard beyond the three-mile limit (three miles away from a coastal shore) but it is still better not to throw many things overboard. Organics are fine, but plastics should never be.

Most wheeled living solutions should have regular trash disposal options as they move about. Please consider the impact on the world that your waste and usage has.

Trash Compaction Sample Options

$30; Easy Pull Can Crusher

Just a simple device for crushing metal cans.

From www.acehardware.com

$120; Household Essentials Trash Krusher; manual

A trashcan arrangement with integral compaction capability to reduce garbage size.

From www.householdessential.com

$1429; Krushr 12 Inch Trash Compactor; electric, 270W

An electric version. Much more expensive, but the power draw is low and this may be suitable for those not capable of using the manual compactor.

From krushr.com

Black Water

We eat, and so also need to eliminate waste. Your mobile living situation must account for this process in some manner or another. While distasteful, human waste treatment and disposal is essential and it is best to have some integrated solution in place, preferably one that is viable both for normal residents and for guests.

Wastes which are usually solid (feces) or liquid (urine) have distinct properties. As such, they may be treated separately or instead in mixed form (slurry), which itself has different properties than either component by themselves. Urine is actually sterile as it leaves the body. Feces which is kept dry will decompose with much less odor than when wet. Slurry is both more disgusting and a greater health concern than either component when they are separate.

While unpleasant to deal with, human wastes are composed of chemical compounds, nutrients, and biomass and can be processed according to those components. There are good reasons for our instincts to consider them unclean and to hide them away, but those reasons do not preclude careful and reasoned methods of waste processing.

Holding Tank Systems

The standard for mobile living solutions has generally been to store human wastes as slurry in a holding tank, with or without added chemicals, to be pumped out as needed and when possible for disposal. This works, and with care it can work well. It is not necessarily the optimal solution. Slurry gives off much more smell than either component alone and can actually provide optimal conditions for bacterial growth. The tanks take up a significant amount of space. Though even when other methods are used, having this method in place as a backup, perhaps in smaller form factor, may be desirable in order to accommodate guests or for emergencies.

Holding Tank System Sample Options

$150; 10 Gallon RV Holding Tank (for gray or black water); 36" x 13" x 6"; polystyrene resin
Standard type plastic holding tank for wheeled platforms.
From www.ntotank.com

$182; Domestic 310 Toilet 302310081; for permanent installation
A toilet designed to accommodate the wheeled market. Suitable for draining slurry into a holding tank.
From www.thetford.com

$169; Ronco 10 Gallon Marine Holding Tank; 26" x 11" x 11"; polystyrene resin
A very similar holding tank to the wheeled option above but marketed for marine use.
From www.tank-depot.com

$137; Albin Pump Marine Toilet Manual
A manual pump marine toilet. The pump arrangement is designed for minimal water use, which saves drain on freshwater tanks and also reduces volume requirements in black water tanks.

From www.boatersland.com
$241; Albin Pump Marine Toilet Electric Silent 24V
An electric pump marine toilet.
From www.boatersland.com

Combustion Toilets

Some people prefer combustion-based waste disposal. This method uses heat, which may be supplied by a fuel or by electricity, to burn the waste to ash. Fumes are vented. Thus no holding tank is required, freeing up space, and there are no unpleasant byproducts to deal with. The theory is sound, but results may vary based upon what setup you use and your needs. I have read about varied results using this method, from perfect operation down to very poor and only half-burnt. There are various commercial solutions to consider or one could devise their own method. Regardless, this type of waste disposal is energy intensive and thus expensive over time. Electric options will require a very robust electrical system. LPG combustion will be somewhat more energy efficient, but all the usual safety concerns of LPG apply and this use will be a drain on your fuel supplies.

Combustion Toilet Sample Options

$3385; TinyJohn by EcoJohn; LPG
LPG burning combustion toilet marketed to the wheeled community.
From shop.ecojohn.com

$1929; Incenolet Model CF; electric, 2000W
A popular electric combustion toilet.
From incinolet.com

$4200; Comfort by Cinderella; electric, 2000W
A more expensive option that claims to provide an equivalent experience to that of a standard residential toilet. That is, with no significant impact on interior climate in terms of heat and humidity.
From www.thecabindepot.com

Compost Toilets

Compost-type waste disposal is rising in popularity. It has many desirable characteristics but also certain drawbacks. As mentioned above, feces and urine behave differently when not combined into slurry. There is less smell. There is less micro-organism growth and fewer of those organisms are harmful. There are space savings. Against these, we must also consider that more care and attention is required. You may also have to innovate your own solutions to address what smell there is.

In the compost method, urine is kept separate and stored, to be disposed of much like slurry with the holding tank method. Something like peat moss or coconut coir is added to the feces and mixed, to absorb excess moisture and begin the composting process. The compost mass is kept aerated, with a vent and usually also a fan (drawing a bit of electricity).

Depending on the design, these processes may be either more or less automated. Commercial compost toilets or heads do seem to be relatively expensive at this time, though it is a one-time cost. It is also entirely possible to design and build your own solution. Urine diversion may be a difficult aspect of this, but you can find toilet seats for sale with integrated urine diversion functionality.

The produced solid compost, once the composting process is complete, is actually just soil and may be disposed of accordingly. It may also be used as actual soil and a growth medium for plants, though never directly to grow plants for human consumption. It is safer by far to keep a remove in the life cycle, for instance using that compost to grow plants that feed animals that in turn feed people. Traditional Chinese agriculture referred to composted human waste as 'night soil' and used it as an integral part of the fertility cycle for thousands of years.

Compost Toilet Sample Options

$129; Urine Diverting Seat — Privy 500
This could be a good option for completing your DIY compost toilet. Even if not, the design is interesting and may be used as a template. The diversion portion is just an inset under the seat.
From compostingtoiletusa.com

$925; Nature's Head Composting Toilet
A popular type of composting toilet.
From www.natureshead.net

$1775; Sun-Mar Mobile
Composting toilet marketed for wheeled living.
From www.thecabindepot.com

$1029; Air Head Composting Toilet
Another popular brand.
From airheadtoilet.com

Cassette Toilets

You may also consider using a cassette toilet or a portable camping toilet. These are similar to tank holding systems in that the waste is mixed, but they are much smaller and the waste 'cassette' or tank is removable for dumping. When you desire to empty them, you simply pull out the tank and take it to a dumping station or just to a public restroom. I have noticed that many people will only use the built in tank for urine collection. Feces can be dealt with otherwise, such as bagging or cat-holes or public toilets. This will obviously be more suitable to wheeled living than marine living, but in this way you can avoid slurry generation and the related concerns.

The cassette toilet is distinguished from the camping toilet by being permanently affixed to a specific location. They will often have some plumbing in place to provide a flushing action as well. Cassette systems may also offer spare cassettes to change out for extending storage capacity.

For either of these, the holding capacity will be limited. As such, they will need frequent emptying with use. They will also need frequent cleaning or rinsing to remain sanitary. No chemicals will need to be added, but you may want to put in small amounts of fragrance or cleaner to help with odor. A bit of white vinegar is said to help a lot for urine smells without being overbearing.

Cassette / Camping Toilet Sample Options

$27; Rothco Portable Camp Toilet
Basic small camp toilet. Really just a folding seat arrangement for bagging waste.
From www.rothco.com

$65; Camco 41541 Standard Travel Toilet
Portable toilet with integral holding tank.
From www.amazon.com

$177; Eathtec ETEC Portable Toilet Bowl
Similar in size and design to the option above, this product touts a proprietary non-stick coating for ease of cleaning and long use.
From easilycarried.com

$119; Porta Potti Curve 565E
A simple portable toilet with an alternative form factor to fit different spaces.
From www.walmart.com

$513; Thetford 32812 Cassette Toilet
A full cassette toilet designed to be permanently installed and plumbed, though also has wheels for easy movement.
From www.amazon.com

Other Considerations

At sea, human wastes may be pumped or otherwise discarded overboard. Inland or in coastal waters this is illegal. Some types of tank systems will use chemical treatment to reduce bacteria. Use of these systems (Type I or Type II MSD) will mean that waste can legally be discharged overboard in some inland waters (sounds, bays, rivers, etc) but not others (No Discharge Zones or inland lakes).

Use of chemical treatment (the blue stuff) to disinfect and reduce odors has been standard for wheeled tank systems. Compost toilets are growing in acceptance and popularity on the RV scene and will be less expensive over time because they do not require this additive.

References and Further Research

Appelhof, Mary and Joanne Olszewski. *Worms Eat My Garbage, 35th Anniversary Edition*

Hall, Peggie. *The New Get Rid of Boat Odors, 2nd Edition*

Elwell, Don. *The Floating Empire composting toilet book*

Baird, Gord and Ann Baird. *Essential Composting Toilets*

rvshare.com/blog/rv-gray-water-tank/

www.boatus.org/study-guide/environment/laws/

www.doityourselfrv.com/rv-toilet-etiquette-tips/

www.boatus.org/study-guide/environment/waste/

youtu.be/jipI9D72tkA

Discussion on wastage and other concerns while boondocking on wheels.

youtu.be/vN7v46Sn3Ds

Good summary of toilet options for wheeled living. Much is also applicable for marine use.

youtu.be/aCRFJqxga3E

Pair of videos which offers an in depth look at the standard marine head and tank arrangement and periodic maintenance concerns. To me it presents compelling reasons for switching to a compost toilet or other non-tank option, at least for the primary use toilet.

Fulfillment Levels

Low: No significant provisions for gray or black waste. Use other facilities or bury with a shovel when necessary. Bag up any trash and place it in a convenient disposal bin. You might have a camp toilet or just some bags for emergencies. You might have a bottle to capture gray water under a sink arrangement.

If you rely on using the facilities that other people already have in place then you need not design your own solutions into your platform. This will of course either tie you to civilization or reduce you to primitive methods.

Medium: Place and plumb a graywater tank suitable for your sink and/or shower needs. Use only environmentally friendly cleaners. Establish garbage procedures and consider limited composting. Recycle when possible. Have one or more set options for black waste collection and disposal.

In this manner you will be able to account for all wastage products within your mobile solution, for appropriate disposal when possible.

High: Keep excess graywater capacity for your needs, fully plumbed for storage and draining. Use only environmentally friendly cleaners. Establish garbage and compost procedures. Recycle when possible. Have at least two options for black waste collection and disposal.

These are only incremental upgrades from the medium fulfillment level, if that. Most concerns will already have been covered.

14.

Health

Improving or maintaining physical and mental health is aided by diet, exercise, and mindfulness. For long-term health, we should consider environmental impacts on our bodies. Any medical concerns must also be addressed.

Diet

Try to eat healthy. This will be different in practice for everyone, but will always mean avoiding sweets and 'junk' food and alcohol except in moderation. Dietary needs will vary from person to person and you must learn your own. What balance of protein and energy and nutrients do you need? Does this change based on your activity? These things will also change over a lifetime or even day to day. Don't get into habits that ignore your current needs. Find good compromises between what your body wants and what you are willing or able to provide for it. Also consider that many processed or prepackaged foods contain additives that can overwhelm your senses and spoil your taste for natural foods. This will go away in time if you avoid those food additives, enabling you to better enjoy natural foods.

Exercise

Some amount of physical exercise is also important. Space may be limited, but there is always enough space to do something to elevate cardio-vascular activity. Elevating the heart rate for at least ten minutes at a time twice a week is enough to improve. There will be more gain if this is increased.

Exercise may be combined with useful work such as pumping water into an overhead tank or even generating electricity. A modicum of strength training, to improve and maintain an acceptable level of physical strength, may be attained simply by pushing, pulling, squatting, sitting-up, or otherwise moving the body around against some resistance, even if that resistance is just the force of gravity. A few minutes a day is all it takes.

Physical exercise need not be muscle intensive and can be based around simple body movement instead. Like Tai-Chi. Or dancing. Or playing an instrument. Muscular strength and endurance are increased by forcing the muscles to do work, but muscular grace is increased by moving the body through detailed motions. The structure of nerves that branch throughout our muscle tissue will grow and even shrink over time just as muscles themselves do. Facility at detailed work or grace in motion is dependent on that nerve structure and will require practiced repetition of the motions in question.

Mindfulness

Mindfulness is my general term for mental health. You might also think of it as having peaceful awareness or proper state of being. Regardless, do not ignore this critical aspect of your self. We can never escape our own mind. Try to experience the full force and extent of your emotions and feelings, rather than blocking them out or seeking to numb them in some way. We have these things for a reason. Even pain has purpose. Stay whole in yourself and become something different and greater by riding out the shocks and travails of this life with a sense of mental balance. Learn to adapt to your mental states in order to accomplish whatever physical tasks might be required of you regardless of your mental state. The mind-body relationship is almost infinitely adaptable. Please think on these things.

Sun Exposure

Most environmental health concerns have been at least touched upon in other sections, but one large one that is often neglected is sun exposure. Do not neglect sun protection and general skincare. Those living the wheeled or marine life will be spending a lot of their time exposed to the sun. Over a period of years this can cause many problems—just ask the longtime cruisers out there. You will still get a tan if you use sunscreen and wear light clothing when out in the sun. It will just take a bit longer. Try to pace your solar intake. A certain amount of sun per day is desirable, but too much will overcome the body's capacity to adapt and may lead to long term damage. Use lotions and cremes to help out the repair process.

Medical

Mobile living means being out of range of established medical care facilities, at least from time to time. And so any injuries or illnesses must be treated with supplies on hand, at the very least in terms of first aid and possibly for very much longer. A basic first aid kit should be considered the very minimum in terms of necessary supplies and more will definitely be recommended. Knowledge coupled with appropriate supplies will be the best defense against possible medical emergency. There are references which can be used to increase your knowledge, some of which I have detailed below. You should also be aware of preexisting conditions and the general state of health for all persons on board or in the vehicle and plan accordingly.

References and Further Research

Cohen, Michael Martin. *Healthy Boating and Sailing*

Alton, Joseph, MD, and Amy Alton, ARNP. *The Survival Medicine Handbook*

Auerbach, Paul S., MD. *Medicine for the Outdoors*

Wilson-Howarth, Jane. *Essential Guide to Travel Health*

www.sailingtotem.com/2014/04/healthcare-while-cruising.html

winnebagolife.com/2016/01/health-insurance-challenge-coverage-for-full-time-rvers

matchamotovan.com/vanlife-cost-health-insurance/

gnomadhome.com/vanlife-anxiety/

youtu.be/3dqXHHCc5lA

Tedx Talk. Argues a link between nutrition and mental health.

youtu.be/v6g4jefalgI

Options and ideas for healthcare planning while living nomadic on wheels.

youtu.be/DxV6qKbZrHw

Examples for health routines while on the road.

Fulfillment Levels

Low: Make no provisions. Maybe you will get lucky and nothing bad will happen.

Deliberate health care is not necessarily required. Though it is highly recommended.

Medium: Try to eat well, as much as possible. Get regular exercise. Pay attention to your mental states. Keep your relevant medical supplies on hand. Keep emergency medical supplies.

Maintaining a good state of health requires some thought and effort. These should be integrated into both your living solution and your daily routine. This may not be easy, but the results are well worth it.

High: Make extensive efforts to have a healthy diet, to exercise, and to address your ongoing state of mental health. Keep redundant medical supplies on hand, including normal and emergency supplies.

Maintaining a high state of health may (or may not, for you) require a high level of commitment and resource use. I still consider the results to be worth it, but this level of commitment is not for everyone.

15.

Pests

Insects are no joke. Some bite and some don't, but all of them can be annoying. There are many different kinds which vary from locale to locale. Always try to to take a look at what insect control methods the locals are using. They have spent a lot more time and experimentation on the particular problem than you have. Insects do tend to come in two main varieties—those just after food and those looking for a new home.

Food hunting insects, such as mosquitoes or gnats, will be attracted by their food source. Unless you can get rid of that you will need to use an active repellent of some sort to push them away or a screening arrangement to keep them out. Keeping things clean and sanitary will reduce the appeal for many pests. Clean and dispose after food prep and eating, keep any garbage or compost sealed away, and so on. Insect netting can be very effective and you may consider both temporary and semi-permanent arrangement depending on conditions where you are.

Insect repellents come in many varieties and, given the ongoing market, there is active research in this field. Keep an eye out for new solutions. It is best to use the chemical varieties in moderation. I have personally had some success using mixed essential oils as an alternative to applying chemicals.

Those insects looking for a home can be a serious problem. Termites will actively destroy your living solution and things like roaches can be very troublesome and persistent. Roaches in particular seem to be endemic around both wheeled and marine living groups. Consider insect deterrent measures before you have a problem with them. They are much easier to keep away than to get rid of once established. Work up a plan for pest control as part of your own integrated living solution.

Other pests can include rodents, birds, and even sea lions. Each will cause their own problems and each must be dealt with in a particular way. Rodents can be a real problem for electronics, as they like to chew on wires. For each type of pest, consider the problem logically. Every creature has its own needs and if they are bothering you or infesting your home they are doing so to fulfill those needs. They each have their own distinct life processes. Deter, trap, eliminate, or encourage them to leave accordingly.

Bed bugs can be very annoying and ruin much of the pleasure you take in your living space. Prevention will be the best measure, as they can be extremely difficult to get rid of, especially if you are trying to use non-toxic solutions. Be careful what fabrics you bring in, especially bedding. Wash first if they are used. Be careful about guests. If they have different cleanliness standards than you then you may wish to take precautions. See the video linked below for a demonstration of using heat to get rid of bed bugs.

Diatomaceous Earth

For general insect control and deterrence, I have had some success using diatomaceous earth. Also called insect dust or insect powder, this is a fine whitish substance composed of some of the debris from ancient seabeds. It can be spread around or sprayed in areas that might have insect problems. A very light coating is enough. The dust acts by scraping at the exoskeleton of insects, piercing their moisture barrier and leading to dehydration and, shortly, death. It is effective against a wide variety of pests (almost anything that has an exoskeleton). It is, however, almost entirely ineffective when wet. So it should only be used in dry conditions. This does not mean that you cannot put it places that will become wet at some point—many people use the dust in their gardens to eliminate pests. For the amount that is used, diatomaceous earth is very inexpensive and can be re-applied as needed. It will remain indefinitely in dry areas, forming a barrier against insect encroachments.

There are some types of diatomaceous earth that can be somewhat damaging to the lungs and should not be used around people. Always use the food-grade variety to ensure that this is not a concern. You still should not breathe large amounts of it, but doing so is only a minor or temporary irritation. Otherwise it is safe to use. Some people eat the stuff for nutritional purposes.

References and Further Research

Olkowski, William, Sheila Daar, and Helga Olkowski. *Common-Sense Pest Control.*

blog.goodsam.com/creepy-crawlers-ban-bugs-from-attacking-your-rv

www.tripsavvy.com/keep-your-rv-pest-free-505133

rvshare.com/blog/how-to-prevent-pests-and-bugs-in-your-camper

insectcop.net/spider-bird-control-for-boat-dock

www.godownsize.com/mice-boat-guide

youtu.be/vRO0PbCHDgA
Talk and coverage from some longtime cruisers on boat pest management.

youtu.be/4qCyuwfuaqo
Look at marine pests—taking care not to spread species to areas that you should not.

youtu.be/V1vcCgwuY58
Detailed consideration of how to remove bed bugs from a van. An interesting method, and may be effective if done with care.

Fulfillment Levels

Low: Make no provisions, except trying to keep things clean.

Some people are never bothered by pests. But the longer you live in the same platform, the more likely you will be to have some sort of pest problem. Better to take precautions and also have some solutions in mind.

Medium: Keep things clean and food sources sealed away. Maintain some non-toxic preventative measures, such as diatomaceous earth. Have some plans for pest removal if they do infest.

Prevention will always be more effective than removal, but this does require an ongoing effort and having specific measures in place. Moderate solutions will likely be all that is required.

High: Be very strict on cleaning and food storage and preparation. Have redundant preventative measures in place. Have redundant plans for pest removal should it be necessary.

If you are very much bothered by the thought of pest infestation, it is possible to ramp up your prevention measures and also to try to quickly remove the pests should they occur. Often this will mean having redundant solutions, rather than using only one.

16.

Address

Even while traveling indefinitely, we still have to interact with some of the people and services that assume (and sometimes require) that you have a home address. Whether you do or not. This section is about ways in which the person living mobile might be able to manage a static address at the same time.

We can break this down into two major concerns: a place to have your mail sent and a place where you can claim permanent legal residence (or domicile). Whether you can use the same address for both of these or if you actually need to spend any time at your official domicile will vary from place to place according to local regulations. I hope any international readers will forgive me, but I am unable to give more specific information for anywhere outside of the USA. Within that country, requirements will vary widely from state to state, and some states are definitely more willing to extend domicile rights to those living mobile.

Mail

This will always come down to having a specific place that your mail is sent, from which you either pick it up yourself of have it sent on to you. The best way to do this reliably is with a paid service. There are many businesses out there which offer mailbox and mail forwarding services. Usually this is for a monthly or annual fee, which may range from $100 to $300 a year, depending on location, services furnished, etc.

You could instead rely on friends or family to do this for you. For a short period of time or if you have a very specific understanding with the person in question, this can be fine. For longer periods or with people that you know will not give it much attention, things often turn out less than fine. What starts out as a favor can quickly turn into an imposition or worse. So, even if you are using that place as your legal domicile, I would suggest that you at least consider also contracting a mail forwarding service to handle your post.

That may cover a place that you can have mail sent before it is sent on to you, but you must also make arrangements to receive that mail wherever you might be found currently. This is generally a simpler matter. If you are staying somewhere that offers mail services (such as a marina and some campgrounds), just use them. If you are boondocking or living at anchor, stipulate that the mail or package should be held for pickup at the final distribution location. This could be a Post Office or a package shipper store (UPS, FedEx, etc). Hold for pickup is almost always an option, as it does not cost the delivery service any extra and may save them delivery costs.

Also, you need not have packages or even all mail forwarded to you through your service. Instead just have whatever you can sent directly to where you are, or even sent to be held for pickup where you are going to be soon. Which will save you postage costs from the forwarding service.

Domicile

Domicile is the term used to distinguish a permanent legal residence from a temporary residence. Your domicile state will be your state of permanent residence for census purposes and for other matters of legal authority. This has to do with the divided sovereignty of the United States between the federal level and the level of the individual states of residence. So, every American (legally) will have a domicile in one of the states or territories of the United States, to which they intend to return even if they spend their time traveling.

Establishing this can be a simple or complex matter, depending on the state. South Dakota (especially), Texas, and Florida are very popular states for nomads to establish legal residence because it is much easier to do so and maintain than for other states. Nevada, Wyoming, Montana, and Tennessee require somewhat more difficult procedures, but are also popular states to use for residency for particular reasons. What state you choose will depend on a number of factors and will be highly specific to your own needs and preferences.

Florida caters to people living on boats in various ways, but car insurance is very expensive there and government charges and fees for services tend to be rather high also. Texas is very attractive for the RV crowd, but does require yearly vehicle inspections (unless you don't enter the state). South Dakota may actively desire to gain citizens which live elsewhere most of the time (and you only have to go back once every five years), but is somewhat remote and the winters can be harsh. It is possible to reach South Dakota by boat, as the Missouri River (which branches from the Mississippi River at St. Louis) is kept navigable up to Sioux City Iowa, at the South Dakota border, and remains open water for another fifty miles until you hit the dam at Lewis and Clark Lake. None of the big three (FL, SD, TX) have state income taxes.

You may have other considerations that will put your domicile elsewhere, of course. These three states are popular because they make it easy to establish domicile even if you do not have any property. If you do have property elsewhere, or if you are willing to spend a bit of money to buy some (a small piece of unimproved land might only be a few thousand dollars), then you can use that to establish residency in any state of your choosing.

You could also ask friends or family if they would mind if you claim their address as your legal residence (this will be more cordial if you do not also want them to handle your mail). Lacking those, you could find someone who will 'rent' you space for a nominal fee, with the understanding that you will never actually show up but they will permit you to claim residence there. In this case be sure that you get something in writing, like a lease or rental agreement, to be able to defend your claim legally. If you do use these approaches to claim domicile in a certain state, be sure that your state will permit this. Some will require a certain amount of time spent living at that address (up to half the year). For this and other reasons these approaches may be something of a legal gray area.

One of the reasons that the big three states are so popular is that they each have clusters of mail forwarding service providers which will also assist you in using the address they provide to establish and maintain your domicile. Which is legal in those states. So, for one rate you will have both your mailing address and legal residence. There are other requirements which vary by state, but the better providers will explicitly state what those are on their website. South Dakota, for instance, requires that you spend at least one day every five years in that state (which you prove with a receipt from a motel or campground) to get and renew your driver's license. Americas Mailbox, Dakota Post, and Your Best Address will be happy to walk you through this and any other requirements. Texas and Florida have similar services that are easy to locate with a web-search.

References and Further Research

www.liveaboardhq.com/how-to-get-started-liveaboard

www.lifesaport.com/home/2017/10/24/legally-speaking-how-the-law-can-apply-to-being-a-liveaboard

gnomadhome.com/vanlife-mail-and-packages-for-nomads

twomeander.com/how-to-establish-a-legal-state-residency-domicile-as-a-nomad

www.escapees.com

americasmailbox.com

youtu.be/jntFI_5FiA8
Detailed discussion of US State residency while living mobile.

youtu.be/Z0zpGH0rXWo
Comparison video on residence (domicile) specifically for the RV perspective.

youtu.be/-8BJDLROpnI
Mail solutions for mobile living.

youtu.be/XylgnHXA0go
More detailed discussion on mail services while living mobile.

Fulfillment Levels

Low: Hit up friends or family for a place to call home while you are living mobile. Also ask them to forward your mail to you.

This will work, depending on the state, at least for a time. Can become iffy after a while for things like vehicle registration, auto insurance, health insurance, etc.

Medium: Maintain or establish domicile in a state of your choosing, but one that you can meet the legal requirements for on a yearly basis. Set up paid mail forwarding.

These steps will cost you a bit more (in terms of money) but will also put you on firm legal ground and provide for professional level mail services.

High: Take the extra step and buy a piece of land in order to have a home base. Also use a mail forwarding service.

You will occasionally have to stop by your property, unless you have all of your affairs taken care of by an agent of some sort, but doing this will expand the number of possible states for your residency. It can also be very nice to have a patch to call home and to store all of your excess stuff on.

17.

Stopping

Even though our living solutions are to have mobility, they will still be stationary more often than not. This section is about finding places to not be mobile for a while. I will consider wheeled parking first. And this will always be parking, whenever you are stopped, but we can further differentiate in terms of whether you are parking in places that people normally park, or camping, or renting space to have your vehicle, or even living full-time (for the moment) on a patch of ground.

Wheeled

The best full-time spot to park your mobile life will always be your own land. Many people who are able find it very nice, though not essential, to have a home base to come back to from time to time. This can be anything from an actual house all the way down to a bit of undeveloped land that you purchased just for this. There are even survival shelters for purchase, bunkers really, that you can keep as a home base to come back to at need or as desired. As an alternative to your own land, you may have a home base on someone else's land...preferably with permission. If you have friends or family who might not mind extended visits from an occasional nomad this can be a good way to have a place for repairs or to rest up or even to winter over.

Renting

If you are not so fortunate, there are also paid options for extended parking. You could rent or lease a bit of ground for parking, provided that all legal requirements are met and all parties involved are clear on the terms of the arrangement. This could be with a private party or instead something like lot rental in an established mobile home community. It is also common for large commercial campgrounds, like KOA, to offer monthly or longer rates for extended stays. You can find the same sort of arrangement, complete with amenities, at RV parks or campgrounds throughout the world. Rates tend to drop the longer the stay that you are willing to commit to, but you will always be paying more for less than you would receive when signing a static apartment lease, for instance. Such is the cost of mobility.

Camping

You could instead spend your parking time camping, by which I mean that you are parked somewhere for a limited time either for free or at the cost of a nominal fee. In terms of wheeled living, staying at a commercial park or 'campground' with established amenities is not really camping—it is renting, even if only for a day. This type will instead refer to dry camping, boondocking, or staying at rough sites such as in a state park or national forest.

There may or may not be running water, toilets, or trash receptacles. Generally this sort of parking refers to the use of public lands that mandate a maximum period that you can stay before leaving, but there are also many private undeveloped campgrounds out there.

Other Considerations

You could also park for a time in places that are actually established parking areas, though generally used by local residents or with the understanding that there is some definite purpose for the parking. Like a trip to the store or street parking next to an apartment or to catch a movie. In these situations, there tends to be some gray area in terms of the legality of parking overnight or sleeping in the parked vehicle. In some places it is definitely illegal or not permitted and thus you should not do it. In most places however there will be some ambiguity, whether deliberately or as a matter of convenience for the locals. If you are parking on private property you should always have written permission from the owner to do so. If you are parking on a public street or other public area you should follow the local regulations.

There are two ways to approach parking in these temporary locations—by stealth or openly. Stealth camping, or parking, exploits the concept that that which is not forbidden is allowed. The stealth camper scouts out a location and parks there, usually just overnight for a place to sleep, without troubling others. Provided that such stealth campers are doing no harm and do leave promptly, there are many places that this can be done without undue concern on the part of the locals or of the camper.

Open overnight parking tends to be a bit more involved, but is generally a bit safer and often quite acceptable as well. This option tends to be more viable in smaller towns or in areas that do not have problems with vagrancy. You can simply ask about overnight parking from a resident, a local police officer or fireman, at a church or library, or even at the local post office. Be open and respectful. Present yourself as the good neighbor that you hope to be, even if it is only for a day or three. Most locals will only be concerned that you are not there to cause trouble and that you will only be staying a short time.

For actual locations on overnight parking, you should always consider local conditions. That which will work in one area may not in another. Parking in urban areas will be very different from rural areas. Small towns will be different than large ones. Your type of vehicle will also restrict your options. Parking is usually best in places that your vehicle will blend in.

Closed, abandoned, or undeveloped areas may be a good bet. Or next to an industrial park. Near a city or county park. Near large apartment complexes. Twenty-four hour shopping areas. Car dealerships, restaurant zones, hospitals. Casinos. Police stations or fire departments (with permission). Airports or other transportation hubs, such as train or bus depots, or even a park and ride lot. On residential streets, though not blocking anything and not right in front of a home. Highway rest areas. Truck stops also tend to be a good place to park for a time. In the past they have been grubby places and not fit for most people, but now most are safe places that welcome travelers and provide good amenities. They offer an excellent place to get a shower on the road without having to get a motel room—and the facilities are usually cleaned after each use.

Other Options

Working back to actual camping, there are also many different options. Public lands are good for extended stays, often allowing you to stop for a week or two or even three. In the United States at least these tend to be much more common the further west you go, but there are public lands in every state. Consider national parks and state parks. National forests and state forests. National, state, or local recreational areas or monuments or fishing areas. BLM (Bureau of Land Management) land. Lands operated by the Army Corps of Engineers often permit free camping. Wildlife management areas and national or state river areas. Public beach areas. County or city parks will often permit camping, especially in more rural areas. The TVA (Tennessee Valley Authority) has established a number of visitor areas for camping throughout that watershed. Other damns and water works not administered by the Corps of Engineers do so as well. Various conservation areas also permit camping. Private campgrounds without amenities may be found almost anywhere.

Regardless of whether you plan to live or rent, camp or just park, always try to plan ahead. There are various guidebooks out there. The internet offers many ways to scout out places remotely. Google maps satellite view and street view can give you a feel for a place, though the photos are often dated. Niche.com and other sites can give you a way to consider crime rates and other statistics. You can make connections with locals before arriving with social networking or hospitality sharing options like couchsurfing.com or boondockerswelcome.com. Planning a trip or a leg of your journey may seem to take away from the adventure and spontaneity of living mobile, but even if you want to be spontaneous (or lazy) you should always have some sort of backup plan in place in case expected opportunities do not materialize. We can only be mobile for so long before stopping. Have some place ready to park before you really need it. Desperation will do far more harm to that adventurous spirit than planning things out will.

Parking Sample Options

$87; Nashville KOA; 1 night, Pull Thru full hookup RV site; water, electric, tv, etc; Tennessee
From koa.com

$40; River Road Camp; 1 night, tent camping w/electric; Central Texas
From www.riverroadcamp.com

$20; Rocky Arbor State Park Campground; 1 night, truck camper; Southwest Wisconsin
From wisconsin.goingtocamp.com

$0; Nelson Creek @ the Fort Peck Project, US Army Corps of Engineers; North Central Montana
From corpslakes.erdc.dren.mil

Marine

Marine stationary places should be easier to find, but good ones may actually be fewer. This will be heavily dependent on how long you are capable of being out away from shore support, which will in turn depend on the capabilities of your various living systems. It will also change dramatically depending on your current location. There will, however, be only so many ways for a boat to stop moving. You will either be beached or on the hard, anchored, moored, or docked. That's it.

Docking

You may dock at a marina or instead at a private dock. For most people it will be at a marina. Marinas are the standard public access point for any given locale for access to and from the water. All recreational, cruising, or liveaboard boaters will need to visit a marina from time to time. They are safe harbor, gas station, shopping, showers, laundry, and gateway to the landed world all rolled into one. They also tend to have or be near repair or haul out facilities. Almost every marina will have a different policy regarding long-term stays, especially in regards to living aboard. All of them welcome (and will charge for) short term visits. Marinas will always be the most expensive way for a boater to remain still, but they do have many attractions and amenities as well. Consider your marina options carefully. If you want access to shore power or water lines, it will be at some dock, and usually at a marina.

You may also have the opportunity to utilize a private dock, either for free or at an agreed upon rate. Having your own waterfront dock would be ideal of course, but is not likely for most of us. Some of those who do own their own dock, however, may find that they do not use it very often or even at all. In which case they might be amenable to other using it. These can be informal arrangements or setup as leases or rentals. There are many resources out there to find a dock for your boat—the first one will usually be to ask at a local marina, either regarding their docks or private docks in the area. Online, you can utilize such resources as marinas.com, dockskipper.com, piershare.com, snagaslip.com, and find-a-mooring.com, among others.

Mooring

To moor is to attach to something that is permanently or semi-permanently affixed to the seafloor but has no direct connection to land. It can also refer to a designated anchorage field. Some people will also talk about mooring to a dock, but here I refer to a non-landed connection.

In addition to their docking spaces, most marinas will also offer mooring space for rent at a lower price. Many other entities have privately owned moorings that may be rented out, such as yacht clubs or canal associations. It can also be possible to establish your own mooring in places where this is permissible, though there may be registration fees or a waiting list to get on. Construction can be as simple as filling a barrel with concrete and dropping it overboard with a chain or line attached to a mooring ball.

Anchoring, in contrast, will involve a temporary fix on a given stretch of seafloor, by a line directly attached to the boat. Depending on conditions and local regulation, you can anchor in one spot for years at a time—or just a few minutes. Boats anchor many places. This is the heart of the great open freedom of boat living. Just drop your anchor and you have found a new home, wherever you may be...in theory. In practice there tend to be a great many restrictions, from both natural and artificial causes. To anchor, you must be in a relatively shallow bit of water, else your line will not reach to find purchase. You should also be sheltered from any more violent aspects of wind and wave. These conditions tend to be found near to land, which places a boater within the legal restrictions of the regional governing body. California, for instance, restricts against long-term anchoring along its coastline.

On the Hard

Putting your boat on land (deliberately) for a time may be called beaching or being on the hard, but I will consider these as quite separate actions. Being on the hard refers to having your boat hauled out of the water by a crane or hoist arrangement and placed in one spot. For some this will be for storage, perhaps over the winter. For others this will be a chance to get at the bottom of the boat for repairs or maintenance. Regardless, most boats should be hauled out on occasion even if only to check on hull condition or to clean off the bottom.

Beaching instead refers to putting your boat on dry land without the crane or hoist, such as by moving onto a gentle sandy beach or just waiting for the tide to go out in a spot you know will dry out. Some boats are designed to be beached and others are not. A fin-keel monohull sailboat will not hold together well during a beaching attempt. Many catamarans are built with beaching in mind, as the hull-form lends itself to the process. Some boats which are not specifically built to be beached may survive doing so in extremis, especially if most of the weight is first taken out of the vessel.

Beaching can be a good way to stop moving for a time if your vessel can handle the process—if the hull is built so that all of the weight can be supported by whatever the very bottom part is. You may want to get at the underwater hull without bothering about a haul-out, or do repairs that cannot be done underway. You may want to stick around a place even though you know the tide is going out. You may just want to put the thing on land for a while for a break from the incessant movement. For whatever reason, having the ability to beach your boat as desired can greatly increase versatility.

Marina Sample Options

$160; Safe Harbor Marina Bay; 1 night, 40ft boat, dock slip, full hookup. Near Boston, MA.
From shmarinas.com

$40; Sea Hag Marina; 1 night, 40ft boat, wet slip, +$5-9 for electric. Steinhatchee, FL.
From seahag.com

$486 (+ electric); Richardson Bay Marina; 1 month, 36ft boat, dock box. Near San Francisco, CA.
From www.richardsonbaymarina.com

References and Further Research

Hinz, Earl R. *The Complete Book of Anchoring and Mooring.*

Wright, Don and Joyce Wright. *The Wright Guide to Free and Low-Cost Campgrounds*

Hudson, Mike. *How to Live in a Van and Travel*

Nicholas, Mark. *The Essentials of Living Aboard a Boat*

dbscweb.files.wordpress.com/2013/08/bradney-mooring-and-anchoring-leaflet.pdf

www.outdoorsy.com/blog/ultimate-guide-finding-best-spots-park-rv

mywilddreams.net/2017/10/27/vanlife-how-to-where-to-park-and-sleep-in-cities

thedyrt.com/magazine/lifestyle/boondocking-guide-free-camping

youtu.be/aSLPAQGsPUk

Remote anchoring advice from an experienced sailor.

youtu.be/oqPiP2JYVNc

Breakdown of one couple's vanlife parking experiences.

youtu.be/aT_zFOOMWfA

Same topic as above, but from the RV perspective instead.

Fulfillment Levels

Low: Do minimal planning ahead of time as to where you will stop. Park as you please; drop anchor when you wish.

In the very short term or for occasional use, this may work fine for you. If traveling far or extensively, better planning and care are required.

Medium: Plan out your route, possibly with alternatives, ahead of time; include places to stop as part of the planning. Have a list of general places you can stop for a while and also specific places for a given area. Have reference materials, with you or online, to direct you to stopping places at need.

These are much better solutions, and with not a great deal more effort. A bit of planning can be a great help, even if you end up changing things around en-route.

High: Have extensive plans for multiple alternatives. Keep both lists and reference materials for stopping places. Reserve in advance whenever possible.

A high level of fulfillment for this need will not necessarily cost any more money and may end up saving you quite a bit of money and time both. The difference is in the level of effort that you are willing to put into planning and contingencies. Plans can always go awry, but having them will almost always be better than not.

18.

Security

Security, in ourselves and for our property, may be the primary human need. Everything you have, you can lose. For some things this may be acceptable, but for many things having some security arrangement in place will be worthwhile. This can be a simple as having memorized the local version of '911' and having a phone nearby. It can also be as complex and thorough as you are willing to put in place. Given legal requirements, unless your travel is purely local then your security solution should not include firearms—which will generally be unnecessary anyway. For our purposes we will consider security to be systems and plans that we have in place to help keep us and our property safe and free from duress.

There will be legal requirements, which will vary extensively from place to place and may impact what security arrangements you have made. That being said, it is very possible to have measures in place which are, or which can be argued to be, legal anywhere. Locks, discrete and non-intrusive sensors (such as motion detectors, cameras, audio pickups, etc), emergency communications pathways, fire extinguishers, alarms, trip-lights, etc, are all passive measures and to my knowledge are legal anywhere. Many forms of passive security can have a deterrent effect. Something as simple as keeping valuable items out of sight can be very effective in avoiding the interest of would-be thieves. As you will be sleeping inside, consider installing bolted latches that can only be released from the inside.

Beyond legal requirements, there are also ethical considerations that you must consider when planning your security. Causing harm to others when not justified or when not sufficiently justified is wrong whether it is legal or not. In situations of danger or where security is compromised, the relative balance between ethics and security may shift, but never lose your moral sense completely. A sense of the balance between practicality and morality is one of the key components of civilization.

In extremis, there are various active security measures which are permissible (and may or may not be legal—know the laws where you are now). Consider that a boat may rig a pressurized water pump/hose system for cleaning the exterior of the vessel... and that may also be useful for 'gently' and safely pushing overboard any uninvited guests. A wheeled living solution may also rig a water pump to draw on stored water from tanks, but the water supply might be less than desired. Compressed air, which is not as useful as water in itself as a motive force, can still be used to impel various objects. Consider that a small bean-bag, when impelled sufficiently fast, can be a very effective deterrent. Care must be taken in aiming—a minor bruise to the torso may translate into a more extensive injury to the face. Drills and practice with your specific security arrangements will improve competency and help avoid accidents.

It will be prohibitively expensive to fully armor your solution against determined attackers, but most security concerns will be a matter of predators trying to profit by taking what is yours. Resolve these by making it clearly unprofitable for those individuals to attempt the matter. Deter them, by such means as motion lights, alarms, cameras, or simply by appearing to be a strong target. Predators seek out weakness, but all they have to go on is appearance. Appear to be strong and they will often look elsewhere.

When you are confronted with determined attackers, think carefully before risking your life to defend your possessions. It will be better, in most cases, to attempt to escape if at all possible. If that is not possible then it is the time to attempt non-lethal defense measures such as those discussed above. Failing that, it becomes appropriate to attempt more stringent measures.

Digital

Do not neglect your digital security. Even if you do not wish to integrate together your various systems you can still suffer in various ways from having a data breach. If you do integrate then such a breach may be nearly catastrophic. Have some sort of last ditch measure in case of actual control loss for critical systems (such as putting everything completely on manual). Measures such as this should really be in place regardless. The ability to tweak the autopilot from your tablet is nice but must never be the primary method of steering.

Have some barriers in place for remote access to your devices and systems—passwords or biometrics or both. Utilize a VPN (virtual private network) when online. VPN services are inexpensive (you should not depend on a 'free' one) and greatly increase anonymity online.

Backup your data locally. Even if you have some sort of online or cloud data storage you will not always be able to access it. It is not necessary to electronically integrate your systems to have an integrated mobile living system in place, but even if you are not integrated electronically then you will have some reliance on computing. If you do so integrate then a system crash can be catastrophic...but may be recovered from if you have backups. Redundantly store your work on a flash drive. Have a dedicated storage drive (or two) just for backing up data in down hours on your server or central PC. Keep a copy of any operating system or important software on disk or flash. Copies and redundancy are critical to electronic security. With them data corruption can be annoying. Without them data corruption can be far worse.

References and Further Research

Emerson, Clinton. *Escape the Wolf*

www.thefitoutpontoon.co.uk/safety-security/secuirty-onboard

www.saltwatersportsman.com/fishing-boats/marine-security-systems-boats

www.tripsavvy.com/installing-an-rv-security-system-2912514

camperreport.com/5-great-security-system-options-for-an-rv-and-what-id-pick

www.wired.com/2017/12/digital-security-guide

rorypecktrust.org/freelance-resources/digital-security

youtu.be/BIZDPKRE3tk

Breakdown of security concerns at anchor for one cruising sailboat.

youtu.be/fHQtQWdVsh0

Safety tips for solo female van living

youtu.be/jMyex5vk5yY

A collection of digital security tips for when you are traveling.

Fulfillment Levels

Low: Keep valuables hidden inside. Keep doors locked when possible. Have some emergency plans. Maintain some degree of awareness of your living platform and surroundings.

Security itself can be greatly increased with just these few measures. They do not take much effort or time and will quickly become habitual. Habits may keep us safe even when we do not have time to think.

Medium: Keep valuables hidden and locked away inside. Have both locks and security latches on all entry points, or some way to otherwise block off large windows. Have an emergency escape method. Have some way to confront intruders in case the escape method fails. Have some ways to deter people from becoming intruders. Consider electronic security arrangements. Protect and backup all digital systems.

This is a bit of a list, but most of these measures are inexpensive and will not require much effort once in place. Deterrence will be the most significant concern, but have backup solutions for serious intrusions.

High: Everything above, but put more into it.

At a medium level of fulfillment all security concerns should already be addressed. Increasing your fulfillment level will be matter of spending more time or money or energy budget for what you consider to be better solutions. Dealing with security will always be a matter of balance. Basic measures are relatively inexpensive, but the sky is the limit on how much you can spend.

19.

Space

The less space you have available, the more important it will become for you to plan out and organize what you do with it. Living mobile will almost always reduce our available space. Wherever we go, part of the point of taking your home with you is to have a place for your stuff. This section will look at the need for storage and space planning.

Space for storage and also for living activities will always be more limited in mobile living solutions. The cost for increasing space is often disproportionate to the gain. Doubling the size of a boat, for instance, will more than triple the total costs involved. Because of this we must be more frugal with the space we have and also become more used to being confined. Space considerations for mental comfort and equilibrium seem to vary a great deal and are strongly impacted by early childhood experiences. This need can be changed with effort and time. The mind itself takes up no room at all. We can learn to make do with less or to do without.

As for material objects, there will be definite limits in what can be kept and what not. Mobile living requires that we reduce how much we have and the size of those things. Almost any one thing can be kept if you are willing to make the trade-off, but choose wisely. In addition, most things are given more space than they really need, which can be reduced by designing and building custom storage solutions. Think spatially and there will almost always be something you can do to get a bit more storage. Consider that any given open space can be converted to storage. Place hooks for hanging things, install shelves, build storage racks, install drawers or cabinets...there are many possibilities if you are willing to make the effort.

For marine living, extra space must always be reserved to keep accessible those things which are required for working the boat or for emergencies. Things which are not used often or not critical for time can be stowed away deep, but don't bury your life-raft or medical supplies or anything else of immediate importance.

Wheeled living will offer more options for storage, as you may be able to put things on the roof or hang them off the back or even tow a trailer just for storage. Just remember to consider the impact on fuel efficiency and to keep the rig safe.

For all living solutions, it can be very important to have a 'salon' space which is kept open normally but is variably used for specific activities or projects. Even if you have very little space in your dwelling, do not make the mistake of packing things in until you have no open area at all. Your salon can serve the purposes of a dining room, office, living room, garage, playroom, and more, but only if you keep it open for all of these purposes instead of crowding it with the accouterments of just one of them.

References and Further Research

Sandenburgh, Roberta. *Small Space Living*

unclutteredsimplicity.com/storage-solutions-for-small-spaces

rvshare.com/blog/rv-storage-solutions

www.sailingchance.com/smart-boat-organization-hacks

blueturtletrawler.com/boat-interior-storage-ideas-or-where-to-put-all-your-stuff

youtu.be/aK-VdF6JXAk

Breakdown on some storage solutions for the uniquely humid environment of a sailboat.

youtu.be/p0pZuQIhUy8

Van build video that highlights the importance of planning and deliberate storage solutions. Custom builds can really maximize space.

youtu.be/VE_QnCrJb6o

Interesting collection of space planning and storage ideas.

Fulfillment Levels

Low: Use what you have or what is convenient to build, but otherwise don't plan out your space deliberately. Come across your space management and storage solutions organically, as they occur to you.

This will work, but is far from the best way to maximize your space.

Medium: Make some alterations to existing structures to help accommodate space needs. If building, take care to plan out storage solutions and layout. Have a plan for where you put things and how.

This is much better, and fulfillment at this level will greatly enhance space options for most people.

High: Make extensive alterations to existing structures to fully accommodate your individual needs. If building, fully plan out and customize storage solutions and layout. Have a comprehensive and detailed plan for where you put things and how.

Even when living mobile, those who are very detailed oriented and organized can still have the meticulous spaces and order that they crave, given sufficient care and planning.

20.

Philosophy

We will all have some mental pattern or ideology by which we organize our understanding of experiences. Philosophy may be understood as being some structure of thought that helps give meaning and direction. It is a matrix that we use to help perceive and understand our existence. 'Philosophy' as a term might mean many other things, of course, to many different people, but this is the definition which I will focus on here.

We all need some sort of philosophy and at any given time we all have one, whether we think of it that way or not. Try not to get hung up too much on your own philosophy. Everybody has their own and none of them are perfect. This is because philosophy itself is a human invention. We are all both flawed and limited; our philosophies will reflect these limitations.

Despite having flaws, philosophies are also very useful. All perception, all understanding, everything we experience, is filtered through our paradigms of thought before it ever reaches the consciousness. A given paradigm may be more or less useful to help you act in a given situation, to improve your understanding of this realm of existence, to decide whether you have positive or negative experiences.

Actively examining our own philosophies and those which others have written of over the years can be beneficial for everyone. I suggest to you that doing so periodically is both a beneficial use of your time and also an important aspect for any integrated living solution to include.

Some of the references I have included below are in text form—books or websites. Books on philosophy will be the richest and most detailed medium out there, but philosophy itself is about thought alone and books are only one possible medium of exploration. Many people are putting their thoughts out there in video format. Representational artists seek to convey a bit of their life philosophies with the art of their pictures, paintings, or sculptures. Most online blogs contain at least a bit of philosophy, and some of them have a great deal more.

References and Further Research

Baggini, Julian and Peter S. Fosl. *The Philospher's Toolkit*

Solomon, Robert C. and Kathleen M. Higgins. *A Short History of Philosophy.*

www.philosophybasics.com

https://newmediarockstars.com/2014/10/the-7-youtube-philosophers-you-just-cant-miss

youtu.be/iZ8so-ld-l0
A brief illustration of some thoughts from Alan Watts.

Fulfillment Levels

Low: Let it sort itself out in your mind and behind the scenes; let your thought be shaped or influenced by others.

This is the approach that most people take. Also the easiest. Just do nothing at all and the need is fulfilled—though poorly and haphazardly, at best.

Medium: Go a bit out of your way to learn about the variations of human thought. Take some time to think about your own life and experiences.

This is a better approach and will be a satisfactory one for most people out there.

High: Read the great philosophers. Consider the philosophical impact of your own life and the leanings of your own thought, extensively. View thought-provoking aspects of the world through the lens of your understanding of philosophy.

I may be biased, but I consider more philosophical thought, up to a certain point, to be better. It is one of those things that you get more out of the more you put into it. Most people will not see the need for devoting themselves in abundance to the many aspects of thought, but those who do may find that the work itself is its own reward.

Part Two—Builds

21.

The Minivan Conversion

For this first sample build, I will start with the most basic and inexpensive platform from which to start living mobile. One can also live in a car, but for the most part a car will not be any cheaper to purchase and maintain than a minivan and will have significantly less enclosed space to work with. It is still possible to turn any vehicle into a mobile living solution, given sufficient creativity. This conversion will look at a minivan, but don't let me stop you from tackling any conversion that you consider viable. One hopes that many of the ideas given in this sample conversion will be applicable to other small vehicles as well.

Cost alone may not be the sole consideration when choosing to create a home from a minivan or similar vehicle. The interior space is limited, but still more than adequate to meet the life needs of an individual, especially when combined with shopping and other services common to settled population areas. The small form factor of the vehicle makes for superior mobility, increasing options for driving and parking over those of larger vehicles. Minivans can also be very low profile, increasing privacy and supporting alternative living options.

Platform

In favor of looking at a very common option, I have chosen to (hypothetically) convert a Caravan. More specifically, a 2012 Dodge Grand Caravan. Your choice may be for a different make or model, older or newer, etc, but I think this gives a solid middle-of-the-road option for comparison purposes. Also, I owned a similar vehicle for a number of years.

Specs

3.6L VVT 24-Valve V6, 283 HP @ 6400 RPM, 260 Ft-lbs Torque @ 4400 RPM
Max towing capacity: 3600lbs.
Front wheel drive
6-Speed automatic transmission
20 gallon fuel capacity, estimated mileage 17 city 25 hwy
Exterior dimensions 202.8in length x 78.7in width (plus mirrors) x 67.9in height

Interior height 39.8in (front) to 37.9in (rear)
4dr SE trim. All standard options.

Note that this vehicle has Stow 'N Go seating, which means that all of the rear seats fold down to be flush with the floor. You may choose to keep the seats in such a case, which will have implications for resale value, or you may choose to remove some or all or them to increase storage area. For vehicles without this feature, you will want to remove all rear seating from the minivan—and possibly the front passenger seat as well. For the purpose of this build I will remove all of the rear folding seats in order to increase storage space but leave the front passenger seat in place. It can be nice to have a passenger from time to time.

Purpose

I must first decide what purposes I will put my living platform to. This really should begin before acquiring the platform itself, but for this first build let us say that the van being used is my best (or only) option. It happens.

So, my central purpose will, of course, be to live in the minivan. Let us say for this build that it will be primarily an urban living platform and will be kept stealthy so as not to bother the sensibilities of others. This will have a definite impact on systems design and what fulfillment levels I choose to meet each of my life needs. The urban environment is rife with alternative services. I will still want to retain as much independence as possible though, so will try to have short term or emergency solutions even for those life needs that I will normally be meeting outside of the van platform.

If instead I were to design the build as a campervan and would expect to frequently be rough camping or otherwise in wilderness areas, my build strategy and equipment list would be different. By setting the definite goal of having a stealthy urban mobile living solution I am able to maximize what limited space and options my chosen platform has. And every mobile platform, regardless of size, will have limited space and usage options. As this is a hypothetical build and my readers may choose to go a different way, I will still try to note some alternative solutions that may be better suited for other purposes.

Planning

The next step will be to plan out which life needs will be met at a given level of fulfillment. In Part One of the book, on life needs, I ended each section with a brief consideration of possible fulfillment levels for that life need. In order to better plan out my living platform, I will now proceed to categorize my life needs for this platform according to whether they will be met with a low level of fulfillment, a medium level, or a high level. This will be different for every platform and for every purpose a given platform is devoted to. For my particular minivan build I will try to minimize expenses and will need to minimize space usage and visible modifications, so will not be able to reach high levels of fulfillment unless such can be accomplished without violating those stipulations.

High fulfillment: Health, Philosophy, Planning, Stopping

Medium fulfillment: Address, Applications, Pests, Space

Low fulfillment: Air, Cooling, Electricity, Food, Heat, Networking, Propulsion, Sanitation, Security, Structure, Wastage, Water

Some of these choices are a bit arbitrary, in that I am not doing an actual build and cannot plan out absolutely everything. Some of them may change over time or even with the seasons. Health options will be greatly increased as I will be staying close to urban services and need not work out most solutions in my own platform. Most of the low fulfillment levels are as such for the same reason. I could probably get by with a medium level for Planning and Stopping, but taking them up a notch will not cost me extra money or space—only extra time and effort. If I find that I need the extra capacity for my Applications, I can always beef up my Networking fulfillment level accordingly.

Notice that I have chosen a low level of fulfillment for both Heating and Cooling. This might presume a level of stoicism, depending on climate, that is not realistic for most people, but I instead will suggest that I need not be in the van during waking hours. Things will be cooler at night and I should be able to get by with a small fan in hotter times, or at most with a small evaporative cooler. For cold weather there are good insulated sleeping options in the camping market. A zero degree sleeping bag will suffice for most winters—though any water in the vehicle, that is not also kept in your sleeping bag, may freeze. For more serious winters a small diesel heater can be installed. One of the videos in the reference section shows a minivan build that is successful even through Canadian winters.

Build

This is also part of our planning, really, as we are engaging in a hypothetical build, but will deal with the more hands on things in order to prompt the required responses.

Preparation

Once you have the seats out of the van and have removed any residual hardware, you must consider what other initial preparation to do to the interior. You may not choose to remove anything else before building up, which will work fine for this vehicle. If desired, you may choose to strip out the carpeting in order to put down your own flooring. For most minivan builds, I would suggest not doing so. The carpet in place has been chosen for durability, to resist moisture, and also has insulation already packed below it. The irregular shapes and floor levels will complicate any re-flooring process. It may still be desirable to put down removable rugs once your build is complete, however. The interior headliner and wall panels should be left in place unless you have a good reason not to. Seat-belt hardware should also probably be left in place, as possible. The belts can be kept out of the way and these installations may be useful for other purposes, as they are load bearing points. For my build I will leave all other fixtures in place, once the seats and associated hardware are removed. As necessary, I will consider added fixtures to maintain access to the Stow 'N Go storage wells.

At this point you have an open canvas and you can choose whatever configuration you like to complete your living solution. I think a minivan build lends itself to having temporary or at least removable arrangements in place, so for my sample build I will focus on those. Depending on whether you are building a campervan or a vehicle more for urban living, your own design choices may be wildly different than my own. I hope that my ideas may still spark some like ideas for you.

Fixtures

Next step will be to consider anything that is to be altered or permanently affixed. If you are going to be adding electric lines or water lines you will want to plan their routing now. The windows should be tinted for a good minivan build, but you will also want to at least plan out your window covering method while you have the space open. Then, look at how you can screen off the front driving area with its large untinted windshield from the rest of the van. This will add privacy and, depending on how you go about it, can help with temperature regulation.

For blocking the windows, I would suggest either reflextix insulation covered in cloth or Mylar sheeting quilted into cloth—preferably sewn in, whichever type you choose, but you could get by with a careful tape job. The reflective barrier will help to keep solar heat out of your living area and the cloth will make it easier to handle, as well as being decorative and less glaring than the Mylar alone. Use Reflectix if you want a stiffened material and Mylar if you want a pliable one. As an alternative to having a thermal reflective barrier you could instead cover flexible foam in cloth. The outer cloth facing at least should be black or some other dark color, but decorate to your own taste and certainly use any color you like for the interior facing. You could also put in small flaps as view-ports in strategic places.

There are many ways that you might affix them in place, and your method will depend on the specific materials and layout of your build. Again, you could get by with taping them in place, but I really would not suggest it unless you do not mind constantly fiddling with the things. A better way might be to screw short fasteners into place at intervals around the window in question and to attach your custom window shade to them with tied string or cords (sewn to your cover). This will keep it firmly in place but also allow you to raise or lower it for partial shade or detach it completely. You could also adhere a strip of velcro to the top portion for a tighter seal, or indeed all around the window. Velcro alone might be more to your taste, but do consider the permanency of the adherence and whether it gives the effect you wish. Also, be wary of cracking the vinyl or other material when attaching fasteners. Drill first, if possible, before screwing, and never place significant weight on the fastener. Go slow and be careful not to drill into wires or other important things under the surface.

You will want some sort of curtain to screen off the front of the vehicle. I suggest Mylar quilted into dark cloth, but sewn in panels perhaps one foot or eighteen inches wide and long enough to be just above the bottom level of the front seat or seats. The Mylar will help with heat from the sun but will not block off airborne heating or cooling from the front vents. The narrow panels will allow you to access storage in the seat-backs and from any bags hung off the back of the seats. They will also allow a modular opening to the front when you want one. If you like you could put velcro in select places along the edges or just simple ties, to make the curtain panels into one sheet when desired. The same methods can be used to fasten the curtain panels at the sides of the interior.

If the panels do not go all the way down to the floor it will be easier to access the space under the seats and also reduce the chance of them getting stepped on and torn or just dirty—though if they do go all the way to the carpeting then less cold air will be passed through between the front and back. The rod to hang them by could be just PVC pipe or a shower curtain rod or something sturdier, cut to length. Take care again with the vinyl when affixing the rod ends. Consider putting cross-supports to take advantage of grips or other hardware already in place. If necessary, you could even put vertical rods down to the floor, which might save you from drilling into the van interior structure. Remember to extend the curtain or curtain panels above the rod so that they brush the ceiling. Also, I would purchase a shade for the front windshield in addition to these measures.

Now I would run the wiring for any solar panels that are planned. You should be able to get away with slipping the cable through the flexible seal at a side or rear door, but you may instead choose to drill a small hole for the purpose. Either method has drawbacks. If you are going to designate one side door as not to be opened under normal conditions, it may be easier to weatherproof a small divot at the top of that door than to drill and seal a roof hole. Though roof holes can be adequately sealed if done properly.

Also at this point I would install one or more small 12V DC fans at the ceiling level to help with cooling and airflow. If there is a center-line storage/utility header they could be attached to that; if not they could be attached at grip points or clothes hooks. Such fans are easy to find at boating stores. As an alternative, you could rig mountings for PC case fans, which also run on 12V DC. A small DC light on a swivel or flex mount might also be a good idea. This light and the fans could draw off of a house battery if you choose to add one, instead of potentially draining the starter battery. If you do not want to bother with extra wiring, you could instead opt for USB powered fans and lights. There are many available, marketed to office workers and the tech crowd. They will still need cords, which you will want to route down along the interior sides if drawing from a house battery. If drawing from the vehicle starter battery there may already be USB ports in place.

For my hypothetical build, I will not be doing wiring or solar panels or a house battery bank. These needs, kept modest, will be met with a small portable power station, which will be charged from the vehicle alternator when running. My chosen vehicle comes stock with a 160A alternator (at 12V) which should be be more than sufficient to keep this power station charged even with short daily drives. From this power station, I will be able to keep my electronics charged and have one or two small fans and led lights which will be clipped in place as needed. For extended computer use I will also want to be able to plug in elsewhere, at a cafe or library. I will still have to be careful of my power draws. Should I wish to upgrade at some point it is still very possible to have a full house electrical system in a minivan. Further details will be offered below.

I will also go with quilted Mylar for both my window covers and front curtain (in addition to buying a windshield cover sized to my vehicle). Yes, this will involve some measuring and cutting and sewing. Anyone can sew, if they are willing to take a bit of time. The materials are very inexpensive. All I will need are some space blankets, a small roll of cloth, a needle, some thread, and a bit of velcro. I will make window covers for the rear and side windows and attach them at multiple points around the windows with small screw-in hooks for short cloth extensions sewn out from the covers.

The front curtain will be overlapping quilted Mylar panels with two or three velcro spots along their lengths to enable fastening them together. If I do not want to use the velcro I can just rearrange the panels so that the non-velcro facings are touching—there should be enough overlap that cloth friction will keep them in place otherwise. The panels will be sewn to length and the rod will be whatever I can find that will fit (such as a cut length of PVC from the hardware store) and attached however seems best. The curtain panels are not heavy so I should be able to manage with short screws into the interior van panels. Shower curtain hardware or closet hanger hardware may be substituted instead. You may be able to use one of those spring-loaded shower rods, but should still do something to help keep it in place at the bracing points.

Furnishings

There are a great many different configurations that you may utilize for furnishings and their arrangements. I will lay out several different options and then continue with my hypothetical build along a recommended route. Thus far all work has been sewing (or taping) and installation of hardware, with limited skill required. The best furnishings will be those which have been designed and constructed for your specific space and layout, but you can get by with only prefabricated items, perhaps slightly modified in some way.

At this point you will have to designate what access arrangements you will have. That is, will you keep one side door for general access and let the other be blocked off during normal operation? Will you need an isle that passes through to the rear door, block off the rear completely, or place movable storage in the way so that you can get through when you need to? I suggest allowing one slider to be blocked off, but still open-able for access to storage from the outside. The curved area left will still offer a bit of vertical space, perhaps for a small shoe rack or other thin vertical items. I also suggest not blocking the rear door off completely. Having to crawl through or filling space with removable items would be fine, but there should be some normal access from the interior of the vehicle. Say that it is pouring down rain outside and you want to get something out of your 'garage' space in the rear storage well. This will be much more comfortable and private, though not necessarily convenient, if it can be done from within the vehicle.

The bed arrangement will dominate the remaining space and also determine further storage options. If you do not want to build, you could place in a futon or a cot or modular shelving. The most common build option is to put in a wooden bench of some sort, cut to size, with padding on top for a mattress. You could also consider a hammock or even some type of fold-down bed. I would not suggest just stretching out on the carpeting. It will do in a pinch, but will cut into your storage options and the flooring tends to be irregular, making for uncomfortable sleep.

Using a futon as both bed and couch is possible, though for a minivan build the space will be too tight for me to recommend it. You will need to keep extra open space to allow the futon to fold down to bed mode. Normal storage options will be constrained accordingly. It may still be possible to put in some sort of rack or shelving for storage above the futon level. If you are able to sleep on the futon in couch mode this may be more viable. In that case simply fix it together and in place, perhaps with zip-tights or cord, and plan on using all space around it as static storage or living area.

A cot might be a better option, as being considerable lighter and also permitting more space underneath for storage. Because of the lighter weight you may want to brace it somehow or otherwise stop it from shifting about. As the flooring may not be level, and also to increase storage space, the cot legs can be raised up by cutting PVC pipe to length and sliding the resulting short pipes onto the feet (perhaps with a bit of padding to save the carpet).

As an alternative to a cot, you could put in a freestanding hammock. They come in a variety of shapes and sizes; some are very simple frames and may even be portable. When not in use, the netting can be put out of the way to free up space. Still, these can be uncomfortable for sleeping over extended periods and will take up more space that could instead be used for permanent storage.

A fourth no-build option would be to purchase modular freestanding shelving. These are durable plastic or wire units which can be assembled to whichever number of levels is required. You will want to use two levels with the shelves set end to end, two or three shelves long, along one side of your space. Plastic types may have ready-made slots for joining units horizontally. Wire types will need to be joined together with fastenings—I might suggest paracord ties or ziptights. You could even add a third level of shelving on one end of your bed. This would leave a sitting area during the day and provide a place to slide your feet at night. Be certain that the shelving you purchase is rated to support your entire weight, along with a safety margin of 50% or more. Once in place, you will have permanent storage areas under your bed and you need not worry about converting your space for sleeping every night.

I consider the modular shelving to be the best of the no-build options, but it will still be less than ideal because the shelves are square and everything inside a minivan is curved. Also, such shelving cannot be cut down to specific lengths or widths. If you build your own or have built a bed solution you will be better able to take advantage of all available space and otherwise suit your needs. I have seen people install slat-style wooden benches that can be extended for sleeping or to serve as a desk chair. You could instead make a folding bench that can be tied up into a chair during the day. A static wooden bench bed could have custom shelving curved to the contours of your space, with built in drawers or cabinets wherever practical. These options will be more expensive, in time or money or both, but also offer many more possibilities. If you are willing to put your own hand to it you need not invest in expensive tools. All tools required can be rented, often from the same place you are buying the build materials.

As an alternative to a wooden bench, you may consider putting in a fold down bed of some sort. That is, a bed which is normally stored in a vertical orientation but is folded down for sleeping, perhaps supported by cord or small chains. Given the curved interior and limited headroom found in minivans I do not consider this to be a particularly good option for this platform, but you may find it works for you. Perhaps you are fine with a narrow sleeping platform or need significant open space when not sleeping.

For both shelving and custom builds, some sort of mattress will be necessary, likely cut for both length and width. Consider foam pads or mattress toppers or just plain upholstery foam, in layers if desired. Once you have them cut to size they could be sewn into a cloth case or, keeping cleaning needs in mind, sealed into plastic sheeting which could then be covered with normal bed-sheets. Just wrapping the mattress layers in bed-sheets might be easiest but will also be less stable.

Other furnishing will follow the same pattern as above, in that you will be able to get by, sometimes quite well, with some pre-made arrangement from another source, but the best way to maximize your space and suit your particular needs will almost always be a custom built arrangement. Given this, I think that for minivans some sort of modular and removable installation is still desirable. That is, if you are custom building you should still make the furnishings removable and not drastically alter the interior to install them. This will help to retain the modularity that makes use of a minivan so desirable. The interior is already finished and is suitable for a variety of purposes and conversions—do not destroy this capacity by making alterations in large ways.

For these reasons and for simplicity, I will continue with my own sample build by using modular shelving as a bed, laid long-wise from the back of the passenger seat toward the rear. This will be wire shelving for strength, in a single layer. The front unit will be 48in x 24in and the rear unit will be 36in x 14in. They will be the same height with the standard poles, 36in, as the support poles are separate and fit various shelf sizes. They will be tied together, top and bottom, with paracord, but only at the center front so that the shelves may be pivoted. The seven total feet of shelving will just fit lengthwise into my build vehicle, if the passenger seat is shifted forward. The rear unit may need to be braced over the cargo well. Note that this will leave just over one foot of clearance below the ceiling (at the highest point) for sleeping, which will probably not be acceptable. Given that, I will cut the support poles down to 24 inches, which will put the shelves about halfway up. This leaves roughly two feet of vertical sleeping space and the same amount of storage area below. Cutting the support poles will be done in stages so as to allow me to test various heights for suitability. Even if the poles are not meant to be cut down they can still be made to work when truncated. JB-Weld and/or epoxy and/or duct tape and/or screws can make for a very strong joint, though you will not be able to easily take it apart later. Painting or covering after the cutting and joining is finished can improve aesthetic appearance.

The above configuration was made using off the shelf components (from menards.com, total cost ~$95) but it is also possible to have a custom shelf built for not a lot more. At www.theshelvingstore.com I price a 24in wide by 72in long by 25in high shelf at around $150. Plus shipping and taxes. I will continue my build with the initial arrangement, however.

For sleeping, I would suggest some flat rigid material placed over the shelf, with any padding above. This could be a cut sheet of plywood or structural plastic or fiberglass laminate, with layered memory foam or just a camping pad above. I will not specify for my build as this will not effect the rest of the conversion, and in any case this can be changed out easily.

With the bed and under-bed storage in place approximately half of the available rear space has been taken up. This also establishes a sleeping/lounging platform and almost 28 cubic feet of permanent storage area under the bed. I would suggest the use of both tote bags and small shelving units to help keep things organized. Two feet or more of shelf clearance is also plenty of room for a cooler or some storage totes.

The advantages of this type of arrangement, which may be the modular shelves I have suggested here or just a cot or instead a fully custom designed unit, are that pass-thru ability has been maintained, that only half of the space has been taken up, and that no exterior access is required to prepare for sleeping or do other things. I have seen other arrangements which block off rear access or turn the whole rear area into a bed with storage underneath, but these seem less versatile to me, at least for a minivan. With a larger van or other vehicle other arrangements become more viable. Disadvantages include that the static placement reduces access through one side door and may complicate your ability to get at underfloor or side panel storage. I have tried to account for these difficulties by only joining the shelves at the center front, which will allow either end to pivot out in order to get by it or underneath it.

Everything else in the space should be portable, in that you are able to move things around with relative ease. If you want to put in something else heavy, like a portable fridge/chiller unit, consider some sort of slider arrangement so you can move it around. You may even fit one under the bed, but you must be able to move it in and out without difficulty. The area between the bed and the other slider door up front should be kept open to maintain ease of entry and egress, but the remaining rear space in line with the driver's seat still offers plenty of room to serve living needs.

Most minivans will have an open space over the wheel-well framed by a rear side window. You often see cup-holders or a flip open bin here. That short platform can be utilized as a stable base for permanent fixtures. It could also be extended slightly to increase utility. I have seen people bring a full counter and sink out from that area. You could instead just place something like a blue water-can sideways on it with a strap to hold it in place. Keeping with my theme of a minimal build home, I suggest putting a wire rack, very like the shelf bed but smaller, in this space to extend the usable surface. In my build Caravan, there are two top seat-belt links, already designed to be load-bearing, to the front and rear of this window/wheel-well area on that side. Cord run down from these links will serve to support all of the weight of the shelf. You will still want to do something to keep it in place, perhaps by putting a line of velcro along the back edge or instead drilling a few more small holes for fasteners. Because this is a wire rack, the cup holders and other spaces underneath can still be utilized for thin objects like toothbrushes or kitchen utensils.

A shelf which extends just a foot out from this support area, held up by cords to the seat-belt links, will be around 18in deep and at least that wide but still permit an open isle (though a small one—if you need more consider a less deep shelf) between it and the shelf bed. This would be an excellent place to mount a water jug or canister, like a Berkey filter arrangement. You could place a portable sink like a freestanding camp sink just underneath the spigot for a ready-made faucet arrangement. With a little cutting and attachment you could instead mount a sink into the shelf extension itself, with a graywater bottle down below. In short, this area can function as the heart of a kitchen and wash up area, all without having to build anything complex. This 'counter-space' will even accommodate a one-burner propane stove.

Establishing a seated area in the van for productivity or general entertainment may be difficult, but is still possible. Most collapsible camp chairs will still fit in the remaining width of the area by the slider door and can be coupled with a folding desk or tray table.

You could also use a folding chair instead of a camp chair and could rig a swivel table, using something like a fishing down-rigger attached to the side of the shelf bed, as a workstation. Some sort of work arrangement will be necessary, as the high bed and low ceiling will make that an unsuitable area for seated pursuits. Though you could always use the front driving area.

For mobile living in a vehicle this size, I would suggest that a small camp toilet, used sparingly, is the most appropriate way to account for elimination needs. If you are urban living you should use restrooms elsewhere most times. If you are camping out you should follow the local guidelines, but many places will permit burying human waste. This is not to say that other arrangements are not possible. I have seen people using padded plastic buckets, lined with new bags each time, to meet this need. I have even seen one person rig a full shower and toilet arrangement as the entire back end of a minivan build, utilizing the extra space afforded by a storage well.

Other furnishing may be ad-hock, or you may go a completely different route than my sample build. Regardless, keep in mind that you do not have to, and should not want to, fit everything you need to get by into the minivan. For the space of a camping trip, sure. For full time living, no. Instead, use it as a base of operations and reach out to other services to meet needs that cannot be accommodated in such a small space. Have a gym membership or go trail running for your exercise. Shower at the gym or have a camp shower that you take out of the minivan to use. Keep a few simple, non-perishable foods on hand that you can cook inside, but keep most of your food prep and eating out of the vehicle, either by using restaurants or public parks in urban areas or just cooking out elsewhere. While it is possible to fit an entire apartment into a minivan, I suggest that you can best maximize the space available if you keep your need fulfillment arrangements within the vehicle as simple as you can.

Electronics

You can get by electronically and in terms of networking with minimal arrangements. A cell phone with a data plan for hotspot data, a laptop or tablet, and a small power station will keep you connected and permit some productivity. You will be limited in power use, however, as all electricity will be drawn from the very limited power station. You should not draw from the vehicle starter battery at all if possible, or only very little. Mostly the power draws should go the other way, in that you should have some device that will let you charge your starter battery from your power station, or have a portable battery jumping device. Do not threaten your mobility by trying to draw off of the starter battery when the vehicle is not running (when the engine is running you are drawing off of the alternator instead).

To meet increased power needs, you can take advantage of that roof space. For a minivan build there is room for at least 200 Watts of solar, obtained from various possible configurations. This will be different but is still possible if there is a roof rack. Regardless of your own arrangement, you should always be able to fit at least one solar panel on the roof. Consider that putting your panels full-on to the angle of the sunlight will greatly increase power generation. This can be done with a raising mount build, but for a minivan I would suggest just making it possible to take your panel from the roof and prop it against the vehicle for a better angle. This can be done simply by including a bit of extra cord and making the fasteners removable and replaceable. If you want to stay low profile, you can mount flexible panels directly on the roof. There need not be any fasteners, as you can get by with just adhesives, but I would suggest at least a few screws toward the front where the wind-stream will be coming from while driving. I have seen other arrangements where standard type mono- or polycrystalline panels are mounted on top of the roof rack. Such an arrangement, even if not removable or tilt-able, will likely generate more power than flush mounted panels because they will stay cooler being up off of the roof. At the cost of being somewhat more obvious and taking up the roof rack.

It is possible to have these panels charging the starter battery of your vehicle, but that is not recommended. Instead, and to take full advantage of this solar power you will need to have a house battery bank or at least a 'solar generator'. It should be deep cycle, but beyond that will be a matter of choice. I would suggest either AGM or a Firefly or, the best, LiFePO4. It is possible to build your own LiFePO4 (100Ah) battery from cells for around $600 or to buy one for about $950. A Firefly will run around $500. A deep cycle AGM will be about $250. The LiFePO4 will last the longest, by far, and will also furnish more usable power and charge much more quickly (depending on available power). You can run heavy draw power needs, like a microwave or toaster oven, off of a LiFePO4 battery without damaging it or reducing usable power.

Obviously this is an investment and only you can decide if it is worth the expense. You will need a charge controller off the panels, possibly a DC-DC converter to link to the vehicle alternator, an inverter, and some battery management system, which along with the batteries add up to a considerable expense. Properly cared for, though, it should last for years, probably longer than the vehicle itself. Consider also that you could easily double the battery bank capacity by adding a second battery, or more, without otherwise altering the system. It will be entirely justified, and the system may be reused, if you are planning for longer term off-grid power needs. So, if you plan to move up to a sailboat, for instance, overkill on your minivan power system will be justified because you can re-use the components. Quality electronic components can last for twenty years or even longer.

Alternatively, you could emplace a more limited system with a shorter expected period of usable life, at significant cost savings. I will posit another build based around an AGM deep cycle battery instead. Note that you can only expect to draw around 200 watts continuously from one of these, or twice that if you add a second one. That is not sufficient to power a microwave, but will do fine for a smaller chiller fridge. All components will be less expensive, as there is no need to account for LiFePO4 chemistry attributes.

So, the solar panels are the same, but you can go with a less expensive MPPT charger. There can still be a cross draw from the vehicle system when the alternator is running, but just using a battery isolator rather than a DC-DC converter. The battery can output to an 800W inverter (over-sized to allow for additional batteries). A separate battery charger will permit shore charging of the house battery, or the starter battery if desired. Total cost of this reduced system will be $1030 ($450 for the solar panels, $30 for the charge controller, $250 for the battery, $50 for the battery isolator, $60 for the inverter, $50 for the charger, $40 for the battery monitor, and $100 for various supplies and wiring). So, for less than half the price of a quality LiFePO4 system you can have a usable house power system. Note that you will need to carefully monitor your power draws. You will also be far better off adding a second AGM battery to share the load. Dropping one of the solar panels will also save in cost, but you should have both if you plan on having two or more batteries.

Even without a house system, you could add some power capacity cheaply with portable folding solar panels and portable chargers, or of course the portable power bank that I am positing for my 'no-build'. Being careful to grab power from a portable solar bank whenever there is sun or charging off the vehicle alternator will suffice for modest electrical needs. This should be enough for a phone and camera and tablet and laptop, etc. Electronic devices are tending to become more and more efficient. Do take note of the information feedback that your power sources offer, enabling you to better plan your power use.

For external networking, once you have the battery capacity in place, I would suggest a mobile hotspot from something like a broadband modem or Skyroam Solis, unless you find your needs are met just by a cellular phone plan. You could increase your range whenever parked for a time by using a directional antenna. Note that this is not a booster. A cell signal booster will amplify on a single band and is good for increasing upload speed, but may do nothing at all for download speed. A dual band directional antenna, in contrast, will increase the useful range of cellular signals, up to five miles or more depending on the model. I would suggest a mounting that can be taken down and put up, perhaps a small swivel on a suction cup that can be stuck on the roof. Directional antenna do tend to be rather noticeable. For a lower profile option consider an omnidirectional antenna. Range increase will only be one mile or so, but they are much lower profile and can be mounted permanently. Wifi antennae will have similar impacts for your wifi use within that frequency range, but useful range will always be lower than with the cellular bands.

My no-build external networking will be accomplished with a mobile hotspot device. This may change monthly as I will likely be paying attention to the best deals. Living urban means that I will be much less dependent on trying to find signal and so will mostly be concerned with data rates and prices.

Summary and Conclusion

My high fulfillment needs of Health, Philosophy, Planning, and Stopping can all be managed by the described platform, provided that it stays within an urban environment and has access to services. Planning and Stopping can be accomplished solely with internet use and time spent, as well as actual driving in the case of Stopping. Health and Philosophy can be accomplished by frequenting gyms or health clubs, stores and restaurants, libraries and public parks or gardens, etc. Emergency medical supplies will of course be kept in the van.

The same for my medium fulfillment needs of Address, Applications, Pests, and Space. Address can be met by using a local mailbox service and possibly some other formal arrangement for a legal address as described in that need section. Applications can all be accomplished using electronics devices, either inside the van or at cafes or libraries, etc. Pests can be taken care of with careful Sanitation practices and also by keeping an eye out for nest building on the exterior, perhaps with a bit of diatomaceous earth inside as well. Space will be solved by the described furnishing arrangements and also by use of custom storage solutions to fit the available spaces.

My low fulfillment needs of Air, Cooling, Electricity, Food, Heat, Networking, Propulsion, Sanitation, Security, Structure, Wastage, and Water, may also be met to a sufficient level. Air and Cooling will be covered by the mentioned clip fans, in conjunction with the integral vehicle systems and the windows. Electricity has been discussed in detail. Food will be obtained elsewhere and either eaten there or with minimal preparation in the van. Emergency supplies will be kept on hand. Heat will be addressed as needed with temporary solutions (clothing and blankets and hand-warmers, etc), though as mentioned a permanent heater installation may be considered if necessary later on. External Networking has been discussed and internal Networking will be addressed as needed beyond existing device capacity. Propulsion will be integral to the vehicle and will be maintained but not otherwise messed with. Sanitation will be handled by keeping things clean inside as possible (wipes, a few cleaners, possibly a small vacuum—which some lucky minivans will already have included) and by showering elsewhere using services such as a gym membership. Wastage will largely be handled elsewhere, but there will also be a small camp toilet in the van for emergencies or urine. Garbage and graywater in the van should be minimal and easily handled. Water will be accomplished by using bottled water, the mentioned Berkey canister, and possibly camping water bladders. I may also consider a pressure pump camp shower for general use or emergency showers.

And so we have a minivan mobile living solution. I will leave the rest up to your imagination. Do remember to fulfill your needs with the minimalist solutions which are suitable to this platform. You may have noticed that I have designed all of this around single person occupancy. This is because I do not consider the platform to be suitable for long term habitation for more than one person. It is certainly possible, especially in the short term, and especially if the two people in question are smaller in stature and/or not very space conscious. For such a compressed space, however, living issues more than double if there are two people instead of one. Cleaning and sanitation (and the smells), food preparation, sleeping arrangements, productivity setups, etc, can all be accommodated, with difficulty, in fair weather and foul, for a single person. Or for two people for a short period. Or if only using the platform as a campervan instead of a full living solution. Try it out if you don't believe me—but in the meantime, I hope you all enjoy the mini-vanlife experience.

Note, however, that my build van has a towing capacity, as do many other minivans. There must be a tow package equipped already or you could weld or bolt one on, but being able to tow a small trailer changes the dynamic considerably. While it would reduce your parking options, it would also defer most of your storage needs from the minivan compartment itself, freeing up space for a larger bed and so on. This would not be suitable for long with my urban stealth theme, but you may find that it fits your build perfectly. In addition, if you are staying in a fixed region for a time you may consider renting a storage unit to increase your stuff capacity, which could also be used to store a small trailer used to shuttle that stuff between regions.

References and Further Research

www.gettingstamped.com/diy-minivan-camper-campervan-conversion

www.your-rv-lifestyle.com/how-to-live-in-a-minivan-camper-successfully

www.thewaywardhome.com/san-francisco-couple-buys-used-van-converts-it-for-200-to-travel-the-us

mybackpackerlife.com/canada/minivan-camper-conversion

www.parkedinparadise.com/stealth-camping

www.doityourselfrv.com/van-dwelling-mini-van-getting-started

youtu.be/Z8CENn_WY6k

This is that video I mentioned above featuring a diesel heater installation. Also a good build in regards to several other features.

youtu.be/eMbaenvfHNM

A rather different approach and more focus on aesthetic appeal.

youtu.be/25VBk8AOqRQ

A build example with a strong no-build focus.

youtu.be/8eP6ic-NyWs

This video is also mentioned above. The van features a full bathroom and shower in the back end.

youtu.be/s0wnLOlCaR8

Another tour from the same channel. This van has a number of innovative features that are worthy of consideration.

youtu.be/m2KkPVOvVQA

An interesting setup that has been professionally designed.

youtu.be/qfIWjVnueSI

Another take with a more modular setup for short-term use, but very well designed for specific needs.

youtu.be/PT8qOPA1zFk

A good build inhabited by an intelligent individual that clearly spends time thinking about things. Worth watching to the end.

22.

The Van Conversion

A full size van will offer considerably more space than a minivan. It will likely have flatter surfaces and exposed metal frames that will support a more permanent build style and the necessary attachments. Your fuel economy will be lower than a minivan can achieve and all of the components and maintenance for the van itself (tires, etc) will be more expensive, but a platform this size can accommodate the life needs of more than one person much more easily. For a single person, the space available is luxurious in comparison.

Van conversions are still suited for stealth builds, though they will tend to blend better into different settings than will a minivan, such as industrial or commercial areas. This is true at least for the commercial type vans I will focus on. It is still possible to find a full size family style van to convert, but these have become rather rare and they are mostly run down. In addition, a bare-bones cargo van will be much less work to strip out in preparation for a full conversion. It will also be cheaper to purchase because of that lack of furnishings.

Platform

For this build, and this one will be a full build, I have chosen to convert a 2012 Chevy Express Cargo (extended wheelbase). This is a solid vehicle and has common availability. It can be found at multiple price points and in various conditions. The towing capacity is very high, the best in its class. It will not afford standing room for many people, and the factory installed systems tend to be somewhat basic, but I do not consider these drawbacks to outweigh the benefits of the platform. Standing room is nice but will not be a concern for most living activities within the van. The vehicle systems will be largely superseded by systems installed for a build—just make sure yours has cruise control and air conditioning for at least when the vehicle is running.

For your own build, standing room and a more open platform may be a much greater concern, and so you will want to go with a different vehicle to start. The Mercedes Sprinter is a very popular build platform because of the higher form factor. The Ford Transit is another option. For me, and for the purposes of this particular build, standing room alone is not sufficient to draw me away from the potential benefits of the Express platform. Each build should be a fully integrated solution, from start to finish.

Specs

4.8L GM V8, 280 HP @ 5200 RPM, 295 Ft-lbs Torque @ 4600 RPM
Max towing capacity: 10000lbs (Max payload 3259lbs)

Rear wheel drive
6-Speed automatic transmission
31 gallon fuel capacity, estimated mileage 11 city 17 hwy
Exterior dimensions 244.1in length x 79.2in width (plus mirrors) x 82in height
Cargo area to front seats 146.2in length x 53.4in height x 52.7in width between wheel-housings (total cargo volume 313.9ft³)

Seating

Two seats max, unless you install more in the back. You may or may not choose to keep the passenger seat. I have seen someone remove it to make room for a small refrigerator. If this suits you then go for it, but I would suggest that keeping the passenger seat in will be better for most people. You will not be likely to have any rear viewing capacity without your side mirrors, so for driving safety you will need to keep the top half of that space open anyway. It can also be nice to have company when driving, even if only once in a while. There is plenty of room in the back for a refrigerator.

Purpose

As noted briefly above, this platform was chosen to maximize the potential outcome for this particular build. The previous minivan sample conversion focused on an urban stealth vehicle and made a number of design compromises to take advantage of the urban environment. This van conversion will also be suitable for urban environments and will make some compromises in order to better blend in for casual parking, but will be designed as a fully encapsulated solution, as possible, rather than one which depends so heavily on the use of outside services. As such, it should be suitable for travel anywhere and with unlimited range, doing equally well as a campervan or for urban living. It is a hybrid design and so will not be perfectly suited for any one task, but will do at least moderately well at any of them.

So, the central purpose of the vehicle will be to have a fully capable living platform, with systems suited for extended living in various environments. With the larger starting platform this is just possible, though it will be both more expensive than the minivan build and also more difficult to design well.

Planning

In order to meet the more ambitious purpose of this build vehicle, I must achieve higher levels of fulfillment for many of the life needs. As possible, of course. Space constraints, and the requirement to work within a budget, will always limit what we might wish to do when living mobile. That is not to say that I cannot take advantage of outside services when available. The point here is to achieve a platform that is fully capable but not necessarily one suitable for full-time non-stop living.

High fulfillment: Electricity, Heating, Planning, Space

Medium fulfillment: Address, Air, Applications, Cooling, Food, Health, Networking, Pests, Philosophy, Propulsion, Sanitation, Security, Stopping, Wastage, Water

Low fulfillment: Structure

Looking at each need and keeping my platform purposes in mind, I have categorized fulfillment levels according to what I consider possible. In keeping with the goal of a hybrid living solution with across the board capabilities, most fulfillment will fall into the medium or moderate category.

I will be relying on the basic structure of the van itself to hold together without alteration, so I had best choose one that is in good condition to begin with (and keep up maintenance as possible).

The electrical system will be designed and installed from scratch and will need to be robust enough to meet a broad spectrum of requirements. For this build it will not have the reserve capacity to meet really high demand draws, but should still be extensive. Planning will need to be very careful and meticulous in order to achieve the somewhat ambitious goals of this project. Likewise space considerations will be very important in order that I might fit in everything that will be required.

Heating fulfillment is a special feature of this particular build. I will get more into this below, but the platform lends itself to this goal. Say that a good part of why I chose this platform is for this reason and also that I anticipate especially strenuous heating needs for the vehicle operating environment. You can likewise choose to stress some particular feature in your own build according to your own needs or desires. This is almost always possible, though it will come at a cost and probably also decreased capabilities in other areas.

Build

Preparation

Needless to say, the best time to address any mechanical problems or intended upgrades in the integral vehicle systems is before starting work on the rest of the build. Do so now.

This is a used cargo van so I would suggest a very thorough cleaning after that. If there have been any hardware installations such as shelving units or racks you should remove them before cleaning—unless you think they will add to your build. There may also be a divider with or without a door between the driving and cargo area. If it works for your purposes go ahead and keep it to save time. If it is metal then this will permit easy drilling and attachment points. Even if there is not a door in place you may consider cutting an opening rather than removing the partition entirely. For my build I will posit just a bare cargo space and no partition. There will also likely be rubber mat flooring down. Unless it is in terrible condition I suggest leaving this in place. It will add insulative qualities and you will generally want to put your own flooring down overtop—the rubber will serve well as an under-layer.

The next step will be to check the entire vehicle, including all exterior seals, for water leaks. I skipped this step for the minivan build because those are generally light wear and any leaks should be readily apparent from water damage to the carpeting or by other indications. Cargo vehicles, in contrast, tend to have much heavier wear and leaks may go unnoticed because there may not be anything that will show water damage. You should have done an inspection before buying (even if you sprang for a new vehicle), but a further inspection now for any leaks and also anything that will be easier to repair when the vehicle is in this state can pay big dividends down the road. Utilize a water hose and also a spray bottle. Any water which gets in should be stopped up. Do not neglect the undercarriage.

Before installing insulation, you will want to work out routing for any exterior wiring and also install any vent fans. Depending on the type of insulation that you use, you may never want to pierce that layer after it is in place. Spray foam, for instance, is some good stuff with useful qualities, but it needs to be fully sealed away from living areas and should not be disturbed after installation without great care. So, I would strongly suggest that you consider wiring needs for solar, fans, and exterior lights or sensors such as cameras or motion detectors, even if you do not intend to install these things just yet. Wires run to the exterior can be easily covered over with a small blank cover or lid until needed. This is also the best and only time that you should install roof vents. You should have at least one. I suggest that two would be better, located at the front (just behind the driving area) and rear of the vehicle.

For my hypothetical build vehicle I will be using spray foam insulation that I will not want to disturb after it is emplaced and so am putting a high stress on cutting and preparing all holes and passages beforehand. You may or may not have this consideration for your own build, but it will still be better to cut all of the holes that you need or may need in future at this point of the build. Yes, it can be somewhat nerve-racking to put holes in the vehicle body, but it is a common practice and there will be little danger of leaks provided that established procedures are followed. Carefully followed and done properly, that is. The RV and camper markets are very experienced in these matters and you should follow their practices for you van build.

Before cutting your roof vents you should also plan out your maximum solar layout —meaning the most that you can cram onto that roof. You may choose to install all of it or none at this time, but you should still account for the wiring paths now. If you would need to pierce insulation to run wiring you may even want to run it all now and keep it up there covered up, depending on what method you are using to keep your holes from leaking. It may instead be possible to put the necessary wiring through your roof vents. Keep in mind that solar panels come in square form factor, both flex (flat) and rigid (raised), usually around 50 watts. You could fit one of these square panels on either side of a roof vent, in addition to any oblong main panels. For my build I will posit a max solar emplacement of three 200 watt panels between the front and rear roof vents and four 50 watt panels flanking the vents—two each in front and back. This will give me 800 watts max solar power which I price at roughly $826 ($190 each for the large panels and $64 each for the square panels). These specs are for monocrystalline. If you must have a lower profile, I price a 680 watts max flexible panel setup at about $1130 ($250 each for three 160 watt long panels and $95 each for four 50 watt square panels). That is, I calculate that this is the maximum amount of solar that will fit on the roof of my sample build vehicle, with two standard fourteen inch opening roof vents. The long flat roof is one of the drawing points of my chosen vehicle. Vehicles with a shorter wheelbase or a raised ceiling will likely be able to fit less solar up top. Given that I will want all of that solar for my planned build, I will go ahead and mount those seven monocrystalline panels (about two inches thick—still pretty stealthy given the height of the cargo van) and run the wiring, after installing the roof vents.

So, even if I do not intend to install all seven of those panels immediately, I will go ahead and run the wiring now, before installing insulation, and also cut holes and install two roof vents. One vent will be center-line in the back and the second will be just behind the driver seat in the front (offset to match the shower space). These will be low profile vents, which will reduce the air draw but also keep them less noticeable.

I will also cut holes suitable for both power and data transmission wiring, which may be used for cameras, external light, antennas, or other things. These will be at all four top corners of the vehicle, covered over on the exterior with small sealed plastic blisters. Inside, I will emplace small pvc pipes so as to be able to run any wiring without disturbing the insulation. So, what I will end up with will be short pipes that will pass through the insulation and to the exterior of the vehicle, where they will be capped off until needed. These pipes can be filled with silicone for now, which will be easy enough to remove later at need (or otherwise blocked off as you choose).

In addition to those preparations, this is the time to decide whether there will be any other holes in the insulation required. Do you want an exterior door to access graywater collection jugs? Black water cassette bins? Both? Do you want a shower drain directly underneath, or instead to a graywater collection tank? How about a shore-power hookup plug? For my build I will drill a hole for a shore-power outlet in the rear floor near the passenger side and also drain holes for the shower just behind the driver seat and for the sink graywater tank (which means I must already have their locations worked out). For the moment the shower drain will be posited to drain into a graywater collection tank mounted in the undercarriage. The sink graywater collection will be a small tank (or bucket) underneath, but will also be drain-able by a valve which can be released as appropriate. This could go down to the undercarriage graywater tank. I intend either a compost toilet or cassette toilet which will emptied from the interior, so will not need further openings. There may be one or more networking antennas installed, but the wiring can be run through one of the top corner holes already placed.

As another step before insulation, you will need to decide what to do with the passage between the driving area and the living area of the van. Some sort of insulated barrier is recommended. You will lose quite a bit of heat during the winter and gain even more during the summer through those big windows and limited insulation in the front portion. This could be a full wall with a door in the middle. You could instead opt for an insulated curtain like the one I suggested above for the minivan. In addition to a shade for the windshield, that is. The full wall will take up space and cost more and be inconvenient... but will increase privacy and security and be much more insulative. I will go with the full wall for my build, as detailed below in the insulation section, in keeping with my design choice to emphasize full insulation. Instead of a door, however, I will have two quilted Mylar curtains, one on either side of the wall itself. The curtains should allow easier pass-through and the double layer of Mylar with a small air gap in between will form a nice insulated barrier.

Insulation

You will want to have some insulation. There are many ways to do this, but I will go with 1-2 inches of spray foam insulation for the walls and ceiling and possibly doors, which will then be sealed away entirely from the living area with a second layer of solid flat insulation combined with tape and sealant. In this way you will achieve the benefits of the spray foam (high r-value, moisture resistant, fills all the gaps) without having to worry much about off-gassing or any long term health concerns, as it will be sealed away from the living area. The foaming itself should be done in a professional manner, either by yourself or hired out. Full PPE will be required. It should be very fully cured before continuing work.

Over top of that I would suggest any type of insulation which will form a full seal over the spray foam. The idea is to fully seal it away, so you could use tapes and flexible adhesives to finish the barrier. The second layer need not be thick or even highly effective as insulation. Most of the work is being done by the spray foam, with just a bit extra and better coverage being provided by the secondary layer.

There are other ways to get heat resistance without the hassle of the spray foam. Some of them will provide better acoustic resistance as well (though not if your second layer is an acoustic barrier). The primary draw of the spray-foam is the moisture resistance it will offer, by filling up all the cracks and crevices to prevent condensation formation against bare metal on the interior of the van.

You could instead go with rock wool (superior to fiberglass) insulation, which has adequate properties and will be less expensive, or something like 3M 600L Thinsulate, which will do about the same though with thinner layers and will be more expensive. You may still want to use the Thinsulate in tricky places like the doors, or better yet stuffed rock wool covered over in Thinsulate, even if you go with spray foam for the rest. I do not really suggest something like Reflectix for insulating the metal van body. If you have windows (which my sample vehicle does not), then by all means make Reflectix covers for them, but it will not be very effective as insulation for the rest of the build. This is because the Reflectix will need a layer of open air to be effective, but leaving that air layer will encourage condensation on the interior of the van, leading to moisture buildup, rust, mold, etc.

Above, I posited a full wall between the driving area and the living area. If your van already has something there, like a wire-mesh barrier, then great, just start with that. If not you will need to build from scratch. The door size will be non-standard, so you may want to just frame in the doorway and hang double curtains, one on either side, for now—as I posit for my own build. If you find you want the door later then it will be relatively easy to add. The same cannot be said of the wall, which should be done now if at all. Luckily the walls, ceiling, and floor already give the limits. If you start with the door frame all you have to do is fill in the middle.

I would start by leaning the front seats back slightly to give a limit. Then, build a full wall frame out of (thin) metal framing, accounting for the door in the middle and fastened as well as you can without compromising the structure of the van. You may even be able to weld it on. Use quarter inch plastic utility panels (as an alternative to plywood) for the wall facing in the vehicle compartment. Paint as desired. Notice the effort to avoid using wood for anything except inside the insulated, ventilated living quarters by using metal framing and plastic sheeting instead of a wood frame and plywood. This will also save space, as the materials are thinner.

As yet another step before insulating, you will want to work out the layout and design, or at least attachment points, for all of your fixtures and built-in furnishings. Consider pre-drilling holes for attachments, though doing so will require precise planning. My build van has metal ribs which the exterior body panels are fastened to, on walls and ceiling, all down its length. It also has exposed beams running where the sides meet the roof. These are my load bearing attachment points, so I will plan out all use now and either pre-drill and install fastenings which will pass through the insulation or, at a minimum, mark exactly where those holes will be so that I can find the spots after the insulation is in place.

So, I will first work out the weight needs of my utility area for shower/kitchen/etc which takes up roughly one fourth of the van space directly behind the driver seat. The floor will support most of that weight but things will still need to be attached up above. I also plan overhead storage in the rear area, which will be supported by the roof ribs, so will mount fasteners now as possible. I will also go ahead and add extra light fasteners to floor and walls and doors for mounting things like trash cans or clothes lines or similar needs. In particular I will emplace overhead fasteners in the rear center as I plan to have a hanging table. Try to plan out every fastener that you will be putting into the walls or ceiling. This is tedious but will pay off later.

For my build I will (finally) proceed with my insulation installation by using the spray-foam for the walls and ceiling and all the little cracks, inside the beams, etc. This must be closed-cell spray foam in order to provide the moisture barrier which is its main draw for my build. For tricky bits with the doors and around my vents and wiring and the drain, I will put down enough 3M 600L to match the depth of the spray foam. Over top of that I will put extruded polystyrene sheet foam (XPS).

Prior to that Thinsulate and XPS, and to help with condensation on the areas that I cannot put spray foam (like the ends of metal ribs and over the wheel-wells and certain areas of the doors), I will apply several coats of Liquid Rubber Waterproof Sealant. This is expensive to use in quantity, but will provide a moisture barrier and protective coating. The same can of sealant will also be sufficient for the seals up on the roof around the corner holes and solar wiring and vents. The wheel-wells will need their own boxes packed with rock wool overtop later, but for the time being just the Liquid Rubber will do. This sealant is interior safe and should have no side effects (after appropriate curing).

The XPS layer should then be sealed off with foam board adhesive caulk and builders tape, with the intent of making as full a barrier as possible against off-gassing from the spray foam. This should be a complete covering except for at the door in front, double door in back, and barn doors (or slider if you have one) at the side, with holes for the vents and wiring and drains as noted. It should be a flat box, ready to receive flooring, wall panels, and ceiling boards. For my van build anyway. If you have windows this stage will be a bit different. Consider using somewhat extended window boxes so that you can have plants and such there. You will also want to at least consider removable reflectrix covers for each window. You will get better results from the heat reflective barrier that it makes if you leave space in the middle—so those plants should still be fine.

Flooring

The flooring installation for my hypothetical build will be a bit more complicated. The goal will be to have radiant heat laid down the center-line of the vehicle under the flooring. There are various ways to accomplish this and also the other requirements for the bottom of the interior build space. I have seen installations which embed the tubing in existing foamboard insulation, ones which run the tubes through and around a metal framework forming an air space, and even the use of spray-foam to fill in around the tubing. For my build I will posit embedding the tubing into the main XPS insulation of the floor—which will be a double layer of XPS. I think the double layer, which will double the possible R-value of the insulation, will help with shock absorption over time and so better protect the tubing from wear.

So, before starting I will already have the basic rubberized flooring that came pre-installed in my build van. If you do not have this then you will want to do something to coat the bare metal and provide a moisture barrier. The Liquid Rubber mentioned above will work for this, or you could go with a different product. The goal will be to achieve a full moisture seal and no more. Depending on the condition of my existing floor covering, I may choose to add more to achieve that seal.

Next will be to put down a full layer of XPS insulation across the floor, cutting as necessary to get around the wheel wells and to account for the holes and piping already mentioned. This layer should be adhered down somehow to reduce slippage. I would not suggest excessive adhesive use, just make sure it is reasonably well tacked down. If you use too much adhesive you will be kicking yourself if you ever have to take up this layer. Seal all of the edges and cracks—this is the primary insulation layer for your flooring and should be as complete as possible.

Next I will put down a second layer of XPS. This layer will not be firmly affixed down. It should be attached, but some play will be desirable. This second layer will have grooves cut into it in which the tubing will be embedded. These groves should be carefully sized to fit the tubing. That tubing may be any sort that will work but the standard is to use a specific type of PEX flexible tubing that is designed especially for underfloor radiant heating applications. It should be orange in color. Before you cut your grooves in the XPS, test your tubing to see what degree of flex it will easily handle. The thinner diameter tubes will flex easier. The grooves themselves may be cut with a hot wire, though in that case you should be careful not to inhale the fumes. You could also use a rotary tool such as a Dremel. Also, depending on the diameter of the tubing you choose, you may be cutting into that first layer of XPS in order to get the tubing fully below the top level of the second layer of XPS. This is intended and one of the reasons I went with two XPS layers for my build.

I will run the tubing loops just down the center-line of my build, but you may also consider drawing the tubes along any surfaces you especially want heated, such as under or beside a sleeping area. Regardless, this should comprise a single long section of tubing and the ends must be brought back to roughly the same point—wherever you will place the heating and circulation elements. For my build this will be just under the sink in the kitchen area, as I will be able to use the existing drain for the sink to handle any leaks in the pipe fittings of the tubing system.

Once that radiant system is in place I would suggest laying down the flooring. This is a bit backwards from residential practice, but the XPS will need to be protected during the rest of the build. It has excellent compressive strength which is part of why it is suitable for flooring, but can be pierced relatively easily. You especially do not want to risk the tubing being damaged. The flooring on top will help to distribute weight and will protect everything underneath. Tarps can be laid down to help keep it nice until the build is finished.

For my build I will go with vinyl click-lock style flooring. This wears well and will not be affected by moisture. It looks nice if done well and does not give much when walked on. It does not require adhesives or mechanical fastening, though I would use some adhesive on the tiny bits in small spaces like between the wheel-well and the side door-well. It will also be stronger, though slightly thicker, than something like sheet vinyl. I will lay it across the entire floor, drilling to pass through my prepared holes for plumbing and the shore power wiring, working as close as possible around the wheel-wells and the side entry-well. To give me something to adhere it to that is not the XPS, I will lay down 10-mil sheet plastic just over the XPS.

Go with whatever flooring suits you. Sheet vinyl is cheap and durable. You are inside the insulation layer now, so something like wood or bamboo should work—though fastening it down might be an issue. A layer of sheet plastic like I posit using will act as a further vapor barrier to protect the wood. You could even lay in a tough carpet if you want. Synthetic carpeting will absorb moisture which can then be dried out with fans. It can be better to catch spills that way than to let the liquid run where it will. I intend to use rugs over the click-lock flooring, which will serve the same purpose but with more versatility. They will also help to protect my knees as I move around the interior, as there will not be sufficient headroom for me to stand.

Notice that all of my furniture and fixtures will rest on top of the flooring that has just been laid. None of them should rest on the portions of that flooring that has the PEX underneath. This should be fine as long as I am careful about weight distribution-no sharp feet against the floor if possible, only broad boards. XPS has a high compressive strength value and the double layer will increase this capability.

The side door-well is a bit of an issue, as it cannot really be properly insulated. This will be more of a problem for keeping the van cool than keeping the van warm, as cool air will drop down there while hot air will tend to rise up. This is in keeping with a build that is more suited for heating than for cooling and the cooling losses must be accepted as part of the compromises of the build.

Interior Layout

The remaining space is roughly twelve feet long, just over four feet high, and just under five feet wide. The only significant intrusion into this space so far is that of the wheel-wells. Thin material will be used to panel the walls and ceiling, in order to preserve as much space as possible.

Standing room will only exist for shorter people. Anyone taller than four feet or so will be moving around at a crouch or on their knees (hence the rugs over the flooring). This lack of headroom is part of the compromise from using this type of vehicle rather than something with a taller profile. Though there will need to be care when moving about, this is still plenty of interior room for one or two people to engage in indoor living activities.

The space framed by the side door and any door between the driver area and the living area will be kept open to facilitate movement and provide a space for temporary activities. The front passage door, if built, should be narrow—just enough to pass someone turned sideways. This will free up space to bring the bathroom/shower partition over to just past even with the driver seat armrest.

The bathroom/shower itself will take up the space back from the partition wall for about three feet, from top to bottom. This will be a sitting shower for most people, so I posit placing a flip-up bench inside over the toilet, to be raised when using the toilet and lowered down when showering. One of the two roof vent fans will be in this shower stall. There should be at least a small lip at the bottom to catch water. I would suggest a curtain instead of a door here. The space is already tight enough and the fan just overhead will help quite a bit with any smells.

Switching to the back of the van and the bed arrangement, we come to the largest single layout decision. Sleep one person or two? Pass through or not? Bunks or full bed or giant bed? How to account for a lounging area as well as a sleeping area? Where to put a workstation?

The answers to these questions will be largely up to individual needs and personal preference—as with everything else in these custom builds. I see that most van builds out there tend to have a full bed across the back, so for variety I will posit two bunks, long-wise, placed just over the wheel-wells. The passenger side bunk can be a bit longer than the driver side, which will be shortened just a bit by the kitchen fixtures between it and the shower unit. This way the insulated boxes over the wheel-wells can become part of the support for the bunks. If the space under the bunks is enclosed, possibly with flip up access by lifting the mattress and a lid, then that area can become a storage chest. The space that is left other than the wheel-well, anyway. Because of that intrusion from the wheel-well, it might be better to divide the under-bed storage into sections, with separate lids. The bunks themselves could have a tilting backrest arrangement to facilitate lounging. They would be narrow, between two and two and a half feet wide at most, but this would permit a feasible walkway between them.

As an option, a board could be fitted to bridge this gap as desired. The mattresses could then be pushed together to make a larger bed. That joined bed might look a lot like the single big bed that I just diverged from and with less storage underneath to boot, but there are important differences. Having two bunks can be very desirable if there are two people in the van who do not want to sleep 'together' or to share a bed. The separation is largely psychological but still important. Also, this makes for two distinct lounging areas. With some padding in place along the wall, either or both of these bunks can be couches at need, with room for several people to sit, though with cramped footing.

Also, for my build I will posit that the board sized to fit between the bunks to form a single bed can also function as a hanging table. I have seen other people have this as a floor mounted table instead. But I like the idea of being able to raise this up to the ceiling or down to the bunks instead. The fasteners on the ceiling were already mentioned above. The rest can be accomplished with cord and hooks.

The entire top rear quarter of the van then becomes a potential storage space, other than the center area taken up by the hanging table. Though you could also have loops of cord underneath the table to increase storage options. Not all of it on the sides can be used for storage, of course, unless we only want crawling space into those bunks. But some combination of permanent and temporary storage is very feasible. Say that you want to designate one bunk as for sleeping only. Leave a gap for adequate breathing room and use the rest of the space (above) as built storage—shelves or cabinets or both. You could instead, in order to preserve two lounging areas, do this with only the bottom third or half of the overhead bunk space. That is, place built storage over where the feet and legs rest, supported between the bunk and the roof ribs, with the leg space open to the center of the vehicle. I like this option because tv or monitor screens, for entertainment or productivity or both, could be mounted on the side of the storage unit and watched by someone lying or sitting in the bunk. Netting or lines or just hooks could be put above the remaining open areas to facilitate temporary or movable storage.

Back to the kitchen area, we have at most four feet of length to fit in everything we need. More likely this will be three and a half feet, unless you plan on a very short bunk on that side. It could be made deeper than the shower stall if you want to truncate that instead. This is still plenty of room for a sink and a range and some counter-space as well, but I would suggest only having the sink be a permanent emplacement and using movable appliances for all other cooking and food prep needs. You will appreciate having the increased counter space. Keeping most appliances portable can also be very handy for when you want to cook outside. This still leaves room for cabinets and a fridge underneath and also cabinets up above, against the ceiling. I suggest covering the back, top, and sides of the counter area with something like stainless steel sheets. This will greatly improve safety and also increase utility because you can use magnets to keep utensils and other things on that surface. Plan out whether you will be using the kitchen while standing, kneeling, or sitting in a chair, and judge the counter height accordingly. Just keep enough room below for your chosen fridge.

For my build, at least part of the cabinet space above the counter area has a special purpose—a freshwater storage tank. This will feed both the shower and the sink faucet, providing a certain amount of water pressure from gravity. As such, my sink 'faucet' will not be part of the sink unit but instead a flex line that comes down off of the tank. This will be a plastic storage tank, 10-15 gallons, sized to fit the space. To refill, a small electric sump could be used to pump water up out of a jug, with a manual pump kept as backup or for exercise. Another, smaller, storage tank for graywater will be just under the sink. A P-trap or S-trap on the sink drain will help reduce any odors from that tank. If desired, a filter arrangement can be mounted near the freshwater tank, with water which is being fed into the tank by pumping forced through those filters before it gets there. This will not take up much room and can be placed just under the tank cabinet as a separate inset or instead incorporated into the overhead cabinet.

So, fresh, gray, and black water storage and removal have been accounted for. Airflow has been accounted for. Sleeping and some workspace has been accounted for—a swivel desk in an appropriate place may also be desired. Your electrical setup is the only other system that needs permanent locations. Everything else that you want to fit in can be moved around as desired. Consider improving your space usage by mounting things to unused surfaces. If you have barn doors, you could affix trash and recycling bins to them. Or anything else that you don't mind swinging out into the world. Same for the rear doors. If you don't mind losing some entryway space, there is room for a coat-rack or small closet just behind the passenger seat.

The shower space would be more complete with a small vent-line running from the toilet up the back corner to the roof vent, with one or two small DC fans integrated into it. This will help with any undesirable smells that might arise from the toilet. Most compost toilets will require this sort of aeration—those that do not strictly require it should still be vented anyway.

Once the electric system is in place and the walls are ready to be paneled, my build will go with plain vinyl paneling for both walls and ceiling. Durable, cheap, and easy to clean. Many people prefer the feel of wood for their living space, which is also a viable option given the good insulation and airflow of this build. Wooden panels or slats will take up slightly more room and will require more care.

Electricity

Electrical Needs Planning

The end goals that your electric system are to provide for should be carefully considered before designing the system itself.

With this build, I will want a number of lights to help make up for the lack of windows. Most of them will be LED, but at least one incandescent reading light will also be included. I find the warm light of incandescent to be comforting at times. So, one light in the bathroom, one over the side entryway, one over the back entryway, one above the front portal. Two in the kitchen area, two or three around the back area, and a reading light for each bed/lounger. This sounds like a lot, but each light should be small and efficient. All together, they should provide full illumination for the van even with all of the odd angles of the overhead storage.

Next, for the fans. In addition to the overheads, which for me will be reversible to put air in or out as I like, there should be smaller fans down below for directed air. I would suggest one at each bed and another in the kitchen. One or two more small ones should vent the battery compartment. This will help with temperature control for the batteries, which is a much bigger deal than most people realize. If you have a permanent location for propane storage, there should also be a special spark-less fan venting that compartment directly down and out of the vehicle. It would be better to store propane out of the living area, but that is not always possible. It is safe to use if you take the proper safety precautions.

Any refrigerator will take a chunk of power. A fridge can also greatly improve quality of life and most people refuse to live without them for any extended duration. This build will have one, preferably a DC side-door but maybe just a mini-fridge. I say side-door because they can still be very efficient and the convenience would seem to outweigh any incremental efficiency from a top-door fridge that will take up extra space or need a special drawer.

Other than those, every appliance will be plugged in as needed. The kitchen setup provides a lot of counter space, so there could be an electric hotplate or portable range for cooking in addition to any propane setup. One could find storage space for a microwave, toaster oven, blender, coffeemaker, etc. Even an electric space-heater could be managed (though propane will be much more efficient).

This build will also have a fairly heavy electronics load. Altogether this is a rather ambitious potential power load and will require an electric system to match. As used, that is. All of the mentioned electric loads can be turned off without much harm, except for the propane safety fan.

Electrical System

Given maximum projected needs, a much larger system will be required than for the minivan build. Safety considerations, which might be glossed over for a much smaller system, must be observed. This includes over-voltage protection and full breaker panels for both the DC system off of the house battery bank and the AC system off of the inverter. All wiring must be correctly sized to meet expected amperage loads.

AC outlets should be wired in to convenient areas, but there need not be many of them. One on either side of the kitchen, which will also cover bathroom use. One at the base of each bed. One on each side up top in back for mounted electronics. USB or other DC power-ports should be put in as convenient as well—this will reduce conversion losses for DC needs like phone charging.

Your inverter should be sized to meet the highest expected power draw, with extra capacity on top as a safety margin and to reduce wear. Multiple inverters can also be wired in sequence to share heavy loads between them.

A significant battery bank will be called for. It should be LiFePO4—a lead-acid bank large enough to meet heavy power needs will be too big to store in this build. However there will be greater economies of scale if building your own LiFePO4 bank from cells.

A good solar charger will be required to take advantage of that sweet 800W rooftop emplacement. Depending on climate, those panels will go a long way toward keeping the batteries charged.

The link to the vehicle alternator will be less significant for a larger battery bank but should still be emplaced. A full DC-DC converter will be required for this to step up to an appropriate charging voltage for the LiFePO4 bank. You may also consider a hardwired link to the starter battery for charging purposes, but for my build I will omit that step.

To allow shore power I would suggest your inverter arrangement be combination inverter/chargers instead. This will permit an automatic switch between battery use and shore power (which will then charge the batteries). Depending on your electric use and the weather shore power may be your main charging source, which helps to justify the higher cost of the inverter/charger.

Estimated Electrical System Costs

500Ah battery bank at 12V: $2800 if built from cells (with BMS), $4800 if assembled from retail batteries.

3000W inverter/charger: $1300 (Victron Multiplus); a second unit can be added if necessary—note that the battery bank is capable of a 6000W or higher draw.
Victron Smartsolar MPPT charge controller: $580
Victron Energy Orion-TR DC-DC converter: $120
Victron Battery Monitor: $210
Assorted system materials, from wires to plugs to fuses to panels: $600
Estimated total: $5610 (or $7610 with pre-made batteries)

So, this will be a significant expense. This can be economized, but the only good way to do so is to shrink the size of the battery bank. The other components will all be needed for a range of battery sizes. I would really prefer to double the size of the battery bank, but that can be done later (extra battery space should be planned for). If properly emplaced and not damaged during use, however, this system should last through at least ten years and perhaps as long as thirty years.

Note that I have gone with all Victron electronics for this build. Doing so insures full compatibility among the components and also permits easy expansion. As noted above in Part One of this book, there are several other companies which have full electronics product lines that will provide the same benefits. The use of Victron here is just an example of a unified build.

Internal networking for this build can all be wireless, or if I choose to I can run cables around the interior. External networking should be more established than that for the minivan build. I will posit two omnidirectional antennae on the roof in order to extend both wifi and cell signal range. They can be placed where desired using the corner holes already cut and ready. Internet access will be wifi when possible and via a cellular data plan otherwise.

Summary and Conclusion

Notice how the entire build fits together from beginning to end. The vehicle choice, interior arrangement, electronics system, water management, and storage solutions have all been fit together into a cohesive living solution, planned together in order to meet desired needs. In this way you can fulfill all life needs in a select manner despite the limited space of a mobile solution. Some things have been sacrificed and others gained in return—every choice in a build is a trade-off.

The final build will be fairly nondescript from the exterior, in that solar panels or other emplacements on an apparent contract vehicle are not uncommon. There can be discrete cameras at all four top corners, blended against the solar panels, to provide full circle exterior viewing coverage for the occupants. Exterior lights, either motion or command or both, can be installed. You may also consider a speaker system or even a full I/O audio system along the roof edge.

Note again the impressive towing capacity of the vehicle. Any number of things can be towed behind it, from a storage trailer up to a full camper or a car hauler or even a boat. Mileage will suffer, of course, but the capacity is very nice and can greatly extend living options.

The interior is highly insulated. This will make it feasible to both heat and cool with portable electric arrangements, which will make the van much more livable in extreme climates. The radiant system discussed can be used as either a primary or secondary heating element. It can feasibly be used to offer some cooling action as well, though the placement of the tubes will reduce efficacy and if cold water is circulated through you should also act to reduce humidity in the van interior. Headroom is limited for this build, but all living needs can still be accommodated within—easily for one person, and for two people with a bit more care and inconvenience.

This is an electronics heavy build that is somewhat more suited to urban environments than for camping, but could be used for either. Estimated cost range for total build, if all or most work is done by owner, $25-35k. Less if going with a less expensive initial vehicle, more if the converse. Not bad for a small RV, and this platform is much more versatile than a larger solution—even if somewhat cramped.

My high fulfillment needs of Electricity, Heating, Planning and Space have all been accommodated as described above. More planning than just this will be required, of course. In order not to bore my readers even further I have left out details such as finish work and specific utility and electric appliance choices and siting. I think I have covered here everything which is particular to the build and that will need to be especially considered.

My medium fulfillment needs are also capable of being met. For Address with this build I would establish residence in Texas or Florida or South Dakota and use a mailing service. Air is met with the vents and fans described—filters can always be placed over the established vents to increase air quality. Applications will be handled by user electronics and whatever other materials I choose to incorporate (a small library, etc). Cooling is only met with the described fans, but I could also use an evaporative cooler or, in extremis, rig up an air conditioner using cardboard, tape, and the passenger window in the driving area. Food preparation and storage can be handled in the described kitchen area. If I chose I could also manage some small food production, such as meal worms or plants under a grow-light.

Health needs can be adequately met—there is no specific provision for exercise, but this can be done in the open space by the side doors. Networking has been described at the end of the electronics section. Pests can be reduced by keeping things clean, but for this more complex build I will be careful to put preventative measures in place, such as diatomaceous earth for insects and poison bait for rodents. I lowered my Philosophy fulfillment level to be in keeping with this hybrid build and that can be met with some time spent in thought and a little reading. Propulsion is handled by the integral vehicle systems, but in order to keep my platform moving I will want to be very proactive with maintenance for all vehicle systems—motor, tires, windshield wipers, etc. Sanitation can be handled with described systems, with the exceptions of laundry which will have to be done by hand or by using outside facilities.

For Security, I would be careful to place bolts on the inside of all doors in order to reduce entry options for intruders, in addition to any other appropriate measures taken. Stopping can be handled with research and goodwill—this platform is reasonably subtle in appearance and, provided that the exterior is kept clean, should not provoke too much reaction in most places. Wastage can be handled with described systems, which will have at least moderate capacity. Water needs will be fulfilled by the overhead water tank at the shower/kitchen junction.

References and Further Research

faroutride.com/build-journal

outboundliving.com/van-living-diy-camper-van-conversion-guide

divineontheroad.com/build-a-van

meanderingexplorers.com/build

www.theroadisourhome.com/2017/11/15/van-build

gnomadhome.com/build-your-van

thevanual.com

mowgli-adventures.com/campervan-conversion-guide

livelikepete.com/category/van-build

www.parkedinparadise.com/how-to-live-in-van

www.spintheglobeproject.com/how-to-build-a-camper-van

saraandalexjames.com/van-build-layout-guide

youtu.be/4hD19_0jl68

A carefully planned build and well presented, though I would be concerned about moisture getting to those frame boards over time. This channel has a number of van conversion videos.

youtu.be/o1Hv5MoEKV0

A touring van conversion by a German couple with a rather different style.

youtu.be/O3LUnrbhXlU

A campervan showcase with build and design choices.

youtu.be/OigUyvSOV0Y

A campervan tour, but built with hybrid uses in mind.

youtu.be/KC2SCZL1QWc

Tour of a fully capable ProMaster conversion. Channel also has a series of videos showing the full build process.

youtu.be/I-F-h8zMcJE

Build video for converting an older full-size family van. Good channel in that it shows specific methods for obtaining desired results.

youtu.be/Plc4RKwxtvU

A similar vehicle to my hypothetical build (regular wheelbase), though as you can see they have some very different design choices. A good build considering the working conditions.

youtu.be/8epCqUxFrWs

Another Express build (extended wheelbase). I have doubts about the efficacy of the reflective insulation, but if that is what they want it will still be better than nothing.

youtu.be/3ADBOGJu_v0

Another Express build. This conversion is very well designed for a low-budget build.

youtu.be/8V-dPgooqMg

Yet another Express build. Sorry to put so many, but it really is a good platform and I want to show the different ways you can build one out. This build video shows a very different and also interesting style.

23.

The Truck Conversion

A truck conversion will by nature be much more modular than using a van or minivan. The main components of frame/chassis, motor/drive-train, and the box for the living area can all be changed out without violating the build. That is, you can pick a different frame/chassis to start with and then switch out either the drive-train or the box area or both. I say 'box area' in reference to any payload that is mounted on the chassis behind the driving area, that is not integral to the function of the vehicle, but that is still a unified part of the total vehicle. If you are very skilled and adventurous you can even build your own truck from parts.

For a conversion, you could start with a regular pickup truck, strip off the bed, and build or place a box onto the chassis. You could instead keep the bed and the whole truck and build or place a box onto the truck bed. You could find an old box truck with a blown motor, replace the motor, and use the box as your living space. Or any combination therefrom. A truck has the same essential components as does a van, but the setup is much more modular as the various components are made at the factory to be assembled from standard parts into multiple the configurations that are needed for work trucks.

Platform

For this sample conversion I will start with a retired u-haul moving truck as the basis for the build, with the assumption that the drive mechanicals do function. These types of trucks are very common and can be found for sale in a wide variety of conditions.

Specs

20ft truck, with storage size equivalent 10ft x 15ft x 8ft
Max towing capacity: 7500lbs
Rear wheel drive
40 gallon fuel capacity, 10 mpg max
Interior box dimensions: 19.5ft long (top) x 7.75ft wide x 7.15ft high. Deck length 16.8ft
Total storage volume: 1016ft^3
Cargo area access: full vertical raise roller door, with pull out ramp.

For simplicity I will assume that the box deck is flush, with no wheel cutouts. Given this initial platform, which is much like a blank canvas for your build and is suitable to being either a stealth vehicle or full on RV, I will attempt to note specific design options as we go along that are more suited for one type of conversion or the other. I have gone with a twenty foot u-haul for this build, but you could easily go down to a fifteen footer or up to a twenty-six footer—they are all standard models. The fifteen will have the same mechanicals but a smaller box, so the towing capacity will increase to 10,000lbs. The twenty-six will be beefed up a bit mechanically and also somewhat heavier to go along with that increased space.

Purpose

As I went with a stealth build for the minivan and a hybrid build for the van, I will set the purpose for this build as a full conversion into a camper vehicle. That is, the purpose of this build will be to create a living platform that is primarily for rural or wilderness use. It will be street legal, of course, and so can drive anywhere, but no extreme measures will be taken to maintain a stealth platform.

Given the size of the initial platform, there is more than enough room inside to fulfill a variety of living needs. It will be a fully capable living platform and one suitable for extended boondocking and wilderness exploration.

Planning

With this purpose in mind, I will stipulate that the truck will haul a trailer as part of its normal configuration. The truck itself is not suited for off-road travel, but it can provide a good base for such and if an ATV or equivalent off-road vehicle is towed along with the build then such needs can be facilitated.

Beyond that capability, however, we must provide for many of our life needs to be met at a high level of fulfillment in order to accomplish the stated purpose of the living solution. This will be more expensive and require careful planning, but given the size of the base vehicle the goal is quite possible.

High fulfillment: Applications, Electricity, Food, Health, Networking, Pests, Philosophy, Planning, Water

Medium fulfillment: Address, Air, Cooling, Heating, Propulsion, Sanitation, Security, Space, Stopping, Structure, Wastage

Low fulfillment: (None)

This is a wheeled vehicle and I will provide for redundant communication options, so I should not be too far away from aid if something goes drastically wrong. So, even though I am planning a solution for extended wilderness living I can still get away with moderate solutions in many areas. These fulfillment levels would be quite different for a marine solution with extended cruising in mind. This camper vehicle is unlikely to sink at any point, for instance.

Food, Water, Health, and Networking will thus be the most important needs to be kept fulfilled, with Electricity and Applications running just behind as being supportive of those solutions. Planning should be highly stressed for this build purpose, as it will often be out of range of immediate support. Pests will need to be deterred and prepared for beforehand, as the platform will often be out of range of shopping. I may have some slight bias toward a high Philosophy fulfillment level, but I could argue that it does not cost much and can be nearly infinitely rewarding.

Many of the needs I categorize here in the medium fulfillment range could be further stressed for a high fulfillment, but in order to keep costs down I have attempted to plan for merely adequate (though still satisfactory) levels of fulfillment, at least when off-grid. Things such as full air conditioner units, which may be run briefly but not extensively when relying on self-generated power, can be used as much as desired when hooked into shore power.

Build

Initial Preparation and Design Choices

I think that the greatest strength of this particular build platform is that it is suited to be built and furnished with standard residential materials and products in most respects. You will still need a mobile electronics setup and obviously will want to go with smaller appliances suited to an off-grid build. But the box itself is already constructed to be weather-tight and the amount of open, already squared-off space inside means that pre-made doors, cabinets, etc can be used. This will save a great deal of time and preclude the need for much of the custom building. Furthermore, there is sufficient open area underneath which is high enough up off the road that it is feasible to run plumbing and electric lines down there—provided that insulation and possibly heating tape is installed on the plumbing. Much like a residential crawlspace. There is even space down there for full fresh, gray, and black water tanks. Though I would still suggest keeping at least freshwater tanks up in the insulated box unless no freezing temperatures are anticipated. Keeping under-mount tanks heated may be too large a power draw.

Doors

Door placement and options will be the first design choice. It is possible to not alter the initial setup at all—just keep the rear slider and use that for all access to the back. Some people go this route. It simplifies insulation concerns and keeps the build entirely enclosed. It is less work. Personally, I would strongly suggest that a second method of egress and entry should be considered. These trucks are designed to be easily latched and locked from the exterior—which could lead to some bad situations. Even without malicious intent being involved, the rolling door could get stuck at times.

Every other door option will involve cutting into the box, but some approaches will be easier than others. If possible, it would be nice to have access directly into the cab of the truck through a doorway. Some vehicles will accommodate this and some will not. Doing so may not be feasible because of a full seat in the front and will involve weatherproofing and insulating an all new seal. You may instead consider a hatch passage from the roof of the cab into the top overhang portion of the box. This will involve cutting both the box and the cab and also carefully weatherproofing against blown in weather while driving, but should be at least possible even if you cannot work in a pass-through door down below. It would provide a good emergency passage even if not frequently used and would not be apparent to casual inspection.

You could also cut an escape hatch through the bottom of the box area. This will be the simplest and easiest method to insure the ability to get out if the rear door is blocked. It will somewhat complicate flooring and insulation, but not overly so, especially if it is only intended for emergency escape instead of as a reusable portal.

You could also cut an RV style doorway into the side of the box. I have seen this done coupled with retracting electric steps that automatically slide underneath whenever the vehicle is put into gear. Your steps could just be fold and latch instead (you will need steps) but having such a doorway can be the most convenient method to get in and out. RV/camper doors are standard and, within reason, secure portals. If you go this route then you would be sacrificing some stealth attributes, but you could also use this as the main entry instead of the rear roller door.

The rear area could then be walled off entirely, with just a bit of space left back there for a utility area. You could also sacrifice that interior space altogether and fix the door into place, even remove the tracks. Then, the entire rear face of the box becomes a place to attach appliance and storage bins without sacrificing aerodynamics. If blocking off the rear door I would also add an escape hatch somewhere inside the box to preserve egress potential.

For my sample build I will cut a door into the box side. This will be on the passenger side as far forward as possible. The portal will be reinforced as necessary and feature a standard RV/camper style door, opening outward to preserve interior space. The lock, however, will be upgraded for better security. Outside, there will be simple fold-and-latch steps to facilitate entry. This door, combined with the rear access which will be left as pass-through for my build, solves the need for having a secondary way out in emergencies.

As an alternative method, I could leave the box intact on the side and cut a hatch in the flooring roughly in the same area. It should be clear just underneath. The mechanicals will all be concentrated down the center-line, which leaves plenty of space along each side for other purposes such as an escape hatch. This would be mostly for emergency use, of course, and much less convenient than having a door in the side. But for a stealth build such a compromise might be a better solution.

Windows

It will be a relatively simple matter to cut and install windows in the box sides, and they could be located almost anywhere you wish—as long as you keep in mind that the box sides themselves are part of the integral weight-bearing structure of the box. The box is held together at least partially by the stiffness of the material (steel) and the integrity of the panels themselves. Any cutting will violate that integrity, which must then be compensated for by a corresponding reinforcement. There will be framing type material along the edges of the box, but especially for longer boxes the sides are at least helping to hold themselves up and to support the structure.

Thus the door I posit to install will need a reinforced frame that assumes the structural burden of the cutout section. The same must be true of any window emplacement. For my build I will also posit a long window, on the driver side, which will be just above the kitchen counter. This should be cut and installed now (thus I should know exactly where and how high the kitchen counter will be) and will need to be reinforced even more than the door, as the long horizontal profile will violate more of the panel integrity than the vertical doorway. For this reason I will have a vertical strip of reinforcing material (steel, to match the panel) which will bisect the window, in addition to added reinforcement along the edges of the cut opening. This will interfere with the view a bit, but not much.

With this window and the door on the passenger side, there will be at least some natural lighting of the interior, as desired. You should also have a cover or curtain for the window(s) for privacy.

Roof Vents

Having at least one roof vent will be almost essential for this conversion. I would suggest two in order to enable both in and out air-flows at once. They could be placed center-line to minimize visibility from most angles. I will again posit one for the shower/bathroom and another as close to the rear as the roller door permits, but both center-line. The bathroom will be set flush against the raised front and the second vent will be five or six feet back (the roller door rail area will be boxed off), which should still permit adequate airflow to minimize condensation buildup and improve the atmosphere.

Layout

Do plan your layout as soon as you know your vehicle dimensions, and before you make your first cut. This is the only way to maximize available space which, though extravagant in comparison to the van builds, is still limited. Will you compartmentalize, try to keep open spaces, or have some mix of the two?

I will try to find some compromise between the two. Keeping as much storage space as possible is important, but your living solution should not make you feel like a hamster in a maze, crawling between separate spaces. Though it can be important to have distinct partitioned areas in order to allow separate inhabitants at least the illusion of privacy.

The top area above the cab is a ready made space to be converted between sleeping and storage as desired. The space is roughly square, so a sleeping mattress could be easily flipped up against the front wall. Even with insulation this space will be over seven feet wide, sufficient to accommodate sleeping as well as a storage box along one side. This could be the main sleeping area for adults or children, or instead used as storage and auxiliary sleeping for guests or during certain climate periods (hot air will rise).

The space just back of that will be, from passenger to driver side, the exterior door with a flush mounted ladder up on the right as you enter, the shower stall, and the joined toilet space. The shower stall will have a roof vent directly up, so that overhead will be at least cluttered. You could squeeze in some room for utility space there by truncating the vent dimensions, you could have the shower space go all the way up, or you could run a full size vent straight up. I will keep the vent as a closed box, fourteen inches square, running down from the roof vent to a normal height shower stall with a top. This vent will be as far toward the passenger side as possible.

Such will allow me to keep a large chunk of space between the vent and the driver side wall, above the toilet, for other purposes. This will be increased further because the toilet side of the bathroom will be sitting room only—though with a curved transition rather than squared. I will go with a compost or cassette toilet again (preferably compost), with a separate vent tube-line run along one edge of the space up to the roof vent, with two or three small fans inline in that vent tube-line for this build. There will be no separate sink in the bathroom, but it is entirely possible to rig the shower faucet for easy hand washing. You could instead have a separate faucet set lower but off of the shower water line, with a truncated basin and drain to reduce splashing. One could even place a ledge and a mirror on one side of the shower stall.

Directly above the toilet space (if carefully braced) is room for a one or two hundred gallon fresh water tank. Or less if preferred. Even a two hundred gallon tank (which I would not go with; it will weigh in at around 1800 lbs full) would still leave room above it to permit top filling and storage space accessible from the top area. I will posit instead a one hundred and five gallon fresh water tank in this space, with dimensions 39in x 26in x 26in. Bracing will be tricky, but the tank need not be kept totally full under normal conditions. Placing the tank here will give a gravity feed to the lines, precluding the need for a full pressurized water system. Filling the tank could be accomplished either up above or (more likely for normal usage) down below by a small pump. If an entire enclosed, reinforced box is built for the bathroom area, or at least the toilet area, the weight of this tank can be distributed across as much floor space as needed so as not to threaten the integrity of the truck itself at any one point or to push the floor insulation past its compressive load capacity. The weight can be spread onto the entire area under the toilet, the shower stall, and under the kitchen counter if needed. This will require a bit more in the way of materials and careful planning, but is very possible. Alternatively, or as you calculate what weight your structure can hold, go with a smaller water tank.

Moving toward the back from there, I would keep the center-line along the roof as open space, or perhaps equipped with storage netting or lines. This would be an excellent space to dry the laundry if it cannot be done outside, or to be used for other temporary purposes. The second vent fan will be in this zone just in front of the end of the roller door when it is rolled up. It will be necessary to frame off the roller door space, but I would suggest putting one or more close-able vents into that space in order to dry out condensation buildup or to vent as desired. The center-line along the floor will be the main walkthrough for the cabin.

For my build, I will keep the very rear near to the roller door as utility space. This will be two and a half feet deep and all the way up, with a full bulkhead wall between it and the living area. The wall will have a door in the center and windows on either side. The door itself could be opaque or instead transparent glass or plastic as desired. A transparent door and any windows can be tinted to permit vision from one direction but not the other, eliminating the need for any curtains. One or more air conditioning units, standard residential but smaller for lower wattage, could be mounted in or above the windows. As an interesting alternative, you may consider using a sliding glass door, like people put as access out onto their patios, as your main rear entry. Many of these come with screen doors fitted as one of the sliders.

In between that bulkhead and the bathroom should then remain a space longer than eleven feet for this vehicle, even allowing for insulation. The kitchen area will be on the driver side to allow easy routing of water lines from that overhead tank. I will posit a convertible table/bed just behind the kitchen, as a second sleeping area and also the main lounging area. Underneath the benches will be storage chests. With six and a half feet of length for the table/bed this will permit over four feet of counterspace for the kitchen.

The other side may be setup as desired. This could be an enormous amount of storage space. For my build, I will budget sufficient space for a rear-facing productivity area (a simple desk arrangement) just back of the ladder up to the loft on the passenger side, clear of the side door but with the option to use that space when desired for more chair room. Just rearward of that will be a utility closet for a small clothes washer, with a cabinet up above.

If I assume two and a half feet of lengthwise (front to back) space for each the doorway, the productivity area, the washer cabinet, and the rear utility area, I will be left with just under six and a half feet of length along the passenger side to configure. For this I will posit long storage shelves on the bottom portion and storage cabinets on the top portion. One or two of the shelves could be high enough opened up to be used as extra sleeping space when needed, or as another work area in addition to the table, kitchen, and productivity space. This will complete my layout planning, enabling me to move on with the build.

Preparation and Insulation

As with the van build, a full inspection should be undertaken prior to building, followed by repair of any issues that inspection turns up and a thorough cleaning.

You may consider two or three layers of Rustoleum or a similar paint type on the inside of the box, after stripping out any unnecessary items or trim and cleaning it up. The paint would act as an initial moisture barrier for any leaks that develop and also help to preserve the metal against inevitable condensation. This would not have been feasible for the van build because of all the pockets and grooves. Also, the spray foam was fulfilling a similar role.

If there are wooden trim pieces on the sides they should be removed unless you judge otherwise. The bolt holes for their fasteners should be reused for your own attachments. If the flooring is wood planked instead of just sheet metal you will have to judge its suitability yourself. I would remove it in preparation for a material which will not be damaged by trapped moisture over time.

For insulation I would suggest just using extruded polystyrene foam sheets (XPS) for all surfaces. This type is versatile and durable, as well as being thin to save space and easy to handle. Its good compressive strength makes it suitable for the floor as well as the other surfaces. Cut any planned holes in the box before insulating, but it is much less important to do all of these first for this build. The XPS should be cleaned up after cutting, but does not represent any potential health risk when penetrated.

For my build, the two roof vent holes (standard 14 inch) have already been mentioned, as have the door and window. There should be further holes cut up top for any planned solar wiring, antennas, and lights, cameras, etc. If you want a cassette toilet that empties through an exterior hatch you could cut that now. I have also seen people put a water fill port and even a shore power port in the side, like some RVs have.

For under the box, this platform could manage a black water tank for a standard RV type toilet and a graywater tank for the sink and shower. I will posit putting a small graywater tank directly under the sink, but with a y-valve that permits draining to another graywater tank underneath the box. The shower could also have a y-valve, though located under the floor drain, to permit draining into that graywater tank or just draining underneath when that is appropriate. Insulating and heating this tank would be difficult, so care should be taken in cold weather, but it does increase graywater storage options.

Regarding the floor insulation, I would either hold off on placing it down or instead put down flooring just after doing the insulation. This could be temporary flooring only, as the purpose here is the protect the XPS from getting torn up.

Building the Space

The shower stall, the kitchen cabinets and sink, any other cabinets, and the bulkhead door and any windows can all be stock items from the hardware store. All other fixtures will be built to fit the space, unless you find something that already fits. For my sample conversion, I may be able to go with stock shelves for the passenger side storage and I may not, depending on how they fit the space.

For the walls and ceiling, you could use just thin plywood panels if you like, but I would go for vinyl panels instead. To me, the moisture resistance and overall utility is better than having the warmth of wood everywhere at the cost of more maintenance. But go your own route. Do strip planked cedar walls if that seems better to you, or just plywood and paint.

I would also put the vinyl on the ceiling, but it could be argued that having something that will breathe better up there is a good idea. I have seen a nice box truck build, made on a small budget, that used stained two by four planks as the ceiling. The wood ceiling looked nice and really set off the whole build even though the walls were all just painted plywood.

For the floor, I will go with the same click-lock vinyl as my van build above. You could go cheaper or more expensive, but to me the combination of qualities, and especially the ease of installation and re-installation, is quite desirable.

After walling over the insulation and painting the surfaces as appropriate, you will need to work out pathways for your electrical wiring and plumbing. Given the nature of the build—sheet metal, flat board insulation, covering—it is not feasible to sink switches and outlets into the walls. Consider instead whether you wish to mount each item out from the walls or ceiling or instead set into one of your fixtures (cabinets, etc). An outlet or light switch will not take up very much room inside a cabinet. On the other hand, if that wall space was going to be empty anyway, why not use it to mount electronics? Full box mountings are available for various electronic fixtures. Wiring can be disguised in hollow trim pieces or just put under plastic covers. It may also be possible to run the wiring itself behind the paneling.

Given the placement of the water tank in my build there should not be any exposed plumbing, as it will run straight down to the shower. The sink piping can be worked through the storage cabinets above the kitchen counter, as those cabinets will be right next to the water tank. I think for this build a faucet coming down from the cabinet above the sink also makes sense, though it could easily be run down to an in-sink faucet instead.

For the main table/bed, it seems easiest just to have the table itself drop down as the center of the bed. You could instead go with a sliding slat arrangement, but then you would have to set the table aside somehow. Though if you keep the wall above that space mostly open, the table could pivot up and latch in place. This would facilitate using the space as a lounge area. It would also mean that the table could be shaped any way you like, instead of made only to fit the space between the benches. Regardless of what method you choose, cushions can be made to shape by cutting up foam padding and sewing it into cloth covers.

Electricity

Electrical Load Estimates

I have mentioned the roof vent fans and inline fans for the toilet vent. You may also want to have a fan mounted up top in the loft. Down below, you could get away with just using a portable box fan or two, moved around as desired in that center isle.

Lights should be mounted up in the loft, in the ladder/door/productivity area, in the bathroom, in the kitchen, in the dining/lounging/sleeping space, in the utility zone outside of the bulkhead wall, and anywhere else desired.

The small washer has been mentioned. There is room in the kitchen for a good sized (though still mini) refrigerator. Other compressor loads (meaning high draw) will include any air conditioning units or heat pumps and an air compressor if you keep one.

If using electric heating and/or cooking that draw must be factored in. Also consider any appliances that might be wanted—coffee maker, ice maker, food processor, microwave, toaster oven, etc.

Once you have considered all of your potential load sources calculate your maximum possible power usage, in the depths of winter or the height of summer, and see if it is feasible for you to install an electrical system which can handle the load. My build posits an ambitious electrical and networking setup and so will have a robust system.

Electrical System

It would seem a great shame to waste all of that open space up on the roof. Monocrystalline or even polycrystalline panels will only stick up a couple of inches at most, so it should be fine to use those if you keep them a bit back from the edge, even if you want a stealth build. The efficiency will increase if they are raised a bit up off of the roof by something that will permit airflow. This could be squared plastic pieces or anything else that will let air pass along it and will remain a stable base for the panels. The airflow underneath will reduce heat buildup in the panels; heat buildup will reduce electrical output efficiency.

For my build I will posit 1000 watts of solar from five 200 watt monocrystalline panels. They will be raised a bit for better cooling, but will be set a bit back from the edge so should not be very noticeable from the ground. This is a respectable amount and should help a great deal with power needs. There will also be room left on the roof for more if needed. I price the five panels at around $1000.

This much solar will require one or more charge controllers rated to at least 100 amps if we assume a 12V system. I will go with two Schneider Electric (Xantrex) MPPT 60 charge controllers, at $1100 for both. Yes, this is more than for the panels themselves, but still necessary to get the most output from those panels and to have an enduring system. It will also permit adding more panels later.

I will posit a 1000Ah battery bank, but this should be kept expandable if more capacity is desired. Priced at $9500 if using retail batteries and $5500 if built from cells.

For power conversion, I will use two stacked Xantrex Freedom XC 2000 inverter/chargers. Multiple inverters, if compatible, can share electrical loads between them. The Xantrex systems are fully compatible and programmable solutions, comparable to Victron Energy systems. These will set me back $680 each or $1360 for both. If I find that I have higher inversion needs, say if I want to add a tumble dryer to the build, I could add a third Freedom XC unit. Shore power can be fed to these units in order to charge the battery bank when it is available.

For taking some charge off of the vehicle alternator I would go with the same Victron Orion-Tr 12/12-18A DC-DC converter as the van build. This is suitable for isolated charging (to the BMS) and need not be linked to other electrical system components. You could also use a Renogy Board 20A DC to DC battery charger. Unless the alternator is upgraded though this should never be a primary charge source. You may choose to do without it altogether.

Xantrex also offers a full range of accessories, such as control panels, battery monitors, and relays. Estimated costs for rounding out the system and putting all wiring and circuit protection in place: $800. For a total system cost of around $10,000 ($14,000 with retail batteries) for the components. But this is a top of the line system designed to last for decades and through multiple vehicles if necessary. As with any build, you can go with a less expensive system if you are willing to accept fewer capabilities and decreased expected system lifespan. Even with this system as described you can lower or raise the cost by shrinking or enlarging the battery bank capacity. You could also have more or fewer solar panels on the roof, which would alter how many and how well rated your MPPT chargers should be. All I can do here is to describe for you a nominal system based on average usage considerations. You can and should tailor your own electrical system to your own load calculations.

For this build, it is entirely feasible to factor a generator into the power equation. One can easily be fit into the storage area outside the bulkhead. If you are willing to go for heavy generator use, you can shrink your battery bank in half or even by three-fourths. You will still need stacked inverters capable of handling your max power load, but the system dynamic can be changed considerably.

Summary and Conclusion

This build is a predictable expansion on the van and minivan builds. The major differences are the amount of space available and the subsequent alterations to design and usage which become possible. Otherwise it is still a vehicle, mobile by virtue of an internal combustion engine and mounted on a frame kept off the ground by compressed air tires.

The largest expense after the base vehicle itself, and possibly an even larger expense than that, is the off-grid electrical power system. Most of the extra expense for this system derives from the need to generate and store power on-site. Reducing power consumption needs can thus go a long way toward reducing the cost of your build. Looked at from the other direction, it is possible to utilize any electrical appliance in your mobile living system that people have for static living systems—provided that you are willing to absorb the higher cost of keeping it powered (and to devote the space onboard for it).

I have been trying to scale my sample vehicle electrical systems to fit the space and projected needs for each build, but you need not follow this progression for your own build. If your power use is light, then just have a couple of solar panels on the roof and a 'solar generator' setup for power draws. Or scale up from there. Just be aware of the capacities and requirements of each component of your system.

With the extensive electrical system projected here, and appropriate electronics, this vehicle build will be capable of meeting my high fulfillment needs of Electricity, Applications, and Networking. I can have a central house computer in addition to user electronics to coordinate internal networking needs and run productivity, educational, and entertainment applications. External networking can be handled with wifi and cellular signal, as with the van build above, or scaled up with satellite communication.

There is quite enough extra space on board to keep extra water stores in addition to the main tank already mentioned. Sufficient filtration and purification can be installed to meet any requirements. There is also plenty of room for food reserves and redundant preservation and cooking requirements. With this power system there can be a separate freezer in addition to the main fridge. There is even room for food production, such as from a small hydroponics system, if desired. So both Water and Food are covered.

The other high fulfillment needs of Planning, Health, Pests, and Philosophy can all be met in the space available by designing and sourcing specific system components. The varied food options will make for a healthy diet. Exercise can be accomplished in many different ways and redundant medical supplies can be kept on hand. Pests can be handled with both preventative measures and by keeping elimination materials on hand against need.

Address will be handled the same as described in the van build. Air control will rely upon the fans mentioned, with the option to add filters as desired. Cooling will also rely on those fans, but there can also be an air conditioning unit mounted in the rear bulkhead to the utility area. Or, better yet, two, with one to be run while off-grid and both together to be run while on shore power. Heating has not been specifically mentioned and in any case should be tailored to anticipated need. The flooring insulation can be doubled so as to permit radiant heat as detailed in the van build. A wall-mount propane heater is appropriate for this build, as it can be vented into the utility area and it will be fairly easy to cut into the flooring to provide a safety drain against leaks.

Propulsion will be handled by the integral platform systems, which themselves should be subjected to regular thorough maintenance. No matter how good the rest of your build is, if the truck breaks down then you are going nowhere. There should be full spare tires mounted where possible, in addition to keeping appropriate tools and common spare parts on hand. Sanitation can be handled with described systems. Security should be analyzed and designed accordingly, but this will be a matter of making minor adjustments rather than major alterations. There is the power capacity for a full electronic security suite for this build, especially if high efficiency electronics are used. All data feeds can be routed through the house computer.

Space needs have been thoroughly accounted for, though this will change depending on the specific sizes and preferences of the actual inhabitants. Stopping needs will be met with external communications and planning. Some Structure issues have been noted, but fighting corrosion and otherwise maintaining vehicle integrity will be an ongoing concern, especially with an older build platform. Commit to regular inspections of the entire exterior and as much of the interior as possible. Solve potential problems before they become an issue, not after. Wastage concerns have been noted and may be fully met by the build described. Keeping an extra camp toilet will also be a good idea.

A box-truck build can be a suitable living solution for multiple people or just one, at a fraction of the cost of an RV or towed camper. And you can still tow a camper or another vehicle behind it. This cost savings is derived from a willingness to build it out yourself (or with help) and to design features that are tailored to you, rather than to a marketing demographic. Numerous compromises are required to reach this tailored build. I have posited toilet solutions which may not be acceptable to many people wanting to live the RV life, for instance.

Regardless of your build choices and compromises, I wish you the very best in your own mobile living truck build. Enjoy the open road.

References and Further Research

www.vanchitecture.com/2017/12/15/16-gorgeous-box-truck-camper-van-conversion

camperism.co/2018/07/07/25-awesome-box-truck-conversion-ideas

tinyhousetalk.com/box-truck-converted-into-amazing-diy-off-grid-solar-motorhome

www.curbed.com/2018/7/27/17617598/camper-conversion-skoolie-diy-vanlife

imgur.com/a/Dmlel

itstillruns.com/convert-box-truck-motorhome-6308063.html

tinyhousetalk.com/cheap-diy-box-truck-motorhome-conversion

www.doityourselfrv.com/u-haul-box-truck

www.wildwewander.com/diy-truck-camper

campersmarts.com/truck-camper-guide

www.desktodirtbag.com/build-pickup-truck-bed-camper-guide

outdoorfact.com/how-to-build-a-lightweight-truck-camper

www.doityourselfrv.com/truck-camper-pop-top

youtu.be/I6UsKNYpnWg
Tour video of a nice box truck conversion.
youtu.be/KOiLCGb2R20
A build video for the same type of truck (UK Luton truck).

youtu.be/7ohdKusa6zg

A build video for a U-Haul conversion (smaller size than my sample build).

youtu.be/1G62JHALM5Q

A tour video for another U-Haul conversion (larger size than my sample build).

youtu.be/DllYl1z1KF8

This is a single video of a multi-part series showing the full conversion (and structural extension) of a box truck into a mobile living solution. This video gives a good idea of the build methodology, but also check out the others on the channel.

youtu.be/vn73KzgXKgI

A showcase video with different truck camper builds.

youtu.be/nMTIxlwSDIQ

A build video for a very solid truck camper.

youtu.be/b6UVNkP5QzI

A tour video for a custom truck camper. Nice build with some good features.

youtu.be/ENZ2KjlN71A

Another tour for a custom truck camper—Alaskan style.

24.

The Electric Trailer Build

This is my last wheeled sample build for your consideration; it will be a bit different. Instead of positing a self-powered solution for integrating mobile living, this build will try to offer an example of a mobile living solution that can be accomplished from scratch—or at least from more basic components. It will (mostly) not be capable of independent motion, but should be suitable for towing behind any number of vehicles. This can afford a very desirable level of versatility for your mobility solutions.

I will start from basic components, trying to give you an idea of what materials, tools, and expertise will be required for each step. You may instead choose to begin from a pre-made trailer of some sort. I will attempt to insert these possibilities into the relevant portion of this sample build and to iterate how the steps will be different.

There are many commercial travel trailers out there which may also suit your needs, new or used. None of them will be perfectly tailored for you. They can, however, be made so with suitable modification. I hope that even if you do not want to build your own, this and my previous sample builds will still help you to plan out any modifications.

Platform

This time there is no starting platform—we have a blank canvas. Whatever we do come up with will, however, need to meet certain requirements. It will be mounted on wheeled axles of a standard width for road travel. The trailer dimensions should be no more then 28 feet 6 inches long, 8 feet 6 inches wide, and 13 feet 6 inches tall (taken from aaa.com). In order to stay within these dimensions, and for the sake of simplicity, I will posit a trailer build that is 26 feet long, 8 feet wide, and 11 feet high (to the roof). It will be double axle and have a standard hitch at the front.

Purpose

This fully custom build will not be attempted as a stealth vehicle, but will instead be a full travel trailer camper. It is possible to build out any number of trailers for inconspicuous living, and I will try to provide links at the bottom and notes along the way to help out such an endeavor. You will need to sacrifice certain features and capabilities in order to do so (no windows, etc).

So the purpose of the build will be to have an individually tailored mobile living solution capable of being towed around by a variety of towing vehicles. It will be outfitted for both off-grid living and to receive full shore hookups when available. I will posit two long term adult inhabitants with extra accommodation for guests and/or children.

Given the specified trailer dimensions, the final build will probably end up being somewhat heavier than desired for light towing vehicles, so I will attempt to work out the systems required to make this trailer self-propelled. That is, one or both of the axles will be equipped with electric motors, in order to assist the towing vehicle in propulsion. The goal will be to reduce the apparent pulled weight of the trailer down to 3000lbs or less, after the trailer assist is added in, in order to increase the number of vehicles that can be used to tow. That should also reduce strain on any towing vehicle and, once energy reclaimed from regenerative braking is considered, increase gas mileage. This will however be an attempt at a theoretical build and will not include actual experimentation. It is hoped that the theory itself will be informative and helpful to any reader considering such an option.

Planning

Given these purposes, I will plan my need fulfillment levels accordingly. Some of these levels may be higher or lower according to personal taste and the requirements of the inhabitants. Given the large amount of space offered by the platform and the already robust electrical system that the propulsion assistance will require, most or all needs can be fulfilled at a very high level if desired and if budget permits.

High fulfillment: Air, Applications, Cooling, Electricity, Food, Health, Heating, Networking, Pests, Philosophy, Planning, Propulsion, Sanitation, Security, Space, Stopping, Structure, Wastage, Water

Medium fulfillment: Address

Low fulfillment: (None)

This build will be somewhat extravagant as given here, in that almost every need is being met at such a high level of fulfillment. Address can be bumped up as well by acquiring a property somewhere to use as a home base. In part this is to end my wheeled sample build sections by showcasing the results that can be obtained with fully custom solutions. You may miss out on certain cost savings that bulk manufacturers obtain, though you can save in other areas by skipping standard options that you do not want or need. It will certainly be more work to do a custom build. But you can have a stronger and more durable build, which may cost less in terms of cash, and that is fully and intimately tailored to your own particular needs and desires.

Build

Axles

The first components to look at will be the axles, or axle if you will only have one. All of the weight of the build must be able to rest on the axles, which must also have more capacity beyond that weight as a margin of safety. Which and how many axles you choose, however, will be a function of how heavy the total weight of your build will be. At this stage you should look at axle options and must choose axles of a specific length and dimensions, but not necessarily a specific product. That is, your trailer frame will rest on these axles, which frame will have specific locations on either side for the spring centers, which is where the frame will actually rest. There will be standard axle sizes that you can use for planning out the frame.

Your frame will rest on the spring centers, but the axle will continue outward another foot or more to the hub face. The tire itself, when mounted on the hub, will extend a bit beyond that hub face and different tires will have various diameters. All of these measurements must be taken into account when designing the frame and body of the trailer. The frame will rest on the spring centers and the body must encapsulate the tires without touching them.

For this section on axles, I will focus on non-powered versions for those looking to build (or further understand) trailers without any power assist. There will be a section below that more fully explores swapping out or modifying in order to add power assist.

For parts, you will need the axles themselves, complete with any brakes, the springs and hangers, and any tires. To give you some idea of the costs: I price an axle kit on amazon at $1924 for a two axle package, rated at 14,000lbs total capacity, 95in hub-face measurement, 80in spring center measurement, permitting a frame width of 6ft 10in. $1849 for the same kit but 75in hub-face, 58in spring center, 5ft frame width. $1664 for a two axle package, rated at 10,400lbs total capacity, 95in wheel hub, 80in spring center, etc. $605 for a single axle by itself, rated at 7000lbs total capacity, 95in hub-face. All of these axles have electric brakes included.

I take from this that I can build a frame that is six feet ten inches wide with a reasonable expectation that it will work for some axle, provided that I keep total weight under 14,000lbs and keep in mind the weight-bearing attachment points. Less weight than that really if I want to be able to tow the thing with anything smaller than a big truck. I could purchase my intended axles now, but it might also be better to wait until I have a better idea of the end weight of the trailer.

The priced examples given are intended for custom trailer builds or for replacements and the sizings are standardized. Given the stated final dimensions of our build, there will be an overhang of the trailer body past the frame for the largest example axle (6ft 10in frame), roughly 7in past on either side. This is workable, but not ideal as the tires will intrude into the living area. If staying with these easy-order axle options we could shorten our trailer width, or we could instead seek out a shop or other outlet to order custom axle lengths from.

Once the frame is built the axles will be installed by attaching at four points for each axle—the spring ends. This will be a pivot bolt which will permit the springs to move with the trailer. That is, the largest spring will be the only point that is actually attached to the trailer (at both ends). The other (leaf) springs will be clamped to that large spring. All of the springs together will be hung just below the axle by two large u-bolts which secure them to the axle. These critical points must be made strong, of course, but gravity and friction help quite a bit to keep things in place.

All of this thus far assumes that the axle types are leaf-spring axles, which are the most common for trailers. You could use torsion style trailer axles instead which will mount slightly differently. The leaf springs could also be flipped over from how I have described (to be over-slung), which will tend to raise the trailer up a bit higher. For more information on this and much else about trailers and axles, see the second website listed in the references section at the end of this build.

Frame

The frame can be built however you like, as long as it has edges that can be brought to fit the spring attachment points. Most trailer frames are made from c-channel steel beams (shaped like an elongated squared off C) which are welded together into a box framework. Additional c-beams or i-beams, also welded, are run across the center of the box to increase strength. Once the box is built, two additional beams are welded into a triangle at one end to make a place to mount the hitch (standard trailer, not goose-neck or fifth wheel).

In order to complete this step, you will need to source the steel beams. These beams must be capable of supporting the total weight of your build at any given point. Otherwise they might break in half on the road. This need for strength and durability is why steel is used for such things. Make sure yours is thick enough to bear the weight. Cut the beams to size and grind and prepare the surfaces for welding.

Next, you will need to be able to weld the steel beams together into a coherent whole. Each weld must also be capable of supporting the entire weight of the build... otherwise it will break in half on the road. This is the step which will stop most people from attempting this type of from scratch build. Welding is a skill which takes years to fully master. I could not do this now, and would not want to try to do so without a great deal of practice. I have welded before, a few times, poorly, but good enough to make simple repairs. I would not attempt to weld together the foundation for my mobile house without both significant need and a great deal of excess care and/or supervision.

After welding you should smooth any rough surfaces, scour off any rust, and paint the frame. Use at least two coats, primer followed by overcoat. This is the last time you will be able to get at the entire frame so take some care with it now.

Alternative to this point: order a custom trailer frame from a job shop. There are many places that will be happy to do this work for you and will do a professional job.

Alternative #2: buy a trailer, something flat like a car hauler, which you can use as the foundation for the rest of your build. Modify as necessary then move on to the next step. A 7ft x 20ft steel deck car hauler trailer rated at 10,000lbs might run you $4000. You can find a smaller one, for half that price, which might still be capable of supporting your build.

I will posit a custom frame as the base of my build, just short of the dimensions given above for trailer length and width and suitable for mounting on my chosen axles. Given my stated dearth of welding ability, I will source this frame from a local job shop. Once they have it welded and mounted on my axles I can see to the painting and other finish work myself. As preparation for building up, I will check over the entire surface for rust or other imperfections and scour or smooth before applying two or three coats of the appropriate paint.

Building Up

At this point you will have a bare frame on wheels or maybe a finished flat trailer. Take stock of all the things you still need to make it road-worthy. Tail-lights, brake-lights, and turn-signal lights, unless you will be adding these after the trailer body is in place. Wiring for those lights and also for the axle brakes. Reflectors along the sides. A hitch mounted up front for connection to the towing vehicle. A standard plug adapter to link the electronics to the towing vehicle. License plate or other registration, depending on your local regulations.

With those in mind even if not yet installed, plan out the frame and body of the trailer superstructure. How you go about this will depend on the materials used for those purposes. You could continue upward with a steel frame and sheath that in more steel if you want, or instead wood or plastic or aluminum. You could instead make an aluminum frame and sheath that in those same variety of materials. You also could fabricate panels that do the work of both frame and sheathing and emplace those. Fiberglass or other molded laminates may also be used, but I would suggest doing so in a manner which makes sense for a one-off build—construct a structure out of your coring material and then glass over that for strength.

Design will also change a bit based on materials used, but there are several possible shapes. You could try for an Airstream-like build, with all curved surfaces (this will be difficult to achieve). You could just make a squared box sitting on top of the frame (this will be much easier but have increased wind resistance). I would suggest a compromise such that most of the shape is an easy to make box and the front portion is either curved or a triangular shape to reduce wind resistance. A triangular forward hitch mount frame would seem to lend itself to a triangular forward build structure, but this will cost you some interior space. Also consider having a horizontally flat forward edge but slanted back slightly, top and bottom, on the vertical axis—many commercial travel trailers use some variation on this. The roof should be flat, or nearly so, to accept solar panels and other fixtures.

If you built your frame from scratch and already have the welding equipment and expertise, the easiest way to build up might be to weld on (lighter) steel beams going vertical and then some more going horizontal across for the roof. To complete the frame up front slope a beam slightly forward on either side, two thirds of the distance to being level with the bottom frame, from the top. Then do the same for two beams from the bottom, at the same angle and one third the distance to level with the top of your superstructure. These four beams should meet; just bring a horizontal beam across to join the two sides at the junction. Add more beams in the middle of the formed box as appropriate for support and also for a place to fasten panels and interior fixtures.

Sheathe over this superstructure frame with thin steel sheets, either welded or riveted or even bolted on. Or use any other type of suitable flat sheets and attach appropriately. You could also do an aluminum frame, though it would be mechanically attached to the steel trailer frame instead of welded on. You could instead just build a wooden frame and put panels on that. Many people in the 'tiny house' movement are following this route. For a mobile living system that will expect to remain mobile over an extended period I would suggest not using wood for anything structural. Use metal and then protect it from the elements or instead something inert like plastic or laminate.

As an alternative method for building up, rather than the frame and cover approach, you could instead build the superstructure from a laminate that is both strong and gap-bridging in itself. That is, you could build the full structure out of a coring material, like plywood or balsa or plastic or even foam, and then glass that over with a stiffener and resin laminate (both inside and out). Care would have to be taken to fully encapsulate the coring material, especially on the bottom where the laminate structure will need to be bolted to the steel frame. You will also have to re-encapsulate the core whenever you cut or drill into the laminate. But this can make for a strong weatherproof structure and, depending on your cost of materials, may be much cheaper than other options of comparable strength. Metals and good wood are becoming more and more dear as time goes on. Fiberglass and plastic resins actually seem to be getting cheaper. It is also possible to frame in with metal and then 'skin' over with laminate panels.

Alternative to this point: buy a cargo trailer—a blank box ready to be customized. A 7ft x 20ft cargo trailer might run you $7000 or less. An 8.5ft by 28ft cargo trailer might run you $9000 or less.

To continue my sample build, I will construct the base for my superstructure. This will be the part that rests on the frame and so will bear the entire weight of the trailer at any given time. It will also serve as the bottom encapsulation of the coring material for the uprights. Directly between the frame and this base will be a thin layer of durable rubber, which will reduce shock to the laminate. Otherwise the base will be bolted down to the frame. The base will be constructed of fiberglass, wrapped thick around a core board and set in epoxy. The core will be drilled through to attach to the trailer frame and must be re-encapsulated at every hole. The laminate will be strong but inelastic, so washers should be padded and care should be taken not to torque down too tight. Use a thread-locker as these bolts should then be sealed over to protect them from corrosion.

Next, I will construct a temporary frame out of two by fours to support the skin of my build until it can be glassed over. After this is in place, just resting on the base, I will glue thin (1/2in) plywood sheets over top of this temporary framing. Use of glue will hold the panels in place without the complication of using through fasteners. There will be no bends in the plywood, so glue will be sufficiently strong to hold it. After the exterior is finished, the glue can be sliced with a thin knife to remove the temporary frame members. Between the superstructure base and the wall panels there will be wooden strips, also encapsulated, to help spread the weight of the walls.

I will then 'paint' the plywood with epoxy to seal it and prepare for glassing over. All places where two panels are joined (or along the bottom strips) should be sealed with thickened epoxy to both seal and strengthen. Next, I will apply a fiberglass laminate to the entire exterior. I think two layers of tri-axial set in epoxy, should be sufficient. Then I will cut a door in the side and proceed with the interior.

To increase strength, I will make thin 'stringers' before glassing the interior, by putting up strips of wood as coring up the four corners, along the roof edge, and also at intervals along the roof and sides. This will somewhat complicate the glassing process, but you can help the transition and eliminate voids by making a thickened epoxy seal all around the stringer cores that will act as a sort of ramp up and down for the fiberglass.

So far I only have one hole in my sample build—the door. As I glassed over the interior, I should have been careful to fully seal the edges of that cut and glass them over as well. This is the point that you may want to cut any windows and also any secondary egress points and any access panels.

To protect the epoxy from UV damage and also to smooth out the surface, the next step is to apply a coating onto the entire surface of the laminate, inside and out. This will be a non-structural thickener of some sort, such as epoxy mixed with micro-balloons. Once this thickener is applied and dry it can be sanded smooth to prepare the surface for painting. The paint, inside and out, must be a UV blocker type in order to protect the epoxy, which may weaken over time if subjected to UV radiation.

Glassing the interior ceiling will be a pain, as epoxy is a liquid before hardening. Use a thicker epoxy or add just a touch of thickening agent, or both. Peel Ply can be very helpful. You could also pre-imbue the fiberglass with epoxy, roll it up into a bundle, then unroll it slowly along the ceiling, using your roller to smooth it onto the surface along the way. The colder the temperature is the thicker epoxy will get, so you could time your work to do that bit at a cold moment. Different formulations of epoxy will also have a different thickness at a given temperature.

Note that when working with epoxy every precaution should be taken to keep it, and the fumes, off of your skin. So for my sample build I will be in full suit and gloves, with a breath mask and face shield. For the inside ventilation will be a problem, so I might even run an airline to the outside while working in there. This may seem excessive and be certainly be uncomfortable to work in, but epoxy sensitization is no joke. A lot of people have gone without precautions when working with epoxy and have become sensitized—meaning that they can never work with it again without getting an allergic reaction. There may also be long term health effects from excessive exposure. After the resin is fully cured it is inert and safe to handle.

This construction method is labor intensive, as you may notice, but it does have several advantages. It is very strong and will resist most types of damage. It is impervious to weather. Any repairs can be accomplished by you and need not be hired out. The materials are not costly. It is also a pretty simple matter to cut small holes later on, as long as the proper steps are taken to protect the inner layers. This construction method is usually limited to marine use, but I have chosen it for my sample build here to point out that it has applications for wheeled mobile living also.

Cutting and Filling

Next is to plan out and commence with cutting doors, windows, ports, utility openings, etc, unless you have already done so. I suggest that you have a very good idea of the final internal and external layout of your trailer before you start the first cut. Measurement, and planning, will save a lot of hassles and also help reduce mistakes. Depending on your build methods, this step might be done at different times. It is easier to construct a laminate structure intact without worrying about holes and extra edges, but you could still cut every opening before putting down any laminate. You could also build the whole structure intact, as I have suggested for this sample build, before cutting the appropriate holes.

You should be able to source all of your individual fitting items from manufacturers for or suppliers of the RV/travel trailer industry. You can also choose a type of travel trailer that you like and use it as a base model, with variations as you find something you like better or an easier way to fulfill a certain need. This sample build, for example, thus far bears a strong resemblance to an Impression 25RB.

It is possible to build or modify a stealth-type trailer as your mobile living solution. In that case you will want to have all of your roof emplacements be low profile and have all of your utility ports be located underneath the trailer. It might be better to settle for semi-stealth, keeping the sides or just one side smooth while putting what you like on the roof and the other side. That way you could have a roof-mounted air conditioner and/or heat pump, vent fans, monocrystalline panels, etc. If you must keep the trailer lower profile you could follow part of the box-truck build and keep a sectioned off utility area at the rear of the trailer. Air conditioners, propane tanks, and vents can all be put here instead of the more traditional mounts. If you make a vent inlet underneath the forward portion of the trailer and another one, just a subtle louver overhang, at the top rear you could maintain full ventilation from front to back without a standard roof vent.

As of now, for my sample build, I have only a laminate box on a frame, so there is still plenty of work to do. The rear of the box was glassed over without any allowance made for doors, but that is fine. Part of the beauty of laminate epoxy construction is that you can always go back and change things later without sacrificing strength or integrity. If surfaces are prepared correctly new epoxy will bond just fine to old epoxy.

So for the rear doors I can just cut out what I need from the rear facing of the trailer box. The doors can be mounted on the flange that I leave up and that which I cut out will become the new doors. All of the coring must be re-encapsulated and glassed over. The same for any holes that are drilled to mount hardware. Every cut surface must be filled and smoothed and painted again so that all epoxy is protected from sunlight. This is a lot of detailed work and you may not consider the method to be worth it. In that case, just alter your plans for the initial build to leave this space open. That will save you from cutting a door to get inside for the interior glassing. However, you will need to fabricate the door panels separately instead of using the cutouts.

I then have rear barn doors and a side door on the passenger side near the front. Say I also build that side door from the panel section I cut out for the door opening. I will also want at least one roof vent, but to go any further I will need to plan out the interior layout in order to integrate that with the exterior fittings.

Layout

I will have a utility space in back, just inside the rear doors, four feet long and the width of the trailer. This will give me a place to mount air conditioning units and propane tanks as well as for general storage. At the top rear of this space, just above the barn doors, there will be a long vent hole. This will be screened and partially covered over on the outside, to keep bugs and rain out and reduce visibility, but will provide constant ventilation. When cutting the doors I left a flange on the sides and top and a small lip on the bottom, for structural reasons. This vent will be in the top flange. There will be a full bulkhead wall between this utility space and the main cabin.

The bathroom will be located in the front section of the build. This in turn will be sectioned off from the rest of the build by a full bulkhead wall and door. For this build I will posit a cassette toilet on the passenger side of the bathroom space, with an exterior access panel to remove and empty the cassette. Constructing this will be a matter of cutting the panel out, re-finishing it and that area, and putting it back in place but on hinges and with a latch. Inside, an insulated box will be made for the toilet/cassette division. So the shower will be against the driver side. There will be room for a sink as well and some storage space.

Just back of the bathroom on the passenger side will be the side door. Just back of that on the same side will be an oblong tinted window looking onto the kitchen counterspace. Opposite the kitchen counter on the driver side will be a convertible table/bed, with a walkway in between.

We will be constructing all of this in an 8ft by 26ft area, minus the thickness of the walls and any insulation. If we account 4ft for the rear utility area and the same for the bathroom, we are down to less than 18ft of length. We can apportion 7ft of that to the table/bed on one side and the same on the other side for a spacious kitchen, past the side door. The remaining 11ft, minus what was used for the insulation and the bulkhead walls, can be apportioned as desired. I will put a triple bunk arrangement on one side for extra sleeping space followed by storage cabinets. On the other side I will posit more storage configured as convenient, but also a washer/dryer space, an extra freezer, and a desk area to use as a workstation. There will be an open walkway in the middle for full pass-thru to the rear doors.

With the internal layout planned I can get back to cutting and filling holes. There will be one roof vent fan above the bathroom, set back a bit from the front so it will be just inside the door for the bathroom. There will be two further roof vent fans, given the length of the trailer, one just inside the rear bulkhead and another above the rear of the kitchen area. This should still leave plenty of space on the roof for solar and any antennae or other electronics.

I will follow standard practice in designating the bottom of the trailer as utility systems space. Given our nominal height of 11ft for the trailer, if we assume 2ft of ground clearance and assign just under 7ft for cabin height, we are left with just under 2ft of vertical space, the length and width of the trailer, for this bottom area. It will be insulated and heated right along with the rest of the build, will also be largely sectioned off by the cabin floor. There will be access panels up into the cabin and to the exterior as appropriate, which I will need to cut and refinish as I did for the cassette toilet access.

Systems

Heating

This build platform is very well suited to a radiant heating system. I will be building in flooring for the cabin anyway—the tubing for the radiant heat can be incorporated into the floor. If the tubing is tacked up to the bottom of the floor it will warm the cabin as the heat rises and also keep the underfloor spaces warm.

Secondary heating can be provided for by means of an air duct system run through the same underfloor spaces. This will be routed through a propane (LPG) heater. The air duct system can also be used for air filtration and cooling.

Water

Given the build size there should be more than one water tank. I will posit at least one tank placed up in the cabin overhead, to provide gravity fed water when that is desired. There will also be two more tanks in the underfloor area. All tanks will be linked for cross-filling and there will be one or more inline water pumps. There will be an exterior port to fill one of the underfloor water tanks. A low-power electric water heater will provide warm water when desired. The propane heater could also be used for water heating, to get hot water.

Wastage

The cassette toilet has been mentioned. A camp toilet could be used as a secondary solution for black waste, but the cassette systems will mostly sell extra cassettes, so capacity can be increased by having extra cassettes on hand. One or more graywater tanks can be placed in the underfloor space, with drains for disposal when appropriate.Solid waste can be sorted and compacted, with either a manual or electric compactor.

Networking

This build calls for a full wired internal network, which can be used for information flow and also command and control of any networked components. It can also be used for device internet access.

External networking can be fulfilled by several possible solutions and should be tailored to the needs of the inhabitants. I would want to have wifi with range extender, cellular with range extender, and possibly satellite.

Propulsion

Now for the power assist. Wheeled electric vehicles have been powered by placing an electric motor in one or more wheel hubs, by placing a motor in the axle that runs between the wheels, or by placing a motor in the same place as a standard internal combustion engine—under the hood.

In all of these cases gearing systems are used for mechanical power transmission of the rotational force generated by the electric motor. Gearing can also be used for the purpose of increasing torque by reducing shaft speed without altering power output—dropping down to a smaller gear will increase the rotational force (torque) that is produced.

For this custom build we could order custom hub motors mounted to a custom axle, or instead a full powered axle arrangement...but that would be more expensive than the rest of the build altogether. Instead, I propose replacing one or both axles of the trailer with an axle that is already mounted with a driveshaft and geared power transfer arrangement. The junk yards are full of these, as every rear wheel drive vehicle uses a driveshaft and rear axle to transmit the force generated by the engine to the rear tires. Skipping the junk yard, we could find a number of aftermarket drive-axles, new or used, from many different retailers.

The only trick would be to source an axle that will fit the trailer build. But since we are still in the planning stage we could just start with the dimensions and attachment points of the axles when designing the trailer frame. In any case the frame would have to be redesigned in order to accommodate the electric motor mounting. This could be kept parallel to the wheel axle (flat driveshaft in relation to the ground and located under the frame), but it seems to me that doing so would subject the electric motor to unnecessary exposure to the elements and also the risk of damage from impact. Instead, the driveshaft could be run up at a shallow angle and made to protrude into the underfloor compartment of the trailer superstructure. This should make no difference in the power transfer to the wheels. With the upward shaft angle both axles could be motorized, instead of just the front one. This would also make it easier to match the axle sizes, as they could be identical parts.

With the axle in place the mechanical problem becomes a matter of coupling the output shaft of the electric motor to the drive-axle. A gear reducer may also be considered, in order to increase torque output and reduce motor output speed. Because the turning speed of the driveshaft will be the same speed as the rotational speed of the tires (unless there is a reduction in the rear differential), this should be matched to desired wheel speed. The range of rotational speed of the electric motor used will have a direct correlation to the range of the rotational speed of the tires. This must be calculated when choosing the mechanical parts of the system.

It will start at zero, of course, but you will want the tires to be able to rotate at the same speed that the tires of the towing vehicle do. So the nominal speed of the electric motor will need to correspond to the maximum expected vehicle speed. And you will not be able to go any faster, so there should be some excess capacity. For example, if I want to go 60mph with 30in diameter tires, they will need to rotate at around 700rpm. If the electric motor used has a max rotational speed of 3600rpm, then the cumulative gear reduction ratio can be no more than 5.1 or the tires will not be able to rotate fast enough. If the motor has a max rotational speed of 1200 rpm, then the cumulative gear reduction ratio can be no more than 1.7. So choosing an appropriate gear ratio will be a matter of balancing desired maximum tire rotational speed against the added torque of a gear reduction. In this application extra torque is desirable to assist in acceleration of the trailer, though it will limit top speed. Also, the lower the fraction of maximum motor speed that is being utilized, the lower the electrical power efficiency of the motor will be. So you will want your maximum trailer speed to be somewhat close to your normal cruising highway speed in order to keep the electric motor use efficient.

With the motor and power transmission to the tires in place, we must also account for control of the motor and powering the motor. Source an appropriate motor and controller, or two motors and one controller. One VFD (variable frequency drive) controller can be used to handle both motors if you have a motor for each axle (though it must be able to handle the full power load for both motors). Remember that the trailer need not be able to move fast on its own, only take some of the load off the towing vehicle. Something like two 30HP motors would be plenty; you could likely get by with two 10HP motors. This choice will depend upon the final weight of your trailer as built. Set up cooling arrangements for your motors and the controller, with air or liquid cooling.

The command interface used for the motor controller will need to be run to the driver seat of the towing vehicle. There are a number of ways this can be accomplished. If you plan to tow with the same vehicle often then a plug adapter could be fit in right next to the plug for the trailer brake lights and turn signals. The towing vehicle could then have appropriate controls installed and the wires run to those. It may instead be possible to enable remote control of the trailer power assist by using a wireless interface. This will require custom programming and a designed interface, but should work and will permit use for any number of towing vehicles. Alternatively, just have your motor control interface on the end of a long flexible cord that can be taken forward and through the window of the towing vehicle. This method will be more robust than the wireless method and will also permit use with any towing vehicle, but will be somewhat awkward in practice. Minimal controls required will be a throttle control for the motors and possibly a toggle to trigger regen.

You will also need to provide appropriate electrical power to the motors and motor controller. Higher voltage will be better, in order to keep amp draws down. You could go as high as 700V or so, which will really reduce amp draws. For safety reasons and because the motors used will be fairly low power, something 72V or less is more appropriate. Keep in mind that the motor controller will require a very specific input voltage and your battery bank must be designed in regards to your chosen motor controller.

Electricity

I will posit a main house battery bank, which will also be used for propulsion, at 48V. Power for the drive motors will come directly off of this bank. AC power will be inverted off of the battery bank by an inverter/charger, which will also charge the battery from either shore power or an optional generator. This will be multiple cascaded inverters if necessary. All DC loads will be run through DC-DC converters in order to step down to the desired voltage. Though DC appliances will be 48V where possible in order to not have to run everything through a converter. Alternatively, depending on system needs, all DC loads can be run through the AC system—this will involve power losses, as all DC power will be inverted twice, but a DC-DC converter will also convert to AC and back to the appropriate DC voltage, entailing those same power losses.

The battery bank will need to be somewhat large. I would suggest at least 200 Amp-hours at 48V. 400 Amp-hours would be better. Which would require the equivalent of sixteen standard batteries. More than that would be even better, and the battery bank must be lithium in order to keep up with the high draw of the propulsion motors. On the bright side, the large battery bank should be more than capable of keeping up with house loads.

For charging, this build will require a good sized propane (LPG) generator, the mentioned shore power capability, and also a large solar panel installation. There should be room for fourteen or fifteen 200W monocrystalline panels on the roof, even working around the vent fan openings. If they are wired in three clusters of five, providing around 60V each and rated for 1000W, they can be run down to the battery bank, each cluster through a separate controller, and provide a good charging voltage for the 48V bank.

I will not go any further into the required electrical system components. There is enough here for the broad outlines and this build is too hypothetical at this point to provide extensive detail for all of the various configurations. If you have propulsion motors then the electrical system must first be sized and tailored to furnish power to those. If you do not have propulsion motors then your system must be designed to handle what loads you do expect.

Summary and Conclusion

This final wheeled build is somewhat lighter on detail than the others, but I think I have given enough here to establish the necessary concepts for the build. Every custom build will be different in particulars, but all of them will follow certain parameters which I think have been made clear here. Your build must be a singular integrated solution in which all of the major components are designed in conjunction. One thing leads to another, from the drive-train to the frame to the superstructure to the electrical system.

The more that you want your build to be capable of the more expensive it will be. The propulsion system for this build as stated, and the required beefy electrical system, will cost several times more, alone, than the rest of the build put together. Largely because of the cost of the batteries, but the other major components are also expensive. All of which is unnecessary if the towing vehicle is capable of towing the full weight of the trailer...which will be made somewhat heavier anyway because of the extra components to provide propulsion. Doing away with the electric propulsion, which may be unnecessary, will save considerable amounts of both weight and money.

There is a middle ground. The drive axle(s) alone will add some weight to the build but not a great deal. What if we design the 'propulsion' system only to provide regen power when braking, with no expected contribution to motive power? In effect this will mean connecting a generator to the driveshaft instead of a motor. There will be no need for high power motors or an expensive controller, only a toggle set to bring the generator into load whenever it is desired to slow down the joined vehicles. And every time power will be put back into the battery bank.

Alternatively, do have some propulsion but size the motors and battery bank at a lower level. Smaller motors will mean a less expensive controller and also less weight. This will save considerable costs and still provide some motive force and regen capability. Just use in moderation. If the battery bank gets low, only use the motors for regen until levels raise back up.

A custom trailer build, or even a converted trailer build, is more than capable of meeting all life needs at a high level of fulfillment. I have provided one example here of a build method that can be accomplished by one individual who is willing to learn and take care (and time) with the build. Above all, I hope that I have stressed the need for extensive planning. A good plan, considering every aspect of the final product, will not itself make for a good build. But a good build may well be impossible without a good plan.

There are many different options for living mobile on wheels. This is just one of them...and possibly not a very good one. In part this electric trailer build is included here to work through the possibilities, for you and also for me, of what we can do with our current level of technology (at least that which is available to civilians) and what it will cost to do so. You can have a self-propelled trailer with an electrical system capable of handling almost any power draw—if you are willing to pay for it. If not, there are still many other possibilities to consider.

References and Further Research

drivinglaws.aaa.com/tag/trailer-dimensions

mechanicalelements.com/trailer-axles-101

www.consumerreports.org/other-motor-vehicles/beginners-guide-to-rv-trailers

mechanicalelements.com/how-to-setup-a-trailer-frame

rvshare.com/blog/homemade-camper

rvshare.com/blog/custom-teardrop

camperreport.com/travel-trailer-camping-guide-beginners

newatlas.com/dethleffs-electric-coco-caravan/56056

www.gorv.com.au/world-first-hybrid-drive-caravan-system

youtu.be/PmeDIQqtYil
An informative video that gives a close look at the components of a trailer axle.

youtu.be/iEtZ0Ioiy24
Shows a steel trailer frame construction.

youtu.be/bHF-qr0Z5AA
A travel trailer build from scratch.

youtu.be/AWbGoRzvFPg
Video series on building a larger enclosed trailer.

youtu.be/cxT2gcyCvvE
Picture time-lapse of a nice looking teardrop trailer build.

youtu.be/o9x3J84CrN0
Time-lapse of converting a cargo trailer into a camper.

youtu.be/Xx9OmerbnS4
A cargo trailer conversion series.

25.

The Sailboat Refit

There are several different rationales that might lead you to choose a sailboat as your marine living platform. You might already know how to sail and enjoy doing so. Perhaps you like racing or the social aspects of the sailing crowd or even just enjoy solitary sailing—but you choose sailboats for preference rather than other considerations. You might instead be drawn to the romantic aspects of the platform—harnessing wind and wave to explore the world beyond the horizon. These and more will always be valid reasons and people will continue to spend millions on fulfilling their sailing dreams. But many people choose sailboats over other marine platforms because it is the least expensive way to get started in long distance cruising. Though not the easiest. For shorter distances or if you will only stay in one area a motorboat will be much easier.

Sailing is a skill. It is not difficult to get started and, given a sufficient amount of practice, there are no barriers to expertise that cannot be overcome with time and dedication and a modicum of intelligence. Getting that practice can be the sticking point, as it will always require that you are out on a boat sailing. This is not something that the majority of people are able to do as part of their normal lives. But it is at least possible to achieve for anyone with access to a boat and a body of water.

Once you have a boat though, and are able to at least get around without managing to sink, the distance you can go will not be limited by fuel or your cash reserves as such, but instead only by any navigational barriers and the cruising capacity of your boat. The world itself opens up before you and new horizons beckon...or at least that is the dream that gets many people into a sailboat. In practice, there are any number of further considerations and limitations, which may or may not push you right back out of the sailboat life.

In a way you could think of sailboats as entry-level marine living. It is possible to get by with very little money once you have your platform kitted out. Some people have been known to set out sailing and just earn what money they need as they travel. And acquiring a used sailboat is fairly cheap—much cheaper than buying real estate. With the increasing number of remote work options out there this becomes more and more viable. As global broadband internet access efforts come to fruition you will truly be able to get online and work anywhere in the world, on land or at sea. All you have to do to get started is find a cheap boat to buy and move on in, right?

Not so much. If you are extremely lucky, as in winning the lottery lucky, you will find a seller who does not care about money and who will sell you a fully cruise capable sailboat in good condition for a dollar. Otherwise you will have to contend with the strange conditions of the boat market, the high costs of parts and labor for marine construction and repair, and the constant corrosion and wear that boats are subjected to in a marine environment. Really you will have to deal with these things anyway once you have a boat, no matter how good the initial condition. Maintenance is ongoing. Damage can occur at any time. And the cheaper the boat that you initially acquire is, the less value there will be in the boat and the more money you will have to put into it over time.

But don't let me discourage you. If you are dedicated and engage in careful planning, if you are willing to learn and to do work on the boat yourself, and if you operate within carefully defined and limited goals, then you can engage in marine living in a sailboat quite successfully. Every aspect of a sailboat can be repaired or redesigned by the owner. Every need has multiple possible solutions.

Platform

Most sailboats are monohulls. There are many reasons why you might prefer a multihull instead and if so I encourage you to read on to my other sample builds, but for most people getting into sailing, especially for those on a smaller budget, it will be with a monohull.

What this means is that all of the boats that you may be looking at will have certain aspects in common—really much more in common than they have differences, at least in terms of the configuration. They will all have an elongated inverted bowl shaped hull that is designed, on the whole, to keep water on the outside and so stay floating, and also designed for movement in only one direction. They will all have at least one mast on which to mount the sails, and usually a large rotating boom as well. And they will all have a large amount of ballast weight at the bottom in order to counterbalance the forces upon the mast(s) and so keep the boat from flipping over when the wind blows. These major design points will determine the capabilities and also the limitations of the platform as a whole.

Beyond them, however, there is a very wide degree of variation within the monohull genre. Boats have been designed for racing, for cruising, for day sailing, and for other purposes. Boats will be shorter or longer, which will often though not always correspond to the boat overall (encapsulated space) being smaller or larger. A longer boat may be narrow and so have less interior space. This is especially true for racing boats that are designed to move through the water easier. Maximum speed for a displacement style hull will largely be determined by length, but a narrower hull form will have less resistance to movement through the water and so will be able to get up to hull speed more easily. So if you want more interior space for a given length do not go with a boat designed for racing.

The length of your boat will have a large impact on costs for maintenance and upkeep. Marinas and boatyards scale their prices according to the length of the vessel. So a forty footer will end up paying more for services than will a thirty footer. Of course, the forty footer will also be able to sail faster and will (probably) have more interior space than the thirty footer. More interior space means greater capacity to fulfill living needs. This is just one of the many trade-offs involved in choosing a boat.

I will not get too far into further describing the variations in the monohull platform, as that would require a book of its own to do properly. Instead, I will allow the particulars of my sample refit to suggest to you further differences. For every specification that I mention below, there is another boat out there where someone did things differently.

For my sample refit I have chosen a Catalina 30. This is a good solid platform for long term living, for one or two people. It is easy to sail but also has a substantial amount of interior room for a thirty footer. These are very popular boats and thousands were produced. They are widely available and can be obtained at low prices, but are also pretty well built and will be durable if properly maintained.

This is an entry level platform and a small boat, all things considered. Almost everyone who has lived on a sailboat has at least occasionally desired to move up to a larger boat. Some people seem to think about nothing else—which is a waste of time and energy if you ask me. But do consider a larger boat first if that is at all within the scope of your budget. This size is about the smallest that I would consider for long term living, for one person and certainly for two people.

Specs

1982 Catalina 30 (Mk1)
Standard mast, standard keel, no bowsprit.
Hull type: monohull, fin keel with spade rudder (wheel steering)
Rigging type: masthead sloop
Length overall: 29.92ft
Length at waterline: 25ft
Beam: 10.83ft
Max draft: 5.25ft
Interior headroom: 6.25ft max
Displacement (total): 10,200lb
Ballast weight: 4,200lb
Fiberglass construction with lead ballast
Power: Universal 5411 diesel auxiliary propulsion, 21 gallon fuel capacity
Water tanks: 43 gallons
Designed by Frank V. Butler and built by Catalina Yachts.
Price estimate: I have seen these listed, in usable condition, between $6k and $20k.

This boat is nearly forty years old, so every single aspect of the boat should be inspected and may need repair or replacement. Say for the purposes of this hypothetical build that I just dove right in and bought a (very low priced) boat at my local marina. It was floating when I bought it, so I know that much, but everything else is in unknown condition. I could instead have had a full survey done (which can be expensive and so not justified for a cheap boat) or at least used a guidebook about how to do my own survey. Doing so will save time and money and may give you some idea about what you will need to do to the boat to get it ready to go. There will always be something. But I know that not everyone will do this so I will start out as the proud new owner of a boat that I have not even set foot on.

The main exterior spaces are the rear cockpit, possibly with a Bimini or awning over it, and the deck forward. Inside, there is a kitchen space, a quarter berth under the starboard side (on the right, facing forward) of the cockpit, a nav station just forward of that and opposite the kitchen, a settee to starboard forward of that, and opposite a port-side table/bed. There is a head (toilet/bathroom area) just forward of the table/bed, with storage opposite, and a v-berth forward of there, with tankage or storage underneath. The settee and benches of the table/bed also have storage or systems underneath. The wide beam of the vessel makes for an open, roomy feeling interior.

Purpose

So what do I want to do with my boat? If all I want to do is live at the marina in the same slip it was in when I purchased, then the boat systems will matter much less than interior alterations. If I just want this thing for day sailing or weekend trips out, I will not require very robust systems at all. But if I plan on extensive cruising of any sort then there will be much to do. Say that I do plan on deep sea cruising. This boat was not really designed with that in mind, so I will have to make compromises (and be very careful about rough weather), but the platform is capable of doing so. People have sailed around the world in smaller boats and ones more lightly built.

Planning

Given that stated purpose I can work on planning out my need fulfillment levels. Most solutions will be somewhat different from those of the wheeled solutions, and very different in some cases, but some of these will be met in the same ways and even with the same components. So if you are moving from a van to your sailboat, for example, you can bring a lot of your stuff with you, such as your Electricity and Networking and Applications components.

High: Planning

Medium: Address, Air, Applications, Cooling, Electricity, Food, Health, Heating, Networking, Pests, Propulsion, Sanitation, Security, Space, Stopping, Structure, Wastage, Water

Low: Philosophy

I have gone against the grain here and relegated philosophy to a low level of fulfillment. Perhaps the planned journeys will inspire greater need for deliberate thought. Extensive travel certainly seems to have that effect on many people.

Planning will very much need extensive efforts. The theme here is global cruising on a budget, so a dearth in material things must be compensated for by careful planning and full awareness. To include an understanding of the conditions which may require abandoning the project or altering goals.

But most needs will be met at a moderate level of fulfillment. Which may be borderline to requirements in some cases, given the purpose of extensive cruising, but should just make fulfilling that purpose possible. With luck.

Major design choices have already been determined by the platform itself. I will not be doing extensive alterations to the hull itself (else I should have chosen a different boat) or the rig (which is just possible, but in most cases should also mean choosing a different boat). Auxiliary propulsion can certainly be altered, and I will include a section below about optionally switching to electric drive for the propeller. The internal layout will not be significantly altered, though some areas will be repurposed. The water, plumbing, toilet, kitchen, and electrical systems will all be thoroughly overhauled, and I anticipate replacing most or all system components. This is a forty year old vessel, and while some things will still work fine and others may have been replaced over the years, no single thing is likely to be in optimal condition.

Refit

Hull and Deck

The first consideration will always be the hull of the vessel. It will not float for long without an intact hull and nothing else is possible without a floating boat. This boat has a two part hull, which is not uncommon with fiberglass production built boats. The deck itself is one piece, and is joined to the lower hull (otherwise just called the hull proper) at the top edge of the flat area. The lower hull down from there is all one piece.

In the water, you cannot do much exterior work on the lower hull, only cleaning and emergency patching. Out of the water (also called being on the hard) you can do whatever you want to with it, as long as it is ok with the owners of the boatyard or other place you have it sitting. Many of the things mentioned below, especially interior work, can also be done while in the water, but I will assume from this point forward that I have had the boat hauled out and am working on the hard.

The lower hull itself has two main exterior sections—that which is normally below water and everything else which is above the waterline. Boat waterlines are part of the design and very noticeable when hauled out as there should be a distinctive painted demarcation. Above the waterline, the hull should be checked for soft spots and the condition of the paint. Alternatively, strip all of the paint off in order to get a good look at the structure. Any repairs at that point can be done in epoxy, regardless of the initial resin used. This will involve sanding smooth any holes or bad spots, tapered down to the hole or center, and then building back up with the appropriate type of fiberglass, layered and embedded in epoxy. After that hardens fully, the surface should be sanded smooth again and prepped to receive paint. If you are working with epoxy then the paint must be UV-blocking or it will weaken over time. Afterward you will need to repaint the hull above the waterline.

The hull below the waterline will have a more complex shape, but the procedures for inspection and repair are similar. You can check for soft spots or obvious damage with the paint on, but to make a really thorough inspection you must first strip off the paint. Damage to the fiberglass can be handled the same way. The keel itself for this boat is a shaped piece of lead which is bolted on to the fiberglass hull. The join area is subject to cracking and separation and should be carefully inspected and repaired, by removing the keel if necessary. The keel should also be faired and sanded very smooth before painting, or repainting, as the lead surface itself is pitted and was originally only rough faired at the factory.

Other areas to note are the support for the propeller and the rudder mounting. I have seen some Catalinas which hang a rudder off the back and control it with a post and tiller, but this boat has a wheel arrangement and the rudder is below the hull. The rudder mounting on the hull is a high stress area and should be inspected. The rudder itself is subject to very high stress and should also be carefully inspected. There will likely be some play in the rudder stock, but anything more serious should be addressed. The propeller shaft is run out of the hull at an angle just behind the keel. Close to the propeller is a metal piece that comes down from the hull and is also bolted on above. Bottom paint has different requirements than paint that will normally be above the water and should be chosen accordingly.

There will also be a number of thru-hulls, both above and below the waterline. The propeller shaft itself is run through a thru-hull and has a special arrangement to stop water from getting in while still permitting the propeller to spin. All other thru-hulls should be simpler, in that they do not need to rotate, but they will still wear out over time and need replacement.

The hull/deck joint/seal should be a noticeable band running all the way around the top outside edge of the hull. Sometimes it is painted for accent. The hull/deck joint on the Catalina 30, like many other production boats, is of a type that is not very strong flexurally and will allow leaks in heavy seas or with things mounted off the rails, so I may need to redo the entire thing. Which will be a long and painful process. This is probably the worst job about using one of these boats for extended cruising, but it must be done unless I do not mind water coming in every time it rains or every time the boat has a sharp heel. Not to mention problems with mildew and general humidity control. I have lived on one of these boats, briefly, and would not have wanted to take it out of harbor without redoing that joint. For my sample build I will pull up the whole deck, clean up the joint, and redo with a full glassed joint. As an alternative that would not require raising the deck up, you could remove the screws that were used to seal the joint by the builder, repair and reinforce the fiberglass, drill out the holes wider, and sink actual bolts through to backing plates in the interior. This will not be as strong as fully glassing the joint to form a monocoque hull, but will still be very much better than the original design.

And while I am at it I should also inspect the deck itself, which includes the cabin top and the cockpit area as well as the flat bits forward. The deck will be cored fiberglass in places, unlike the mostly solid fiberglass of the hull, and any leakage will have severely weakened the coring material, which might be either plywood or balsa. Any holes in the deck will probably entail much more extensive repairs because the coring material for that section may be ruined. Just assess the full extent of the problem, cut out the bad parts, and rebuild with your own glass and coring. Pay careful attention when inspecting the area around the mast, the chain plate and cleat mounting areas, and also the seat areas in the cockpit and the wheel pedestal mount. These are the highest stress parts of the deck other than the joint with the hull.

Do not forget some kind of non-skid additive to the deck paint or finish. There are various methods for this but the simplest is just to add a bit of sand to one of the upper paint layers. It has previously been popular to surface the upper deck of even fiberglass boats with something like teak flooring. This can be nice and will offer a pretty good surface grip, but if this has been done to your boat more than ten years in the past there are likely to be problems forming.

The stanchions (safety rail upright supports) may need repair or just reinforcement. As I will want to mount certain hardware on them for offshore cruising I will look into reinforcement while working on the rest of the deck.

As a final note on the hull, I would at least consider stripping the entire outer hull down to the glass (while I had the deck raised up anyway) and adding two or three reinforcing layers of bi-axial or tri-axial fiberglass embedded in epoxy. This will strengthen the hull against the strain of off-shore cruising without having to alter the interior. Another (possibly better) option might be to reinforce the hull interior at the existing stringers or by adding new ones, but this would involve extensive tearing out in the interior. Layered epoxy on the hull will also stop any chance of hull blistering, though this is more normally accomplished with the use of epoxy based undercoat layers before painting. While I was doing this I would also enlarge upon the drain arrangements for the cockpit, which is large enough for this model that it may endanger the boat if filled with water due to heavy weather.

Ports and Hatches

The door into the cabin from the cockpit (otherwise known as a companionway) is the main way in or out of the interior, via steps just inside down to the cabin level. Fortunately it is a wide doorway. Given the age of my sample boat and the various ways I have seen people attempt to cover the companionway opening, I will posit that a complete rebuild of the doorway and door will be required. Which is nice in a way because it will allow me to tailor my solution to my own preferences and also to increase the security of the boat with robust locking arrangements.

There should also be at least one hatch forward on the boat deck. Depending on your latch arrangement this may not permit egress, but in any case should be designed or redesigned as an alternative point of entry or exit. It is also a fairly simple matter to retrofit older Catalinas with the better vent hatch arrangements found in newer models. I will posit one vent hatch installed just back of the mast in the main cabin, rebuilding the main portal hatch above the v-berth, and installing two solar vent/fans, one in the head and another opposite that just starboard of the head.

Together with the doorway to the cockpit these hatches should provide more than adequate ventilation for the interior, even in bad weather as long as drainage is accounted for. To complete the airflow arrangement some kind of air cover will be needed for the cockpit, which will form a negative pressure zone when the front hatch is open and so make for some (unpowered) airflow even in mostly still air.

To fulfill this and other purposes I will posit a full hardtop with front windshield for the cockpit, with heavy synthetic side covers (and possibly rear) that can be drawn back or removed. As permitted by the line and winch arrangements. For visibility the side panels should be the type with transparent plastic set into the center of the panels. This is very non-standard for the platform and will require a custom build, but will facilitate sailing in rough weather and give me a place to mount solar panels, in addition to improving airflow. Having a sunshade for the cockpit is also nice. There should be plenty of space for this underneath the boom.

All other ports in the deck should be inspected. Mostly this will consist of the windows in the main cabin and in the head, but there are also the fill-ports for fuel and water and the plug for shore power and one for waste pump-out. The windows (also called port-holes or just ports) are likely to be a problem area and will need repair if not full replacement.

Steering, Mast, Sails, and Rigging

The rudder itself and mounting should have been inspected as part of the hull, but that still leaves the wheel or rudder staff arrangement and any autopilot. Given that my boat has a wheel already, if there is no autopilot in place I would go with an on-wheel type, which could be wired down through the wheel pedestal. In addition I would carefully check over the wheel-rudder linkage hardware.

The mast for this boat is an older style and may need replaced unless it is in good condition. Non-anodized aluminum was used, so painting is appropriate for both mast and boom. The mast compression mount (down through the cabin to the keel) will originally have been wood, so that will most likely need replaced as well unless it already has been. At a minimum it should be inspected and reinforced. Regardless of whether I will be replacing the mast and boom, all joints and hardware should be inspected and replaced as necessary.

The original mast spreaders for this boat were wooden and should be replaced regardless of condition for the purposes of off-shore cruising. The standing rigging (the wires coming down from the mast) will also be replaced regardless of condition, and I will go one gage higher as the original design was somewhat weaker than will be desired.

The chain plates that the standing rigging are attached to, for this vessel type, have been known to become damaged or even fail outright. As part of the deck refit, I will re-set (or replace) the chain plates and also insert aluminum reinforcement plates underneath.

The sails should be inspected and repaired, if possible, or otherwise outright replaced unless relatively unused. I think that I will be able to get by fine with two sets each for jib and main, as long as they are new, and will not otherwise bother with additional sails. My preference is for roller furling arrangements and I will put that in place if possible, but will otherwise keep the sailing mechanisms as originally designed.

The lines should likewise be replaced if at all worn and extra line, sufficient at least to redo the entire running rigging, should be kept on hand. Winches and cleats should likewise be inspected and repaired or replaced as necessary. I do not mind manual winches and so those will be used for preference instead of powered winches. This will help to save on power draw for the build.

Navigation

Navigation instruments should be carefully inspected. As this is an older vessel I may consider upgrades even if current electronics are in good condition. There should be at least one compass on the wheel pedestal and possibly more elsewhere. The sonar (depth finder or fish finder) will likely need to have an installation on the outside bottom of the hull, which will require either its own thru-hull or at least a cord run up the side.

Things like sonar, radar, and satellite weather are luxuries, but do not require overmuch power draw and can be very useful. This boat will have sonar, radar, and a satphone that gives weather reports. Sonar is inexpensive and useful. Radar can be a very important navigational boon in low visibility conditions, but I will choose a lower power version to save on power draw and also cost, even though this will limit range. Longer range weather information can be obtained from the satphone. All of these will be fed into a chart plotter if possible, or a separate multi-function display if not. I will still keep a chart plotter with a full load of digital charts for my area.

Food and Water

Kitchen appliances will be a toss up and dependent on the condition of what is installed. Original equipment for cooking was a gimbal mounted alcohol stove, I think. I may keep that if in good condition but would rather not, as the alcohol can be hard to find and cooking with it can be tricky. There is a good-sized refrigerator/cooler compartment but I would probably have to redo the hardware entirely for full refrigeration. I will do so, also checking over the insulation while disassembled.

There should be two sinks and one tap each for fresh and salt water. The metal sinks will need to be checked for corrosion and the drains and lines inspected. The taps and lines will also need to be inspected. Most likely I will end up replacing all of this hardware except possibly the sinks and taps themselves.

There is a good sized fresh main water tank (under the v-berth) and should also be a secondary tank (perhaps under the starboard settee), but I will still keep at least ten gallons (two jerrycans) of reserve water. The water tank itself and all fittings and lines should be inspected and replaced as necessary. There should be a small 12V water pump for moving the fresh water around. This is unlikely to be in good condition and will need replaced along with any other old electronics.

There may be a small water heater located under one of the cabinets in the kitchen. I would inspect this for condition along with the rest of the water system, but as a matter of personal preference may choose to remove it even if in ok condition. I opt for cold showers and extra storage space is always nice.

Sanitation and Wastage

There should be a foot pump at the kitchen sink for drawing in raw water. I would also want to install a hose in the cockpit for general purposes, possibly with the option of switching between salt and fresh water streams. The freshwater option could be run from existing water lines and would be pumped by the freshwater pump mentioned. This would not work for the saltwater and I would not want to put in an extra thru-hull, but an inlet hose could be lowered over the side. Or I could just use the same thru-hull as the inlet for the sink tap. For preference I would install another small pump suitable for salt-water, wired somewhere near the kitchen/cockpit companionway and normally kept switched off. With careful plumbing I could manage both pressurized salt-water for the cockpit hose and also a smaller stream at the sink tap—though in this case the tap itself would need to be redesigned and the foot pedal done away with. As an alternative I could manage without the saltwater shower option for the cockpit and just use one of those hand-pump camp showers for salt-water spraying while at sea. While in harbor a portable powered water pump could be used, or I suppose also at sea when I have extra power to burn.

There is no provision for storing graywater onboard this boat and no good place to put a tank either. The sink will drain directly out a thru-hull on the side, above the waterline. The drain in the head (for the shower) will go into the bilge and so will the drain below the icebox/refrigerator. From there the bilge pump will kick on, once there is enough water in the bilge to activate the switch, and put it over the side out a thru-hull. So I will be careful about the cleaners and soaps I use and hope for the best. I also prefer a dry bilge and will be showering in the cockpit when possible (which will also drain overboard, by necessity). The ice-box will have been redone as a refrigerator and will have minimal liquid drained—just some condensation and anything from spills.

There should be sufficient power for a small clothes washer, but finding room to put one will be more difficult. I might consider placing one in the v-berth. This will make plumbing easier as the main fresh water tank is right there. If I put it into the spot next to the head it should be clear of the overhead hatch and also still permit one person to sleep in the v-berth. It could be drained into the bilge as well, but if I did go ahead and install a washer I might also consider a thru-hull above the waterline for draining. The better option might be to skip the washer and just use the trusty bucket system for laundry. Clothes will be hang dried regardless.

The Catalina has a small hatch for garbage in the kitchen area that leads to a space under one of the cockpit lockers. This is convenient and I may keep the arrangement depending on any modifications I might want to make in that space. Larger solid waste will be stored as possible for proper disposal.

As designed, there is a small marine toilet in the head, with tankage underneath the port salon seat. This system may or may not be in good condition, but if any salt water at all had been run through it for flushing purposes then I would want to do a full overhaul of the system while I had the boat apart. If keeping the marine toilet I would set it for freshwater flushing only.

But I might instead opt to install a compost toilet. Urine could still be routed to the holding tank and would require minimal amounts of my precious fresh water for flushing. Or that tank could be removed altogether in order to free up space. Solids would be composted. There should be an existing vent line for the holding tank which could also be used to vent the compost head. Though I have seen it suggested that this vent should be up-sized and run out its own thru-hull for better venting, as Catalina seems to have vented the holding tanks for their earlier models into a railing stanchion. The compost toilet could also have secondary venting through the solar vent/fan that I mentioned installing at the top of the head/bathroom.

Auxiliary Propulsion

The auxiliary engine for this line of boats is set a bit forward under the kitchen counter, rather than back under the companionway stairs. This is better for weight distribution, I gather, but the cabinet in which it is located is a very tight fit for the engine and noise suppression can be difficult. Especially for the diesel versions. The fuel tank will be located somewhere under the cockpit and usually under the quarter berth.

If keeping the engine, I would want to do a full tear-down and rebuild. Especially if it was the original engine. This would give me a chance to try for some soundproofing in the engine housing and would also let me get at the stuffing box and the interior portion of the propeller shaft.

The boat is under powered with the original engine, so I may consider an upgrade, especially if there are significant problems with the existing diesel. For this boat replacing the engine might be a better course than switching to electric propulsion, for several reasons. The propeller is on a long shaft, which may be strained too much by the high base torque of an electric motor, but the angle is shallow and the prop is pretty close to to the hull, meaning that this is not a great candidate for switching to a larger propeller in order to take advantage of the torque characteristics of an electric motor. There are also limited options for generating electricity. This will make for much shorter range under auxiliary power and also require careful budgeting of electrical power. If the engine is in working condition or I can locate a cheap replacement in good condition I will probably just stick with a diesel.

Still, electric propulsion is much nicer to live with and it will be very possible to make the switch. The electrical systems will need upgrading anyway. If switching to electric I will first strip out the fuel tank, engine, transmission, and shifter linkage, and will then tie off all engine electronics and controls for possible reuse with the electrical motor system. The fuel tank can be replaced with a (custom sized) water tank, which will allow me to do away with the water tank under the starboard side settee without losing any capacity. With that space opened up I will dedicate all space under that settee and the nav station for batteries and electronics.

A 15HP electric motor would be more than enough for this boat. 10-12HP may also be sufficient. You could even drop down to a 5kW (~7HP) motor and still get by. I might go with something convenient like the 10KW (~13HP) Brushless Sailboat Kit listed on this link: www.thunderstruck-ev.com/sevcon-brushless-sailboat-kit-10.5kw.html.

Though I may instead source my own components. A gear reduction may be in order for this installation, but 2:1 should be enough and more than that would risk warping the propeller shaft. Mounting would require replacing the existing engine mounts, which to do properly would mean stripping down to the inner hull and building back up. All new components together will weigh less than the engine being replaced, but proper mountings are still essential for controlling vibration. Also the angle of the output shaft for the new motor should be perfectly aligned with the propeller shaft, though offset for the gear reduction.

Given that this will be the largest and most important power draw on the boat, the battery bank will be tailored to it and all other loads will be converted down to an appropriate voltage. That is, the propulsion battery bank will be wired at 48V DC, which should be able to feed to the motor and controller without any conversion losses. The cable will need to be routed straight across the center walkway, but that can be covered over easily enough. Depending on the overall needs of the rest of the electrical system, I may keep the propulsion bank wired separately and have a separate battery for house loads (under the nav station cabinet).

So, if I have four 100Ah batteries wired in series at 48V for propulsion, the electrical motor will be able to run at full output for just under half an hour. Actual practice will allow several times as much range, as full output will not be required to achieve hull speed except in very heavy seas and anyway dropping down a knot of two from hull speed might require only half as much power draw. But clearly either very careful (and infrequent) motoring will be called for, or else a larger battery bank. If I want to be able to motor frequently then I should stay with diesel for this build.

If switching to electric propulsion I would want to prop up as much as possible to take advantage of its differing characteristics. An electric motor will not stall out when switching into reverse and also provides full torque output from a standing start. So I would want to install the maximum propeller diameter that will clear the hull sufficiently to reduce vibration and will also want a heavy pitch and either three or four blades. This will be discussed further in a later section in the book, but increased thrust from more efficient propellers is where electric propulsion can really shine.

Electricity and Networking

Given the age of the boat, a full electrical upgrade will be required. Other than wiring in good condition and switches and panel facings, everything should be replaced. This means all breakers, all relays, all fuses, and certainly all of the outdated lighting should be switched out for modern equivalents. Some of this could be recycled to help defray costs. Before doing this I will want to plan out all electrical loads and also work up a circuit and wiring diagram for future reference.

For this build, I will require power and wiring for any electric propulsion (or otherwise for starting the motor), internal and external lights, any fans, the refrigerator, the water pump(s), the bilge pump(s), any electric appliances or devices, navigation and Applications electronics, and any electric roller furling devices (which can run at 48V and will only draw 800W or so, briefly when in use).

Except for the propulsion motor this is not a heavy electrical load for a modern boat, though I could certainly use up quite a bit of power with appliances if I wanted to. There will be no bow thruster, no electric winches, no water-maker, no air conditioning (unless on shore power), and no electric heating except possibly small on-demand devices. There will be a substantial number of electronics, but these can be very efficient and not all of them will be in use at once.

Regarding those electronics, navigation and autopilot may be routed to a multi-function display, or better yet two concurrent displays located at the nav station and on the wheel pedestal. Chart plotting may be included if possible or on a separate display. I will also want such house electronics as a central computer, two or three monitors mounted on the walls, and a series of speakers around the interior. In addition I could have other small user electronics. The navigation electronics could then be interfaced to my central computer for programming and alternate control and display. Barring Starlink or some similar internet option, external networking will be limited to wifi and cellular when those are in range, other than the satphone already mentioned. It should be possible to route the data from the satphone into the central computer for ease of use.

Other than the required electrical wiring, interrupts, and safety devices, I will also need such equipment as inverter/chargers, a solar charger and any other charge controllers, battery management, and any DC converters, in addition to the batteries. Electrical safety and corrosion control are particularly important in the marine environment and will significantly increase the complexity of the electrical system and also the expense, but are entirely necessary and must not be skimped on.

There will still be a need for power generation. Around 400W of rigid solar panels can be mounted on the hard top I posited constructing above the cockpit. I could also mount two or more wind generators, located on poles at the rear of the cockpit or fastened to the mast. These together should keep up with normal electrical loads for lights, electronics, etc, but will only put a dent in heavy electric motor use or significant appliance use. With steady offshore winds much more power can be produced by wind generators, but in that case I am likely to be sailing anyway and will not need much extra power. If the wind dies I might want to motor, but then I will not be getting any power from the wind generators. The solar alone will only be enough for a trickle of power for the motor. I could also draw from regen while sailing, but this boat has a pretty low hull speed (6.7 knots) and will not produce very much power except in sustained high winds, and once the battery bank is full then the regen will not be required.

There is room in the port-side cockpit locker to install a small generator unit, but together with fuel this will take up most of the locker space that could otherwise fit other necessary equipment. You could instead use the existing fuel tank from the replaced motor to fuel the generator. Instead of locating your secondary water tank in that spot, it could be located under the port-side settee of the table/bed. Which would require removing the black waste holding tank from that location and going with another option such as a compost toilet. So, with a sufficient number of compromises you could have a small generator with enough fuel bunkerage to run all day and then some and which could power the electric motor, alone, up to perhaps four knots boat speed.

Other Equipment

Heating for this build will be provided by a solid fuel combustion heater (charcoal, briquettes, scraps of wood, etc). This could be mounted on the bulkhead forward of the port-side settee, next to the table fold-up position, or on the cabinet forward of the starboard settee. Heat shielding will be wrapped around the back and sides and the bottom, which will also serve to capture spilled ash. It may be vented through existing vents or instead through a dedicated opening in the deck. This should be sufficient heat to keep the boat above freezing even in very cold temperatures. When on shore power, electric space heaters can be used as well if desired.

There will be no attempt at insulating the boat. A certain amount of insulation is already provided by the hull itself and in any case the hull will be tightly sealed and airflow controlled. The tight spaces and structure of the build are such that full insulation will be impractical. I may consider insulating the hull-side exterior of any water tanks, but that is all.

Bow anchor, chain, and rode will need to be inspected and replaced if necessary. I will also want to have a full spare on hand for each of these components, in addition to a smaller anchor kept in the cockpit area. A hand-crank anchor windless, with mechanical advantage, will be fine for my purposes.

In addition, for the purposes of cruising I will want to have full emergency and safety gear on board. A lifeboat with EPIRB, in addition to whatever dingy I decide on. Personal flotation devices for each person. Safety harnesses and lines. Medical supplies.

Emergency food storage and water production (solar still). Sea anchor or parachute. An extensive electronic library so that you have references for many things. Etc.

Summary and Conclusion

And so there you have it—that which is required to turn a mid-sized sailboat like the Catalina 30 into a blue-water cruiser and a comfy, if somewhat cramped, home. Personally I consider the quarter-birth aft under the cockpit starboard-side to be the best area for sleeping, so would turn that into my bedroom with the v-berth forward devoted to storage. There is a great deal of customization such as this that I have not gotten into for this build—make alterations to suit for own desires. I have also not even touched upon certain of the needs fulfillment topics, such as Pests. Please refer to the needs sections for more information.

Notice that this required a similar amount of effort and materials and money as would be needed for an entire new boat—provided that you did the work yourself. Most systems were replaced and other systems had to make compromises in order to stay within the limitations of the platform. For these reasons and because such a goal really does exceed the initial design considerations of the platform, I do not recommend refitting a Catalina 30 or similar vessel for extensive cruising as has been detailed here. Even with the profligate measures, themselves compromises, that I have outlined here, the end result will be borderline for that purpose. However, this is still a very good platform for moderate and coastal cruising or for any lesser purpose. If your goals fall within that range then you can scale back on most of these refit procedures and still get by just fine.

References and Further Research

Calder, Nigel. *Boatowner's*

Casey, Don. *This Old Boat, Second Edition*

Casey, Don. *Don Casey's Complete Illustrated Sailboat Maintenance Manual*

Berman, Peter. *Outfitting the Offshore Cruising Sailboat.*

sailboatdata.com/sailboat/catalina-30

www.thunderstruck-ev.com/sevcon-brushless-sailboat-kit-10.5kw.html

www.practical-sailor.com/sailboat-reviews/sailboats-21-30ft/catalina-30

www.practical-sailor.com/sails-rigging-deckgear/improve-your-catalina-30-upgrading-the-worlds-most-popular-30-footer

www.spinsheet.com/boat-reviews/catalina-30-used-boat-review

www.docksidereports.com/hull_to_deck_joint.htm

mycatalina30.wordpress.com

www.catalinadirect.com/shop-by-boat/catalina-250/engine/fuel-tank-17-gal-c-250c-30-w-inspection-port

refit.guide

mrandmrshowe.com/lifestyle-blog/empress-sailboat-interior-refit

www.cruisingworld.com/classic-plastic-refit-on-budget

www.cruisingworld.com/how/refit-reality-check

youtu.be/_v9_vmKMja4

A tour video for one Catalina 30.

youtu.be/AT1wWsXJl5Q

A second tour video, 1982 model.

youtu.be/b3k_xiBTWNQ

Interesting refit job on a derelict Catalina 30.

youtu.be/lkXi6TC9c_w

A short video detailing the refit of a neglected Catalina 30.

youtu.be/SEkJ1SbwyrY

Extended slideshow documenting the refit of a wooden sailboat.

youtu.be/l63GDdzyoTI

Informative video on one couple's search for a liveaboard sailboat.

youtu.be/PQyn02VT1jY

Video with a more detailed discussion of what to look out for when boat shopping for a liveaboard.

youtu.be/Au6R7PLrLbo

Tour video for a sailboat outfitted as a global cruiser.

26.

The Motorboat Refit

If you want to live on a boat that moves and do not want to sail, it will be a motorboat. Yes, it is possible to live on a boat small enough to paddle or row, but I will not consider that to be a serious option. Motorboats can be all shapes, all sizes. Boats for living aboard and keeping mobile in will be more restricted in hull-form and I will focus on the most likely market candidates. For now anyway. The next few build sections will examine ideas for custom built marine living.

Going the route of refitting a used motorboat may or may not be more expensive than doing so with a sailboat. The boat will have bigger engines and possibly more than one, with corresponding cost increases for the engine itself and also for every component in the propulsion system, but you will not have to worry about masts and rigging and sails. Mostly the costs involved will depend on the condition of the vessels in question and the components you choose as part of the refit. Operating costs, once the refit is complete, will be higher. The primary expense for a motorboat over time will be fuel costs, and the more you cruise the more it will cost you, in addition to wearing down the components of the engines. This contrasts with a sailboat which, under sail at least, may have no ongoing expenses at all other than maintenance and replacement for worn out parts.

It is possible to switch a motorboat to electric drive systems. I do not consider it practical, at this time, to generate sufficient electrical power onboard a typical motorboat to power those drive motors except with a generator unit. There are limited areas to emplace solar panels and most smallish motorboats are more suited to inland and coastal waters that will not have sustained winds to draw on for wind generators. You may be able to generate sufficient power for house electrical loads with renewables, but nowhere close to what will be needed for propulsion. This leaves fuel powered generators for a serial hybrid drive system. Which is possible, but not really practical, as efficiency losses in such small-scale systems will mean that you require even more fuel than before going to electric drive, and the boats themselves will not be designed to take advantage of the best strengths of electric propulsion.

Electric propulsion boats are very possible—many large ships operate on serial hybrid drives—but in order to be a good solution the boat design and operating conditions must be tailored to play to the strengths of electric motors. I recommend electric propulsion for (some) sailboats and not for motorboats, unless custom built for the purpose, because it will be a secondary propulsion system for sailboats and also because the motor power ratings will be much lower for auxiliary motors and so efficiency losses will be less of a concern. This does assume that we are talking monohulls. If you find yourself refitting a lightweight multihull boat, then by all means consider electric drive. I will have a full section later in the book exploring the strengths and weakness of electric propulsion in some depth. But the vast majority of motorboats will be monohulls or equivalent and not really suited for electric motor re-powering at the current stage of available technology.

Platform

A vessel that relies on motorized propulsion alone instead of also (or only) using sail will still have many of the same internal systems as a sailboat, but will have very different operating characteristics and operating parameters. It will feel different, will move differently, and will be able to go different places. But it will never be able to move without fuel (or battery power) and without the engine (or electric motor) running.

Unlike sailboats large enough to live on, which will always have displacement style hulls, a motorboat may be a displacement vessel or a planing vessel. There are also semi-displacement hulls, or semi-planing, which are not perfect for either role but can do both adequately. A displacement vessel will always be limited to a certain speed (hull speed) because of the characteristics of the water that it moves through. Water does not compress very much and so a vessel passing through it will reach a certain point in speed (largely determined by the length of the vessel) at which water resistance to its movement is too great for it to go any faster. A planing vessel, such as a speedboat, will instead be shaped in such a way (and be light enough) that when sufficient propulsion is applied it will rise up partially out of the water and so be much less restricted by water resistance. Higher speeds become possible. These hulls will be either flat on the bottom or, more commonly, come down to a shallow point in the center. The more power that is applied by the propellers at the rear the more of the vessel rises out of the water and the higher the speeds that can be obtained.

Planing and semi-planing boats must go fast in order to achieve their cruising speeds, which will require higher horsepower engines and more fuel use. Full planing boats in particular are unstable, especially in heavy seas, if they are unmoving or are not moving fast enough to make plane. A semi-planing hull can be much more stable but will not plane as well and so will be limited to somewhat lower speeds.

A full displacement hull will always be slower, but will be more fuel efficient because of it. For living aboard, you may consider a tug or trawler or even a houseboat with a displacement hull. For cruising long distances a trawler boat will be ideal, and might use somewhere between two and four gallons of fuel per hour. Trawlers are built heavy to withstand rough seas and have slower but more efficient engines. There are some newer trawlers out there billed as semi-displacement, but this is mostly a marketing compromise and they will be more expensive, with bigger engines and more fuel use, and with somewhat less room inside due to hull-form changes. They can go faster than a normal displacement trawler because of the changes, but at high cost.

Then you have the proper motor-yachts. These will have hull-forms that range the gamut, from full plane all the way down to full displacement. For this refit I will be focusing on the cabin cruiser type of motor-yacht, as being large enough for long term living and also capable of some cruising. They can also be obtained more cheaply on the used boat market and I will consider a cabin cruiser as an entry level vessel for marine motorized living.

Pretty much all of the cabin cruisers are semi-displacement, with an irregular hull-form. They will have two best speeds for cruising, in terms of fuel use, based on whether they are planing or displacing water at the time. At displacement speeds this will be dependent on what the hull speed of the boat is and the best cruising speed, or sweet spot, will be somewhat less than hull speed. At the planing sweet spot the same boat will be going around three times faster through the water but will also be using about twice as much fuel in terms of distance (half the miles per gallon obtained). Which is a nice increase in speed for less fuel use than you would expect, but still limits cruising range at planing speeds to less than it will be at displacement speeds.

For this hypothetical refit I have chosen a Chris-Craft 42. Which is even older than my sailboat build but should also have very strong (even overbuilt) fiberglass. So even if all other systems are in poor condition, at least the hull will be (should be) strong. It is also a double cabin vessel and has a lot more room aboard than any comparably sized, and especially any comparably priced, sailboat.

Specs

1969 Chris-Craft 42 Commander
Hard top glassed doghouse
Hull type: monohull, semi-displacement
Length 42ft
Beam 13ft
Draft: 38in
Displacement: 25, 621lbs
Fiberglass construction
Power: 2 inboard Detroit diesel motors at 258HP each, 200 gallon fuel capacity.
Water tanks: 120 gallons
Price estimate: I have seen several of these listed, between $17k and $40k, depending on condition.

Like the sailboat refit, I will assume nothing about the condition of the vessel, though for your purposes you really should have a very good idea about the condition of the boat, and what you will need to do to it, before you buy it. There will always be something.

The main exterior spaces are the top steering platform/bridgedeck/doghouse and open patio behind it, an open deck forward from there above the front berth, an open deck at the front of the boat at the lower exterior level, and full length walkways to either side between the cabin and the railing. The only open surface at the rear, at the level of the walkways, is a small ledge. Inside you have the central salon, which includes the kitchen in the forward portion, the engine room below and accessible through a hatch in the salon floor, a full double berth in the rear with adjoining bathroom and closet space, and the front v-berth cabin with adjoining bathroom.

The big draw with this particular design is that it has two full private berthing areas complete with separate bathrooms. This is the shortest Chris-Craft type that offers this feature and sacrifices have been made in other areas in order to accommodate the extra berthing. The main salon space is adequate and feels roomy, but the engine area is decidedly cramped (though it will not feel that way if you are switching from a sailboat) and there is a definite lack at the very rear where other models fit in a porch or well or some kind of swimming access. Still, boats get more expensive with more length and the extra private berthing capacity is very nice to have.

Purpose

This boat is not suited for extended cruising in the open sea. It has some stability from the wide beam (for a monohull), but has no substantial ballast for its weight (though the large engines provide quite a bit) and will have limited cruising range even with the large fuel bunker (because of those large engines). For weekend trips or inland cruising or coastal cruising it will be very suitable. It is a perfect fit for the Great Loop and other rivers and lakes. I think it would be fine in the Caribbean or even the Med or Baltic, with proper care.

For this build I will posit outfitting the boat for extended coastal cruising, which might mean the Great Loop or instead island hopping around the Caribbean. In either case it will always be in range of a place to refuel and never be far from help, should that be required. This will be well within the design parameters of the vessel, but careful attention must be paid to the weather when not in sheltered waters.

Planning

Given that stated purpose I can plan out my need fulfillment levels accordingly. This vessel has two to three times the internal room of the sailboat refit above. It can also expect to have access to shore power to recharge batteries, among other amenities, every time it goes in to refuel. So, though many systems may have similar design requirements to that of any other boat build, the increased space and differing operational parameters will lead to significant differences in the final product.

High: Address, Air, Cooling

Medium: Applications, Electricity, Food, Health, Heating, Networking, Pests, Philosophy, Planning, Propulsion, Sanitation, Space, Stopping, Structure, Wastage, Water

Low: Security

I have lowered the Security fulfillment level here, as this vessel with this purpose is a good candidate for that variation. Notice that for Security, there is a distinct difference between low and none. If you will never be out of range of assistance and do not make yourself a target...and never stray from safer areas...then basic precautions should be sufficient, unless you are unlucky. Also, the large number of windows on this build will rather complicate physical security arrangements.

Address has been bumped up here for similar reasons. This is a shallow draft vessel and could have a home dock along a river or lakefront in any of over a dozen American states or even in multiple countries. See my later section on extended navigable inland waterways throughout the world.

Air and Cooling can both be met at a high level because of the initial design of the build itself. It has a fully enclosed living quarters and is well insulated. Air conditioning was a standard feature when new. It has the potential to have air filtration and treatment taken to a high level. There can be air conditioners (modernized and more efficient units) in each cabin and also in the main salon.

All other needs will be met at a moderate level of fulfillment. Structure is borderline low, in that no real changes will be made, but since this is a refit the entire structure will be carefully inspected and may need repair. Stopping will only have a few options at any given time—you know that you will need to be able to make it to the next fuel dock and must plan your route accordingly, but there will be only a few docks within range of the vessel at any given time. Given the age of the boat, Applications, Electricity, Heating, Networking, Propulsion, Sanitation, Wastage, and Water systems will all need to be thoroughly overhauled and upgraded. Food will mostly be met with specific practices, but there is a large kitchen that can be fully equipped. Health needs will be fewer because of keeping in range of assistance. Pests must be accounted for but that will also largely be a matter of practices. Planning can be lower for this build without great risks. And Space must be accounted for, but there is a great deal of room aboard (for a boat) and it will not be critical to use every little nook and cranny.

Refit

Hull and Decks

The outer hull has the same two main sections for this boat—that which is below the waterline and that which is above. These will be of one piece but will be surface treated differently. Below the waterline the hull has a very irregular shape in order to facilitate planing without entirely losing stability at displacement speeds. There is a sort of smoothly curved mini-hull in the center portion, which comes down to a narrow edge to form a keel shape from front to back in the center bottom. That part also has short extrusions (mini-bilge keels) about halfway up on either side and running from front to back. These help to reduce rolling movement from side to side but do not resist forward motion. To either side of that center portion are flat-bottomed hull sections that sweep from front to back until they meet the center at the flat square transom. This will enable to vessel to rise up on its own bow wave and achieve planing speed. Not perfectly, because of the deeper center curved hull. Just as motion at displacement speeds will be less than ideal because of the flat side sections. But the compromise shape makes for a boat that is adequate in either speed range.

Above the waterline the hull-form is much more regular, with a smooth graceful curve on either side back to the transom. This is interrupted only by a few thru-hulls and also by large air intake vents on either side in front, near the top, to supply the engines. The paint above the waterline should be in good condition and if so may be left undisturbed. If not it will need sanding and re-painting, but there should be no need to strip all the way down to bare glass. Just make sure you use a paint that will bond to what is already there. In any case all thru-hulls and openings should be inspected and repaired as necessary.

Below the waterline, given the age of the vessel, there will be an unknown number of paint layers and it should be stripped down to the glass. Which will mean a lot of work with a small orbital sander, given the irregularities in the hull shape. After this is done and the glass itself has been inspected and repaired as necessary, apply two or three epoxy barrier coats, bottom paint, and an anti-foul which conforms to current best practice. A good anti-foul choice will depend on your operating conditions and location and also how often and how much bottom cleaning you engage in. There are many comparison resources available online which are easy to find. I do urge you to consider the potential environmental impact of your chosen coating.

Thru-hulls below the waterline will need special attention. They must be checked for damage or wear, bedding integrity, and any corrosion. The electrical system will be redone, but corrosion spots below the waterline can tell much about stray currents. If any thru-hulls need replacing do not skimp by buying cheap replacements. Good bronze or polymer parts should be used—these tend to cost about the same, though there may be market or local variations in price. An all polymer setup can simplify corrosion concerns, but bronze will be more resistant to impact and with a properly designed electrical system there should be no stray current to induce corrosion. I know that many people use good stainless steel for thru-hulls...but I hesitate to do so. It will resist corrosion but never as well as bronze, and in low-oxygen water, such as may be found in many river systems due to field runoff and rampant stimulated marine growth, stainless steel can develop significant problems. But if it is sufficiently cheaper than the better alternatives you could always budget multiple replacements.

The rudder and propeller systems should also be cared for at this point, in addition to any hardware emplacements such as for sonar or an electrical discharge plate (for lightning).

There should be no special problems with the hull-deck joint for this particular vessel design, but this remains a high stress area and it must be fully inspected and alterations should be considered. Common builder practice is to use the screws through the rub rail as mechanical attachment through some type of fiberglass filler at the junction itself. Which is a poor way to go about it but saves on labor costs. It will be difficult to get at the inside with this build to replace the screws with bolts and backing, and it will probably not be worth it to fully strip and redo the seal inside and out, but the joint can still be strengthened (and resealed as necessary) by removing the screws and rub rails, stripping the area down a bit, and resealing with epoxy and synthetic fiber strips (aramid or Spectra or similar products). If the epoxy is still tacky when you replace the rub rails and put the screws back in there should be no damage to the new seal from those fasteners (though getting them back out will be more of a chore). The synthetic fibers will resist fracture from stress much better than fiberglass and the epoxy itself is many times stronger than the original polyester resin. Any changes you do make can be covered up by the rub rails.

The decks above are likely to have more problems. They will have been more lightly built than the hull to begin with and may even be cored, with a material subject to water damage, in places. The worst problems will develop right along the outside edge of the lower deck and also at the rear upper deck where the rails (stanchions) are mounted, and especially at the very front where the anchor and windlass and main docking cleat are located.

I would suggest reinforcing every second or third rail stanchion with aluminum backing plates, once any repairs have been made. This will reinforce the rail strength, making it feasible to use that area for hardware mounting and also guarding against future damage. You could so reinforce every stanchion instead but there are a lot of them and that much is probably unnecessary. I have also seen structural wood, made nice to look like trim, placed all along the stanchion line at the outer edge. The wood is fastened to the deck and the stanchions are fastened to it—so all lateral stress is borne by the easily replaceable wood instead of the fiberglass deck. Though keeping this method sealed properly may be an issue, as the wood will flex differently than the fiberglass and will also move and swell or shrink with weather changes.

Other than that the decks themselves should be checked for any damage and also for whether repainting is required. If you are going to repaint then stripping the decks down to glass will make inspecting deck integrity much easier, and you will be more likely to successfully locate any problem areas. Existing hardware mounts on the upper deck should be inspected and you must also work out what older equipment you will be eliminating and what new hardware you will be mounting.

Consider that a short mast could be mounted near or on the pilothouse. This would increase instrument and signal range and the mast could be designed to pivot down in order to maintain current overhead clearance. Two masts, one on either side of the pilothouse, would give more mounting space and also look more symmetrical. This would help to free up space for potential solar panel emplacement. You could also mount one or two wind turbines on pivot-down masts somewhere along the lower deck walkways near the transom. At the back of the pilothouse is another good place for wind turbine masts. These masts could be located at or even replace a reinforced stanchion.

Ports and Hatches

There is a large hatch above the front cabin, a few vents, inlets for shore power and food and water, and an outlet for pumping out black waste. These should all be checked for damage and replaced as necessary. Since you will be doing deck work anyway this is also a good time to go ahead and redo the seals for each and every one of these. They might be fine, but you don't know how long ago they were sealed or how well or what stress they have been subjected to since. Best to take care of a potential problem area now while doing the rest of the refit. During heavy rains or a storm is not the best time to find out that your front hatch leaks down onto the bed in the v-berth, or that your water inlet is letting in moisture and causing mold in the mechanical spaces, or that your shore power cover leaks and causes a short every time it rains. Etc.

The biggest concern for this part, though, will be the doors and especially the large number of windows all around the cabin and up in the pilothouse. I think that I can safely guarantee that on a fifty year old vessel at least some portion of this will need extensive work. Most likely it will be best to redo all seals, just as with other exterior ports and fittings. Flexible sealants tend to degrade over time and in any case much better products have been developed since this boat was constructed. This will include re-glazing the windows, though make sure that whoever does the work does not use household silicone as a sealer. Marine grade silicone is much better suited to the boat environment and in any case only marine grade sealants should be used. The aluminum structural material for the doors and windows should still be fine, though it should be carefully checked for strain and also for corrosion where it has been sealed away from open air. Aluminum in constant contact with moisture and especially stagnant water has a tendency to corrode. While you are going about this you may decide to reconfigure the arrangement of the doors. The slider type doors in particular seem to be susceptible to damage from careless use or the seals wearing out and I have seen cases where people have converted them to swinging doors or just sealed them off entirely. This is the best time to look at existing doors and decide whether and how to reconfigure them.

For this particular boat I will also suggest extending the pilothouse hardtop to the rear of the top deck. This will require a custom fabrication of new fiberglass paneling and mean reinforcing the stanchion mounts, but half of that work will have been done already while working on the deck. Flat fiberglass is the easiest to construct and you can make a simple one-off female mold out of plywood and plastic sheeting, with boards fastened at the edges to define the boundaries of the panel. Matching the existing supports for the pilothouse hardtop may prove to be the most difficult part and will likely require custom work from a job-shop if you want cosmetic perfection.

Propulsion and Steering

There should be two rudders, one just aft of each propeller. The rudders for this boat will be subject to very strong forces while underway and should have been stoutly built to begin with, but fatigue over time will have degraded strength in all of the materials used. They are also free-hanging (no skeg) and subject to impact damage. A complete rebuild may be required, but probably it will be sufficient to sand or grind down surfaces and reinforce with epoxy and new fiberglass. Just be careful to keep the original shape and to smooth and repaint all surfaces. That is, if the metal pivot and forward post section of the rudder are in good condition. If not, a new rudder, or else a full disassembly and rebuild, will be required. The steering system will also require inspection, at a minimum, and overhaul as necessary. Find out what method is used to make the rudder turn when you turn the wheel and check it for any problems.

The propellers, shafts, and exterior shaft mountings should also be cared for and repaired as necessary. These are high speed shafts, so any cutlass bearings will take a lot of wear and replacement should be considered. This is also the best time to consider whether to change out your propellers for a different type. The sacrificial anodes—which will be zinc or aluminum or magnesium depending on what type of water you cruise in—should be replaced unless in very good condition.

The engine compartment, despite being the heart of the vessel, is seldom thought about and often neglected. Doing so will be easier for this boat as it is hidden away under a hatch. Most people spend far more time on the cosmetics of a boat than they do on the mechanicals but very few people will bother to keep a clean engine compartment. After five decades and multiple owners, this one will require a thorough cleaning. Which will be a two part process, in that a rough cleaning should be done before any mechanical work just so you can really see things and what you are doing, but a second and much more thorough cleaning should be done after everything is back together. After that, you only have to worry about cleaning up each individual mess that you make, else soon enough you will be back to the same mess that you started with. Which will put people off of taking proper care for boat components that are kept down in the engine room.

Anyway, there will be five main sections down in that space. The central area which is open for access and also to allow the erstwhile boat mechanic to catch a spot of rest—in addition to housing the engine starter batteries underneath. A corner for each of the two engines, which will be crowded in. A corner for the generator and house battery bank, usually port-side forward. And the starboard-side forward section for everything else, including the water pump and heater and pressure tank. Some more electrical system components will also be scattered around that forward section.

The engines for my chosen boat are the original diesels. Gasoline engines are also frequently found on these types of vessels. In either case, if you are lucky then your motors are in good condition and will only be in need of maintenance. For me, it is just possible that the two fifty year old diesel motors in my boat, if they have been properly cared for and seen relatively light use, will still run. But most likely they will need to be rebuilt, or else replaced even if they do run, in order for me to fulfill my purpose of coastal cruising. Either of which options will be a chore and a half just to move things about in that engine compartment.

For removing the engines entirely, you can build a scaffold and beam arrangement that runs all the way through the boat at the level of the doors and windows (which will be removed, along with the safety railing) and rests on the ground. With that in place, the floor in the salon will need to be taken up in order to lift each engine, dissembled as far as possible, straight up. Which can be done even by one person with a strong enough chain hoist and mechanical advantage. You will also want your beam to be equipped as a gantry (with railing) that will allow the hoist to slide over and out of the boat. All of this can be done by a single person just for the purposes of the job, but do take care to design and build each component to bear the weight of the very heavy engine blocks—don't just guess and do leave a safety margin. More people will make for lighter work and a crane or backhoe will be even more help.

If you buy a motorboat, unless you just sit at the dock, you will be continually sinking money into the propulsion system. Most often this will be for fuel, but every individual component for an engine will need to be serviced or replaced after a certain number of hours of running time. Which will go far beyond oil changes. Do obtain any possible manuals for your particular engines. Do perform regular maintenance and also keep spare parts on board. Don't skimp on maintenance and repairs. If you wait for something to break down before fixing it then you have already more than doubled your repair bill. Properly maintained (and modified) engines will use less fuel over time and will have fewer problems. I will not claim that they will have no problems—you signed up for that when you bought the boat. But the central ongoing problem of your boat—propulsion itself—can be made manageable with proper care. And sufficient money.

Interior

The boat will have been insulated when built, but that will also have degraded over time and replacement should be considered. I have seen boats of this type where someone, the builder or one of the owners, used fiberglass batting for insulation. Which tends to gather moisture over time in high humidity environments, such as a boat, and provide less insulative value even while it becomes moldy from the moisture buildup. I will posit dismantling the interior and redoing the insulation. Which will not be a fun experience overall but will be much less messy than redoing the decks outside. If fiberglass batts were the original type I will switch them out for mineral wool batting, after cleaning things up and inspecting the uncovered areas. If something thinner was used for the original insulation then I would switch in something like polyiso board or XPS. Taking this step constitutes a complete tear-down and rebuild of the interior, so you may not want to go this far in your refit, but say in my case that I needed or wanted to redo the interior anyway. This would also be a good time to redo or at least inspect the wiring and the water piping.

When re-assembling the interior, I would want to make certain changes in layout and furnishings. I have noticed that many of these cabin cruisers will have the main salon furnished with regular furniture, but it seems to me that this is a waste of space when built-in furniture can provide so much more encapsulated storage room. Perhaps I have spent too much time on sailboats, but I would go ahead and do this for at least the dining area and part of the lounging area of the salon. This should not restrict future access to the engine room as long as that is taken into account with the design and attachment points of the furniture. The beds should already have under-bed storage, but any dressers and shelves will also be built-in or at least attached. The kitchen cabinetry and counters will be revamped, and any issues with the fixtures (stove, sink, etc) or needed replacements will be accomplished.

I also note that none of the overhead space is being utilized. Something like a hanging rack above the kitchen counter would improve space usage, as long as it were made strong enough for rough waters. It is also possible to mount flat things, like flatscreen televisions or computer monitors, into pivot-down boxes on the ceiling. This will save space at floor level and such an arrangement could be used in the salon and also in both bedrooms, for Applications purposes. For that matter wall mounts could be installed instead in locations where that is preferable.

Water, Sanitation, Wastage

The entire water system, from the storage tanks (I hope there is more than one) through the engine room and various pieces of equipment there and to the end use outlets, should be checked over...and replaced with new components. Yes, you could keep the old pieces that are still working, but those that are metal will be subject to fatigue and corrosion and those that are plastic will be degrading by this point. The pump and pressure tank and water heater should be fine to keep, if in good condition (and after cleaning out), but all lines and fittings and tanks should be replaced. This will take care of any buildup of contaminants in the system and also permit you to design in extra filtration and otherwise to customize your system.

While doing so you could consider whether it is feasible to add in graywater tankage. Probably this will not work out without cutting into fresh water tankage, and in any case it may be complicated to manage pumping it out when desired, but it will be a much more feasible option with this boat than it would be on a sailboat. The showers and sinks could also probably use some work. For convenience, I will want to install an outdoor hose on the forward deck above the v-berth and perhaps another one at the rear of the pilothouse area.

Black waste will have been taken care of with standard marine toilet arrangements. There will be two separate tanks, as the toilets are on opposite ends of the boat. If you are compost toilet friendly this is a good time to switch out the marine toilet from one bathroom. The other could be kept as standard for guests or other use, but it will need to be thoroughly inspected and overhauled. The space saved by switching one toilet to compost can be devoted to another water tank, a graywater tank, or other equipment.

Electricity and Networking and Navigation

The electrical wiring itself may be salvageable, depending on what what used during building, but pretty much all other electrical components should be replaced. The system itself should be redesigned at this time, as new loads will be added and some old loads will be eliminated.

Solar panels can be added to the top of the (extended) pilothouse roof and more can also be placed just in front of the pilothouse. Wind power may or may not be added, depending on wind conditions for expected cruising grounds.

The generator below-decks (if there is still one there) will need to be subjected to the same rigorous examination and rebuild as the propulsion motors. It can then be integrated into the electrical system. With an integrated internal network the generator can be programmed to turn on automatically if specified conditions are met. Like the house battery bank running low. This could be dangerous if the system is left on and the boat is unattended, but should be fine if someone is able to monitor things and the automation will increase convenience. With further network integration that monitoring could be done from a remote location.

As no electric propulsion is contemplated and there is a generator onboard, the house battery bank need not be overlarge. 5-10kW hours should be plenty. Large air conditioning and heating loads will rely on having the generator running anyway. A larger battery pack will mostly be a convenience for this build. Though a significant power reserve should still be kept to insure that vital electronics are not depowered.

External networking for this build will rely on cellular data, unless for some reason wifi is also found to be useful. Internal networking will consist of two parallel systems—one for propulsion and navigation equipment and another, less robust system for Applications uses.

Navigation equipment should be checked over and replaced or modernized as necessary. Some things, like compasses and tach gauges, will never cease to be useful. Other items, like thirty year old gps units or that non-functional radar unit, can be gotten rid of. All sorts of new multi-function display screens and useful gizmos are available. These should each be considered for actual use value. The more important ones, such as radar and sonar and charts and gps, are essential for any extended cruising effort.

Other Equipment

There is no good place to store a dingy on the deck, but the hull sides are high and mounts for hanging a dingy could be installed when the stanchion work is being done. I would suggest a vertical hang, such that one side (port or starboard) of the dingy hangs against the hull toward the waterline and the other side is up close or above the deck. This will somewhat complicate launching and retrieval, as compared to hanging the dingy level with itself, but will also reduce load on the mounts and increase docking options.

Full safety gear will be required, though if this will be for river travel I think we can do without the life-raft and EPIRB. Redundant sensors for smoke and monoxide and CO_2 should be mounted in appropriate places. If propane is used aboard then an entire safety system for that will need to be planned out and installed. I would suggest instead using diesel fuel for cooking and heating purposes for this boat, or else electric, as this will simplify safety requirements and the diesel is already available.

The anchoring system will need to be inspected and overhauled. This boat weighs almost three times what the last refit did, so the anchor and all attachments should be three times as strong. And there should still be redundant equipment in case the primary anchor is lost. Different types of holding ground will also be encountered, so different anchor types should be considered. The only normal use for line on the boat are the docking lines (and the dingy), but extra line should also be available on board. Stuff happens and it is good to have sturdy rope when it does.

This boat is also a good candidate for an air compressor. There is room to put one down in the engine room (just). The compressor could be used for scuba or dive lines or just for general purposes. Compressed air is handy stuff and uses will range from cleaning out debris to running power tools to pressure washing the deck and the hull.

Summary and Conclusion

This build will be more expensive to refit and to operate than the sailboat refit, or even a comparably sized sailboat. If you must have a motorboat then a low speed displacement vessel will be a much better choice in terms of cost outlay over time. Cabin cruisers are compromise vessels and suffer from a number of shortcomings in consequence. There are pretty cheap to get ahold of, however, and do have varied purposes that they are suitable for. It can be nice to go fast. Though 'fast' is a very relative term in the marine world.

Another viable liveaboard option is something like a cuddy cruiser or small cabin cruiser. This refit used a boat that can be likened to a two bedroom apartment. A smaller cabin cruiser can be similarly likened to a one bedroom apartment. And a cuddy cruiser is a lot like an efficiency apartment. A small one. But for a single person it will be more than enough space to live. A smaller boat will be less costly in every respect and will have increased mobility.

References and Further Research

commanderclub.com/page/42-commander

captainjohn.org/GL-Boat.html

www.pbo.co.uk/gear/pbo-great-uk-antifouling-showdown-26053/3

www.powerandmotoryacht.com/maintenance/refit-guide

yachtsurvey.com/usedboats.htm

www.mby.com/maintenance/refurbishing-classic-motor-yacht-16304

youtu.be/HOeEDIGIbXw

Tour of a somewhat smaller Chris-Craft.

youtu.be/CgUTYqZHzwQ

Very detailed video tour of a high end motor yacht, with full explanations for every boat system.

youtu.be/16HAp_P7VQs

Brief video discussing a wooden boat restoration.

youtu.be/BBm_lPIqHfs

Good look at some of the exterior refit procedures.

27.

The Riverboat Build

These next three sample builds are a bit different, in that they posit building a marine platform for mobile living from basic materials instead of altering an existing build. Custom built watercraft can have greater variation than road capable craft, which must all follow certain shape and size restrictions. I hope to showcase some of that possible variety with these sample builds.

This first will be the simplest in form. The intention with it is to offer a paradigm for craft that can be (relatively) easily built from materials, but that can still offer capabilities similar to, or even better than, commercially produced watercraft. It will not be intended to last forever, but will still be solidly built (hypothetically) and carefully designed.

I have a preference for multihulls for most applications, but this build will be a monohull. Less stability will be required, as the craft is (mostly) intended for inland water travel, and for certain applications monohulls remain the superior design choice. Perhaps you have width restrictions—the UK narrowboats must not exceed seven feet in width, else they cannot pass all of the canal locks. Most are built to a total width of six feet ten inches. Monohulls are also better at supporting and transporting heavier loads for a given size of vessel. A multihull must support more weight above the waterline and be heavier built the more weight they do support, but a monohull carries most of its weight, both structure and cargo, below the waterline where it is actually supported in part by water pressure on the hull. Heavier loads are not normally a requirement for residential craft, but it is still nice to have extra capacity.

Please do keep in mind that anything I am able to include here will not be sufficient on its own to set about the building process. My primary intention is to share ideas and to give examples of possible method. Other resources should also be consulted, some of which will be referenced at the end of this section. In particular I would suggest at least consulting a naval architect or engineer before finalizing any build plans. They will charge to look over and improve upon your design efforts, though not as much as for furnishing a custom design, but they will also be able to point out any flaws and concerns for your build. Better yet, do consider commissioning a custom boat design. This will be somewhat costly, though not nearly as costly as the rest of the project, and you will be able to stipulate your own design features and build materials, in consultation with a person who has acquired expertise in these matters. Better design will also save costs and headaches down the road.

Coming to know just what design features you do want is part of what this book is all about. Read on, if you will, and explore with me different options for this type of build.

Purpose

This platform will actually be intended to fulfill a similar purpose as the last sample build, the motorboat refit. This is, it will be intended for extended cruising in areas of protected water, such as lakes and rivers and canals and inter-coastal waterways. I think that with a custom design it can be made far better in such operations, with less cost over time, than any stock boat you may find on the market. This is particularly true in the case of propulsion, which will be specifically designed for energy efficiency in use.

I will also include thoughts on...extending the range a bit, shall we say. It is possible to modify even a river craft for the purpose of global voyages, but it will also be best to incorporate this possibility into the original design, particularly in regards to the load structure of the hull. Even if the full modifications will not be made during the initial life of the vessel.

Design Choices

Dimensions

Other than making sure the boat is longer than it is wide, dimensions will be up to the designer. It should be quite a bit longer than it is wide. The width of the vessel determines much of the resistance to movement as it travels through the water. Wider beam, more resistance. A wider beam will also increase stability and resistance to rolling over when water or wind impacts the side, so a compromise must be found between stability and water resistance when choosing the width. And of course the width will be a major component of the total volume calculation for the interior of the vessel.

Stability can also be added in other ways. A keel, which is an appendage of the lower hull that extends out into the water, will increase lateral stability even better than a wider hull. The flat surface of the keel will resist motion through the water. A ballasted keel, such as are used for sailboats, will even further increase stability, in that the weight concentrated at the bottom of the boat will resist forces that try to swing it upward and to one side or the other. Traditional keels will also increase the draft of the boat, but not all keels do. A split keel, which will have two keels that start on either side of the hull and extend down just a bit past the hull itself, can provide even more stability (and let the craft sit upright on land) and not increase depth. Some catamarans utilize mini-keels, which are long shallow extensions on the bottom of the hull and provide more stability without greatly increasing depth. Bilge keels may also be used. This is similar to a mini-keel, but is instead a flat extension run along the side of the hull and acts to resist any rolling motion of the boat from side to side. A keel on the bottom of the boat can also be desirable to protect the propeller from impact or grounding damage, even if placing one will unnecessarily increase the draft.

All of that is in regards to side-to-side, lateral, stability. Front to back stability will be a matter of the length of the vessel. A longer boat will be able to better resist pitching forward or back in the water, from wave action of just the force of the wind. Length, at least for a monohull displacement vessel, will also determine the maximum (within practicality) obtainable speed, or hull speed, of the boat. A longer boat will travel faster through the water. However, the length of the vessel will also be the most important factor when determining how strong the hull must be built. The center of the hull, lengthwise, will be the greatest point of strain when the vessel is in motion. If the hull is not strong enough to resist the fulcrum action of the two ends of the boat, it will split in half. So the longer the boat, the more heavily built it must be. This is the largest factor in determining the materials cost of the hull, as a longer hull will require more and sturdier materials in order to increase strength.

Height must also be determined. A taller boat will have more interior space, but will also have increased draft and greater wind resistance. This last is very important for sailboats which must move with the wind—you may notice that most of them are very sleek and low to the water. It is less important for motorboats, though still a factor, as the motor acts in the denser medium of the water and wind resistance can be overcome without too great an effort. In vessels that are not heavily ballasted, increasing the draft by putting more weight above (greater height) can also be a desirable thing. The deeper draft will allow increased stability.

Shape will be the final dimensional consideration. Each part of the boat will have a different impact on the behavior of the boat and must be shaped accordingly. The hull itself must be shaped to allow better passage through the water, but this could be curved or straight lengthwise, and curved or chined or even flat when viewed on end. The Catalina 30 hull swells out in the center, lengthwise, in order to increase interior space. Water resistance is reduced, despite this, by the smooth curve of the shape (and also by the low speeds anticipated). Depending on the building method, curved hulls can be more difficult to achieve, and the benefits are arguable. Many boats have chined hulls, with multiple flat sections laid at angles.

Wind resistance will be determined by the height of the boat, but also by its shape above water and the form of the superstructure. A longer or taller cabin or pilothouse will increase wind resistance, but some height is desirable to improve viability and for instrument emplacements. Concentrating too much weight above the waterline will reduce lateral stability. There will be a fulcrum at the center-line of the hull, from top to bottom, determined by weight distribution. That fulcrum must be kept near or under the waterline.

The bow of the boat, the front which cuts through the water, can have different shapes for different purposes or just a compromise shape that is imperfect but easier to build. A plumb bow, straight up and down, or a tumble-home bow, angled slightly backward going up, will reduce weight forward but can make anchoring more difficult than it has to be. A raked or spoon bow, angled forward from the waterline in either a straight line or curved, respectively, will ease this problem at the cost of a bit more weight forward above the waterline. A bow that sweeps up higher than the deck will take on less water in larger waves, though this will not usually be an issue for inland watercraft.

The stern and transom design may vary even more widely than the design of the bow. A wide full stern will increase interior space, but will also increase water resistance during motion. A narrow stern or one which rises out of the water will permit the water flowing around the hull to pass much more smoothly. This can be observed in the wake of a craft. More wake indicates more water resistance which shows itself the disturbed water behind the boat. It can be nice to have a swim platform or steps down to the water, but this requires a wide and inefficient stern. It also reduces potential area for a propeller or rudder. A stern that sweeps up from the keel or bottom, even below the waterline, will permit a much larger propeller. If it narrows while doing then so water resistance will be reduced. This will somewhat limit interior space in that area, but not necessarily space on deck. That narrow stern section can flare back out above the waterline, into a heart shape, and still permit a broad transom. Consider the stern shape of a Whitehall rowboat or a wherry.

Stern design must also account for the possibility of waves coming up from behind the boat (referred to as a 'pooping' action). A higher stern out of the water will reduce normal buoyancy in that area, but may also increase reserve buoyancy which will lift the stern back up when a wave washes onto it from behind. A lower stern will have increased normal buoyancy (if it has more volume under the water) but less reserve buoyancy when pooped.

Materials

You can try to build a boat out of just about any material. They will all have certain physical characteristics that are more or less desirable for the purpose. But certain materials seem to lend themselves to a given application and these are the materials that get used for boat building.

If I wanted a very durable hull and did not care how much it cost, I would have one built out of copper-nickel or Monel. Large ships are all made of steel because it is strong and can be worked easily (and is cheaper than other alternatives). Most smaller production boats are made of fiberglass which can be pretty easily worked into a mold before hardening and is adequately strong and very long lasting. Many amateur builders use some sort of wood, because it is very strong (in certain respects) for its weight, it is easy to work with and to get ahold of, and it can be cheaper (sometimes very much cheaper) than using another material.

For home builds, the most viable options are steel, aluminum, fiberglass, wood, or a wood/fiberglass laminate. Costs will vary and will depend upon local sourcing options. Steel and aluminum will require welding and can only be easily made into certain restricted shapes. They will also require an internal frame and the hull must be insulated afterward. They will have superior impact and damage resistance in use (steel more than aluminum), but significant efforts must be made to prevent corrosion or galvanic action on the hull.

Fiberglass construction can be made into any shape that you want, but you must have a mold (which will double the materials and work required for a one-off). Coring the fiberglass with something like balsa or foam will not add strength to the hull as such, but it will increase stiffness and also add to the insulative qualities of the hull. Cored areas also require less fiberglass and resin to achieve the desired attributes.

Wood construction (of certain types) does not require a mold, will be self-insulating, and can feel much better to the inhabitants, but wood is subject to damage (rot and pests) over time in a marine environment and will resist impact less than metal or thick fiberglass. It can also be difficult to repair. It is actually becoming more common to build in wood, with the advent of cheap effective epoxies, as the hull can be entirely sealed against rot and also strengthened with a sheathing of epoxy and fiberglass.

A true fiberglass/wood laminate, though, will use a structural wood as the coring material of a full fiberglass layup. This hybrid method (two or three different main ones, actually) can eliminate the requirement for an expensive mold, such as fiberglass normally requires, as the hull shape can be made out of wood, without full framing, and then glassed over. It will also be stronger than normal cored fiberglass, as the wood core will have better structural properties. And in doing so the vulnerable wood is very well sealed away from rot or infestation. I know of one custom yacht that has a double core of mahogany within a full fiberglass layup (glass-wood-glass-wood-glass), for even more strength, redundant damage resistance, and also excellent insulation.

Propulsion

Sail or motor are the most practical marine propulsion options. Though motorists may disagree with the claim that sailing is practical. You could also go with something like a jet drive or even a tunnel drive if you are really creative, but these will be expensive, more complex, and also more difficult to design for than the standard types.

Sail imposes its own requirements on the build. Any mast will be subject to the wind attempting to push it over, especially if you hang a sail from it, and must be counterbalanced in some way to keep the boat from tipping over. Which will also require that the mast and the forces upon it be supported by specific reinforcements in the hull itself. Other than accounting for those points, masts and sails can be mounted almost anywhere along the length of the boat—though some configurations have been proven to be better than others.

Motor propulsion can allow greater freedom in choosing hull-form, but there is one very specific stress that must be accounted for. If you have one motor, then the entire force of the boat as it moves through the water will be transmitted from that propeller, along the propshaft, and into the motor. Which means that the motor had best be mounted very firmly to the hull and that the hull must be able to adequately spread that strain outward from the single point of stress.

You can mount a motor and its propeller anywhere on the underside (or even the side) of the boat where it will fit. Propellers are usually placed at the back because that way the hull forward can protect it from damage, and also because the flow of water from the propeller past the rudder will multiply the steering power of the rudder. But if you did not care about impact damage and/or plan to use side-thrusters for steering, then the propeller and motor could be placed in the front, or halfway down the sides, instead. I have seen a custom catamaran build that used outboard motors mounted in the interior sides of the hulls, that would pivot up into the hull when not in use, for auxiliary propulsion. This method will reduce the steering power of the rudders while under motor power, but since there were two motors spaced apart some steering could be accomplished by reversing one motor or the other.

Interior and Systems

This part will truly be up the imagination of the builder, as long as all necessary systems and components are accounted for. Do you want to steer the boat from the back or from the front? Rudder linkages can be electronic or hydraulic (or pneumatic for that matter) and can be run to any part of the vessel. Sailboats are steered from the back or the middle because wind resistance forward must to be kept down, but many motor craft will locate the pilothouse in the front for better visibility. When reversing, or just for general information, cameras can be very useful when the feed is routed to screens around the pilot.

Tankage, both liquid fuel and water, is best placed near the bottom of the boat, for stability. You must also include one or more bilge areas where water or other liquids can be gathered and pumped overboard.

In general, your interior layout will end up with many aspects that are similar or identical to production yachts. This is just because the systems themselves force a certain layout. Tankage will always be down in the bottom of the hull. All of the food preparation and storage will be concentrated into a kitchen area and all of the personal needs will be addressed in a bathroom area. There will be spaces dedicated to sleeping that also have clothing storage nearby. Etc. The interior layout will always follow a certain logic just because it will be providing for the living needs of people. So it follows that looking at other boats and patterning your layout after one that you like, with a reasonable amount of variation, will be a more efficient way to go about interior design than to start from scratch.

Build

Materials

So, if I were to set about building this boat, I would use plywood sheeting for the hull. That is, the hull will be an epoxy laminate construction of fiberglass over a core of plywood. Many people avoid the use of plywood for laminate below the waterline, mostly because of the reputation for problems that the building method has gained. But it remains a viable possibility—one that greatly eases effort and reduces materials costs for certain hull-forms. Provided that the work is done carefully and well.

The standard for boat uses is marine ply. It tends to be composed of stronger types of wood than normal residential plywood and it is also required to have any voids in the material, especially in the vulnerable edges, fully sealed against moisture. Most marine plys will be a better product (though quality can still vary), but consider that you will be working with epoxy anyway and will have the opportunity to do your own sealing treatments. I contend that, especially when being used as a core within a strong fiberglass layup, any kind of plywood will do, provided that it is well-prepared and sealed with thickened epoxy. When laying glass on any type of plywood you will want to paint on epoxy anyway in order to keep the layup from getting starved of resin (wood will tend to absorb a certain amount of epoxy when it is laid on wet). And I would certainly be inspecting and touching up even marine ply when using that. So for my build I will use three-quarter inch plywood sheets, residential type but of fair quality. I will carefully check each sheet before use and will fill all voids with thickened epoxy. I will also go ahead and seal every edge of every sheet with the same thickened epoxy. This is more effort than might be required for marine ply, but may represent a considerable cost savings given that the entire hull will be built of these.

Dimensions

I started this part with that discussion on plywood rather than stating intended hull dimensions because I will allow those regular sheets, three-quarters of an inch thick, four feet wide, and eight feet long, to dictate the dimensions of my build. Plywood can take a bend if you want, though that gets more difficult the thicker the sheets are. This hull will curve in somewhat closer to both ends, though only with very gentle bends in the wood.

There will also be a reinforced keel for most of the center-line of the bottom of the hull, composed of four two-by-six boards. That is, four lengths of two-by-six boards that are scarfed together to reach the full length of the keel. Each pair of boards will be bolted together for added strength, with countersunk bolts that will be glassed over. The first two will extend an inch or two up into the hull. That will leave about three inches extending below the plywood hull sections which will meet at the center-line bottom at those keel boards. The lower two keel board will extend straight down, as the boat rides in the water, from the other two keel boards. These two will not be mechanically attached and will be intended as a sacrificial loss in case of serious grounding. They will be sealed and attached with thick laminate, to be sure, but should break off, and so reduce pressure on the boat, well before the hull itself is breached. The normal job of this lower keel section will be to improve the lateral stability of the boat and to reduce any rolling action. It will also help to protect a large propeller. The keel as described will deepen the draft of the vessel and so itself increase the chances of a grounding, but most groundings in a river area are much more likely to be in soft mud or sand than on hard rock, and in any case the total draft will still be fairly shallow.

The hull dimensions will be forty-six feet long by fifteen feet wide. The width will be obtained by the four inches of the two-by-six keel boards combined with two sheets of long-wise plywood on either side. The plywood will slant up from the keel at a shallow angle such that a total width of fifteen feet is reached. From there, the hull sides will go straight up. Four sheets of plywood on either side (along the keel) will make up the flat sides length of thirty-two feet, with the remaining fourteen feet of length (at the waterline) devoted to the bow and to the raised stern area which will accommodate the propeller and rudder. Both ends will be tapered inward.

The bow will require irregular cuts of the plywood, but will raise upward and forward from the keel as it narrows inward and comes to a point at the very front. This will be a straight vertical bow for most of its height, but will flare forward just at the top to allow for an anchor chain compartment. It will be somewhat of a blunt bow angle overall, as I will be bringing it from fifteen feet wide to a point within a limited amount of length, but this will be a low speed craft so that will be acceptable, provided that the laminate is made strong enough.

The stern will also narrow somewhat, though not to a point. At the rear edge of the keel, it will raise up (near vertical) to just below the waterline and then angle up and backward (somewhat above the horizontal) all the way to the rear of the vessel. Which will then rise up in a flat vertical transom. The space that is formed by the area under the raised stern will permit a large propeller and also a rudder installation. An extension from the bottom of the keel will extend back to support the bottom of the rudder. With a presumed draft of forty inches, a propshaft angle of fourteen degrees, and a four or five blade propeller, I should be able to manage proper clearance for a thirty-four inch propeller. Maybe thirty-two.

Construction

Plywood lends itself to stitch-and-glue construction, but the size of the boat will make doing that the normal way pretty awkward, so I will start with a temporary frame laid on top of a strong-back. The frame will hold my upside-down hull together until I can get it glassed over and will also help with making the few gentle curves I plan for the plywood. Once the frame is in place I can start with the keel at the top and work my way down from there. Each angle and join between pieces will be filleted and strip-glassed before moving on. This will permit smooth transitions instead of abrupt angles and will make sheathing easier, as well as strengthening the joints.

The fiberglass sheathing of the wood will be accomplished with triaxial fabric. This is slightly more expensive comparatively than biaxial, but I think worth it to add longitudinal strength along the length of the hull, without having to work successive layers at different angles. Axial cloth (biaxial is just two layers of axial run at different angles, and triaxial is three layers all run at different angles) is the strongest type of e-glass by weight and its use will help reduce the amount of epoxy that is required. Even so, the epoxy for this build will end up costing more than the e-glass, and possibly more than the plywood. I think I will use three layers of the triaxial, both outside the hull and for the interior. Maybe four.

Once the hull is glassed on the outside, rolled over, and glassed on the inside, it will form a single monocoque piece. It will also need to be pierced at several points for thru-hull emplacements. Every hole drilled must be bored out nearly twice as wide as necessary for the thru-hull. The remaining space should be filled in with a strong full fiberglass laminate plug. This will protect the integrity of your core if that thru-hull should fail at some point. It will also provide a very strong mounting point for the thru-hull as the glass will be at least an inch thick. You should still use a backing plate for every thru-hull in order to spread out loads and stresses. At no point should any fastener or anything else be allowed to touch the wood cores. It would be very convenient to just screw into the wood, but that will lead to many headaches down the road. Keep your core encapsulation perfect.

The bore for the propshaft will need to be very carefully placed. There must be extra room for bearings and it will also need to account for a stuffing box or other type of seal. The angle must be precisely measured so as to be perfectly square to the hull from side to side and exactly fourteen degrees down (or less) from top to bottom, in terms of the waterline plane of the hull. Above all this area must be heavily reinforced, as the entire thrust of the boat at speed will be transmitted along the propshaft and onto the motor-mounts.

The superstructure for my build will have a flat roof suitable for solar panels roughly fifteen feet above the waterline. This will leave around eighteen feet, altogether, of vertical space between the keel and the roof. I will build this into two decks, upper and lower, the length and breadth of the boat. The lower deck will be fully encapsulated by the hull and entered only from the upper deck. The upper deck will be the superstructure proper and will have an exterior walkway on both sides for the full length of the vessel and also around the front (for a U-shape). This exterior decking and the outer skin of the upper deck (superstructure) will be built the same as the hull (though perhaps with fewer glass layers and certainly with open spaces for doors and windows) and will be fully joined to the hull into a single larger monocoque piece. That should resolve any hull-deck seam issues and also make for a much stronger vessel overall. The roof of the upper deck will extend outward on the sides of the vessel so as to overhang the walkways, with support extensions running vertically between that roof and the deck of the walkway.

This will be a fairly low speed displacement craft, so the boxiness of the hull and superstructure will not present significant problems in terms of wind resistance. It will also be electric drive, so having a large amount of space for solar panels is very desirable. There should be roughly 600sq.ft (15ft x 42ft) of flat space on top of the roof. Minus a bit for navigation and networking instrument mounts and also a feasible amount of walking area, but most of this can be used for solar panels. I estimate enough space for twenty to twenty-five 300W monocrystalline panels. 6000–7500W of solar. Which has a beauty all it's own.

The wood-epoxy-glass construction will need several layers of UV-blocking paint. This will be expensive in itself, but is absolutely essential to insure the long-term durability of the hull. Epoxy is strong stuff and will hold the whole thing together, but will also degrade over time in the presence of ultraviolet radiation. So this aspect of the build will be just as important as the layup for the hull itself. There are different ways to go about this— some paints will try to reflect UV and some will absorb it instead. It may be good for the top coat be a reflective type and any under-layers to be absorption types.

This boat can be made more livable with port-lights and windows, but keep in mind that every (durable, fully sealed) window will add to the cost of the build. And will still be a weak point in the structure no matter what you do. I will posit a modest number of port-lights for the lower deck, all located in the center of a plywood core panel. The upper deck will have a full transparent windshield forward for the pilot station and also a modest number of port-lights (not full windows) along the sides and at the back. Using only port-lights (except for the pilot station) instead of full windows will reduce interior light and may actually increase expenses, but will make for a stronger structure and will also ease security requirements. There will be two full-size hatches (not regular doors but just as big), one on either side of the upper deck. There will also be an emergency escape hatch at the rear of the lower deck, built into the transom a good distance above the waterline.

There will need to be some railing for the upper deck walkway and also some accommodation for an anchor at the bow. The number of stanchions can be reduced or even eliminated, as railing can be built as full glassed horizontal extensions between the upright supports coming down from the extended roof area. My build will do without deck-mounted stanchions altogether. There will need to be some anchor mount hardware. The anchor chain compartment has already been mentioned, but I may also want to add a short bowsprit, which will ease space constraints at the bow.

This build as described thus far will leave very little exterior space for lounging or other outdoor activities. The roof will be largely taken up by solar panels (though you could easily reduce their numbers a bit to fit in a lounging or sunbathing area) and the walkways are pretty narrow. As an alternative to the full box enclosed upper deck, the walls at the rear could be left open to form a porch area. With the length of hull available, this porch could be made as spacious as you like—six feet long for just an outdoor sitting area or as much as twenty or more feet long for a full outdoor activity area. There will need to be support pillars at the corners and spaced along the sides and rear, but cored fiberglass construction is incredibly strong so there should be no structural reasons to limit the size of the porch area. The only consideration remaining will be to keep an appropriate balance between the indoor and outdoor space along the upper deck. I think I might posit a twelve by fifteen feet porch at the back, which will leave me about thirty feet of length inside to accommodate the pilot station and any living areas. Though the interior will be 30ft x 9ft or so, remembering the side walkways. Perhaps a main salon and kitchen, depending on what I decide to place on the lower deck instead. There must also be appropriate amounts of storage somewhere on the upper deck for any emergency supplies and necessary boat materials. Built-in seating in the porch area should accommodate this need quite nicely.

Over time, damage to the hull is close to inevitable. Stuff happens, and the coring will eventually be exposed and take damage. But when it does, as long as you were careful to isolate each core section from every other core section during the initial build, repair can be as simple a matter as replacing the damaged sheet of plywood and redoing the glass overlay. It will not be quite as strong as the original, since new epoxy will not bond perfectly to old epoxy, but it will be strong enough. A 75% bond strength with epoxy is still plenty. Even the keel boards can be replaced in this way.

Tankage and Bilge

The keel board sections that extend up into the hull should have their side areas filled in and the entire bottom center of the hull glassed flat. This will greatly strengthen the keel and also simplify bilge and tank arrangements. The sides of the hull will slope upward, though gently, so all liquids will naturally flow down to the area of the keel. The full bilge thus formed can be left exposed if you desire, but it will be better just to leave the very center area open (for bilge pumps and as an inspection area), leaving the rest of that center-line space for tankage.

This build is actually taller than it is wide, which makes it important to keep some weight concentrated down low in the hull. The rear bottom will be devoted to the electric motor. Forward from there, except for the bilge well, should be built-in tanks. This will allow perfect sizing to the space available. It can also be done using the same methods as the hull construction and when in place the tanks will serve to further reinforce the strength of the hull. These tanks can use the hull itself for their bottoms, but it will be better to lay down plastic against the hull and then build a tank. After the tank is completed, it can be lifted up, the plastic removed, and then lowered back into place.

These tanks can be multipurpose, but can only be used for water, diesel, and sewage. Gasoline tanks cannot be built into the hull with fiberglass, for safety reasons. I would also not want to put sewage this far down, which will complicate venting and pump-outs. For my build I will posit two or three tanks for diesel fuel and the rest for water. Diesel because I will still want a generator for this build and that is my fuel of choice for this particular design. The water tanks can all be devoted to potable water, but I may also choose to experiment with adjustable trim and ballast by taking in exterior water or pumping it back out. The large propeller in particular may require careful management of boat depth. In any case all tanks must also accommodate drain channels to allow any liquids to make their way down to the bilge well.

Propulsion

The single large propeller will be heavy and so will its propshaft. Despite this, furnishing the torque required to get them spinning will not be a significant concern, as long as the motor used is not grossly under powered. The more important consideration will be sizing a motor that is capable of moving the craft at desired speeds.

For this displacement vessel maximum speed will be hull speed, and will be about nine knots for the dimensions given. The power required to move the vessel at that speed will then almost entirely be determined by the weight of the completed vessel—its displacement. I will estimate this to be about fifteen thousand pounds.

With a four blade propeller of thirty-two inch diameter, a 40HP (30kW) electric motor should be plenty for hull speed and some reserve power remaining. Assuming a nominal motor speed of 1800RPM and a 3:1 reduction gear (600RPM max, general use around half that). Based on an AC induction motor with appropriate controller—heavy but reliable. Cruising speed will be just over half power for the motor and will be around eight knots. Which might require about 16kW power input. Even in full sun this will be more than is furnished by the solar bank, but between batteries, solar, and a generator unit this is very manageable. Lower speeds will be obtainable on solar alone, depending on conditions. We could get by ok most times with a 20HP motor instead, but that would leave no reserve and require too much runtime at full output. A 30HP motor might be a good compromise, which will still leave some power reserve but also be more efficient at lower speeds (electric motor power efficiency will tend to drop quite a bit when below 50% capacity usage). Cruising speed with the 30HP motor might be about seven knots instead of eight, but would drop the power draw below 13kW.

This will change based on vessel weight—if we want 40HP at 15,000lbs then we will want 60HP at 20,000lbs and 25HP at 10,000lbs. If anything though I think I might be overestimating the final displacement, and perhaps the draft as well. Which is one reason I would want to run my figures by a naval architect before starting my build. The construction technique of axial fiber and epoxy over plywood is very strong for its weight and so will make for a lighter vessel than one built using mat and roving fiberglass with polyester or vinylester resin (for instance). So I might want to extend my keel deeper to get the draft I want, or would have to go with a smaller diameter propeller...which would require a somewhat stronger motor. Everything is interrelated when calculating boat propulsion.

It may be better to utilize a twin screw configuration with this boat. That is, two propellers. They could be full size or just a bit smaller than the one I have been positing, as they will not be torque limited by the motors. But the motors themselves could be half or less the power rating of the single motor version and still achieve reasonable speeds. Being able to run just on one prop or the other will also increase low speed options. With just a single motor having to stay above 50% power for full efficiency and not wanting to run for extended periods below that because of heat issues makes for a significant boat-speed limitation. Sizing just one motor smaller will reduce power draw and permit a lower cruising speed, but also reduces reserve power potential. So having two props and two smaller motors will increase versatility without becoming power inefficient.

Electricity

Given that main (and only, unless you count strapping the dingy to the side and using that to move the boat) propulsion will be electric, a sizable battery bank will be called for. Which will probably cost more than the motor and controller and gearbox combined, but battery banks are useful for all sorts of things. A 30kWh bank or larger will allow for such conveniences as air conditioning and microwaves and electric cooking, though overindulging will require lots of generator runtime.

Three separate electrical systems will be best—propulsion DC, house AC, and house DC. These systems will connect at the batteries but should not otherwise. The propulsion motor controller will require much higher voltage than the normal DC house system, so I may consider separately configured battery banks, but with some redundant interlink capacity in case of battery problems.

Navigation tools and other instruments will be up to you, but I would want a chartplotter and sonar at a minimum. Short range radar can also be very useful for navigation in limited visibility. While this craft will (probably) not be intended for long-range cruising, spending all of its time in the relatively shallow coastal and inland waters will make close-in navigational concerns very important. I would also want cameras mounted on the boat for screen images of the rear and sides, both normal vision and IR. An IR camera on the front could also be useful, for when you don't want to turn the lights on but still want to check what's out there. Consumer electronics like this will probably not be marinized (though you can make efforts to improve the seals and otherwise protect them from degrading), but basic versions are not expensive and you can keep spares on hand for when they fail. Cameras are just one of the possible benefits of maintaining an internal network for the boat.

Air, Water, Heating, Cooling

As there are two distinct decks, there should be a ducted air circulation system. This will help insure that humidity and odors do not gather in the lower deck to give it a 'basement' feel. The total interior square footage for the boat is not large, about as big as a medium sized apartment, so air movement through the ducts and vents can be accomplished with a pretty low power draw. I would use several smaller fans instead of one big one, as this will give more control over power draws and also help to even out circulation.

Air conditioning and heating can be integrated into the vent system. These will both tend to reduce humidity, but for times when you want neither cooling nor heating you can also integrate a dehumidifier into the vent system. Between the vent fans and a dehumidifier there will be a small but significant drain on the batteries, but the large solar array should help to defray that draw. This is an electronics heavy build and keeping the humidity down will be very important for system longevity.

Heating and cooling during milder temperature periods can be assisted by a raw water heat pump system. This will have a much lower power draw on average than air cycled heating or air conditioning, though you should have those systems as well for extreme temperatures. The raw water exchange element can also assist in cooling the propulsion motor and motor controller, which will be a steady and significant source of heat while under power (though not nearly as much as a combustion engine).

I would also consider a radiant tubing system placed between the two decks (mounted on the overhead of the lower deck). This may seem redundant given the air vent system, but water or glycol are much better conductors of heat than air and this would be a good alternative option to have for nearly passive temperature regulation. Even without a powered heating or cooling element, if the radiant tubing were connected to (though kept sealed from) the raw water exchanger it would have a constant stabilizing influence on internal temperatures. The water under the hull will almost always be cooler than the outside air during hot times and warmer during cold times. This would improve internal temperatures and only require a small pump to keep going.

Given the expected cruising ranges and the large amount of internal water tankage available, this build does not call for its own watermaker. Though adding one may be convenient and will help to reduce dependence on the shore. Other water systems can be fairly simple. A pump will be needed to maintain system pressure and circulate the water, as well as a pressure tank to reduce use time for the pump. I would want a shower on the upper deck and the kitchen up there will need water as well. If there is a marine style toilet then it is best to use potable water to flush it, for the sake of reducing both odors and maintenance needs.

Range Extension

I have never actually seen this done but the concept is sound. I do not mean range extension in terms of increasing cruising range, but instead by way of making the craft suitable for blue water. By adding outriggers to the hull.

So, the idea is that you can vastly improve stability and render this boat fit to motor all around the world by adding outriggers, in effect making it into a trimaran. Unlike a trimaran, however, these outriggers could be collapsible and/or detachable, depending on how you design them and the main boat hull. They could be attached at need for a long voyage and detached as well. Or they could be permanently attached but made to fold in close to the hull when not in use so as to decrease overall beam.

What I mean by 'outrigger' in this case is just something which is buoyant in the water and preferably does not cause drag. So an empty barrel would not do because it will drag through the water and slow down the boat. But something like an old canoe would work as an outrigger (to some extent) because it will not add much drag and will increase buoyancy. In the case of range extenders (really just stability increasers) for a custom boat I would suggest something shaped like a canoe but fully sealed against water—airtight.

This can be built in the same way as the hull of the main boat—epoxy and fiberglass over wood. A hollow sealed shape, say forty feet long or so, with an average diameter of just two or three feet, will have nearly as much buoyancy as the entire hull of the main boat. With an outrigger on either side you can dramatically increase your initial stability (depending on how far out they are mounted) and nearly triple your reserve buoyancy. Consider that the deeper down in the water you try to push these things, the more force they will exert to try to come back up. If you are very careful with your seals they do not even have to be fully hollow and could be used to store equipment. The internal area should still be compartmentalized in case of damage.

The tricky part will be attaching them to the main boat in such a way that they are unlikely to come loose or, worse, damage the hull. The best way for removable mounts will probably be to use large shackles affixed onto both ends of a strut arm, which can be locked onto mounting points designed into the main boat hull and the outrigger. With enough epoxy and fiberglass, the mounting points can be made as strong as they need to be. The shackle must be designed to lock in place without rubbing. There should be at least two struts for each outrigger and three would be better. Given the lengths involved there should probably also be a cross-brace across the strut arms and parallel with the hull. Most importantly though, the boat hull itself must be designed to brace and support the strut arms leading down to the outriggers. This will call for reinforced stringers across the horizontal, vertical, and long-wise aspects of the hull from the mounting points. Each mount may have to withstand a force greater than the weight of the main hull and supporting this must be designed into the monocoque structure of the hull itself.

A Less Likely Possibility

This option is a bit more fantastic but the concept is also sound. Say that you want to be able to move your boat relatively short distances over obstacles that block passage between waterways. In some cases adding wheels to the bottom for an amphibious capability would be helpful, but such a system would be a real nuisance the rest of the time. I have also seen a catamaran that had hydraulic legs that would allow it to 'walk' up on a beach and back out, but a similar system would be very restricted by terrain. My idea here is even less practical than those two options, perhaps, but it would not be limited by terrain at all and would also not impact the normal operation of the vessel. Just attach a balloon to the top.

Or, more formally, deploy a buoyant lifting body from the top of the boat sufficient to lift it out of the water and a certain distance into the air. This can be done, but the resource commitment will be significant and safety will be by no means guaranteed. The equivalent to two or three or four large balloons, made of strong, lightweight, airtight synthetic fabric could be stored in boxes on the roof. A hydrogen generator in the hull could provide the lifting gas for the balloons. Hydrogen will be much more dangerous than other alternatives, of course, but the superior properties that it offers are what makes this scheme just possible for a home builder to accomplish. Raw water hydrogen generators are still very expensive, but the technology is advancing rapidly.

Propulsion while in the air will be somewhat tricky. The main propeller will not work as it could not spin fast enough (and may become damaged if you try). It should be possible to mount small air propellers on the hull that will move the boat short distances in still air. In breezy weather or without worrying about extra propellers an advanced anchor system could be used. That is, place one anchor where you want to go, pull yourself to it, then place another anchor where you want to go next. Repeat as needed. An exotic alternative for this would be to mount some sort of grapnel cannon on the boat that can be used to fire an anchoring point over a certain distance.

Summary and Conclusion

So there you have it. That last section in particular is meant in only a half-serious fashion—the results will probably not be worth the effort and the worry—but I also consider it to be a logical (after a fashion) extension of the appeal for this build. It is well within the realm of possibility for a home builder to add custom systems to their boat that tailor the entire vessel to their needs. Even to the extent of taking it airborne, if desired. Just don't forget strong mounting points.

I have skimped a bit on details, on need fulfillment levels and so on, because I do not want to get too repetitive in these build sections. If you have read from the beginning to get here then you should already have a good idea about what I will have to say regarding various boat systems. If you skipped straight here then please consider reading the specific needs section that interests you and also the prior build sections for more details and ideas. What I have included is what I think will be pertinent to someone considering a build like this and also what will be interesting to consider.

References and Further Research

Brown, Russel. *Epoxy Basics*

Brewer, Ted. *Understanding Boat Design.*

Devlin, Samuel. *Devlin's Boat Building*

Drake, David. *Lt. Leary Commanding*

carveyourcreation.com/how-to-build-a-wooden-boat

www.vicprop.com/displacement_size.php?action=calculate

youtu.be/k0WGFmXe1-4

First in a series of videos showing a building process for a wooden, electric powered boat. Though a smaller one than I discuss above.

youtu.be/ttWDy7GRHjw

Presentation and discussion for a steel kit boat build. Channel has further videos on the build.

youtu.be/sVqIueFKfv0

Good video showing the start of a framed wooden boat project.

28.

The Sailing Catamaran Build

This build section is actually one of the primary reasons that I decided to write this book. This is the boat I have been noodling over for several years. May my readers gain from this long pondering, as I have gained from that time spent in thought.

Platform

For marine living, and especially for a sailboat, a catamaran has much to recommend it. No added ballast is required to balance out a mast, so there is no need to drag around a heavy keel like monohulls do. Stability is instead provided by the spacing of the hulls. So when the forces on a mast attempt to push it to one side or the other, the buoyancy of the hull on that side will resist that force and work to keep the boat upright. The density of the water is so much higher than air and thus the buoyant action resisting lateral forces so efficient that catamarans tend to heel over just a few degrees at most when sailing, as opposed to the thirty or more degrees that a monohull might heel at.

So catamarans will provide flat sailing or near to it. The lack of ballast also helps (very much) to reduce weight. Because of the way the stability works they may also be very shallow draft, and some cruising catamarans draw only two feet or so of water. All of these factors combined make for a much faster craft than a monohull of similar length. It is not unusual to see a catamaran sailing half again as fast or even double the speed of a monohull of the same length. These same factors will act to improve energy efficiency when motoring. Lightweight and narrow and low draft hulls are easier to move through the water and require less thrust. They will not be limited by the traditional hull speed calculations.

Available space is also a big draw. The space between the hulls provides a convenient place to store a dingy. The bridgedeck area makes for a very large interior living space in comparison to what a monohull can provide. The rough figure is that there is about double the internal room available for a given catamaran than for a monohull of the same length. Externally, the increased area provides much better options for solar and wind power as well as offering a large amount of open deck space.

There are some drawbacks to be considered as well, but I think that the positive benefits far outweigh them. These can be boiled down to higher costs and awkward sizing. Build costs will be somewhat higher because the stresses on the bridgedeck and its joints to the hulls will be very high, and so must be met with a stronger build. The increased space will also be paid for by increased materials needed to build it out. Systems costs will increase, though mostly this will be a matter of doubling the number of propellers, rudders, and motors. With electric drive the required motors will be smaller, but two 20HP motors will still cost more than one 40HP motor. And two motor controllers will be required.

However, the build cost can quite easily be reduced by reducing the length of the vessel. A shorter boat can be lighter built in all respects and will also require cheaper propulsion and steering systems. And a thirty foot catamaran will still have a lot more room aboard than a forty foot monohull.

Sizing problems come into play when you try to fit your wide multihull into places that have been designed for narrow monohulls. For navigation this will mostly not be a problem, as most multihulls will still be narrower than commercial traffic, but you will be barred from older canal systems and some rivers. Docking will be the main issue. You might require two or even three monohull spaces to get at the dock and marinas will charge accordingly. Some of them will not be able to accommodate your boat at all. Expect to moor often (though boat systems can be designed to accommodate this and some people prefer mooring to docking). Boatyard costs will also tend to reflect the increased surface area of a multihull, and some lift arrangements will not work for a double or triple hull.

It may also be the case that multihulls are not able to sail as close to the wind and will make more leeway (being pushed aside by the wind action) under sail. I think that this is a bit of a wash in terms of sailing performance and also that different multihull designs can ameliorate these issues. The leeway problem occurs if a multihull has less grab on the water (no deep keel), but this can be countered with daggerboards or minikeels. Some multihulls with alternative mast arrangements (see below) can point closer to the wind, but even those that cannot will still reach an upwind location sooner than a monohull because they can sail so much faster, despite having to cover more ground to do so.

Purpose

This build will be designed from the start as a global sailing cruiser. It will be an off-grid energy platform with multiple renewable generation options. Capable of operating independently from shore for extended durations and in various weather and climate conditions. Fully networked into the global internet for remote applications. Truly mobile living.

These capabilities will come only at some considerable expense, but every one of the need fulfillment levels can be scaled up or down while still doing the job. The hull itself must be fully built out from the beginning, but that will only be forty percent or so at most of the final cost of the build. And hull costs can be considerably reduced by the home builder. All other systems can be tailored to fit almost any budget. And the wind will always be free.

Design

Like the last build (and the next), I will not be getting into every little detail of the design and construction of the boat. I will try to highlight and adequately describe special features and alternative design choices, in addition to showing off the overall build and giving a good idea of what it will look like.

Dimensions

The boat will be 48ft x 26ft at the waterline, for a length overall of 50ft. This is probably an overambitious size for a home build, but as this build-out is hypothetical I am taking a few liberties. 40ft x 24ft would also be a good ratio of length to width. This ratio must be kept pretty low, especially for a boat intended for all weather conditions, as it will be a large factor in the initial stability of the vessel. Initial stability is rather important for a catamaran, as it does not actually have much in the way of reserve stability. That is, it will require a great deal of force to lift one hull or the other out of the water (and more force the wider it is), but once that event occurs then it will take comparatively less force to turn the boat over altogether. So a weather event which is sufficient to overcome the initial stability of the boat will likely be able to complete the process for a full flip, unless you really get lucky and a gust that can lift a hull still falls short of being able to flip the boat. A boat can also be flipped the long way, of course, but this is less likely to happen given the greater length of the hulls. It will be even less likely the longer the boat is, but the length-width ratio must always be kept low enough to improve initial lateral stability.

The hulls will be around ten feet in height in addition to minikeels extending further down and running along the length of each hull. This should put the deck around seven or eight feet above the waterline and offer plenty of interior space in the hulls themselves. Which for my build will also be fairly wide but not overly so. Perhaps around four to five feet. This is a good way to increase interior space and buoyancy, but the wider the hulls the more exterior surface area there will be below the waterline and so the greater water resistance to motion there will be. Narrower hulls will have increased draft to produce the same buoyancy but will have decreased water resistance and likely be a bit faster. For my build getting the most speed is a less important consideration and will be somewhat compromised in several respects. It will still be significantly faster than a monohull for a given energy outlay or wind condition, so this does not concern me overmuch.

Total draft should be about three and a half feet (42in), with the minikeels being designed to make up the difference after hull draft. This is more than necessary for the platform, but is still very shallow draft and will not restrict possible navigation areas very much. The increased draft will also permit larger propellers than otherwise. I will want the minikeels themselves to extend at least one-half of the length of the hulls, roughly centered to make gaps both fore and aft. This is much greater keel length than usual for sailing catamarans, but I consider it an important support of the purposes of this build. It is a deliberate increase in underwater surface area and will somewhat slow the boat, but will also greatly amplify initial stability. A limited amount of drag will be added in the long-wise dimension, but a great deal more drag will be added in the lateral dimension. So any tipping force must be that much greater. This will also reduce the amount of leeward action under sail. And any intentional beachings will be better supported, as the keels will be designed to support the weight of the boat.

The bridgedeck will clear four feet above the waterline and interior headroom will max at around seven feet, for somewhere over eleven feet of total clearance from the water (after the structure thickness). This will mean the bridgedeck is raised three feet or so above the deck/top of the hulls on the exterior. The bridgedeck top will be a flat surface extending somewhat over half the length of the boat. Wind resistance will be higher than ideal with these sizings, which will slow speed a bit when sailing and motoring both, but that factor can be somewhat reduced with slanted or curved exterior surfaces. I will want to have a pretty gentle angle on the front of the bridgedeck in order to reduce wind impact forward. More importantly though, these dimensions will improve quality of life. The high bridgedeck clearance will reduce or eliminate wave slap on the underside and so remove much of the annoyance factor from that. This can also be a safety consideration during serious wave action. A small cut-water will be added to the center-line of the bridgedeck underside to help reduce wave effects even further.

Ceiling height inside is also a very important attribute. Above in my van build section I downplayed this somewhat, but conditions are very different on a cruising boat. Van living includes the frequent possibility to step outside, or in rough weather to leave the van and go into a building. You can still go out on the deck to be able to stand upright on a sailboat, but in rough weather all you will have is the boat and you will not want to go down into the hulls when things are happening topside. It is a very significant factor to have adequate walking headroom in the main living salon on a boat. If I were taller I might even go as high as eight feet of interior clearance.

Mast

The dimensions given above are a little eccentric but not large departures from standard sailing yachts. My mast idea is. I propose what you might call a boxed a-frame mast. So it will be a split mast, supported in two places on the boat, mounted to the exterior edge of each hull a bit forward of center-line lengthwise. The upright mast posts will be straight but move inward slightly, so the top flat horizontal bar of the mast will be about twenty feet long (reduced from the twenty-four feet or so of the mast mounts). There will also be another horizontal bar four to five feet below the top-bar (according to the wind turbine heights, see below), and maybe a third bar about midway between there and the deck for extra side-support. I posit a mast height of around sixty feet from the waterline. With no boom.

There are certain drawbacks to a mast like this. It will have to weigh somewhat more than a single stick mast, as there must be more material up above to support the bridging shape. The larger profile will also increase wind drag and so reduce sailing speeds and impact stability. And it looks strange to the nautical eye. These things are true for standard a-frame masts that meet at the top and the negative factors are even more pronounced with the boxed frame I am proposing. But hear me out.

The weight and drag will reduce speed somewhat, but that is not my primary concern with this build. Stability is a wash, as the spaced bracing on the hulls will compensate for the extra weight and I have already increased lateral drag with the long minikeels. Using this mast will reduce loads on the bridgedeck which must be supported by the hulls anyway, making for a more efficient build structure than a single central mast will. Furling arrangements will generally be easier with it and can be used in all wind conditions, including a roller furling main. The entire rig can be easily controlled from the front cockpit I discuss below, which increases safety in all conditions as well as being extremely convenient for single-handing. It may be argued that sailing performance close-hauled will be improved (though I have also encountered those arguing the complete opposite). Finally, for my purposes, the top horizontal cross beams will enable me to safely mount several vertical wind turbines, in addition to navigation and communication equipment.

This mast will require no stays to the side and no spreaders, but there will be some to the rear and front. For choice the only forestays will be furling sail arrangements (and possibly the rear stays as well if I can work out how to do it and still get some use out of those sails). My preference is for synthetic rigging, though that may not be entirely possible with creative furling arrangements.

For loading purposes and to reduce mast weight and drag, it would probably be better to mount the mast legs on the interior edges of the hulls rather than the exterior edges, but there are a few different reasons for the wider bracing. It allows more room up top to fit in wind turbines. Side stability will be somewhat improved. And I would like to add a built-in system for lowering and raising the mast.

Folding Mast

So, if the mast leg on each side were not directly connected to the hull but instead hinged at the top of a triangular bracing, with support legs extending fore and aft, then the weight of and forces on the mast could be better distributed along the hulls. Also, the overall length of the mast legs would be reduced and it would be more feasible to pivot the mast at those hinges. If the hinge were ten feet off the deck, then the mast legs would be just a bit longer than forty feet. Tilting the mast down at a sixty degree angle would reduce mast height by twenty feet, and of course tilting it down to the horizontal would reduce mast height by forty feet. This would make a great many under-bridge passages accessible to the boat and open up a number of inland locations that most sailboats are barred from.

Strength and durability for the system presents an engineering problem, but one that is resolvable. It will be expensive, as not all required materials will be within the scope of the home builder. The hinge will almost have to be metal, and something better than plain steel in order to withstand the marine environment. It may also require a large gear and pawl arrangement in order to keep the raising and lowering process manageable and help to lock the system into place. I think the actual raising and lowering could be accomplished with electric motors mounted on either side at the hinges. The power draw will be significant but not nearly as much as that required for electric propulsion.

The mast will require bracing when lowered. This could be accomplished with hinged supports mounted on the mast legs, but that would increase overall mast weight and windage. It seems better to build hinged supports toward the rear of the hulls, about twelve feet long, that will normally lay flat on the deck to the sides of the bridgedeck cabin. The mast could be lowered by its controls to a set position and hold there (the system had better be strong enough to hold it in place) and then the operator could move back and swing the braces up into pre-made latches on the mast.

Overall this mast pivot arrangement is overly complicated and will be expensive to build and maintain. I would think long and hard before including it in my build and would need compelling reasons to do so. But is it a viable option. I thought it up mostly because I do not like the height restrictions keeping sailboats out of most river systems. If global cruising is the goal then it would be nice to be able to pass upstream under the annoying low bridges that land-dwellers seem to insist upon. I still kind of like the idea of the triangle arms coming up from the hull for the mast mount, even without the pivot option. This will increase windage a bit and complicate wiring runs, but it cuts the load stress at the hull joins in half and will also reduce strain on the fore and aft stays.

Layout

The piloting and control station will be located at the very front of the bridgedeck and might be seating room only in order to accommodate the sloped front angle. I would want this to be enclosed against bad weather, but also have openings for ventilation and good exterior access in fair weather. So there will be doors (hatches really, and not full size doors and not upright walking passages) on both sides and windows wherever possible. The lines and controls for the sails will all be run to here, in addition to steering and motor controls and instruments and monitors. This area should probably be somewhat narrower than the cabin further back, in order to help reduce weight forward and accommodate the pathways for the side hatches. Visibility will be good for the forward arc, but rear visibility will be compromised and should be replaced with camera feeds. This will improve pilot awareness in fair weather. In foul weather the pilot will be relying more on radar than visual inspection anyway.

Forward of the pilot station there will be some exterior lockers to utilize the final bit of triangular encapsulated space. From there forward there will only be a single trampoline in the center between the hulls and a cross-brace at the front, walk-able and full supported for stays and furlers. I may consider a small bowsprit at the front center off of the cross-brace to improve the forestay angle. The single large trampoline forward will reduce weight but keep the space useful for certain activities. If solar fabric becomes more viable for the average consumer then this net trampoline can be replaced with a solar collector and still be useful as a trampoline. Also, this open space forward between the hulls can be used as alternative dingy storage or even mounting for a larger and heavier boat. Doing so will impact wind and water resistance, but the capability is nice to have.

Many catamarans will run a central exterior support forward from the bridgedeck to the line of the bows in order to run the anchor line, but I think that is unnecessary weight as the twin bows at the front offer a perfect opportunity for redundant anchor capacity. You should not have two smaller anchors and use both, since you will inevitably end up with greater load on one than the other and may end up parting and coming adrift. But you could have two full size anchors, one on each bow, with the second anchor providing a ready backup in case the first anchor fails. It will not be too difficult to attach the anchor line from one side over to the other side cleat so that the actual anchor placement in the water is center-line for the vessel. You could use both full size anchors at once for extra holding power.

I also like the idea of integrating lift points into the build in order to facilitate haul-outs. So the forward cleats could instead be full integrated extrusions from the hull capable of supporting a large part of the weight of the boat. Similar extrusion/cleats could extend up in the rear area of the hulls. You could also put some in the center-line exterior of the hulls but if you have extension (triangle) supports for the mast legs then those will do fine for the center attachment points. With these in place a crane will not need slings, which may not be sized for catamarans anyway at certain boatyards, but can just drop chains and hooks from the central lift point. It is also nice to have very strong attachment points on the boat for other purposes such as mooring and docking and towing. Best of all these lift points can be built of the same materials as the hull.

I would want the pilot area in the front of the bridgedeck to be fully sectioned off from the rest of the interior cabin, with a bulkhead wall and hatch. It will be best to keep weather out of that area anyway, but it will be subject to more weather forces and in case of leaks in can be equipped with its own drains to underneath.

The rest of the bridgedeck space will need to be divided between the main cabin, the porch out back, and the dingy storage. I would want the roof of the bridgedeck to extend well back to just short of the sterns. It can be braced on the side hulls and will shelter the porch area from sun and rain. If well built, it can also help to extend the dingy davits backward a bit and so increase the potential porch area. There will be no need to mount any sort of instruments or equipment here, as everything can be accommodated on the mast.

Inside, I would include a small food prep area in the salon, but would put the main kitchen down in the port-side hull. It is convenient and pleasant to have the kitchen located in the salon area where all the action happens and most of the windows are, but I will need to budget extra space up there for my generator and fuel storage (see below) and still want to keep that main living area as open as possible. The kitchen will be just a few steps down and that passage will be kept as open space.

I will designate the rest of the port-side hull as storage and living space. Aft the motor and its battery bank can be covered over by a raised bed. Add a bit of storage space forward from there and a hatch and you have a guest cabin. Then the kitchen forward from there. I like the idea of having a full shower in the bow, which many market catamarans do. Between the bow shower and the kitchen is plenty of space for a guest toilet and bunks and more storage.

The starboard hull can then be configured as the private quarters. I would have roughly the same layout that side, except there would be a privacy screen in the passage down to the hull and the area opposite the kitchen would be an office/productivity space. The bed would still be aft over the motor and the shower all the way forward at the bow. I may put a compost toilet adjacent to the sleeping cabin for convenience.

Propulsion

The (auxiliary) propulsion system will consist of the electric motors located at the rear of each hull, their controllers, any battery banks, any reduction gearing off the motors, the propshafts, and the propellers.

Before getting into propeller sizing and consequent system design, however, we must first have a better idea of the shape of the stern than I have thus far indicated. I will get into further detail below regarding the actual stern construction, but say for now that the bottom of the stern will be a reverse curve (reversed in comparison to the downward bowing hull), bowing upward and pointed somewhat forward, from just behind the minikeel to the very back of the hull well above the waterline. This will act to reduce interior space and also reduce buoyancy astern, but there is already plenty of interior space, that which remains will be sufficient for the rudder mount (though the top of the stern may need to rise up a bit above the rest of the deck), and the buoyancy loss can be compensated for with the overall hull-form shape. This shape has the benefit of being viable to build without using a full mold or frame. It will also effectively eliminate any worries over hull clearance for propeller sizing.

The propeller diameters can then be any size from around thirty-six inches on down. As this is an energy intensive build already I will want to go for maximum efficiency and will posit the diameters as that full thirty-six inches, with pitch to be matched to propshaft RPM at desired cruising speed. I will also want to use regen under sail so will increase blade area by positing four or five blade propellers. Something like a Michigan Workhorse, designed for heavy duty commercial purposes and so likely to give long service in this lighter application.

The propshafts will need to be something like two and a half inches in diameter (or even larger) to bear the weight of the propeller and high torque strain. There is little constriction on shaft angle on the exterior, other than closer to the horizontal offering better clearance from the rudder skeg, so I will let the motor and gearbox inside determine shaft angle. I may be able to achieve a true horizontal mount, but something like a five to ten degree angle seems more likely. There will be an exterior strut and cutlass bearing to further support each shaft, with two arms running up at an angle to each hull for better support.

These are very large propellers for a dual prop setup on a boat of this displacement, so I will posit gearing down shaft RPM to a max of three or four hundred. This will somewhat complicate the gearing and will require a robust gearbox instead of a pulley arrangement, but I will be able to use less powerful motors to somewhat defray the extra cost. This will limit top speed while motoring, but I will be happy with a cruise speed of around eight knots and the lower boatspeed will even further increase efficiency. I anticipate a sailing speed well in excess of twelve knots anyway, depending on wind.

20HP motors should be fine for this purpose, though I would also consider something like a 10kW as a viable alternative. Those chosen will depend on the final displacement weight of the boat. Permanent magnet type motors are a good fit for this build, though care will have to be taken to not ever over-speed the motors during regen, given the aggressive gearing for the low-speed propellers and higher expected sailing speeds over motor-cruising speeds.

Steering

Steering will be an entirely separate system than propulsion and consist of the rudders and their posts, gearing systems and electric motors, power for the motors, and the control circuits routed to the pilot station. Access to the rudder posts and steering motors will be through the propulsion motor compartment and located at the very sterns of the hulls. It should also be possible to accommodate an emergency steering access point by cutting a removable but sealed port directly above the rudder post, for fitting an emergency tiller. This would be an awkward arrangement but could still provide some steering capability in the case of full electrical power loss. Though as this is a sailboat it is also possible to effect limited directional changes with the sails alone.

I will want full skeg rudders for this build, to improve durability. I may also want to run supports from the rear of the minikeels to the bottom of the skegs, but these would have to be curved down somewhat for propeller clearance and would then be the lowest part of the boat (and increase draft). The extra support may not be worth it and can be compensated for by increasing the strength of the skegs.

Electricity

Power for this build will center around the boat batteries, and I will posit three separate battery banks for this application. That is, there will be one battery bank located at each motor and used primarily for propulsion and a third battery bank for all house loads. This will complicate the electrical system and increase expense, but it will also simplify voltage requirements and provide redundant capacity in the event of one or two banks losing power. All normal charge sources can be input to the house bank and dedicated charge and cross-draw circuits can be run between the three banks, which can be switched on or off at need and utilize programmable controllers. This will also simplify issues with the parallel wiring arrangements that are often used to configure larger battery banks.

The roof of the bridgedeck was specifically kept as a large flat open space for the purpose of mounting solar panels. I will be able to cram in quite a significant amount, as there might be as much as 600sq.ft. I will posit around twenty 400W panels (or equivalent) for 8kW max solar charge. There is room for more than that but this is a conservative estimate. I will arrange the solar installation into small groupings with multiple smaller solar chargers. This will be somewhat more expensive initially, but will provide much more energy in the long term as shading effects from the mast and stays will be reduced. Series connected panels especially may drop out entirely with very little shading, so with one large solar array on top and near constant shading very little power might be produced. 8kW is a considerable amount of solar for a boat and I might be expected to receive as much as 40kWh per day. Average draw will most probably be less than this, but that is still quite enough power for most non-propulsion loads and a good amount of propulsion as well.

I hope to complement this large solar array with a substantial amount of wind power generation. The specific shape of my eccentric mast is almost entirely based upon wind turbine mountings. There will be much more available wind higher up and this build is intended for extensive offshore cruising where there will be steady winds. I will posit mounting multiple vertical axis wind turbines near the top of the mast between the two top crossbars. The top and bottom mount should permit sufficiently strong attachment and reduce the chance of damage to the units.

Vertical axis turbines are generally less efficient than horizontal designs at electrical generation, but there are a number of benefits which make them the better choice for this particular application. They can be much quieter and the distance from the deck may be enough to reduce any noise altogether. They can be designed to not require any braking action in high winds, as the geometry itself can create a vortex and counter force at higher rotation speeds. I can fit more of them onto the mast, given my specific arrangement. They will provide power from any wind direction without needing to move around (other than the static rotation). And altogether I might be able to draw as much or more energy from wind generation as I can get from the large solar array. Very much more in certain conditions and averaged over a twenty-four hour period.

They will have to be built stoutly and so will add to mast weight and somewhat to windage under sail. Though since most of the wind that impacts them will be converted into electricity (or heat), stability will be much less impacted than otherwise might be the case. They will reduce sailing speeds and sailing efficiency, but since they will be generating electricity at the same time then I should be able to get much of that back with motor-sailing. Even more so if I am getting a solar draw at the same time. Despite the auto-braking action of the design, in very high winds the system will be in very serious danger of taking damage. This is actually another reason that I would like to be able to lower the mast down. But in such strong weather conditions every boat will be in danger of taking damage and also every part of the boat. The best option for protecting the turbines will be the same as for other systems—keep an eye on the weather and take shelter when necessary. This system can be made quite robust enough to withstand normal cruising conditions.

Regen under sail will be the third renewable energy option on the boat. This can be a very serious power source on a sailing catamaran with large propellers, as power draws will be increased by the higher possible sailing speeds and also the larger propellers with greater drag potential. This will slow the boat, and between the wind turbines up top and the drag below sailing speeds might be cut in half in certain wind conditions. There may also be a very serious drag on the boat even when not using the system for regen. But under sail at least you might be able to generate more power than the wind turbines and solar panels put together. This does not indicate that the wind turbines should be eliminated, as they will also keep working at anchor and throughout the night.

This system setup with extended renewable power generation options will require certain alterations in piloting behavior. Under sail, for instance, it will be important to use the propulsion motors for either power generation (regen) or propulsion, but not let them sit idle. So if the battery banks are low then regen should be engaged, but if they are full then motor-sailing should be begun. Otherwise the high propeller drag will reduce sailing speed to no gain. The motors need not have a high power draw in the case of 'motor-sailing'. Just a trickle of power, more than compensated for by the solar array and wind turbines, should be sufficient to get the prop spinning at boat speed with no load and eliminate most drag.

I will also propose that this build is suitable for gaseous power generation as a backup system for the multiple renewable options. For choice this would be hydrogen power, and if the price ever comes down enough and safe durable hydrogen systems suitable for marine living are designed then I would be prepared to switch over. No extensive changes would be required for the generator and storage cabinets as overhead venting will already be accounted for by the natural gas option. Both hydrogen and natural gas are lighter than air and float upward. Hydrogen would be even better if the system included the ability to generate the gas from raw water.

So the boat design would be even further future-proofed with the ability to switch to hydrogen power. For the time being however it will be much cheaper and entirely possible to safely utilize natural gas or LPG (propane or butane or both). As an added bonus these can double as cooking and heating fuels, but the primary use will be to fuel a combustion generator for electricity production.

This is one reason why I put the kitchen down in the hull and saved back some salon space. To safely store and utilize LPG on a boat, being heavier than air, it must be kept from flowing down into an encapsulated hull. So I can use it on my catamaran build as long as I keep it up on the bridgedeck and have drain pathways that allow any spilled gas to drop down onto the water instead of into a hull. I will locate my generator unit in a cabinet on the bridgedeck, against the back wall to the porch, and store the LPG in another cabinet right next to it. There will be no propane use down in the kitchen. Any cooking gas will be used inside at the prep station or outside on the porch. A gas heater will also be located in the salon if one is utilized.

Safety can be further increased by designing the generator and storage cabinets to be stronger at the top, bottom, front, and sides then they are to the rear. So any explosion will be channeled toward the path of least resistance which will be the weaker rear (blowout) panel. This will be unfortunate for anyone out on the porch but will save the interior. As an alternative the tops and/or bottoms of the cabinets could be designed to be weaker. This will further complicate the build process and may somewhat weaken other structures, but may still be the better choice. There will already need to be drain vents in both the top and bottom of each cabinet anyway and so some part of an explosion will go that way regardless. Not that I consider an explosion to be likely, with regular maintenance and careful procedures for gas use, but the possibility must be considered and provided for.

This does put the generator unit in the main living space. Gaseous power generators tend to be even louder than diesel units. But the generator cabinet itself can be designed with extra insulation and effective soundproofing. The exhaust can also be muffled and vented under the bridgedeck. There will have to be a dedicated air intake, probably from the top, which must be drained and filtered against water and salt content. Taken altogether the generator noise will probably be louder out on the deck than inside the salon, but in any case can be well muffled.

So the electrical system will actually be four separate systems. An AC house system, run through an inverter/charger which either draws from the house bank or is powered by the generator and charges the house bank in addition to meeting AC loads. A DC house system at 12V, which is directly powered by the house battery bank that is in turn charged by solar and wind power through multiple charge controller units. And two propulsion battery banks at 48V (or higher), which power the propulsion motors and in turn are charged by them while in regen mode. The propulsion banks may also be used for other high draw DC loads. Each DC bank will have a programmable DC-DC converter run between it and the house bank for charging purposes. They may also have a converter run between themselves for cross-draw capacity. Shore power will be run through a dedicated battery charger built around an isolation transformer and only linked to the house battery bank.

I will not size the battery banks here but the bigger the better. Given current battery prices this will be a very significant expense, though I may be able to cut the cost nearly in half with a custom (LiFePO4) build from cells. Fortunately these batteries can be expected to last through at least ten years of use and perhaps much longer. By the time they fail there may be better options for replacement. Safety requirements and other precautions will add considerable complexity and expense to the electrical system, but are absolutely essential for this electric-centric build. Full grounding plates on each hull and lightning rods at the top of each mast leg, with heavy cables run between them. A large number of breakers, fuses, and relays. Carefully planned corrosion defenses.

At least control circuits can be simplified with the inclusion of full internal networking. No need to run dozens of control wires when you can route all of it through a single backbone. Though in this case I will need both an NMEA backbone and a separate system for non-NMEA electronics.

Construction

For this build I will need to have more curved surfaces and otherwise better control over shape and form. Plywood will still be useful for broad flat surfaces, though I may go with a stronger marine ply for this build. For the hulls and other curvaceous areas I will utilize a strip-planking method. This is still a wood-cored epoxy/fiberglass laminate, but instead of plywood actual wood planks will constitute the coring material. Sizing for the planks will be a matter of choice and will depend on what shape you want the hull to be. It is called strip planking because the planks are usually pretty narrow, as in thin strips of wood, but even if they are made narrow for better working they can still be fairly thick to make a good solid core. In any case the width of any given plank is determined by the shape of the hull at that point and how you want it to bend.

There are different methods of fitting the planks together. I will just butt each one against the next and fill the gaps that are formed with epoxy fillets, but you can also shape the sides into hollow and protrusion forms so that there is a smoother interlock from one piece to the next. That might be a bit stronger laterally, but I will be getting most of my lateral strength from the fiberglass anyway.

Regardless of the fitting method, strip-planking requires that you make a framework in the shape of the hull-form you want to achieve. The strips are then attached to the framework by fasteners, which get removed once the hull strips are firmly attached to each other. After the exterior of the piece is finished (glassed over), the hull is turned or rolled over and the interior is finished up. So the framework is discarded after its piece is finished. Though in the case of a catamaran, with symmetrical hulls, the same framework pieces can be reversed and used for the other hull if built in sections.

For choice I would like to try black locust for the hull strips/core, but the black locust trees in North America only grow to a certain size before locust borers get at them, so it might be difficult to find good sized mature lumber. I have read that there are European black locust plantations that are not troubled by the locust borer. The wood is stronger than oak and grows faster, so the Dutch and others plant it as a local alternative to tropical hardwood imports. It is highly rot resistant and should make a good marine lumber choice.

I might also like to try sassafras wood, which is common in the midwest and reputed to make strong durable lumber. If I were building on the west coast I might instead use Douglas fir. In the southeast yellow pine. But in each case I would still compare pricing and quality to imported woods like mahogany and teak, which have been proven to make very good marine lumber.

Hulls

Before getting started I would need to make a strong-back to have a firm level base to use for the temporary framing. If I had the space available I would go ahead and frame up the entire bottom of the boat so that I could get the best epoxy bonds all the way across. That would be at least a sixty by forty foot working area, preferably indoors and with some kind of temperature and humidity controls. The overhead would also have to be tall enough to allow turning the build over, and if I did build the entire bottom at once I must still have some practical way to do the turning over and to move the thing around. Like a hoist and gantry system, though enough hands could probably do the work as well.

So that method would call for a permanent building with some stout hardware hanging from the ceiling and climate control to boot. That would be nice to have, but you can build with less. As an alternative method I could frame in a temporary structure and seal it over with plastic sheeting. Turning could be accomplished by moving the frame out of the working structure, flipping it, then moving it back in. The flip could also be accomplished with a temporary structure, just a scaffold and pulley system. Though it might be best to incorporate that into the working structure itself in the first place, if possible. You might also manage the flip with enough willing hands. Otherwise, just build the thing in sections. Build one hull, flip, build the next hull, flip, then build the bridge between them.

As for moving the thing around...a strong-back is usually made by setting concrete into the ground then directly bolting into that for a firm base. But it could also be done with a mobile frame arrangement, by adding wheels or rollers to the bottom of the frame. This would be much more difficult to work with and would require careful adjustment and probably constant fiddling, but it would permit a rolling frame arrangement. With your setup and intended build method it may be worth it.

Because of my overhanging stern design I will need to increase buoyancy aft and so will have a more rounded hull-form under the waterline than might otherwise be ideal. The specific shape of the hull will thus be irregular and will need to be carefully planned out, built reversed into the frame, and then formed with the strip planks. Which themselves will be scarfed together lengthwise, as I am unlikely to find any good lumber the full length of my hulls. I will not be able to form the irregular shapes required just with long planks, but any gaps will be filled in with shorter pieces that are carefully interlocked into the rest of the strips. For me this will be done with thickened epoxy fillets instead of wood-forming, as the core will mostly be adding compressive strength to the full laminate, but there will be a longitudinal strength factor as well so I will engage in some mechanical interlocks like the scarfing.

From the bow to just aft of where the keel will be, I should be able to make the curves required with single long strips, though more or less narrow depending on their specific bends. The reverse curve for the stern will require new strips which will butt into the longer hull strips. For these I will want to mechanically interlock the wood and also add laminate reinforcement even before the main hull glassing rolls. This will be a stress point but if sufficiently strengthened will not be a weak point.

From this reverse curve on the bottom of the hull, to the smooth rounded sides, to the flat (or slight flare) of the deck at the stern, careful joining and reinforced transitions will be required. But with sufficient planning and effort the final shape can both look graceful and be very strong. One could do the same thing, and other more exotic shapes, with molded fiberglass, but that would not have the added benefits of the solid wood coring. And this way no mold is required.

The minikeels will need to have a gradual transition into the hulls, in order to better distribute force should they be required to bear the full hull weight while on the hard (and also in case of grounding). I think I would also build these as a wood-cored laminate, with long boards oriented along the length of the hull. There will be two separate sides close to the hull, with boards flaring up to starboard and others flaring up to port, and joined to a single board, or boards, extending down into the water as far as is needed to make up my intended draft. Close to the hull this will form an air void, which I may leave as is or instead choose to fill with closed-cell foam. The foam will be messier and almost impossible to clean out if I want to get rid of it later, but an air void may conceivably fill with water after damage and endanger the continued buoyancy of the boat until drained.

As with the riverboat build above, the minikeels will be designed as potentially sacrificial in case of severe grounding, that the main hull itself will be less likely to be breached. So I will first glass over the hull, then build on the keel, then glass over the keel. This will be more than strong enough for normal forces, as I will extend the keel glassing layers some ways up onto the outer hull laminate, but the keel should break off with impact before the hull itself it staved in.

However, a final laminate layer will extend from covering the keels and to well above the waterline, and will be aramid (Kevlar or equivalent) instead of the axial fabric for the rest of the laminate. This will end toward the rear at the stern transition, as that hull area will be protected by the propeller and rudder. This aramid layer will be the most expensive laminate layer on the hulls, but the cost is not that much greater and I think the increased impact and abrasion resistance will be well worth it. It will not really help in the type of serious grounding which might rip off a keel or worse, but should provide excellent resistance to lesser damage sources like a log impact or an accidental scraping-type grounding. In those cases I might lose paint layers but will not have to deal with much hull damage. Which I consider a good investment.

For the main laminate layers, I would use triaxial fabric for choice, but in any case axial fabric, in multiple layers. To my knowledge this is the best compromise available between cost, strength, and weight for a laminate buildup. At least one using epoxy and done as a home build. Axial in epoxy is very high strength for a given weight and fewer layers will be required, which will reduce the amount of resin and fiberglass needed. With a solid wood core stiffness is still very high despite the thinner glassed laminate. The materials are also bulk produced and, while more expensive than individually weaker alternatives, are within the price range of a home builder. I would want to be advised by an expert in the matter, and this may vary for different parts of the vessel, but I think something like four layers of triaxial (inside and out) should be sufficient for this build.

Joining

The transitions between the hulls and the bridgedeck will need to be very strong. The primary strength required here will be in the sideways direction rather than the long-wise direction for the hulls, but long-wise strength will also be important. I will run the core strips straight across the gap instead of following the direction of the hull boards, but will use mechanical bonds at the joinings and heavily reinforce the entire area. As with the sterns, this is a stress point but need not be a weak point. With laminate construction adding strength becomes a simple matter of adding layers of fiberglass.

For the small cut-water I will just add a triangular-shaped piece of wood, long-wise, onto the core before glassing over. This will reduce clearance to the water a bit, but my intended (and possibly overambitious) four feet of clearance is very high up and a few inches reduction in the middle will not matter overmuch. If water does get that high though the cut-water will serve to reduce its impact.

Before discussing the top of the boat I will stress that every single air gap in the coring material, except for the optional ones inside the minikeels, should be filled in with thickened epoxy fillets before glassing over the hull-form. No significant voids should be permitted, as each one will become a potential weak spot in the laminate. The primary purpose of the core is to act as a firm compression barrier for the glass laminate overtop. There are other important secondary purposes, such as increasing laminate stiffness, adding insulative qualities, and increasing longitudinal strength, but without that compressive resistance you might as well not have a core. The fiberglass does have some flex, but if ever that flex potential is exceeded, say by being pushed into an air gap instead of being resisted by a solid core, then the glass will break and most of the structural strength at that point will be lost. I have left some air gaps in the minikeels (or weak non-structural foam), but that is a deliberate aspect of the sacrificial nature of those members and is a special case. The rest of the core, from the bottom of the hulls all the way up, must be a solid piece before glassing is started on that portion. There will be some inevitable gaps inside the wood itself, but this weakness can be reduced by soaking unthickened epoxy into the wood, which will have to be done before glassing regardless in order not to starve the laminate of resin. And of course the fiberglass itself should be carefully rolled on and have no air bubbles.

Top Deck and Cabin

With the bottom finished as much as possible we are done with the temporary frame arrangement and can proceed to flip the thing over and start on the top parts. The core would have been attached to the frame to begin with, but those fasteners should have been filled in and removed as the core became better attached to itself, and by the time the first layer of glassing was finished the frame should have had no actual attachment to the hull-form. After the flipping maneuver is complete, hopefully without mishap and having been planned out before even starting the build, the work may continue. Everything below should be carefully padded, braced, and leveled before moving on.

Before building on any more coring material, the existing core must be filled from this side and otherwise prepared to receive the fiberglass, and then the fiberglass applied. Not all the way to the edges, as that must be kept exposed for continued core building, but close. I will want to go ahead and fully encapsulate the hulls where possible, so that a leak in the deck material will not necessarily spread to the hull cores, but the build process for the top part will be much less regular than the single hull-form underneath. Before doing all of this though the special reinforcement points must be accounted for.

The lift points that I want to put at the corners of the top deck will need to be fully attached to the main body of the hull. Perhaps by sinking a long bolt or two along the core before glassing that portion over. The metal bolts will be fully encapsulated and so will not (normally) be subject to corrosion. They could extend up above deck level and have a third bolt welded or otherwise attached across the gap. This would then serve as a core for the laminate of the lift point. I suppose you could do the same thing with a curved stick of wood —this would not be as strong and a heavier glass laminate would be required overtop, but if the point were ever damaged then there would not be the risk of corrosion. The metal cored staple can be thinner and thus mounted closer to the deck.

The mast mounts will need to be even stronger than the individual lift points. I think that if I were doing single-point mast mounts on either side then I would run an extra core board all the way down to the bottom of the hull and some ways up the other side, using that as the basis for a reinforced stringer to distribute the compressive and sideways force. I would also run extra core boards both fore and aft from there as the basis for a reinforced stringer to distribute front and back loads. Though most of that force will be handled by the standing rigging, each piece of which must also have its own reinforced attachment points. If I were doing a pivot mast or just building up a framework to shorten the length of the mast legs then I would still keep the long-wise reinforcement but run the vertical boards down at diagonals, so there would be one going toward the center of the hull from each mount point that would meet each other and another going toward the end of the hull from each mount point but would still reach the bottom of the hull and wrap around a bit. This diagonal arrangement may actually be better for the single mount method as well, though it will somewhat complicate the internal build.

There will also be gaps in the laminate structure that should be left out before coring and glassing as the build moves upward. Those lockers at the very front of the bridgedeck. The cabin door and window openings. The entire porch gap at the back. Some of these might make more sense to go ahead and build, cut out, and use the panel formed for the hatch or so on, but that will be up to the builder as there are other methods which may be preferred.

The deck itself and other flat gap-bridging areas I will build with marine ply coring, though every critical load point, like the corners of the bridgedeck cabin, will have a solid wood core. All of the structural parts of the interior will be finished up before I cover it over with the deck, but when I do get to this point I will need to insert aluminum mounting plates on top of the plywood, to which railing stanchions can be attached. The mounting plates will be glassed over and the stanchion fasteners run through the laminate down to the plate, but still sealed against moisture. This way the coring material will not be exposed but the stanchions and railing will have a goodly amount of strength.

The hull-deck joins themselves will be full glassed joints. The common core will be broken here (mostly) but the gap will be fully filled with structural fiberglass and resin. The idea is to form the entire hull-form into a monocoque structure but still fully encapsulate different sections of the wood coring as possible. So I will do the same at every spot where the solid wood coring joins up with a plywood cored section. Full glassing for both ends and solid full-thickness fiberglass between with a strong laminate to join them together.

Interior

Inside the hulls, bulkhead walls made of plywood-cored laminate will be used to further increase stiffening and strengthen the hulls against over-flexing. The port-side hull can have three, one on either side of the kitchen space and a third up front sectioning off the shower. The starboard hull can have matching bulkheads, one on either side of the office space and a third one at that shower.

Water tanks will be built into the hull bottoms, though made fully encapsulated and even removable should that be desired. The hulls will be floored off level and with sufficient overhead clearance for standing, which should leave two or three feet of vertical space underneath for tanks, bilge spaces, and general storage. I would not want to keep electronics down there in case of moisture buildup, but it is a suitable area for things like water pumps, raw water thermal exchange units, black water tanks, air compressors, dehumidifiers, (synthetic) line and sail storage, etc.

Cabinets, counters, closets, partitions, beds, bunks, and drawers can be built to suit and made with leftover hull materials, though need not be made structurally strong. Port-side, I will want a standing preparation area in the kitchen and a wide enough passageway that two people can easily get by each other. All of the remaining space across will be counters, stoves, sinks, fridges and freezers, and cabinets and drawers, with the exception of a cutout nook near the bottom of the stairs up with a built-in seat. For the comfort of the cook or for a child to sit and watch without blocking the stairs.

Aft from the kitchen will be the guest cabin, with a bed in the far back. The under-bed space will be devoted to propulsion and the back up under the stern to steering, but there should be room forward from there to include closet space and shelves. I will also want at least one applications screen mounted on the walls or ceiling, in addition to lighting arrangements.

These are long hulls and the kitchen will not be huge, so there should be some considerable space forward from there and before the guest head and separate shower for both bunks and storage space. In addition to any space reserved under the flooring for storage.

In the starboard hull I will want a broad workbench and cabinets and drawer space in the productivity area. As well as mounted screens and speakers and some type of seating arrangement that is both comfortable and will permit passage fore and aft for those who are not utilizing the productivity space. Perhaps a fold down seat (or two) that is padded for comfort. A standard office chair would probably not work very well. This space will be smaller than the kitchen area as I have posited a compost head just next to the master bedroom aft, but there should still be plenty of room.

Forward from there will be a large space between the shower and the productivity area. Room enough for good-sized closets and plenty of other storage. I would also want a dedicated cabinet for electronics—house computer, networking, backup server, etc. Climate control will be important for these delicate electronics in a marine environment and that will be made easier by siting them all in one closed off location. I could mount a very small air conditioner unit, vented through a port either to the deck or the inside hull facing, which could maintain this cabinet cool and dry at the cost of limited power use.

Up in the main salon I have indicated that there will be cabinets in the back for the generator and fuel storage, a small prep area which may have a propane stove, and a forward area sectioned off as the pilot station. That forward area will have a full bulkhead wall made of marine ply cored laminate, with a hatch for passage up offset a bit from center to help clear the pilot seat forward. This wall will be a good place to mount multiple display screens to show various information feeds to anyone lounging about the salon. Such as echoing any exterior camera feeds, showing the current radar or sonar picture, or giving details on battery bank usage and status. This will all be redundant information to what is available to the pilot, but it will be little trouble to echo interesting things into the salon and may help to involve more people in the state of the boat. Beside the convenience factor, of course. Those same displays could also be used for various applications purposes.

There will also be plenty of room in the salon for a lounging area and a separate dining area, complete with under-seat storage which may double as freezer or refrigerator space. I would want to locate the house battery bank in one of these under-seat spaces. Both areas could be designed for use as sleeping couches when there are larger groups of people aboard.

Mast

Probably the best way to get the mast I wanted, as a home builder, would be to order a custom built one out of aluminum from a shop that specializes in making masts. There are more than a few of these places. It would most likely be expensive to have the specific design I want built, given that there are no other masts out there like this that I am aware of and it would really have to be custom. It would not be too expensive to consider, as the individual component themselves could be sourced from standard aluminum mast parts. Aluminum is strong and light and has been proven to be an excellent mast material.

I could also make one up at home, and make it as strong as it needed to be, but a fiberglass or cored fiberglass mast would be very difficult to make and would most likely be heavier for the strength than a custom aluminum job. Especially if I needed to make it hollow to accommodate wiring and cables. It might be cheaper, but would be a lot of work and end up being heavier.

Unless I used carbon fiber, in which case it would both be more work and more expensive. But lighter than aluminum and very strong. I look forward to the day when carbon fiber prices come down from the ridiculous level they currently occupy. But that day is not yet.

Other Considerations

Egress

Thus far there from my description there is only one way to exit each hull—up the stairs and through the bridgedeck. This is not sufficient. I will also posit emergency escape hatches in three locations. Two of these can be managed above the beds in the aft cabins, through to the decks near the sterns. Another can be located on the port-side hull only and accessible through one of the bunks forward. This places an emergency exit at each sleeping location in the hulls.

From a structural perspective I would rather not have any of these. They weaken the structure and can be a pain to maintain or repair. In addition to complicating the build process. But from a human perspective I would rather just sink the whole bloody boat than to unnecessarily endanger someone sleeping aboard. So in they go. Kept latched from the inside of course, and made strong.

The salon will have exits at the front and back already, through the pilot house and out either side or back onto the porch. Because of this I see no good reason to make the side windows able to open and close, so they will be built in. Easier that way, more durable, and less likely to leak.

Airflow

I am of two minds regarding a ducted ventilation system. On the one hand, free-flowing air vents will remove any possibility of full encapsulation for sections of the hulls. On the other hand, the air ducts can be run at ceiling level and if water gets that high then the boat will already be fatally compromised regardless. The overall buoyancy of the boat should be such that it cannot sink unless completely filled with water. Probably not even then, and if it does it will not sink very far. In the case of a turnover, however, ceiling air ducts will act to spread water throughout the vessel—though only at that level.

A ducted ventilation system will assist with airflow and dispersion of heat and cooler air, but there is an alternative that will work almost as well. Fans, larger than would be required for an air duct system, can be placed at strategic points around the boat interior. The fans will circulate the air to every space that is not closed off and serve to normalize temperature conditions throughout the interior. This will be somewhat less efficient for energy use and give less control over airflow and especially air filtration, but is still workable and may be the better alternative for this build. This method, however, will reduce airflow when hatches are closed for privacy.

Also, it will be very important to keep the propulsion areas under the stern beds both cool and dry. For the sake of the batteries and also the motors and controllers. There are ways to do this without airflow or without airflow throughout the hulls. I could mount small air conditioner units into those spaces like for the electronics cabinet. I could utilize a chiller unit from raw water (that may be required anyway depending on the type of motor used). But the easiest way will be to vent that area to the cabin inside, which will then need to be vented into the rest of the boat to normalize temperatures. Humidity control can be aided with desiccants or with small dehumidifier units.

Thru-Hulls

I have not covered thru-hull construction method, but it will be similar to the riverboat build above. Each one must be cut or drilled wider than needed, because the core will become exposed and must be fully encapsulated and the full thickness of the hull built back up out of fiberglass laminate. And then the thru-hardware can be placed and carefully sealed.

The core should not be weakened any more than necessary. Space out the thru-holes and try not to put too many of them in the same core boards. If thru-hull locations are planned out before the build is finished then laminates can be strengthened in those areas. They might become stress points but need not be weak points.

Finish Work

I did not mention painting so far but a great deal of it will be required. All epoxy must be fully protected from UV. Use multiple coats of specific and varied paint types. Barrier coats and then an absorption layer and then a reflective layer, or however you choose to complete the process. Inside feel free to switch to whatever colors you wish, but I would still put down the same protective layers underneath. Outside the color should be white or close to it to reflect as much sunlight as possible.

The hull laminate will need to be faired before painting can even begin. Which will involve a lot of tedious effort first applying the fairing compound and then sanding it back down. There are ways to make the finished paint look as professional a job as the pro builders can manage. Roll and tip and burnish. But this process will start with a carefully faired hull and the end result will depend on the initial fairing.

Summary and Conclusion

So that's my dream boat. At least for now. I will probably think up another wrinkle at some point, and likely I have forgotten to mention one that I have intended to work in. You understand, if you have gotten this far in the book. Boat noodling can be an endless process, which is one of the reasons I have attempted to undergo the extensive research efforts required for this book. Alas, I have not yet been cured of the need, but perhaps by the time I finish the next section...

Seriously though I think that this boat, or some variation thereof, can be an excellent platform for global cruising and can be built and operated even by those with limited funds. Certainly with a smaller cash outlay than will be required for a production catamaran, used or not. The prices on those things are ridiculously high, even by the inflated price standards of the marine market. I may have gone a bit overboard on the described systems for this sample build. I estimate that with certain systems scaled back somewhat and some frugality in other areas then a home builder could manage this build for around sixty thousand USD or less. Not including the costs for an adequate workspace. Which I think is pretty good overall—you can have a boat that is fully customized and better built and much cheaper than an equivalent production yacht. As long as you can manage the simply enormous amount of work that will be required. Practically speaking, this will take months to accomplish, if not years. Though many hands make light work.

This will not be possible for everyone. Or even for very many people. But much of this will also be pertinent information for those who want to modify their existing boat. Or those who might want to buy something cheap and make it better. There are a great many fiberglass boats out there and you can find one that is a good deal to buy. It may not be designed the way you want, but if you modify it using epoxy resin for your laminate then it will already be stronger than the initial layup in one of the ester resins, even considering a secondary bond. Fairing it back to look professional is mostly a matter of patience and care.

You will not be able to core a boat that does not already have one, but you can still add insulation to the interior and strength can be added by thickening the existing laminate.

References and Further Research

Larsson, Lars, et al. *Principles of Yacht Design.*

Rossel, Greg. *The Boatbuilder's Apprentice.*

https://www.boatdesign.net/

catamaranconcepts.com/category/hull-deck-design/bridgedeck-clearance

www.sail-the-difference.com/index.php?id=40

liveantares.com/exterior-images-antares-44-gs

www.glpautogas.info/documentos/11GASOLINE%20AND%20LPG%20comparison.pdf

www.puremajek.com

www.schionningdesigns.com.au/kit-process

buildacat.com

thecoastalpassage.com/cheapcat.html

youtu.be/adNpyoMdnf8
Discussion on mast height in the ICW on the US east coast.

youtu.be/EitqKNsiUOA
Narration and pictures for a scratch built catamaran. Global cruising on a tight budget.

youtu.be/u9F5xbIZbHI
Detailed description of a hydraulic walking system for a catamaran.

youtu.be/5eB0VGCsOPc
The same boat but a narration of the build process. Welded steel.

youtu.be/0ihuOBoL5IM
Picture collage video showing another catamaran build.

29.

The Solar Trimaran Build

This is a concept build for motor only long range cruising. Unlike the sailing catamaran above which attempts to integrate as many types of renewable energy collection as possible, this boat will focus entirely on maximizing solar power collection. So no regen and no wind turbines (though it would not be difficult to add one or two turbines to the build). The boat will be electric drive and will have maximum propulsion energy efficiency, as a displacement vessel. Powered primarily by solar but with a backup generator.

Platform

As a marine platform, a trimaran will have very different characteristics and properties from monohulls or catamarans either one. Like a catamaran, initial stability is achieved by the spacing between the hulls, but unlike a catamaran there is no lack of reserve stability. If you push a trimaran to the side enough to lift one side hull out of the water, then the other side hull will be dipping into the water. The buoyant force from the side hull in the water will be very great and will resist further motion downward. Racing trimarans do manage to flip over but only because they are designed for maximum speed and so reduce buoyant forces (which require greater whetted surface) to the absolute minimum. It should be nearly impossible (barring a hurricane or extremely large waves) to flip a properly designed cruising trimaran over.

This will be even more true for motor trimarans than for sailing trimarans. A motor only boat will lack the top-hamper of a mast and will not be subjected to the wind forces of a sailing vessel. Actually, I do not think that sailing trimarans are well suited for long term habitation. Some people do so, and happily, but it seems to me that they suffer from some of the worst characteristics of monohulls and catamarans both without some of the corresponding benefits.

They do not stay as level as a catamaran, as the central hull acts as a pivot for the side hulls and in any sort of rough seas you can get a bobbing back and forth motion that is distinctly unpleasant. They will heel far more to the side in steady winds than will a catamaran, though still much less than will a monohull. Sailing trimarans at anchor will also tend to bob back and forth. All of these aspects are much reduced for motor trimarans.

Space considerations will not necessarily be mitigated for motor trimarans, though there will be a bit of extra room because you do not have to fit in the accouterments of sailing and all the backup materials. Extra sails and lines and stay materials, etc. But even without these things the hulls themselves will be very narrow in comparison to a catamaran and especially to a monohull. The narrow hulls will reduce living options and storage space below even more than the loss of width because you must still allow adequate passage for a person from one end to the other. In each hull. This problem may be somewhat overcome by the very wide space available for a bridgedeck. Even more so for a motor trimaran because you will be able to build higher upward than with a sailing vessel.

And for daysailers or short cruising trips these are not overwhelming disadvantages. Particularly when you consider that trimarans tend to be roughly thirty percent faster under sail than even catamarans, which themselves might be twice as fast as a monohull. This is not an exact rule, but the different speeds roughly correspond to hull speed calculations for monohulls. A monohull of a certain length will be restricted to a certain speed because of the length of the hull as it passes through the water. A catamaran of the same length will have twice as much hull length altogether, though, because of the double hulls. And a trimaran will have three times as much hull length because of the triple hulls. There are many other factors involved, but generally speaking these ratios hold true under sail.

So trimarans are fast. This will be less important for the motor trimaran that I will focus on here, as it will be a more efficient lower speed craft. It will still be significant because much of that potential speed increase has to do with reduced water resistance which will be important at lower speeds as well. Drag underwater can be minimized, because trimarans do not require any keels at all. Stability is provided by hull spacing alone. A sailing trimaran might want minikeels to be able to point closer upwind, but a motor trimaran will not want any. Propeller drag is also not an issue at all for a motor trimaran.

Overall, less thrust will be required to propel this trimaran hull-form through the water than for a catamaran or monohull of equal displacement. Which will directly reduce energy needs for propulsion. This, coupled with the large amount of potential area for solar panel arrays, is why I think that a true solar electric trimaran is a feasible build prospect for even a home builder.

Purpose

As noted above, this will be a global cruising trimaran. Since there will be no mast to catch on bridges, it will have more potential cruising grounds even then the catamaran build above (barring the folding mast option). Solar power will substitute for wind (sail) power as the method used to escape the range limitations of combustion engine vessels. This will mean electric drive, so this will also be an electronics heavy build. Due to the intermittent nature of solar energy capture, average speeds are expected to be somewhat lower, but there will also be large battery banks and a backup generator to ensure mobility in all conditions.

The goal will be for this build to have a comparable or even lower cost outlay required than for the catamaran build above. In both cases of course many systems may be upgraded over time from the initial build configuration. This upgrade capacity should be maintained or even enhanced by deliberate planning during the build process. Best to plan for future expansions now rather than later even if they are not within the current budget.

Design

My effort here will be just one example configuration for a build suited to this particular purpose. Every build design must entail a series of compromises, a number of competing factors weighed against one another. For the catamaran build above I stressed a flat unbroken expanse for the bridgedeck roof in order to maximize solar collection for that build. This required me to place the pilot station far forward on the single bridgedeck level, restricting direct observation to the sides and rear and indicating the use of cameras to maintain situational awareness of those directions. Here I will design in a modified fly-bridge instead, despite the potential loss of solar collection to the broken roof expanse and potential shading, both to provide unobstructed directional viewing for the pilot and to offer reasonable mounting points for necessary navigational and communications hardware. In addition to increasing living space. The rest of the design aspects will include their own compromises.

Dimensions

I will posit an overall size for the build at 52ft by 32ft. That is, the central hull will be fifty-two feet long overall and somewhat shorter than that at the waterline. The two side hulls will be somewhat shorter in length at the front (five feet less or so) and even with the main hull at the rear. The total width between the exterior of the side hulls will be thirty-two feet. Again, this sizing may be larger than necessary or than possible for a home builder, but that is something that will come out when assessing the actual plans. For now I will dream large.

This is a pretty wide beam for a cruising vessel and I think I could go as low as twenty-five feet instead without worrying about sideways stability, considering the trimaran buoyancy factor. I am going wider, despite the potential for navigational complications and docking difficulties, in order to increase surface area for solar without the structural complications of an even longer build and especially to maximize internal space on the bridgedeck, which will be the majority of the space available aboard. Docking will not be appreciably more difficult for a thirty-two feet wide boat than it will be for a twenty-five feet wide boat—this will be a mooring vessel most of the time regardless. The standard sized river barges in the United States are 35ft wide, so I estimate that navigation will still be possible to the majority of destinations, even if the width of my build will restrict me from certain narrower passages. One can always use a dingy for short jaunts up narrow passages.

The side hulls will measure just five feet wide at most, with an expected draft of a bit over one foot deep. I will want them to have rounded bottoms in order to increase buoyancy potential (and reduce bobbing), even though this will somewhat increase drag while motoring. This is a very narrow profile and it will be a challenge to make use of the space available for any sort of living accommodations, and doubly complicated because I intend a height under the main deck of around five feet down to the very bottom of the hull. As such, I will be designating the side hulls as exclusively for systems and storage area.

The central hull will be both deeper and wider. I will posit a draft of three feet or so under the waterline, and the hull will also be rounded at the bottom. At maximum it will reach about eight feet in width. The interior height will be matched to the side hulls so that the main deck will be about seven feet from the very bottom of the hull. This will permit (low) standing room in some parts of the main hull but not all, as tankage will reduce that vertical space wherever it is placed.

So the openings under the bridgedeck and between the main and side hulls will be about seven feet wide at the most and around four feet high. That width may be excessive and could be reduced somewhat by widening the hulls, but in any case the sloped hull sides up the bridgedeck will reduce this width considerably at the top of the openings. No cut-waters at the tops will be necessary, as any waves that reach that high will already be squeezed and have their force reduced.

The cramped vertical hull dimensions will permit a main deck the entire thirty-two feet width and fifty-two feet length of the boat. Truncated in certain respects, of course. The front portion will curve inward from where the side hulls stop to the front of the main hull, perhaps with a small bowsprit added on for an anchor mount. The rear of the main deck will continue to the back edge of the main hull (raised out of the water to better accommodate the propeller), but the side hulls will have steps down at the rear for better access to the water (and also to mount the outboards discussed below).

There will be side passages along the edges of the outer hulls, an outdoor lounging area in the bow, and a small porch in back over the stern of the main hull, but the entire main deck will have a full roof. That extended roof will be used to mount solar panels. The increase in air resistance at expected speeds will be minimal, as the covered side passages should permit easy airflow, particularly if the front of the enclosed cabin is curved to reduce wind resistance. That enclosed cabin, representing most of the interior living space of the boat, will measure around twenty-five feet wide to forty feet long at the most. Call it nine hundred and fifty square feet.

There will also be an enclosed second level with lots of windows for all-around visibility. The pilot station will be located at the front of this area but still well back from the bow of the main hull. The dimensions of the upper deck will be roughly twenty feet wide and twenty-five feet long. It will have a flat roof to facilitate solar panel mounts. The rear will be located just short of the inward curving roof of the main deck porch, which area on the second level will be utilized for navigation and communication instrument mounts.

Vertical clearance for both decks will be around seven and a half feet. This should put the top of the upper deck roughly twenty feet above the waterline of the vessel. Instruments will be mounted below the roof of the upper deck so even with antennae overall height should not exceed twenty-five feet. Which will be too high for certain low bridges but still a much lower height than any sort of sailing vessel and many other motor yachts.

Solar

In estimating the amount of solar wattage that can be mounted on the boat, I will assume an average size of 6sq.ft per 100W. Smaller panels may give a bit less than that but larger panels, even less efficient polycrystalline, will be right around there or better.

The roof of the upper deck will yield 500sq.ft all for solar. There should be flat roof space from the sides of the upper deck to the edge of the outer hulls, with some wastage for curved transitions. Call it two strips five feet wide and twenty-five feet long, so another

250sq.ft. These strips may be curved for better aerodynamics and aesthetics, so this will be a good place to mount flexible panels. There will also be flat roof from the front of the upper deck to the front edge of the lower deck and the entire width of that lower deck, with some losses because of the curved forward deck not fitting square solar panels along its edge. Call it an average of another ten feet by thirty-two feet of open space, or another 320sq.ft.

So around 1070sq.ft altogether. Call it 17.5kW of solar panels altogether, or something like 87.5kWh per day. More than twice as much as for the catamaran build above, but this will be our only source of renewable energy. This will still not be enough by itself for extended motoring. However, my estimates here are actually conservative for how much wattage can be obtained from just the flat portions of the available mounting spaces. With careful sizing and efficient panels, 20kW or more should not be too difficult to reach.

In addition to this, there is another area that solar panels could be mounted which has not been factored in. I rarely, if ever, see permanent solar installations on vertical surfaces. The sun is usually overhead somewhere, so collection efficiency will be much lower over the course of a given day. However, because energy costs are so much higher on a boat than on shore, it seems to me that even with this collection efficiency loss vertical mount solar panels will still recoup their initial investment costs over a period of several years. And they will boost the overall collection potential of the boat. So I will also posit mounting solar panels vertically between the upper deck and the main deck along the outside edge.

This will not be straight up and down, as I have factored in some gradual transition to the upper deck, but close enough. Because there is an air gap along the sides of the enclosed cabin anyway from the walkways, the outside edges of the outer walkways need not be left open for wind resistance purposes. Some gaps can be left for viewing purposes but they need not be large. The front area where the curved transition to the bow of the main hull starts should be left open, and the rear area will also curve inward toward the main hull stern and should be left open. So I will have about twenty-five feet of length on both sides to mount flat panels. And roughly seven feet of height, which will not quite match panel sizes but I will use it as an average figure. So call the total area another 350sq.ft, for another 5.5kW nominal of solar. If I estimate that these panels will be half as efficient as the horizontal mounts, that will drop my expected daily energy draw from these down to something like 13.5kWh per day. So not a large addition but still significant.

Electricity

This build will need a large amount of battery storage capacity. I will posit two battery banks, one for propulsion at the rear of the main hull and another as a house bank. They will not be sized here, but again the bigger the better. The house bank should be at 12V and the propulsion bank at whatever voltage is best for the motor, though there will be added complications and safety issues for anything above 48V.

I will also posit gaseous power generation as a backup power source for this vessel. Cabinet placement for the generator unit and gas storage will be somewhat more complicated than for the catamaran build, but can still be designed so that any leaked LPG will drop down between the hulls and any leaked natural gas or hydrogen will be vented safely as they rise up. All combustion appliances or engines can be converted between LPG and natural gas use, which will increase refueling options. Upgrading to a hydrogen generation system will also mean switching to electric for appliances, though I suppose some combustion gases could be kept on board for cooking and heating purposes. I will not repeat the extended discussion from the catamaran build again here, so please see that section for further information. Most aspects will be the same, but with the triple hull it may be necessary to make an encapsulated channel across the main hull for any gas lines. This should be a solvable problem of insuring an airtight seal and allowing pathways along least resistance routes for any safety drains down or up. So no pockets where gas can pool. And LPG detectors should still be placed down in the hulls if that is your chosen fuel.

Propulsion and Steering

The main propulsion system will consist of the propeller and shaft, any gearbox, the electric drive motor, and the propulsion battery bank. These will all be located at the rear of the main hull.

I will want the stern of the central hull to rise out the water as with the catamaran build, so there will be a reverse curve from the bottom of the hull to the stern low enough under the deck to give clearance for the rudder hardware. The rudder itself will be mounted so as not to extend past the stern. This will require a large reverse curve for the back of the hull in order to accommodate the propeller and rudder both, but the buoyancy loss will be taken up by the side hulls and the rudder might interfere with dingy use if extended past the stern.

Even with the extra clearance along the hull provided for the propeller by the raised stern, maximum prop size will be limited by the depth of the hull, as I would not want to extend the propeller down past the protection of the hull in front. The limit would probably be something like thirty inches or less in diameter, given the assumed depth of three feet. I could accept this limitation, as that is still a large propeller, or I could extend a support member at an angle downward from the bottom of the hull and toward the rear.

Doing so will increase the depth of the boat, but will permit a larger propeller and also provide a bottom attachment point for the rudder skeg and propeller shaft strut. As this build will be more concerned with propulsion efficiency than keeping a shallow draft, I will posit extending the maximum draft of the boat by another foot, though just at the rear of the main hull, with such a support member. I will also increase the propeller size to thirty-six inches in diameter, with four large blades. This is the same size as the two catamaran build propellers, but less thrust will be required for this hull-form and slightly higher RPM's can be used. Motor cruising speed might still be a bit lower but not much.

But that can be increased with the secondary propulsion systems, if necessary. That is, I would also want to mount outboard motors on the rear inward sides of the side hulls. These would be propane/natural gas instead of electric, so would not be dependent on the main propulsion electrical system for power. Reliance on a single electric powered screw for propulsion may be considered risky for a long range cruiser without the option for sailing. These outboards would alleviate that concern, but their main purpose would be to increase low speed maneuverability.

The awkward steering at low speed and in tight spaces is one of the main drawbacks of a trimaran hull-form. They will generally have the same single propeller as a monohull, with its tendency to walk the rear of the boat toward the direction of turn, but will be much wider and so even more ungainly. The wide spacing of the twin propellers and ability to turn in a circle in place is a major draw for the catamaran crowd. But with twin outboards on the outer hulls a trimaran can do the same thing. In a pinch, the same outboards could also be used to increase speed while out cruising.

For this hull size I would want to mount two 10HP outboards. A Lehr propane 9.9 weighs 88lbs and can be moved around by hand. Together these should give plenty of power to move the boat around harbor or in other tight spaces. Fuel lines could be run from the main generator storage tanks in the deck cabin, but only if they are routed on the outside of the hulls. It would seem a better solution to mount individual fuel canisters back at the outboards, with no path for gas to enter the hull and no long lines to potentially get damaged. If each side hull has steps down close to the waterline at the rear, the outboards could be located just inboard from there on the hull sides, able to pivot up out of the water when not needed and in easy reach from the steps.

The main motor should be sized somewhere between 30-40HP equivalent. I will want propshaft RPM at a maximum of eight hundred and probably less than that. I might expect a cruising speed under eight knots, sustainable in good sun from the solar array alone. This is anemic compared to most motor yachts (though not displacement monohulls), but most motor yachts will have large fuel bills and this boat will just need a bit of propane now and again. With extensive cruising the solar array will pay for itself many times over in fuel costs alone.

As with the riverboat build, it may be better to posit a two propeller main propulsion system instead. Doing so could reduce the steering issues and eliminate the need for the propane outboards, though there will still be some steering problems because the props will be close together. But two smaller motors will permit better low-speed options and also be somewhat more energy efficient than one larger motor. And a lot of boats have awkward steering. It will cost more, as propellers and shafts are not cheap and smaller motors (and controllers) are more than half the cost of one large one. But the result may be worth the greater expense.

Layout

So, steering and navigation will all be routed to the pilot station at the front of the upper deck space. I would want a permanent view-screen at the front of the upper deck, fixed windows on the sides (though perhaps with the capacity to open and close), and a door at the rear in addition to more fixed windows. That door will be the access to the navigation and communication equipment as well as the solar panel mounts on the rest of the upper exterior spaces. The remaining space could be devoted to lounge area but I think this is also a good space for general applications and projects requiring open area. So seating and tables and electrical wiring and network links, but kept more open than not. There will be a full stairway down, starting near the upper deck exterior door and extending forward into the main deck cabin.

That main deck cabin will have doors at the rear onto the porch and also on both sides onto the exterior walkways. The far front will have windows forward but no direct exterior access. This is a good place for a secondary nav station and workspace. The cabinets for the generator and fuel storage will be at the rear of the main cabin, as will the kitchen area and attached dining space. Beyond that many configurations are possible. I would want at least two private cabins and bathrooms, a guest bathroom, and a main salon (which may be the same as the dining area). The 950 sq. feet of this cabin is capacious indeed for a boat and I think would fit everything desired without too much trouble, provided that care was taken to use minimal space for any given need.

There is space in the main hull forward for a private cabin and bath, though with low overhead. The staircase down from the upper deck could just continue downward into the main hull. The rear of the main hull will be devoted to propulsion and I would want the center of it for water tankage and general systems and storage, but the front third could be a cabin space.

I would have access into the side hulls be via hatches rather than stairs down, though I suppose it would not be too much trouble to place stairs along the curve of the join from the hulls to the bridgedeck (as is common). In any case the side hulls will be for storage and utility only.

The main deck will also have the porch at the rear in the curved space available from the rear of the main hull to the stairs down on the exterior of the side hulls. I have not seen this done on a trimaran, as most will also have stairs down to the water on the main hull, but the rear of that porch is a good place to mount davits for raising up a dingy.

There will be walking space (if narrow) from the rear porch around both sides of the cabin to the open (but covered) area at the front of the boat. That open area will also be curved, from the front edges of the side hulls to the front of the main hull. This front area will be the only boat deck edge with full stanchions and railing, as the sides will be mostly enclosed and not need railings and the rear area will only have brief rails where appropriate. There will be a small bowsprit at the very front of the main hull to mount the anchor and windlass. Chain storage will be accommodated by sectioning off the very front of the slanted main bow for a drained storage locker. The remaining interior space in the main hull at the bow might be a good location for a shower.

Construction

This boat can be achieved using a number of build methods and materials. Steel or aluminum or fiberglass or a cored laminate or more exotic materials. Welding or framing or molding or stitch and glue or strip-planking or any other method that works. For myself, I will prefer a wood-cored laminate construction, either strip-planked or stitch and glue. Probably both, where appropriate. These are the methods I consider most suitable for the home builder, in terms of ease of method, manageable construction, costs, and final product quality (strength and durability and appearance).

I will posit constructing this boat in the same method as the sailing catamaran above—strip planked for curved surfaces and support structures, marine ply for flat surfaces where convenient. You could instead do the whole boat in marine ply, with no appreciable loss in strength if you are careful. It would be less work than strip planking, but any damage taken below the waterline will also become a more serious matter. Damage to planks can be uncovered and new planks scarfed in. Damage to marine ply will necessitate replacing an entire sheet at a minimum. You would also have to go with chined hulls instead of full curves with plywood. In either case, for me the wood will only be the coring material for a strong epoxy fiberglass laminate.

Hulls

Going with strip planking for the hulls, the easiest way to begin will be to have a good interior working space (barn, shed, warehouse) large enough to move the entire build around in, with a temporary frame setup for the entire lower part of the boat. So the bottom part will be cored and glassed while upside down, flipped over, and then extended upward into the rest of the build structure. If you must, you could do without the interior space, as long as you have some protection form wind and weather and especially the sun. You will need some method for turning and flipping the build around. As such you would do well to go ahead and construct a temporary shed to do the build in. Unless you choose to construct each hull individually and then assemble them right-side up. In that case you may never have to flip the main build, only roll the hulls around. Glassing in the bridgedeck above where the water will be will be awkward while the hull is right-side up but still possible.

The point here being that there are a number of ways to accomplish your build, and you will outright need very little in the way of established build space, but the less established your build space the less convenient and more difficult the build will be. It is my strong suggestion that you plan out your build space with as much care as you plan out the boat itself. Planning and care will save effort and reduce mistakes.

So, say that I have a full frame for my hulls and bridging and that the core is finished and ready for glassing. I will still want to have a strong laminate overlay, but it need not be as strong, laterally, as that posited for the catamaran build. The hull bridges will be required to bear something like half the force as for a catamaran, given that there are twice as many of them. Yes, there is more weight up above as the cabin is larger and there is a second deck, but there is also no mast and the hull structure need not bear the greater forces impacting on a sailing rig. However, the longitudinal strength required will be determined by the length of the hulls rather than the lateral forces. Given that this boat is even longer than my catamaran build I will need a stronger laminate front to back along the hulls.

And so the varied properties of axial fabric come into play. For the catamaran I used triaxial because it was easier for rolling out and, though I did add an extra layer or two for extra strength, the forces impacting on the hull were assumed to be roughly equal in all directions. Not so for this trimaran. So I might still use triaxial for good multi-directional strength, but I will also add a layer of monaxial (one layer of fibers running one direction) along the full length of the hulls in between the triaxial layers.

Yet another reason to consult a naval engineer or architect before starting. I can guesstimate like this and have rough approximations of how I need to design my build to meet expected loads, but a professional will work the entire thing out mathematically with known values, solve the exact materials that will be needed and where, add in a specific safety margin, and have done. And indeed a home builder can do the same thing if they insist on doing everything themselves, but they are far more likely to miss things through ignorance. But I digress.

I would want to add a layer of aramid fabric to the very outer edge of the laminate for all three hulls. This will be the most expensive layer of the laminate and some will argue that it is not justified, but I consider it an important measure for increasing the impact resistance of a wood-cored laminate hull intended for extensive cruising. If this were a day tripper or a coastal vessel I would not bother. But if that aramid is even once the difference between an off-shore hull breach and just a nasty impact it will have been well worth it. The single outer aramid layer seems like a good compromise to me and after all possibly the best part of a laminate build is that you can incorporate different qualities with different materials. So we have the core for compressive resistance and improved stiffness, the axial fiberglass for general strength enhancement, the aramid for impact and abrasion resistance, and the epoxy to hold it all together. Strong and light and enduring. Beautiful.

Moving on Up

Once the bottom is complete it will be time to flip the build upright. The temp frames can be done away with but the strong-backs should be retained and used to brace the hulls firmly for continued stability. Well padded, of course, to preserve the laminate.

Sheathing for the hulls and bridges will be only half-done at this point and the interior sheathing should be accomplished. After that, work can begin on the main deck. Half of which (the top) will be pretty easy and the other half (the bottom) a major pain. The curvature at the front where the side hulls fall short of the main hull and must curve around to complete the bridge should already have been completed. Likewise the shape at the back where the porch will curve around to meet the side walkways. So the main deck itself will not have to bridge any space and will only be a full (and structurally strong) covering. Building the core of the deck will be a bit of a toss-up for me. Marine ply would be much easier and plenty strong enough, but solid planks are more appealing. Still, I would probably go with the marine ply. Glassing the top of this will be (relatively) easy and should be accomplished after glassing the underside, which will be…a bit more of a challenge.

Not only must the underside of the open spaces be laminated without the ability to stand upright and while trying to convince liquid epoxy to not obey gravity, but there must also be fully encapsulated joins with no air voids where the deck meets the topsides of the hulls and bridges. Doing this all as one piece will be the next thing to impossible. Instead, it should be accomplished one sheet of plywood at a time, pre-cut for a very specific location. Prepare the receiving section perfectly flat, with added core pieces as necessary. Layup wet laminate on the plywood sheet, lower it carefully into place, and glass more to join the surfaces together fully. If more layers of fiberglass are desired to increase the strength of the piece they can be applied and allowed to partially cure before adding the last and putting that marine ply piece into place.

In any case before building the main deck I would want to run solid wood cored structural members up vertically to better support the upper deck. And the same for at least the corner frames of the upper level all the way up to the top roof. Technically this will not be strictly necessary and all strength required can be furnished with plywood cored laminate, but I still have a preference for the solid wood and the frame produced will ease the rest of the build process. Temporary framing will still be required at several points in order to hold up plywood sheets until they can be laminated in place. Also, because epoxy will be used as the binding resin, every bit of extra core utilized will serve to reduce costs. The resin and fiberglass combination will be considerably more expensive than the wood, volume for volume. It will still be required to fully encapsulate all wood, but every time filler is needed then wood should be used instead of extra fiberglass. And wood-cored stringers will add strength more efficiently than just adding another layer of fiberglass.

The multiple levels and extra hull of this build will make the build process considerably more complex than for the catamaran build above. But it can all be accomplished one piece at a time and the shape of the superstructure will not be overly complicated. Working from plans rather than ad-hock will greatly smooth this process, which will be one of the most time consuming parts of the entire build.

Other Considerations

No special escape hatches will be posited for the hull spaces other than normal access points. The one sleeping area I have designated in the front of the main hull will have a full stairway up to the main deck which should be sufficient. In the case that that is blocked, there can still be other access hatches leading up further back along that hull. Alternatively a hatch can be located at the front of the center hull straight up through the main decking.

Deliberate airflow will be particularly important for this vessel structure. There are three hulls and thus at least three bilge areas that should be kept ventilated. The motor area at the rear of the main hull will require cooling and ventilation. And any encapsulated spaces in any of the hulls, especially the side hulls which may not have open stairways, will need to have some sort of arrangement for continual air movement. Stagnant air should be avoided in a marine environment, as humidity will tend to gather and condense and mold buildup will occur.

So I will posit a full ventilation system with vent openings to every encapsulated space on board. Aside from air movement, this system can also assist in heating, cooling, and humidity control. It should also be possible to place valves in the ventilation system that can be closed for a watertight seal, as was not considered during the catamaran build. In this way I can have a vent system but still be able to section it off fully in case of a hull breach.

Summary and Conclusion

This section has really been a redesign and modification of the previous catamaran build. Eliminating sail propulsion and adding another hull mandates certain changes in the build, but most things will actually be the same or close to it. Similar design problems in balancing expected loads, same build style, same overall purpose, etc. I know I have not covered everything, and even less so in the case of this trimaran, but I trust that I have included enough discussion to provide complete pictures of the final products. The rest of this book should help to fill in the gaps, especially if you dive into the references I have added to the end of each section.

These two are just about the most ambitious projects that I would consider as a home builder, especially working alone or with limited assistance. But the builds, and the goals they represent, are within the grasp of the home builder. Especially if you somewhat reduce the vessel dimensions I have given here. This trimaran, if fully designed and carefully built, will function as a global cruiser. As will the catamaran above. All without having to rely on combustion propulsion. Before LiFePO4 batteries and (relatively) cheap renewable energy components these mostly off-grid solutions would still have been possible for some but not within the reach of very many. With existing technology these outcomes are now possible for a great many more people.

References and Further Research

dmsonline.us/why-you-want-a-trimaran

www.boatinternational.com/yachts/editorial-features/galaxy-of-happiness-the-trimaran-taking-yachting-to-another-world—33363

www.boatdesign.net/threads/round-bilge-vs-hard-chine.37594

smalltridesign.com

plougonver.com/home-built-trimaran-plans

www.dixdesign.com/3fold6.htm

edhorstmanmultihulldesigns.com/triplans/index.php

youtu.be/PPKX9rs5DbQ

Animation video for the new Leen motor trimarans.

youtu.be/nVG5SMwxLYY

Tour video of a solar powered motor catamaran. Merge this concept with that of the last video and you will see what I have in mind for this build.

youtu.be/duZQ6kvQNU0

First video in a series about a home-built trimaran.

youtu.be/Lx4M1B3yGno

Video about a custom designed and professionally built motor trimaran. Has some interesting design choices, some of which are within the scope of a home builder.

Part Three—Extras

30.

On Batteries

Battery banks will be at the heart of the mobile living electrical system. Given that I am advocating large, high-capacity banks of very expensive batteries for many mobile applications, I think it best to include this detailed discussion on batteries and their aspects. The more expensive LiFePO4 batteries will only provide a lower cost of energy storage over time if we are able to keep using them for years and years. You will only get that long use with a well-designed and properly maintained system. Some of the information included here is very basic, but all of it is important to understand when designing your own battery banks. I will focus the section almost entirely on LiFePO4 chemistry batteries, but many of the same principles will also apply to other chemistries. All actual practices will vary between chemistries, sometimes a great deal.

How They Work

A battery itself is an electrochemical device designed to discharge current at a specific voltage when connected to an electrical circuit that has a load included. This does not even require that the battery itself form a continuous part of the circuit. Just that the battery negative terminal (from which electrical current flows) be connected to some electrically positive element. The imbalance between the negative source from the battery and the positive receptor will induce a current to flow. Any load source, which is anything connected into the circuit that uses up electrical energy (such as a light-bulb), that is part of the circuit will increase the current flow by the specific draw of that load.

The batteries that we are concerned with will also operate in reverse to this, by accepting current when connected to a circuit that has a charge source connected to it. This in turn need only connect to the battery at the positive terminal (into which electrical current flows). If that positive terminal is connected in circuit to a negative electrical potential, the imbalance will induce a current to flow.

Whether that current will actually flow is dependent on the voltage of the charge source—the voltage of the negative electrical potential of the circuit. A battery will have a very specific operating voltage, usually a bit over 12V (DC, of course). The battery will not accept a charge from any source operating below that voltage. Charge voltages must fall within a very specific range because the charge acceptance of a battery will vary based on charge voltage.

The batteries themselves are composed of individual cells which make up the basic components of the battery. A battery is simply a collection of battery cells which are wired together (or otherwise linked electrically). It is the chemistry of these individual cells which determine the operating voltage of the battery itself. In the case of LiFePO4, each cell furnishes (an average of) 3.2V. So a nominal 12V battery (actually an average of 12.8V) will have four cells or groupings of cells connected in series to make up the 12V. When a charge source is connected to the battery positive, it is the individual cells which accept the current, which must divide out to have voltage over 3.2V for each cell. When a load is connected to the battery negative, each cell will furnish current at 3.2V and at an amperage level determined by the resistance of the load. Though cell voltage will also vary depending on actual state of charge.

Resistance is what limits the flow of current (measured in amperes, or amps) through a circuit. So a circuit with zero resistance will draw the maximum amount of current that a charge source or battery is able to furnish. If you connect a conductor directly between the positive and negative terminals of a battery, you will be inducing a constant flow of current. This will actually be a very bad idea for several reasons. The battery will not charge itself very well if at all because the current will be flowing at the same voltage as that furnished by the battery. This will quickly discharge the battery below safe levels and cause a hazard. Which will be compounded because no conductor is perfect, and the more current that flows through one the more heat will be generated by the resistance present in the conductor. So if this was a small wire that you used it would quickly melt. If it was a larger wire that could handle more current you might instead melt the battery terminals first.

So any resistance in a circuit will limit current flow, but a resistor that is designed as part of the circuit will deliberately regulate the flow of current through the circuit. Because current will flow in inverse proportion to the level of resistance in the circuit. So if you inserted a resistor, such as a light-bulb, into that circuit between the two battery terminals, only the amount of current that the light-bulb would accept will flow through the circuit.

But resistance is not constant. It will vary according to the voltage of a circuit. Higher voltage, less resistance. Lower voltage, more resistance. With batteries or other circuits that provide a constant voltage, resistance can be assumed to be stable. So that light-bulb (which had best be one designed to operate at 12V) will have a constant resistance and permit a constant amount of current to pass. But if the battery voltage drops down lower because of over-discharge less current will flow and the bulb will dim. And if another battery is added in series to double the voltage then more current will flow, the light will brighten, and the bulb may become damaged and cease to work. So it is very important for voltage to be kept constant or nearly so for electrical systems.

Bringing this back to batteries, they themselves will have resistance between the different parts, which altogether is termed internal resistance. So each cell will have a specific internal resistance, each conductor between cells will have a specific resistance, and the battery terminals themselves will also have a specific resistance. Altogether this will add up to the internal resistance of the battery. A charge source into the positive terminal will have current regulated by the internal resistance of the battery. So a higher voltage charge source will induce a larger current to flow into the battery, as that resistance is reduced by the higher voltage. Thus voltage levels will be closely associated with the charge acceptance rate (CAR) of a given battery chemistry. Increase voltage over a given level and the current may be higher than the maximum CAR of the battery, which will quickly lead to heat buildup and damage.

Cells

At this point I will drop down to the level of the individual cells. The battery is only a collection of cells and all properties will be derived from cell properties. With lead-acid battery types this is a less important aspect, because all of the cells are pooled together into a single container and you can only really interact at the battery level. LiFePO4 batteries, in contrast, are just collections of individually packaged cells. Which is what makes it possible to assemble your own batteries.

Cell Balance

Cell balance has to do with how much electrical potential is present in two or more cells at a given time. Charge levels, in other words. If all of your cells are bundled together into a single battery and one cell has less charge in it than the others, then you have a problem. Every time you go to charge then that cell will come up to a lower charge level than the others, and every time you discharge then that cell will drop down to a lower discharge level than the others. Which over time will reduce the useful life of that cell. And every time you try for a deep discharge then you will lose the voltage potential of that cell when it bottoms out before the others. So your 12V battery will drop to 9V and everything in that circuit will suffer the consequences.

Cell Matching

In good batteries this does not happen (much) and you can expect the cells to be pretty well balanced. But the primary reason that this is so is because the cells themselves were matched together when the battery was assembled. Which means that each cell will have about the same amperage capacity. The amps that can be drawn before full discharge. Equally as important, however, the cells must have closely matched internal resistance ratings. Each cell will be (should be) charged at the same voltage level, and if resistance ratings vary then charge levels will vary and balance will be thrown off. The same for discharge, as a lower resistance in one cell will lead to a higher discharge rate for that cell and balance will be thrown off.

Internal cell resistance is not really something you can change, as it is set by the construction of the cell. Different cell chemistries will have different internal resistance levels, but cells of the same chemistry will also vary. Even standardized production runs will produce cells with somewhat varied resistance.

Good practice when making a battery is to start with cells that are very well matched in terms of resistance and that are charged to the same capacity level. The better market battery producers will all do this. Insuring this can be something of a challenge for the home battery builder, as cells are often ordered and shipped over long distances and you cannot test them before they arrive. The only way to get matched cells is to go through a distributor that will test the cells and send them to you matched. Which means going through reputable sources instead of ordering the cheapest cells you can find. Bargain cells are priced that way for a reason (often for more reasons than cell matching alone) and should be avoided by anyone intending long term use.

Balancing

Even with closely matched resistance values, cell balance will tend to drift apart over many charge and discharge cycles. Also, resistance can vary, though slightly, between the individual conductors that are used to connect cells into batteries and batteries into banks. So periodic balancing will be required.

This should only be done periodically, however, as each re-balancing cycle will reduce cell life more than a larger number of normal charge cycles. Occasional balancing is necessary, but each time will shorten battery life. It will do so much less than will leaving the cells out of balance. And better matched cells which are part of better designed battery banks will require balancing less often.

The two methods of self balancing are to top balance or to bottom balance. The balance method that you utilize should be matched to the normal usage pattern of your battery bank. So a bank that goes through frequent deep discharges, to 20% or lower capacity, had better be bottom balanced—the cell capacities matched most closely together at the bottom end of their discharge capacity. Failure to keep cells bottom balanced may lead to some cells dropping out before others with deep discharge and consequent voltage loss. A bank that will more often be kept much closer to full charge should instead be top balanced—the cell capacities matched most closely together at the top end of their charge capacity. Failure to keep cells top balanced may lead to overcharging some cells at full charge and thus increasing the aging rate of those cells.

For most, if not all, mobile living solutions top balancing will be preferred. But this will directly follow from the usage parameters of your cells. If you regularly discharge the cells close to max potential then they should indeed be bottom balanced. Electric propulsion banks that will be heavily drained (usually in wheeled applications) may be one example of this. Better practice will be to maintain higher capacity levels whenever possible, and certainly not to drain cells down past 20% overall capacity. The deeper that you discharge these cells each cycle the shorter the expected cell life will be. Part of the draw of LiFePO4 over lead acid types is that you can go down to 20% or lower instead of having to stay over 50% for the sake of battery life, so use that capacity if you must and if that fits with your charge sources planning. But do keep in mind that longer lasting LiFePO4 banks will never drop below 30-40% and will try to maintain higher charge levels. Which makes top balancing the preferred balance method.

I will not get into actual balancing procedures here, but see the references below for more information.

Battery Monitors and Battery Management

'BMS' may actually refer to several different types of system and can be short for either battery management system or battery monitor system.

Battery Monitoring

A battery monitor is information only. There will be a central unit that keeps track of data feeds from sensors connected to the batteries and calculates values based on those data feeds. So you might have a battery monitor screen output that shows battery temperature values. The monitor system will get that information from temperature sensors connected to either the whole battery or to the individual cells (best is cell level data) and feed it directly to your screen or otherwise use that data to give you an average figure. The other things that a monitor system can keep track of directly are voltage and current flows (amps in or amps out). So you can be fairly confident that the monitor is correct about these things, as long as everything is working properly.

The primary purpose of a battery monitor, other than to warn you about out of range temps or voltage or amp draws, will be to keep track of the charge state of a given battery or cell. How much juice is in there at any given time. In fact most dedicated battery monitors will have this as their sole purpose. To tell you state of charge and track charge usage over time. Many will not even have temperature sensors, though the better ones will or will let you add your own to the system.

There is a problem however, in that a battery monitor cannot ever directly determine how much energy potential is present in a battery or cell at a given time. A battery is not like a tank of water in which you can easily check a fill gauge. There are some indications given by voltage differences, similar to the pressure differences for water tanks. But LiFePO4 cells only really change voltage levels when they are almost fully discharged or when they are actively being charged and are almost full or empty. So mostly what a battery monitor will do is keep track of how much current goes in or out and give you a battery charge readout based on ideal figures. Some battery monitors are better at this than others and will be more accurate over time. Some will be very inaccurate and become less so over time.

Battery Protection

The first (and lesser) type of battery management system (BMS) will actually just be a battery protection device. That is, it will have temperature sensors and voltage sensors and amps sensors for current...and will disconnect the battery from the external battery connections whenever any of these values exceed a certain programmed range. It might also send out an alarm signal to any connected devices, such as a battery monitor. More often the alarm will be sent out at a certain value and battery disconnect will occur at a somewhat greater or lesser value.

So if the battery gets too hot or gets over or under voltage or amp draws exceed a certain level then that battery will drop out of your battery bank. Which can be less than ideal, from the perspective of the operator and for the continued health of the other devices in that electrical system. Though still desirable in certain circumstances. Better to have a battery dropout than to risk a fire or have the battery permanently damaged or, worse, the whole bank. This is really a form of dumb battery management, though the best ones will be programmable by the operator. Some packaged batteries which include a 'BMS' will have this type of system.

Battery Management

The better ones however, and the better separately sold BMS units, will be full fledged battery management systems. That is, not only will they monitor and report and offer overvalue protection, but they will also optimize battery usage by varying cell discharge and charge rates in order to better keep the cells balanced with each other and also have some method to balance our the cells when not in use. If done properly this will greatly improve cell life. Some BMS units will also include temperature regulation options, if connected to variable speed fans for air cooling or cycled liquid cooling solutions.

Smarter systems (better programmed and linked) may actively vary battery loads and usage by communicating with other devices in the circuit to vary or eliminate their power draws. So a BMS that is networked to a compatible inverter unit, for instance, may inform the inverter that loads are too high and request a reduction in power draw. In a similar manner the BMS might be linked to a charger (which could be the same inverter/charger unit) and will work together with it to maximize battery charging efficiency.

So, when purchasing a battery with BMS included or selecting your own BMS, there will be a number of important considerations. Will it monitor values and output them to me? Does it have thermal management? Active or passive? Is is programmable by me? Will it communicate with other devices? What type of overvalue protection does it have? Will it work to balance out the cells, and using what methods? Is is a centralized unit, distributed, or modular? Etc. The cheaper ones will not have the best features, but the more expensive ones will not necessarily do everything you want them to either. The best BMS will be matched to and possibly able to communicate with the rest of your electrical system—part of an integrated solution.

Building

Building a Bank

A well-designed and carefully monitored battery bank may not actually need a dedicated BMS unit. It is (much) better to have one anyway for redundancy and active management options, but you can complete all of the most important features with manual control and system design. In conjunction with a good battery monitor. The monitor can tell you when values get out of range and you can drop loads from the bank by shutting things off or just drop out the bank or individual batteries in it. If you are present and awake. Cooling devices can be passive or manually controlled. Balancing can be done manually, though not the active load variation that a good BMS can achieve.

Regardless of whether you have a BMS or not or what type it is, you will still want to carefully design your battery banks. The most basic concerns will be what voltage the bank will furnish and how large the total capacity will be. Voltage is increased by connecting batteries in series (negative to a positive) and every battery so connected will add its voltage to the total voltage. There are no serious problems with series connected banks during normal usage, but problems can arise if one or more batteries in the series drop out and system voltage is reduced. The only way to protect against this is to have separate battery banks. So your house 'bank' might actually be two or more separate battery banks all configured at the same voltage. That way if one bank loses voltage then another bank can be switched in, either manually or automatically. This will complicate the DC system, and even more so if you want to have multiple banks 'online' at once, but you will also be protected against voltage loss. It will be up to you to decide if that factor is important enough to warrant the extra expense and complexity.

Individual battery bank capacity can be increased by wiring batteries in parallel (negatives together and positives together). Actually, and despite common practice, it is a bad idea to wire in parallel at the level of individual batteries. This is because it is almost impossible to match resistance levels exactly between batteries, given that each battery is a collection of varied cells that are themselves connected and averaged. Each connector inside and outside of each battery will also impact resistance levels. Inevitably some connections will loosen over time and alter resistance, and seemingly identical connectors will have small variations that impact resistance in the first place. So while it is difficult but possible to closely match resistance levels between the cells of a battery, any variation will be multiplied when batteries are connected in parallel. The differences in resistance levels will lead to unbalanced power draws between batteries and thus you will end up with batteries at different charge levels.

The best way to increase capacity is to instead parallel cells to desired capacity and then series together the (low voltage) batteries thus formed to reach desired bank voltage. This is the method used by every electric automobile on the market to form their large capacity battery banks. Parallel the cells first and then series the cell bundles together for voltage. Unfortunately this method will not be possible for those buying pre-made batteries instead of individual cells. And the standard batteries on the market are all around 100Ah, so parallel you must to achieve reasonable capacities.

The easiest way to somewhat ameliorate paralleling problems is to insure equal connections between batteries that are parallel. That is, instead of just putting a bar or series of wires across the negatives and the same across the positives and connecting your DC system to that, you should have each negative and each positive connected directly to a common central point. Thus you will have a common positive and negative from each battery in the bank. This way, draws and charges that go to the individual battery posts will be passively equalized to a certain tolerance depending on the material of the conductors used. The other method, which unfortunately is common practice, will lead to varied draws and charges because current will flow unevenly across the linked terminals. The posts furthest from the system negative will have a lower power draw and the posts furthest from the system positive will receive less charge. This problem is somewhat reduced, but not totally, by linking the system negative to one side of a common negative bar and linking the system positive to the other side of a common positive bar. The variation will not be as bad but the central batteries will still have different flows than the outer batteries.

The other method which can be used to reduce paralleling problems is for BMS units on the individual batteries to be able to communicate with each other and work to keep the batteries balanced in addition to the cells within the batteries. So output and input currents will be varied between the separate batteries and total charge capacity will remain roughly constant. Some BMS units have this inter-connectivity designed in and others can be so linked with dedicated multiple BMS products.

Building a Battery

Of course, it will still be better to assemble your own batteries from cells to achieve desired capacity and build up from there. Also much cheaper, as the cells themselves cost less than prepackaged batteries, even with your own BMS and other necessary components, and the prepackaged batteries with the better BMS units included are also the most expensive ones.

This process will be explained in much greater detail if you explore the references included below, but the basic procedure is thus: buy matched cells, balance them, assemble them together along with your chosen BMS and monitors, and construct an enclosure that serves to contain them and keep them safe and cool.

Sourcing good cells can be somewhat difficult. To my knowledge, all commercially available LiFePO4 cells are currently manufactured in China by a certain number of producers. Sinopoly, Winston, Calb, Lishen, etc. Consumers then have the choice of ordering direct from the producer or buying from a reputable middleman (importer). Results have tended to vary using either method, but if you are careful and willing to pay a bit more you should be able to source decent cells.

Balancing the cells properly will require a dedicated power supply unit, which will increase costs. A desktop power supply is useful for all sorts of applications, however, and can be used to balance multiple batteries over a period of years, defraying that initial cost over time.

Only quality materials should be used for the assembly process. Very high amp draws and inputs should be expected for these batteries, so good solid conductors and connections are necessary. Your BMS may be a full unit or just a 'mini' BMS, but in either case should be rated beyond the full capacity of your assembled battery.

The battery case can be built from whatever materials you want to use or have on hand, but certain properties will be desirable. You will want it to be solid enough to hold the cells together in the event that one or more of them try to expand. It should conduct heat away from the cells as possible but have no possibility of shorting out the electrical connections. It should protect the cells and the BMS from impact damage and possibly from environmental contamination (like humid ocean air or random sprays of water). The case itself can be separate from the battery bank enclosure or they could be integrated together, but temperature and conductivity and physical protection and environmental protection must be considered.

References and Further Research

marinehowto.com/lifepo4-batteries-on-boats

nordkyndesign.com/protection-and-management-of-marine-lithium-battery-banks

www.diyelectriccar.com/threads/bottom-balancing.85458

kwsaki.blogspot.com/2013/01/how-to-bottom-balance.html

www.solarpaneltalk.com/forum/off-grid-solar/batteries-energy-storage/general-batteries/369810-what-is-wrong-with-wiring-batteries-in-parallel

www.smartgauge.co.uk/batt_con.html

batteryuniversity.com/learn/article/serial_and_parallel_battery_configurations

nordkyndesign.com/assembling-a-lithium-iron-phosphate-marine-house-bank

nordkyndesign.com/lithium-battery-banks-fundamentals

youtu.be/w4Wy_dp0ad4

Detailed build video for a LiFePO4 solar bank.

youtu.be/p21iZVFHEZk

Crash test video for Winston LiFePO4 cells. It is possible to destroy these with overcharging, but notice there is no fire even though the gas release indicates thermal runaway has occurred. Winston claims that their specific chemistry has better attributes in this respect which is one reason this video was posted.

31.

Electric Marine Propulsion

This is a bit of a loaded subject. It is certainly a very confused one and there is a lot of conflicting and even contradictory information out there. Some people are very pro-electric drive and others claim that it is just not worth it and are firmly in favor of combustion engines. Given that I am pretty strongly in favor of electric propulsion for some (though not all) purposes, I think that it is important to include this discussion of the factors involved. I will draw strongly on basic principles and the actual physics of boat propulsion in order to attempt to clearly lay out the differences and provide an accurate comparison. This is not meant as an argument either for or against electric propulsion as such but instead is intended to be a comparative analysis.

How Boats Move

Any boat which wishes to move forward in the water must account for the forces which are in play to keep it from moving—it must overcome those forces with a greater force. Here I will focus solely on a fluid medium of still water, though air resistance and the motions of wind and water will also come into play in real world applications. Simplified, then, a boat will have a certain mass and if it wishes to move in one direction it must apply a force in the opposite direction sufficient to move that mass.

Force = Mass x Acceleration

So, if we know the mass of the boat and also how fast we want to move it, then we can determine how much force will be required. However, we will also have to overcome the resistance of the water that the boat moves through. That is, the boat must push itself forward through the fluid medium that has a certain density and that will resist the effort to push it aside. More, the faster that the boat tries to move the higher resistance to motion that the water will exert. This is because water is mostly a non-compressible liquid. It will compress slightly, because of any gases such as oxygen that are dissolved in the water, but on the whole it cannot be compacted into a smaller space than that which it currently occupies. What this means is that every bit of water that the boat tries to push aside must move aside other bits of water in order to have its own space. So the boat is not only pushing at the water right in front of it but also the water on all sides of it. Some of that water also gets pushed up into the air somewhat around the boat, forming waves, but this will never be all of the water moved aside and in any case the water that is being pushed up into the air will also be trying to fall back down due to the force of gravity. This gives us a new calculation.

Force = Mass x (Acceleration – Resistance)

Because resistance to motion increases as boat speed increases, it requires progressively more energy to move the boat through the water the faster that you want to go. That is, it might require three times as much energy to go twice as fast. There is actually an upper limit for the speed that a given vessel may move through the water which is expressed by the term 'hull speed'. This is the speed at which the resistance of the water becomes so great that no practical force is sufficient to move the vessel any faster. There are two factors that determine hull speed. The first is the length of the vessel, in that a longer vessel will be trying to move water aside over a greater span of distance, and the longer wave that is generated by the boat as it passes through the water will permit higher speeds before reaching too high a resistance to move faster. The second is the mass of the vessel itself, in that a greater mass of boat will displace more water, which is an equivalent mass of water to the mass of the boat, and so will have to move more water aside as it moves forward.

So if we want to move a boat through the water in one direction, we must generate sufficient force in the other direction to overcome both the mass of the boat and also the resistance of the water that the boat is moving through. This is regardless of propulsion method. We can also determine that the faster we want the boat to move, the more resistance will increase and thus progressively more force will be required. And that there will be a point where resistance is so high that no further speed increases are possible.

All of this so far has dealt with displacement motion through the water. It is possible, given sufficient propulsion and the proper hull-form, for some boats to rise partially up out of the water and so reduce their water resistance enough to achieve much higher speeds than displacement hull speed. This is called planing, or moving through the water at planing speed. Most of my discussion here will be in regards to displacement speeds, as at this time electric propulsion is more suited to displacement applications, but I will also include some discussion below on the feasibility of electric propulsion for planing vessels.

Propellers and Propulsion

It would be nice to be able to generate force directly, and so to move boats through the water without having to deal with further complications, but thus far no one has managed to figure out how to do that. Instead, the best method that we have determined is to use a rotary propeller to thrust water in the opposite direction that you want to move the boat. That is, a spinning shaft is projected out of the rear of the boat, to which a propeller is attached which thus also spins. The shape of the propeller is such that it gathers water as it spins and forces that water to pass in a single direction. The movement of the water in one direction creates a force in the opposite direction equivalent to the mass of the water times the rate its acceleration—which provides us with a balanced equation for moving the boat.

Mass of the boat x (Acceleration of the boat – Resistance of the boat) =

Mass of the water x Acceleration of the water

On the propeller side, we can leave out resistance of the water to being moved, as to a certain extent this factor cancels itself out. That is, there are multiple types of resistance involved and some of them work in our favor while others do not. First, instead of just trying to push water out of its way, the propeller is sucking in water on one side and pushing it out the other. So there will not be a buildup of resistance to a linear motion as we have with the boat. Second, the non-compressibility of water and general resistance to being pushed around here works in our favor, as some of the thrust obtained from the moving water column that the propeller generates is from the water behind the boat resisting the motion of that water column. Third, the water will also resist changing from a resting state of inertia to an accelerated state of motion, but that will be overcome by the force of the propeller—and specifically by propeller torque. Which is a different calculation entirely and one we will get into in a bit. For now, we can change around these force calculations into terms that are more useful.

Force of the water column =

(Weight of the water / gravity) x ((final velocity – initial velocity) / time)

Whereas mass has been reduced to weight divided by the force of gravity and acceleration has been put in terms of starting and final speed over time. The force of gravity is a known constant at sea level. If we assume that starting speed is zero and that the time passed is one second, we can further simplify.

Force of the water column = (Weight of the water / 32.2) x (Velocity of the water)

Velocity and gravity are both in terms of feet per second, which units will cancel each other out. This means that both force and weight will here be measured in pounds. So if we know how many pounds of water that we want to move, and how fast we want to move it, we will also know how many pounds of force are required to do so. Alternatively, at a constant level of force, increasing velocity will reduce the weight of water moved. And so on. But the most important point here is that thrust generated by a propeller will be a factor of the volume of water passed (water has a pretty constant weight by volume) and how fast it is moving.

Propeller Diameter

There are thirteen or so different properties that distinguish one propeller from another. Here I will focus on three of those, as being most important for our thrust calculations and also to keep this discussion manageable. First, each propeller will have a different diameter. This is also the most important measure for determining displacement propeller efficiency, as I will explain.

The diameter of a propeller is simply the total length across the prop when looking at one of the faces. While it is spinning, the propeller blades will form a circle of swept motion and the diameter of that circle will be the same as the diameter of the propeller. In terms of our water column of thrust, the volume of water which may be moved will be limited by the diameter of the propeller. The circle of swept motion of the propeller will be the same diameter as the column of water being thrust out by the propeller.

But as the diameter of a circle increases, the area of that circle increases exponentially. For example, a 12in diameter propeller will sweep an area of .76sq.ft, but a 24in diameter propeller will sweep an area of 3.14sq.ft, and a 48in diameter propeller will sweep an area of 12.57sq.ft. Because of this we can most easily increase the volume of water being moved by the propeller by increasing propeller diameter. Doing so will take advantage of that exponential growth and so be more effective than other measures.

Propeller Pitch

Each propeller will also have a certain pitch. This can be more easily understood if we visualize turning the propeller on its side so that we are looking at the blades edge on and the propshaft would be running straight from right to left. The pitch is the distance that one of the propeller blades will travel, from one side to the other, as the propeller turns. So, a 12in pitch propeller blade will move across a twelve inch distance, along the curve of the blade, while the propeller spins. A 24in pitch propeller will move across a distance of twenty four inches while the propeller spins. And so on.

Propeller diameter will determine how large a water column can be moved but only in conjunction with pitch. That is, for every full rotation of the propeller, the total volume of water that is moved will be limited to the size of a cylinder of water with a circumference given by the propeller diameter and a length given by propeller pitch. At a certain propeller rotation speed, an increased pitch will mean that a larger amount of water is being moved, which will mean that more thrust and thus more force is being generated.

Increasing the pitch does not help as much as increasing the diameter. There is no exponential growth here—it is a straight linear progression. But if you are already at your max diameter then you can make your propeller more efficient at moving water by increasing the pitch. However, pitch also has limitations that it must meet. The pitch of the propeller has a close relationship with the speed of the boat, in that the pitch is what limits the water speed through the propeller and will do so most efficiently when matched to how fast the boat is actually traveling. Ideal pitch will align the speed of shaft rotation with the speed of the boat and will increase efficiency in the entire motion. For a fixed propeller, this can only be maximized for a single speed—which should be the cruising speed of the boat.

Because water is a fluid medium there will always be some slip, in terms of pitch, as the propeller turns. Less water will be propelled astern than the pitch itself would suggest in the terms that we have been using regarding a column of water, because some of that water will be slipping out the sides of the prop and so on. Calculating actual slip is a somewhat troublesome matter and well beyond the scope of this discussion. I will be using these approximate figures for slip calculation. For speeds under nine knots, slip will require a 45% increase in pitch size and for speeds between nine and thirty knots slip will require a 25% increase in pitch size. So for most displacement craft that would have, for example, a nominal pitch of twenty inches at a given diameter to move a specific volume of water, actual pitch will need to be twenty-nine inches. Faster craft like multihulls will need an actual pitch of twenty-five inches instead of the same nominal twenty.

Slip = 45% under 9 kn

Slip = 25% between 9 – 30 kn

After calculating ideal pitch, increase measure by this amount when sizing actual propeller.

Propeller Blade Area

The diameter and pitch provide the limits on the column of water that can be moved, but it is the blades themselves that actually impact the water and move it along. So blade area will have a direct impact on the volume of water that is actually moved. At any given time a certain amount of water will be in contact with the propeller blades and that is the only water that the propeller will be moving at that time (except for the hydrofoil action—see below). Wider blades will increase blade area and adding more blades can allow more blade area than having fewer blades. A larger center hub will also reduce blade area.

I will assume blade area to have a direct relationship with the volume of water that can be moved by the propeller, in that volume figures obtained from combining diameter and pitch will be multiplied by blade area as a proportion of total area of the circle described by propeller diameter. These will be ideal figures, as will be used for slip, and somewhat rough. But they should be adequate for our purposes. So, a propeller with four wide blades will be assumed to modify water moved by 60% (only 60% of the volume of water that diameter and pitch describe will be moved), a propeller with three wide blades will modify by 50%, four narrow blades by 40%, and three narrow blades by 30%.

Despite this, for very high speed operation narrow blades are actually better. High speed propellers in general focus on increasing force by moving the water astern faster, while low speed propellers increase force by moving a greater weight of water. I will not get into cavitation and other high speed propeller headaches here, but there are various reasons why planing vessel propellers are shaped differently than displacement propellers and have less blade area. But for low speed displacement vessels, with a slow moving prop, more blade area is obviously better. Though depending on prop speed, there can be too much blade area. Every time a blade moves through the water ahead of another blade, it disturbs the water and decreases efficiency of water flow. This effect is compounded the closer the blades are to each other, but it is also reduced proportionately with slower moving blades.

Propeller Efficiency

What we can now see is that, assuming a constant rotational speed, increasing the pitch and the blade area and especially the diameter will increase the force thrust by the propeller. Simply put, larger props will move more water at a given speed. However, the smaller propeller will also be using less energy at the same rotational speed. The force required to turn the larger propeller at the same speed will be greater, because the volume and thus mass of water being moved will also be greater.

The more important point here is that if we instead assume that a larger and a smaller propeller are generating the same amount of thrust but at different rotational speeds, then the smaller propeller will require more energy to do so than the larger propeller—will require more power from the motor. This is what is meant when it is said that larger but slower moving propellers are more efficient than faster moving but smaller propellers. Another way to say this is that with an equal amount of energy being transmitted along the propshaft, the larger propeller will generate more thrust than will the smaller propeller. There are a number of reasons why this is so, but much of it is that the propeller will progressively lose energy efficiency the faster that it turns. There will also be more efficiency losses from heat in the propshaft and at every mechanical transfer point with higher rotation speeds, but this will be less important than the action of the propeller itself.

As the propeller rotates, there are actually two forces which act to move the water. The first is direct push by the blades. The second is a hydrofoil action, in that the moving blades also generate suction and act to pull water into the propeller from the other direction. Much like fans and other aerofoils, the curved blade surfaces will generate zones of low pressure on one side and high pressure on the other. But this will be limited by the even flow of water to the propeller. The faster that flow is the more disturbed the water becomes and so the less efficient the hydrofoil action of the blades operates. The boat hull, air bubbles in the water, and the churning action of the propeller blades themselves all act to disturb the water flow and so to reduce propeller efficiency. All of these negative factors are intensified at higher rotation speeds.

The hydrofoil action itself is also amplified by a larger diameter propeller, because the effect is scaled proportionally to the area that the propeller sweeps. So just as the area swept by a propeller increases exponentially as the propeller increases in diameter, so too will the impact of the hydrofoil action. The larger prop will generate more suction for less energy even before water disturbance is factored in.

Bringing this back to our two major thrust factors of volume of water passed and speed of that water, it will require less energy to increase volume moved than to increase the speed of the water. Because of the relative efficiencies in the way propellers work (at displacement speeds). So large propellers will require less energy for a given thrust value.

Speed Efficiency

Once planing speed is exceeded propeller efficiency principles change a great deal. Super-cavitating and surface piercing propellers can achieve high energy efficiencies. That is, in terms of thrust achieved by the propeller itself. Vessels operating at planing speed are never more efficient in terms of overall energy use to move a given mass over distance. There is a large energy cost outlay to achieve and to remain at planing speed. This is why speedboats are relegated to recreation and military purposes and all waterborne commercial transport goes by displacement vessels. Except for some fast passenger vessels.

The principles outlined thus far indicate that there will be significant energy efficiencies obtained by displacement vessels which stay somewhere below their hull speed and use large, slow turning propellers to do so. This is borne out by the example of large commercial marine transport vessels. They travel faster than most civilian craft because hull speed is more a function of length than displacement, but they do so below max hull speed and with very large props. You can be sure that this is intentional on their part; in that business fuel efficiency can be the difference between profit and bankruptcy.

Power Generation

All of this will depend upon the ability to set the propshaft turning at the desired speed. In order to do so, a twisting force must be applied to the inboard end of the propshaft. This twisting force is known as torque. The propshaft itself, the propeller, and the volume of water encompassed will all together have a certain mass which will be in a state of inertia that resists the motion of acceleration. In rotational problems like the need to turn a propeller, torque is that force which overcomes inertia and accelerates that mass up to speed.

Without torque, the propeller speed cannot be increased. However, the faster the shaft turns (and, correspondingly, the less efficient the propeller becomes) the less torque is required to keep the shaft moving or even to increase speed. The upper end of rotational speed will be limited by available horsepower (or kW)—which is another way of saying that the maximum amount of force that can be applied to the propshaft is the maximum amount of force that can be used to turn it in a given time. The propshaft itself will always turn because of applied torque, because torque is the measure of rotational force and the shaft must be forced in a circle to keep spinning.

Sorry if that last paragraph was a bit circular, but I notice that there is continual confusion (and misinformation) about the differences and relationship between torque and horsepower. They are both just measures of force, or energy. Torque is rotational force, period, and horsepower is force applied within a set amount of time. Kilowatts are only a measure of energy and must be converted somehow to produce force, but the standard conversion ratio for horsepower is given below as 1kW = 1.34HP. The standard measure for torque is 5252 x HP / RPM (= ft-lbs of torque).

So if horsepower is the amount of force applied over time and we modify this in terms of rotations over time, then torque is instant rotational force. Getting back to turning the propshaft, the larger more efficient propeller will have a greater inertia, because of higher mass, and so will require a larger amount of torque to overcome that inertia and accelerate that mass. The smaller prop will have less inertia and will require less torque to get it moving. This is a limiting factor that has nothing to do with energy efficiency, but is the primary reason why almost every displacement boat out there is designed to use a smaller, less efficient propeller at a higher, wasteful RPM.

Combustion Engines

Combustion engines do not generate torque directly (except for rotary engines, but those are rare). Instead, a linear force is generated by the motion of the cylinders as they move up and down or side to side. Those cylinders will be connected to a crankshaft which turns, and the force of that crankshaft as it turns will be the rotational force of torque. The turning crankshaft may also be linked to a transmission system which can gear down for lower speeds (which will mean higher torque as the force is constant but the rotational speed is decreased) or gear up for higher speeds (which will mean lower torque as the converse is true). Most displacement boat transmissions will have a constant gear down ratio, continually lowering shaft speed and increasing torque.

This gearing down is good, and it allows those boats to have larger slower propellers than they otherwise might. However, combustion engines face two significant limitations that limit them to maximum propeller sizes. First, the torque potential that the engine develops has a set curve. Maximum torque is only developed at higher engine speeds. At idle speed when the transmission will be engaged torque will only be a quarter or a third of maximum potential for the engine. It is better to have the transmission, in that it will multiply what torque is produced at a given shaft RPM, but it is also impractical to engage the transmission at higher engine output levels.

Even if going without the transmission, the motor will run straight into the second limitation whenever it tries to apply power to the propshaft. This is that the engine will have a certain minimum speed, below which it will not run—the engine will stall unless the crankshaft can maintain a certain minimum speed. Try to run a combustion engine very much below idle speed and it will quickly die and need restarting. The combustion itself requires the pistons to maintain a certain speed of operation. And the propshaft is mechanically connected, whenever the transmission is engaged, to the crankshaft of the engine and thus to the pistons. So if the propshaft were to stop turning, or to refuse to turn when you engage the transmission because torque loads are too high, then the engine would stall and die.

This is precisely what will occur if the torque that is applied to the propshaft is insufficient to overcome the inertia of the propeller. If the prop is too large for engine torque at idle speeds it will not work. So the engine will be limited to turning a propeller in which the combined mass of the propshaft and propeller and water around it require at least less torque to get moving than will be developed by the engine and transmission at idle speeds.

The actual torque limit is really determined by reverse gear requirements. The engine will also stall if the transmission is shifted into reverse and it cannot furnish the combined force required both to stop the propeller from spinning and to get it turning the opposite direction. This will require even more torque, but must still be done at idle speed to allow shifting the transmission, and will shrink propellers down even further for a given engine. Assuming that they want to be able to shift into reverse without stalling out. It also places a limit on the gear reduction ratio of the transmission. Gearing down more will multiply torque which will be permit a larger propeller, but that larger propeller will have higher mass which will also multiply the force required to overcome its momentum when switching into reverse. So too large a gear ratio, with a larger prop, will still lead to stalling out when attempting to reverse propeller direction. Which is not a good occurrence on a motorboat trying to avoid obstacles.

I say 'for a given engine' because larger engines will furnish more torque at all speeds and so be able to have larger propellers. This seems to be directly related to the mass of the engine. Big heavy crankshafts and pistons and other moving parts will have greater energy of momentum behind them which will be directly transmitted along the propeller shaft to help overcome the inertia of the propeller. But the whole point of this is to achieve better energy efficiency of propulsion by getting to a larger, more efficient propeller. The larger the engine used the more mass that will be added to the vessel, which must itself be reinforced with yet more mass in order to bear the weight of the larger engine. All of this added mass will lead to greater vessel displacement and thus reduced energy efficiency. The gains are canceled out.

Electric Motors

Electric motors operate on entirely different principles. They are in fact torque machines, in that all they do is provide rotational force. The output shaft which provides the turning force is inserted within and connected to the rotor, which itself is inserted within the stator. The stator acts upon the rotor with magnetic fields which cause the rotor, and thus the output shaft, to turn.

Like a combustion engine, an electric motor will also have variable torque. But the torque characteristics at a given speed are very different. Most critically, electric motors will produce high initial torque. It may not provide maximum torque from initial start, but the curve will be much flatter than for a combustion engine and a motor may give in excess of eighty percent of maximum torque immediately. That is, the torque will be available as soon as the motor is powered on, from rest. There is no idle speed and the motor will never stall and die if dropped below a certain speed.

There is also no direct mechanical connection between the drive mechanism of an electric motor and the output shaft. The shaft is not free floating, but is just mounted on bearings and will never actually touch the stator which provides motive force. Taken together these characteristics of electric motors overcome the two major limitations that combustion engines face. Propellers can be made larger than an equivalent HP combustion engine can manage because high torque is instantly available and because there is no stalling problem stopping you from using a larger gear reduction.

There are certain drawbacks to using electric motors. The two main issues are energy storage capacity and lower reserve power. Both of these problems can be overcome but they must be accounted for in system design.

It will be difficult to store as much energy in your batteries as you can in a fuel tank. Even though a combustion engine might only manage to turn thirty percent or so of the energy capacity of the fuel into usable work, the energy density of liquid fuel is so much higher that even the best new battery technology offers no contest in regards to storage capacity. Before stable lithium batteries (LiFePO4) this was a much larger problem. Lead acid chemistries have difficulty furnishing the high amp draws required by electric propulsion. Lithium batteries still have much lower energy capacity than will be desired but they are at least feasible to use. This is particularly true when batteries are used in conjunction with alternate power sources which are not available to a combustion engine.

Electricity can be generated from the sun, from wind, and even from the waves with regen on a sailboat. For extended motor use a generator will still be required, but generators do not have the variable load requirements of a propulsion engine and can be tuned to run at higher levels of efficiency. That gain in efficiency may be lost in conversions and during line transmission on its way to the motor, but with sufficient gains in propeller efficiency you will still use less fuel than would a propulsion engine. And when the batteries are charged you can switch back to using them instead. But the best way to overcome energy storage problems is to have multiple ways to generate electricity. A combustion engine will only have the one fuel source but an electric motor can have multiple energy input sources.

The problem with reserve propulsion power (as separate from energy storage capacity) is actually a couple of different claims. First, that electric motors lack the excess power that allow diesel engines to rev up and power through heavy seas. Second, that electric motors are only suited to going slow and use way too much power when sped up.

Both of these problems do crop up and, I think, are both the result of not planning out the entire installation, from propeller to motor to power sources.

Every conventional boat propulsion system is designed as an integrated system. The engine is sized to the boat and the prop is sized to the engine and vice versa. The boat is built with sufficient hull clearance to fit that size of prop. Fuel bunkerage is calculated to match the intended purpose of the vessel. Engine power levels are also matched to prop and boat in order to achieve maximum efficiency at cruising speed—which automatically leaves reserve power on the other side of the torque curve of a combustion engine.

Very few electric propulsion systems are designed with this level of integration for the small boater. To do the job properly the entire boat must be designed with a particular propulsion solution in mind. You see people who put in an electric motor but keep the same prop, either because the boat they have cannot fit a larger prop or just because they don't know that a larger prop would be a better fit with the new motor. You also quite often see people who abuse their batteries or do not set them up properly in the first place. This second mistake I have addressed in another section. The first I hope will be sufficiently addressed by this section.

Electric motors do have less reserve capacity than combustion engines. A combustion engine can almost always push the RPM's a bit higher in order to overcome increased prop resistance from adverse conditions. An electric motor cannot do this; it will have a maximum motor speed which should not normally be exceeded (though some types are better at over-speeding than others). However, this problem can be resolved by choosing a motor that will allow the vessel to reach cruising speed, in terms of the thrust that will be delivered by that particular propeller and the hull speed of the vessel, at less than the maximum power output of the motor. Does that 20HP motor not have enough excess capacity? Go for a 25HP motor instead. Just like you would upgrade your diesel if you thought it was under powered. There are some efficiency losses from running a motor below full rated capacity, but the same can be said about combustion engines. This will vary by motor type, but an AC induction motor, for instance, may have very little difference in motor efficiency from fifty percent power on up to full rated power. If used with an appropriate controller. Normal cruising speed can be less than full capacity and there will still be excess power for adverse conditions.

I hope that this section will offer some guidance when selecting an appropriate electric motor size for a given boat (there are very few user-friendly resources available on this subject), but what it boils down to is that you will have to measure the forces involved and calculate what that means for your own boat. If you know the boat displacement and hull speed that is a good place to start. If you are keeping the same prop then you will want to get a motor with close to the same HP rating as the engine it is replacing. If you are switching out your prop as well then measure the difference in weight between the two and adjust your torque need calculations accordingly—also keeping in mind that a larger propeller requires a stronger propshaft. If you are building from scratch and planning out everything yourself then you must do the same thing that a naval architect or engineer will do: go back to the basic physics and design your systems according to forces and loads and material strengths.

Electric horsepower is not more powerful than combustion horsepower—and horsepower doesn't turn the shaft anyway. That's all torque. Because of the different torque characteristics of the two motor types, you can install an electric motor rated down to about one third the horsepower rating of the combustion motor it is replacing as long as you keep the same propeller. This will work, because the electric motor will still supply more torque from rest than the engine would have at idle speeds, but the boat will move more slowly and you will have no reserve power capacity. This is the cheap route and is actually a good solution if you have limited battery capacity and are ok with the low speeds. There will be some small efficiency gains from eliminating the mass of the combustion engine and fuel, and more than that in terms of energy because you will be using less energy for the motor than was provided by the more powerful combustion engine. Kind of like trading down from an SUV to a compact car—great mileage, less power.

The problem of electric motors using too much power at higher speeds is mostly a boat problem and not dependent on the type of propulsion. Water resistance continues to increase the faster you go until you hit hull speed and cannot go any faster. So, yes, as water resistance increases the motor will have to draw progressively more power to overcome the progressive water resistance. The trick is to size the motor and propeller (especially pitch) to reach maximum efficiency at your desired cruising speed, which should be somewhat less than hull speed, with some motor power capacity left over as a reserve.

This concern can also be explained because many people have used lead acid battery chemistries to power electric propulsion motors. As I explain in the needs section on Electricity, every type of battery will have a maximum amp draw rate which it will be able to sustain and still provide full battery capacity. Exceeding that amperage is possible, to an extent, but doing so will reduce the total amount of energy you can draw from the battery before depletion. Even Firefly batteries are not really suited for electric propulsion unless you spread the amp draw over a lot of them. Other lead-acid chemistries are even less suited for this application. LiFePO4 batteries are workable, in that much higher amp draws with no capacity loss are possible, but you will still have to spread the draw over a large enough bank. You must pick your specific batteries and design your bank accordingly —some of the cheaper lithium batteries out there have deliberately throttled amp draw capacity.

You must also size your battery bank to meet expected motor draws and have specific charge sources in mind. Battery energy density is still much lower than all combustion fuels and you cannot get as much range out of a battery bank as you can out of a fuel tank. There must be alternate charge sources, whether solar or wind or a generator or just shore power after short jaunts.

Example Boats

Ok, so let's throw in some real world examples (though calculated theoretically) to see what we can actually do with electric propulsion. I will start by picking out a few different boats and showing how you might go about re-powering. For better actual displacement figures, I will add about 10% onto the spec displacements of the boats. First up is the boat from my sample sailboat refit. I will use the speed conversion of 1kn = 1.6878ft/sec.

Catalina

Catalina 30, 1982
Displacement: 11,200 lbs
Hull speed: 6.7 kn (11.31 ft/sec), est. cruising speed 4 kn (6.75 ft/sec)
Universal 5411 Diesel with 11HP
HBW50 transmission at 2.14:1 gear reduction
Propeller: 3 wide blades, 13 in diameter, 9 in pitch
Propshaft: 1 in diameter

There are several re-power options we can go for here, but they will all run into certain limitations in the platform itself. The most important of which are the maximum propeller diameter for the boat and the maximum load on the propeller shaft.

Both of these issues can actually be improved upon somewhat. The shaft can be extended (or just replaced with a longer shaft) which will place the propeller further from the hull and so permit a larger prop diameter. The shaft could also be replaced with a stronger material, which will permit greater torque loads. Lastly, the shaft bore could be expanded, which would mean drilling into the hull and rebuilding the entire arrangement and would permit as large a shaft diameter as might be desired. This last option is possible but not really warranted for an older boat.

The good news for this boat is that the propshaft used is a standard size diameter for multiple Catalina boats. It is the same shaft used in the Catalina 36, which displaces half again as much and has up to a 30HP engine. A new shaft ordered from Catalina Direct might run $400 and can be sized anywhere within a 12 inch length margin. I would not stay with the old shaft for this vessel, especially if it is the original. Metal will fatigue over time even if it is not corroded and an electric motor will place a higher torque load on the shaft.

If we extend the propshaft by about six inches it will be possible to switch up to a fifteen inch propeller, but otherwise thirteen inches will be the limit for this boat. If buying a new propshaft as part of the rebuild a longer shaft is the best option we have to improve propeller efficiency. Pitch could be extended up to as much as fourteen inches but should be matched to intended cruising speed.

This leaves us with blade area, which may be difficult to increase. Four or five blade inboard propellers as small as thirteen inches (or fifteen) are difficult to find and may have to be custom ordered. If you did find a five blade propeller you may be able to move up to sixteen inches in diameter (or fourteen with the shorter shaft), as the extra blades will reduce vibration against the hull and so the clearance margin could be reduced. This last can only be fully determined by actual testing though.

The original 11HP diesel is known to be somewhat under powered for this boat, but I would still not go any higher than 15HP with an electric motor. Larger than that and you run the risk of warping the propshaft under heavy loads. A 10HP electric motor would actually work fine if we are able to prop up to the fifteen inch diameter prop. More thrust will be achieved than the original diesel could offer because of the increased propeller efficiency. Battery space will be limited for this build and it would even be possible to go with a 5HP motor, though I would only do so if keeping close to the mass (weight) of the original propeller arrangement—which may still permit a larger prop diameter. A 5HP electric motor will still be able to generate more torque from rest than could the original diesel at idle speed.

A 5HP motor will have a max electrical load of 3.73 kW (which might mean up to 4 kW from your batteries). This figure will be 7.5 kW for a 10HP motor and 11.2 kW for a 15HP motor—approximately, and this will vary a bit depending on motor type and controller. So if you have a 400Ah battery bank at 12V you will be able to run the 5HP motor at max for one and a quarter hours, the 10HP motor at max for three quarters of an hour, and the 15HP motor at max for just under half an hour. Clearly this will be an auxiliary motor or the battery bank should be sized larger, but the use won't be nearly as bad as this under most conditions. Cruising speed for the 15HP motor might be around 50% power draw, for instance, or possibly even less with the larger prop. This is another reason why using the 10Hp motor instead could be a better idea—electric motors have an efficiency curve and it tends to fall of quickly at less than 50% power. And you should not run the motors, as a general practice, higher than 75% of max capacity for cruising. This will reduce wear and also leave you some reserve power.

Gear ratio will depend on the nominal rotational speed of your chosen motor. This might be 1200RPM or 1800RPM or 2400RPM or 3600RPM or even as high as 6000RPM—motor-speed is highly dependent on the motor build. I will assume cruising RPM for the original diesel to be at about 2/3rds max RPM, so around 2000. With gear reduction this comes to 935RPM for the propeller. If you have the original prop then you will want to aim for the same rotational speed at cruise. If increasing the propeller size you can gear down a bit lower, but not much. So for example a 1200RPM motor will not gear down at all (direct drive), while a 2400RPM motor might use a 2:1 gear ratio. If going with a larger propeller you can reduce propeller speeds somewhat to increase efficiency.

Chris-Craft

Chris-Craft 42 Commander 1969
Displacement 28,000 lbs
Hull speed: 8.6 kn (14.52 ft/sec), est. cruising speed 7 kn (11.81 ft/sec), est. planing cruise 18 kn (30.38 ft/sec).
2 inboard Detroit diesel motors at 258HP each
Paragon P44 transmissions at 2.5:1 gear reduction
Propeller: 4 wide blades, 22 in diameter, 22 in pitch
Propshaft: 1.5 in diameter

The problems for electric re-powering a large semi-displacement craft like this are more serious...and really make the attempt infeasible at this time unless you are fine with only low displacement speeds. But discussing why that is so can also be worthwhile.

If we assume that the two cruising speeds are at 2000RPM and 3600RPM, and that idle speed is about 500RPM, we can try to work out some rough power figures. Say that the transmission engages at idle speed and that we get one quarter potential power at that point—about 65HP (per motor). There is a fixed gear ratio so this will give us a shaft speed of 200RPM at that point. Which means we are developing 1707 ft-lbs of torque at the propeller. Cruise for planing speed will be close to maximum motor power but with some reserve, so I will put that at 230HP. Or 839 ft-lbs of torque at the propeller. So cruise for displacement speed will be at around 120HP, or 788 ft-lbs of torque at the propeller.

Why so much more power to cruise at displacement than for the Catalina? If we figure the torque for the sailboat above at cruising speed, we have about 50 ft-lbs even being charitable. The Chris-Craft is giving fifteen times that amount from each engine. There are several reasons why this much power will be required—and the first is that I am using guesstimates and my figures may be wildly off. Engine tuning is a fine art and I can have no clear idea about how those diesels were tuned to develop power.

There are other factors which are very real though. The craft displaces nearly three times as much as the Catalina. This becomes a progressive burden the faster you want to go and cruising speed is nearly twice what it is for the sailboat. Which means that immediately we must furnish well in excess of six times as much thrust—and probably more like ten to fifteen times as much. The hull-form itself is not as efficient and will increase drag—remember this is a compromise hull that will also permit planing. The propellers will also be pitched specifically for planing speeds and will be (much) less efficient in displacement mode. True, the props are bigger and so more efficient, but if pitched wrong for a given speed then drag will also increase. The Catalina prop should be pitched for perfect efficiency at its one cruising speed.

There is zero room to increase propeller sizes on this boat. They are already perfectly sized for the designed aperture just under the hull and right in front of the rudders. This means that any electric motors we put in will have to match the RPM figures of the diesels, at the prop shaft, in order to develop the required thrust at the two important cruising speeds.

We would have to size our motors to match the horsepower ratings of the original diesels, or at least get close, to allow the boat to make plane. The only feasible single motors I know of at this power range are large three-phase AC induction motors. I price a 250HP Baldor somewhere in excess of $20,000 new. It will weigh 2900lbs. Max power draw will be under 190kW. You may be able to find motors that are designed for marine use and have somewhat better prices or lower weight, but the power draw will be similar. Bellmarine offers a large Shaftmaster motor rated up to 100kW (~135HP). Two of these with the output shafts yoked would substitute the full horsepower for a single one of the replaced diesels, so four of them together would give the boat the full horsepower rating of the original diesels. Figure something like 300kW for cruising at plane.That spec alone would be enough to force me to stay with combustion engines.

You could not run such motors on batteries. There is just not enough room on the boat. This means that serial hybrid power will be required. There is room for a generator in the engine room and one came standard emplaced there when the boat was new. But there is not room for a generator that could supply 300kW of power. In effect, you will need an engine about the size of the two diesels that were replaced combined in order to generate the electrical power required for the equivalent electric motors. You could do this. I think it would take up half the salon of the boat but it would fit. It would not be very practical.

However, there is an alternative provided that you are willing to give up planing speed altogether and also to drop down to a slower displacement cruising speed. The original generator emplacement will have been something like a 6.5kW Onan diesel unit, but with modern units you can get more power in less space. Especially after removing the two diesel motors, you may be able to just fit in a 50kW generator unit. Which will be able to run two 50HP electric motors at about 2/3 power. These will be sufficient to propel the boat. I estimate that, with no other changes, you may be able to cruise at just under the original displacement cruising speed of seven knots. If you were willing to drop down to four knots or so you could reduce motor power and generator size both quite a bit. Replacing the propellers to match pitch to speed will be required regardless.

Lagoon

Lagoon 42-2 2016
Displacement: 29,000 lbs
Estimate hull speed: 16 kn (27 ft/sec), est. cruising speed 7 kn (11.81 ft/sec)
2 Yanmar 4JH45 diesel motors at 45HP each
Gear reduction: unknown
Propeller: 3 blade folding
Propshaft: none—sail drives used

It is surprisingly difficult to find concrete information on production catamaran propulsion specs, but I want to include a sailing multihull in this section. You may immediately notice that hull speed is very much higher than it would be for a monohull. Oddly enough, it has been found that two shallow and narrow hulls that are not dragging around thousands of pounds of ballast can move faster and more easily through the water. The figures I have given here are approximate. One reviewer claimed that sailing speed in brisk winds achieved fifteen knots and that the boat at cruising speed for the motors went roughly seven knots. This might suggest that the boat is somewhat under powered by the motors, but seven knots is a very respectable cruising speed and the system is designed to increase fuel efficiency and thus range under power. Remember that the motors are for auxiliary use rather than primary propulsion.

Even though exact figures are not available, we should be able to manage the same sort of alterations to this boat that we did with the Catalina above. That is, if re-powering with electric, we could increase the shaft length enough to prop up two inches or so. I would also want to increase blade area by going to four or five blades and switch to a standard prop instead of the folding model.

Regen is much more effective at the higher sailing speeds that a multihull can obtain, and the larger blade area will increase that capability. It will also increase drag, but as I suggested in a previous section it is possible to reduce or even eliminate drag under sail by feeding a small amount of power to the electric motors. Just a trickle is enough to get the propeller turning at boat speed, as long as you are not taking on a propulsion load. Motor use will be very inefficient but at very low power draws that should not matter. You can also switch back to regen for a bit if you find that you are depleting the batteries over time.

With propeller efficiency increased somewhat over the stock propellers, we should be able to do well enough switching in 35HP electric motors or equivalent if dropping cruising speed down a knot or so. Two 35HP motors will draw somewhere around 26kW each at full power output, but normal cruising draw will be significantly lower. This can be furnished directly with a sufficiently large generator unit, but a large battery bank will also suffice for limited durations. The motors could also be run from the batteries while they are charged by a smaller generator. If the generator is kept running while using the motors, it will reduce the draw on the batteries and extend range under power. After a time you will need to stop to let the generator recharge the batteries, but this is still a very flexible setup that would not require direct serial propulsion. You could also just size your generator to match the motor power draw at cruising speeds. The batteries would then provide reserve power if more is needed.

A Better Way

So much for the conversions. There are good arguments in either direction for re-powering displacement vessels with electric drive. It provides some benefits but also has drawbacks. The benefits would be much greater, however, and the required motors would be smaller, if it were possible to put in significantly larger and more efficient propellers. Sadly this is not the case for any boat that was designed for combustion propulsion. Making the alterations necessary to have much larger propellers involves significant trade-offs that will never be justified if combustion propulsion is intended.

Shaft angle would not have to change. Fourteen degrees or so is the standard, which is not perfectly efficient but still has no appreciable efficiency loss when compared to five degree shaft angles. Some boats have shallower shaft angles than others, but fourteen degrees is fine and will allow a somewhat larger propeller.

Blade clearance must be kept about the same, but can actually be shrunk a bit with lower shaft rotational speeds. 8% is the minimal acceptable clearance under five hundred RPM, but that is better than the 10% acceptable clearance under eighteen hundred RPM. So bigger slower props will be able to take advantage of a bit of extra space there.

The two primary considerations for propeller space, however, are clearance from the hull and draft of the vessel. Hull clearance being the biggest compromise needed for a custom design. The propellers are located toward the rear and it is possible to design a hull that sweeps upward at the back end and so gives more room for a larger propeller. Doing so will reduce interior space and also tend to limit design choices for the stern emplacements of the boat. This is a design sacrifice—it would mean no sugar scoop steps for a catamaran and will reduce buoyancy aft on any vessel. But it could also double or triple the possible propeller diameter and make for a significant increase in thrust efficiency.

More room can also be had by increasing shaft length, which will compound the effect of the shaft angle. Pushing the shaft back very much will require changing the rudder position and will also entail a thicker shaft that is better supported, but the thicker shaft will be required regardless to support a larger propeller.

Larger propellers will also increase the draft problem. Which is that a larger propeller will tend to be the lowest appendage hanging down off the hull and will be at risk of impact damage. Protecting it somewhat might be achieved with keel shape, but damage to the propeller will still become more likely the larger the propeller is. Large ships, with very large propellers, do manage to resolve this problem quite well however. It simply requires changing the hull shape sufficiently to hide the propeller behind the swell of the hull. Which will be more of a problem for shallow catamarans, but at the same time a catamaran is able to split the thrust load between two propellers and thus they can be made somewhat smaller.

If we could double the size of the propeller on the Catalina, instead of just adding a couple of inches, then a 6HP electric motor would be plenty of power for cruising speed and even leave some reserve. Larger props would not really help the Chris-Craft out a whole lot for planing speed, but they could give a knot or two extra for the displacement option and at a considerable savings in energy output. The Lagoon could get by with 20HP motors, giving nearly twice the range at cruise under battery power and no loss in reserve power for rough conditions, if significantly larger and more efficient propellers could be used.

References and Further Research

Gerr, David. *Propeller Handbook*

Gerr, David. *The Nature of Boats.*

www.sailmagazine.com/diy/fuel-consumption-tug-vs-cruiser

www.passagemaker.com/technical/the-nuts-and-bolts-of-propellers-part-1

sailboatdata.com/sailboat/catalina-30

catalina30.com/TechLib/Propellers/propellers.htm

downeasteryachts.com/wp-content/uploads/2009/11/Universal-Diesel-Model-30-operation-and-maintenance-manual.pdf

www.catalinadirect.com/shop-by-boat/catalina-350/engine/props-etc/prop-shaft-46-14quot-to-58-14quot-for-c-30-c-320-c-34-and-c-36

commanderclub.com/forum

st4.ning.com/topology/rest/1.0/file/get/2057936919?profile=original

sailboatdata.com/sailboat/lagoon-42-2

www.sailmagazine.com/boats/boat-review-lagoon-42

plugboats.com/electric-inboard-boat-motors-guide-over-150-motors

www.youtube.com/channel/UC6BAWH7F1cixqeoS1XlLYww

An archive channel for a solar powered catamaran. Interesting data and setup, though nothing is really explained.

youtu.be/_L1xmG5Kndw

A careful conversion effort using basic components. This couple did end up either warping the propshaft or damaging the bearings after quite a bit of use, but the installation lasted for some while without problems.

youtu.be/gGO4-2SXnqY

A display and discussion video regarding a family converting their sailboat to electric power.

32.

Navigable Inland Waterways

There are extensive cruising possibilities in several parts of the world that do not require any sort of blue-water navigation. Or even coastal cruising in many cases. This section will not be an extended essay but instead more of a list guide for those interested in this possibility. I could find no source in which all of this information together is readily available and so include it here for the benefit of my readers.

North America

The Great Loop is the term used to indicate a popular circular travel route around navigable waters in the United States and southern Canada, but there are many branches and turns that are little known as well as one large system that is not connected to the Great Loop at all.

That being the Columbia and Snake Rivers, which are kept navigable all the way from the Oregon-Washington coast, past Portland Oregon, past Kennewick Washington (the Tri-Cities), up to Lewiston Idaho. This route is kept open by the Corps of Engineers for navigation, with locks and dams, and also for water level control and electrical generation. The hydro power stations along the route provide electricity to a large part of the surrounding area. And you can sail or motor from the Pacific Ocean all the way to Idaho.

The Great Loop itself might be said to begin at Chicago. From there canals lead south to the Illinois River, which connects to the Mississippi near St. Louis. One can take the Mississippi down to the gulf of Mexico, or instead switch over to the Tennessee River for the Tenn-Tom canal and Tombigbee River which joins the Alabama River to enter the Gulf at Mobile Alabama.

From there all the way around the coast to New York State the route makes use of the inter-coastal waterway (ICW). This is a continuous protected channel that runs along the entire coast and permits light craft or barges to transit the coast without (much) fear of adverse ocean conditions. There is also a shortcut across south central Florida known as the Okeechobee Waterway.

The Erie Canal permits access from Waterford NY up to Lake Ontario and over to Lake Erie via the Welland Canal. You also have the option to branch along the Oswego Canal near Albany NY, to get up to the St. Lawrence River near Montreal instead—which will then allow travel upstream to Lake Ontario and over to Lake Erie via the Welland Canal.

From there the Great Lakes are largely open water with the occasional lock between, all the way to Chicago and the start of the Loop.

The Loop forms a convenient circle, but there are also a number of branches that are less used except by commercial craft and locals but still open for cruising and exploration. All of the Great Lakes, of course. The St. Lawrence River empties into the Gulf of St. Lawrence and the Atlantic Ocean. The Upper Mississippi (above St. Louis) is kept open in warmer months all the way up to Minneapolis and St. Paul Minnesota.

The Missouri River, also from St. Louis, is open navigable water past Kansas City, past Omaha Nebraska, and all the way up to Sioux City and the border with South Dakota. Depending on water conditions as some years the Missouri has lower water than others.

From the Mississippi, the Arkansas River is navigable across that state and all the way up to Tulsa Oklahoma. The Red River, which is actually a salt-water river, can be taken across northern Louisiana all the way to Texarkana.

The Tennessee River can be used to access the Ten-Tom and head south, but also offers access upstream of Chattanooga in itself and up past Nashville using the Cumberland River.

The Ohio River, which enters the Mississippi just south of St. Louis, provides access in some form or another to large parts of Kentucky, Indiana, Ohio, Pennsylvania, and West Virginia. That's right—you can take the Ohio all the way up past Pittsburgh and to Morgantown WV and even a bit beyond.

Great Britain

Aside from extensive coastlines, Great Britain also has a large network of rivers and working canals that offer extensive internal travel possibilities by water. These canals are largely the realm of the narrowboats, as many date back to the industrial revolution and are not very wide.

I say Great Britain but really the main interconnected system is down in the England region. Scotland has a few canals across, which greatly reduce travel times by water around the coast, but are not connected to the main canal network in the south. Except indirectly across the Irish Sea or the North Sea. Northern Ireland and Ireland have some linked internal waterways as well. But using the canals in the England region you can explore from Liverpool to London and from Bristol to Hull, with many destinations in between and branches all over.

Russian Federation

The Russian Federation has extensive river and canal links west of the Ural Mountains. With the major caveat that any vessel which travels them must be Russian flagged. Which may or may not bar all foreign vessels and may also be subject to change.

Regardless, it is possible to travel by boat across much of western Russia, from the Baltic to the Black Sea to the Caspian Sea and many other destinations between.

Continental Europe

West of Russia proper, the major waterways of Europe have been extensively linked for water travel and transport. From the Black Sea to the Baltic through Ukraine, Belarus, Lithuania, and Poland. Or up the Danube to points north or back over down through France to the Mediterranean. There are many navigable links through European waters north of the Alps and Balkans, too many to describe here. They also link to the entire Mediterranean world through the Rhone and Danube. All of the Baltic through numerous paths. The English Channel, the North Sea, the Bay of Biscay. And every major river on the continent.

Other Notable Waterways

China has good coastal cruising and also long navigable inland waterways on the Yangtze (Chiang Jiang) River from Shanghai and the Xi River from Hong Kong.

The Mekong River passes through Southeast Asia all the way up to China on the Tibetan plateau.

India has a number of large rivers that have been deepened and are kept navigable. It also has a growing number of canals linking waterways together.

The Nile, Congo, and Niger Rivers in Africa all have extensive separate areas to explore.

The Amazon basin is a very extensive river system which can be traveled by small craft. Further south, the Paraguay-Parana inland waterway covers nearly as much territory.

References and Further Research

www.greatloop.org

captainjohn.org

www.usace.army.mil

en.wikipedia.org/wiki/Inland_waterways_of_the_United_Statescanalrivertrust.org.uk/enjoy-the-waterways/canal-and-river-network

www.ukwaterwaysguide.co.uk/canal-maps.phpwww.britannica.com/technology/canal-waterway/Major-inland-waterways-of-Europe

vagrantsoftheworld.com/russian-river-cruise-st-petersburg-to-moscowwww.eurocanals.com

www.unece.org/trans/main/sc3/where.htmlwww.wwinn.org

youtu.be/hlv2RNE9eLk

Long introductory video to the Great Loop.

youtu.be/rxHIk5ARHLI

1st part of a series on US inland waterways.

youtu.be/gDVdcTFV8Nk

An older video discussing the history of the UK canals.

youtu.be/Cd-7riM3xzI

Documentary film on water travel through Russia. Including much historical commentary.

youtu.be/Jwa_1cifDss

Brief video documenting a trip across the European landmass by water, north to south.

youtu.be/Gpt1zF9CrEU

Interesting and very detailed video discussing canal cruising across Europe.

33.

Protecting Electronics

This section attempts to categorize things to consider for long-term mobile electronics usage. Also some ideas regarding use of often much less expensive consumer electronics in the marine or wheeled environments. Also some information on general power use.

Moisture Protection

Getting electronics wet while they are in use will generally lead to damage because the different components will have specific ways that they conduct electricity and in certain amounts. Water and other liquids may act as conductors with will transmit electrical charges to parts of the electronics that are not rated for that voltage or current load and so will become damaged. So it is bad to get your electronics wet unless they are sealed against moisture, but specifically this is because of random electrical connections that can be formed.

The actual sealing will mostly be a matter of making the device case watertight. So many phones and other portable electronics are rated for various degrees of moisture protection because the case has been sealed somehow to stop the flow of moisture. There are different ways to do this but all of them will fail at a certain point. So a device might be sealed against splashes of water but the seal could fail if the device is fully immersed. Or if immersed at a sufficient depth of water such that water pressure increases enough to break the seal. See the references below for a breakdown of various ratings.

It is possible to add moisture protection to some devices. All you have to do is find a way to fully seal the device against the entry of moisture. So some form of solid or flexible sealer could be worked along every seam. If there is a screen then a clear sealant could be used along the edges. Every port and jack must also be sealed. This method is not a very good solution but is at least feasible to use with certain devices.

A better solution might be to construct a full enclosure for a device that can be more easily sealed against moisture. So a regular computer monitor could be used in the rain or the cockpit of a boat without fear of moisture damage if it was enclosed in a watertight box with a clear front. Care would still have to be taken when routing the power and input cords and it might be a good idea to keep desiccant pouches in the box against condensation buildup. A touchscreen would not be required for control because waterproof keyboards and mice are readily available. So you could have all the functionality and durability of something like a multi-function marine display, which might cost many thousands of dollars, at the much lower rates charged for non-marine electronics (a computer and monitor, along with the right software and components). As long as you carefully design and build your enclosures and are able to properly route the feeds and integrate the software. Alternatively this larger monitor could be set to echo some dedicated display with a much smaller screen—a seven inch multi-function display might cost less than half that of a twelve inch display with the same features. Monitors and even full computers are good candidates for full enclosure boxes, but the boxes must also account for such things as heat dispersion and kinetic resistance.

Corrosion Protection

Corrosion concerns are related to moisture concerns, as almost all corrosion that we are concerned with occurs through the actions of water, but there are different steps that may be taken specifically to address electronics corrosion issues. There are different oils and greases designed to keep away moisture but not conduct electricity. There are various conformal coatings that may be applied for a durable barrier against moisture and even air. There are also conductive greases for high power connections.

Dielectric grease is the standard automotive protection measure used against corrosion of electronic components. For spark plugs and battery terminals and sensor plugs, etc. It is non-conductive and so may interfere with conductivity for loose connections, but with tight metal on metal connections it is pushed aside and remains all around the connection to insulate against moisture and other contaminants. It is also recommended for use in computers and other delicate electronics but mainly just at connection and plug points.

There are many different types of spray-on oils that will displace moisture and remain in place on components until wiped off or otherwise displaced. Some will even work to actively neutralize existing corrosive reactions. This method is suited for broad application and will need to be renewed periodically as a regular maintenance chore. Any oil used in this manner should also have dielectric properties—be non-conductive. Certain products can be used to spray circuit boards to protect against salt air, networking equipment, radar components, and any other open metals that might be subject to corrosion.

For a more permanent coating there are various products known as conformal coatings which may be applied to electronics and circuitry. Many of these are only suited for industrial use and may be part of the process used to 'marinize' those expensive marine products, but other conformal coatings can be easily applied by the end-user. So if you design and build your own house computer or server unit, you can protect the connections with dielectric grease and you can seal the boards themselves with some type of permanent or semi-permanent conformal coating. This is an extra step but an important one for DIY electronics work.

For higher power connections or those that may be somewhat loose it will be better to apply a conductive grease. This is a good way to reduce resistance values at battery terminals or electric motor and controller linkages, for instance. The lower electrical resistance will reduce heat buildup at the connection point and can also save you quite a bit of power over time for high current connections. The grease will also act to keep moisture away and so block corrosion. There are some specialty greases like ceramic heat-sink paste which will conduct heat but not electricity but in these cases the compound you use should conduct both. And the greased connections should still be sealed away somehow from casual touch.

Kinetic Shock, Vibration

Every piece of electronic equipment will have lots and lots of thin metal connections which may be damaged, at once or over time, by impacts or vibrations. Those thin metal connections will themselves still be more resistant to shock damage than the solid circuit boards. Possible methods for reducing kinetic damage include hardening the electronics components themselves, which will not be possible for the end user, and isolating or padding the electronics against the sources of kinetic energy, which will be a matter of locating and building cases and enclosures. So try to site your electronics where they will not be impacted or shaken around any more than necessary. And also tailor your mounts and enclosures so as to protect electronics from impact and to not transmit motion or vibrational forces.

Heat

Heat and vibration are the great long-term enemies of electronics. These will both act to shorten useful life. Great heat, as with extreme vibration or shock, will also act to immediately destroy electronic devices. So if you want your electronics to last longer then you must try to keep them as cool as possible. Air conditioning is a luxury when living mobile and not always possible even for you, let alone your electronics, but there are various measures that can be taken to keep devices reasonably cool.

Often this will involve design compromises. Wooden boxes and enclosures are easy to build, will protect against impact damage, and can be sealed against moisture. But wood is a thermal insulator and will trap heat inside. Aluminum is more expensive and not as easy to work with but is a good heat conductor and will help to keep things inside the box cooler. Iron and steel and other metals will also conduct heat. Metal boxes will conduct electricity as well, which means that bare electronics must be insulated from the case by some material that may not conduct heat...and so the compromises continue.

But cases themselves can only offer passive cooling. Active cooling arrangements will involve managing the flow of air or some liquid to move heat away from components. Air cooling is the most standard practice as small fans are cheap and can be run with minimal power draw. But air is a poor conductor of heat and open air pathways are also open moisture pathways.

Liquid cooling is more complicated to setup and can possibly lead to damage if the liquid escapes, but is a better solution both in terms of heating and in order to seal components away from corrosive environments or moisture inrush. This is also called water cooling, but the liquid need not be water. Other liquids such as certain oils or chemical compounds like antifreeze will have better thermal conductive properties and may be non-conductive of electricity so will be less of a danger if they spill. The PC community has a great deal of experience with liquid cooling of electronics and is a good place to find information.

Voltage Stability

If you are running your electronics off of your own tailored electrical system then you will need to insure that the voltage they receive never goes outside of the designed voltage range of the product. So a device may be rated for 12V DC and so nominally suitable for a house DC system, but unless the design includes a range of acceptance then the device could be damaged by 14V DC or 10V DC...which the voltage of your system may easily fluctuate to with load or charge variations in the circuit.

Devices which are not rated for fluctuating voltages must have additional protections in place to insulate them from system variation. Which will often mean extra devices, adding to system complexity and increasing the real cost of the electronics that require this. For AC electronics this will usually be resolved just by having a quality inverter unit but DC electronics may need extra protection.

Conversion Losses

Most electronics that receive AC power do in fact run on DC, which means that if you are running your system off batteries and providing AC power through an inverter then you will be going through two conversions. No electrical conversion is completely efficient, so there will be power losses every time. The standard figure for a good inverter is 10% loss, so you will be losing at least 20% of power used for standard household electronics. And possibly twice as much.

This problem should be kept in mind and minimized whenever possible in terms of both system design and usage, but there are not really any easy solutions for switching most electronics over to DC power input. Specific DC power supplies are not in high demand and may be many times more expensive than standard AC input power supplies. It can also be easier when a specific DC voltage is required to invert from AC rather than to convert between two DC voltages.

Household Electronics

These will not be designed for any sort of rugged environment but may be protected in various ways against any of the dangers to electronic components, as detailed above. So you can build a PC, carefully and with a specific operating environment in mind, and expect to be able to use it for a long time on your boat or in your wheeled living solution. Other less expensive or less critical devices can be used as is regardless of the environment. They might not last as long but if they can be cheaply replaced then this may be the better option. People use standard laptops and tablets all the time on boats or on the road; even in heavy salt air they might be expected to last as long as people normally use such things before upgrading to the next one.

Automotive Electronics

The automobile industry is much larger than the marine industry and is a continual source of new products in electronics. Which will have lower prices than marine products because of production scale and more competition, though they will also not be specifically suited to the marine environment. They will all be designed to run on DC power and usually now from USB ports. Devices like GPS units, night-vision dash-cams, security cameras and microphones, led lighting, coffee makers, and many different audio system options. Even if you are living the mobile marine life then this is a great place to look for electronics. They will need no more extra protection than household devices and may need less.

Marine Electronics

Some devices will only be made for marine use. Fish finders (sonar), chart plotters, mobile radar, and other items can only be found on the marine market. There are many excellent products that are already fully protected against moisture, corrosion, heat, and impact. Generally sold at a premium to match those impressive features. That is, transducers will be required, as will external radar hardware or gps data, but the signals that these items send out are interpreted and displayed by software programming. There is a video linked below demonstrating a DIY chartplotter device. It is equally possible to develop and build sonar and radar devices yourself that serve the same functions as commercial products.

Solar Panels

Solar panels that are sold for more rugged environments, such as wheeled living and marine applications, tend to be priced higher than their residential or commercial equivalents. In terms of value offered, the prices are higher because efficient panels or specific shapes are selected and because they might have a stouter frame, be more waterproofed, or have pre-sealed electronic components.

It seems to me that selection alone can be accomplished by the end user with a bit of research and that all of the measures used to make these panels more rugged can be matched or bettered with a DIY installation. There are no moving parts, so fully sealing delicate components away will not be a difficult problem to resolve with careful product selection. Framing and mounting will be particular to each individual installation regardless. If the stock frames that your panels arrive with are insufficient then you may build better ones. Alternatively you may tailor your mounting arrangement to reduce vibration damage or heat buildup or the possibility of kinetic impact. These are generally things that you will want to do anyway and the panels arriving with somewhat better frames may not greatly assist the process.

References and Further Research

www.howtogeek.com/209024/htg-explains-how-water-resistance-ratings-work-for-gadgets

geargadgetsandgizmos.com/what-really-is-water-resistant-waterproof-and-ipx-ratings

www.w8ji.com/dielectric_grease_vs_conductive_grease.htm

forums.iboats.com/forum/boat-repair-and-restoration/electrical-electronics-audio-and-trolling-motors/531617-dielectric-grease-on-connections

www.thehulltruth.com/1309211-post1.html

www.dell.com/community/Desktops-General-Read-Only/Corrosion-in-computers/td-p/3679814 electrolube.com/knowledge_base/protecting-electronics-from-corrosive-operating-environments-to-increase-end-product-lifetime-and-reliability

www.powerandmotoryacht.com/electronics/personal-computers-sea

www.boatdesign.net/threads/discussion-multipurpose-onboard-computers-human-inputs-human-outputs.20169/#post-169245

www.boatdesign.net/threads/discussion-multi-purpose-onboard-computers.19458

www.boatdesign.net/threads/archive-onboard-computers.57866/#post-803490

www.custommarineproducts.com/marine-solar-panels.html

youtu.be/mtsW-aNKddQ

Presentation video on conformal coatings.

youtu.be/HOu5hRqSDtU

Demonstration video for waterproofing drone electronics.

youtu.be/ucXwrU5vqVg

An extended presentation regarding heat and cooling issues with electronics.

youtu.be/G6Ys4qQuYPw

Cold plate cooling method. Safe and effective. The cold plate could replace one panel of an enclosure box.

youtu.be/SZqU6Xv31ZU

Chartplotter build using household electronics. Could be made better with some waterproofing of the circuits and dielectric compound in the connections.

youtu.be/ROr1j1cPkRE

Comparison video for use of consumer electronics on a boat.

34.

Mobile Citizenship

For those wishing to live mobile, there are definite limitations in legal and social matters because the traditional pattern of citizenship is one organized around static locales and specific residence locations. As detailed above in the Address section, there are some ways to work around this but they are less than ideal solutions for most people. The only lasting solution for this problem is to formally detach rights and duties of citizenship from local residency or designated location and enable truly mobile freedom in matters legal, financial, and social—to create a new organizational pattern for citizenship itself.

Citizenship

By citizenship I mean not just the status of national citizenship as an identified member of a given country, but also the regional and local affiliations that are tied to it. The USA, for example, will recognize its citizens as those people born within its territorial boundaries or otherwise naturalized, but will also designate and require that each citizen is a resident of one of the states or territories within the country. The states and territories, in turn, will identify their residents in terms of a specific address, a physical location of residence, which in its turn will be under the jurisdiction of local governance in the form of a county or municipality. Part of this has to do with the theoretical divided sovereignty in the US between the federal and state governments, but many other countries in the world organize themselves in the same manner. With regional and local governments having specific jurisdiction over their residents and every national citizen having a specific designated home location.

This traditionally has been how governments keep track of people and also how they manage funding for the various federal, state (or regional), and local services. Anyone who has an identifiable home address may automatically be categorized in terms of who they pay taxes to and how much and in what form. Also what services they are entitled to partake in. And to be fair this is how most people live at any one time—static lives organized around a specific home location. What I am advocating is not necessarily a complete overhaul of citizenship itself for every person (though that may be overdue as well), but instead something like adding a special category that recognizes the capacity for people living mobile to be good citizens.

Citizenship is often discussed in terms of rights—the rights of citizens that are awarded or recognized by the national government. Such as the American bill of rights, etc. However, the very concept of every citizen having rights itself entails that every citizen has duties. If I have a right to free speech, and you have a right to free speech, then reason dictates that we each also have a duty to respect the free speech right of the other. Likewise for every other person. If we all have the right to free speech then we all also have the duty to respect the right of free speech that others hold. Else that right will not be recognized and will be precluded. We often discuss these things in terms of the laws that are passed that may or may not abridge one of the rights of citizens and hold the government responsible for infringing on the rights of citizens, but such would actually be an action by the collection of citizens infringing on those rights. That is, representational government actions, public actions, are in legal fact the actions of the whole body of citizens. Governmental laws which infringe on a given right are in fact a failure by the citizenship to uphold the duty to respect that right.

So good citizenship is that which occurs when a citizen fulfills the duties of citizenship. Those duties themselves arise directly from the rights of citizenship. By extension of this, we may consider government taxes and services in the same manner. Such things are often very abstract and imperfect, but in simplified terms we pay taxes as a duty and partake in government services as our corresponding right. If our government is truly representational then we are in fact imposing these taxes on ourselves in order to endow ourselves with services. Ideally.

The different tiers of government then collect taxes and provide services in accordance with the span of their individual mandate. Which is organized territorially but with distinctions between the national and regional levels. So the national government collects income and other taxes from all citizens regardless of location and then provides global range services to those citizens in turn. State and local governments are generally restricted instead to operating within their own territorial borders, in terms of both taxation and services offered. And to a certain extent they are required to render services even to residents of other states and localities. A local fire department, for instance, will still respond to accidents on major highways even though none of the people involved may be one of the local residents that support that fire department with tax payments. There are many other possible examples of unsupported or shared service use. The operating assumption that makes this shared services system work is that everyone who partakes of state or local services in one area will at least have some home area in which they are contributing taxes. So everyone involved in a highway accident to which local services responded would still be paying taxes of some sort to support the local fire department near their place of residence. A rough balance is thus maintained.

Problem

So the problem of mobile citizenship is two-fold. It is a problem for those living mobile that they are limited by requirements which mandate that they must have a home location, but it is also a problem for regional and local areas that those living mobile may not be contributing tax support in proportion to the services that they partake in. Detaching citizenship from residency upsets the balance that permits services to be rendered to non-locals who do not pay local taxes.

Every person who visits a local area is utilizing local services. Wheeled living depends on the roads, built and maintained by tax money, even if those living on wheels do not actively engage with local or regional government. Local areas are also protected by the deterrent impact of law enforcement services regardless of whether police are actually engaged with. This argument is less clear for marine living but still real enough. Regions and locales work to preserve and maintain waterways and also any time that someone living marine touches the shore they are at least indirectly benefiting from local services. Living marine permits long but not indefinite periods away from shore.

But having a home location also imposes expenses and requirements well in excess of taxes and collective service support. Purchase or lease and maintenance of a physical residence is very costly—for many people this requires more than half of all income earned. Escaping these possibly unnecessary expenses is one of the primary reasons that people choose to live mobile in the first place.

Having to maintain such a residence also requires either occasional trips back home or the hiring of others to manage the residence, and possibly both. All of this would seem to be unnecessary for someone that wishes to live mobile instead and imposes a burden that is not warranted by the duties of citizenship alone.

Resolution

What I would like to see enacted to resolve this problem is a special category for mobile citizens. That is, an opt-in program that permits people to live without a permanent legal residence (domicile) but requires them to maintain a mail service and to contribute to a common tax support fund.

Somewhere to send official mail will be important to have. To some extent this could be replaced in time with electronic services but as yet some things must still be done with hard copy. Requiring that this be done through the Postal Service would help insure compliance with identity and verification checks and could also support a paid expansion of services for that financially troubled entity. Though nothing would stop those living mobile from also contracting a private mailbox service for their normal post. An official mail account could be expanded upon and possibly eventually replaced with an official online account for electronic post, also routed through the Postal Service.

A common fund to help support regional and local services seems like the most practical way for those living mobile to make real contributions to the public service providers that they are supported by. Though this method will still have its challenges. This could be a flat rate charge upon entering the special status bracket of mobile citizen and some small percentage of income earned thereafter. Or otherwise whichever tax method can be found to be most fair to all parties involved. Possibly with subsidies for needy cases.

In these ways all requirements in terms of the duties of citizenship can be met by mobile citizens. We can live mobile and still be good citizens. As yet with citizenship tied to domicile those living mobile have no set means to rationally contribute to local service providers. In consequence they often encounter rejection (and even forced settlement) by others who see them as freeloaders or degenerates. This characterization can become self-fulfilling over time, but that need not be the case. Those who cannot afford or choose not to engage in static housing can also be contributing members of society.

Given the organizational patterns of the United States, this might best be accomplished at the level of the individual states. And as such it need not involve a legal change for all or even most of the states themselves. A federal law altering the domicile requirements and mandating certain conditions and responsibilities for those states that wish to include this new category of citizenship would be sufficient. Those states that wish to change their own laws and actively welcome mobile citizens could then do so. Other states would be free to maintain more strict residency requirements. Those that opt in would be able to share in the common tax fund in accordance with the number of mobile citizens they acquire and those that opt out would be barred from use of that fund. With federal cooperation and in partnership with the Postal Service the mobile citizens would not even have to set foot in that state, as all verification and other requirements could be accomplished at common government facilities.

Alternatively, though this would require (much) more extensive changes in federal law, citizenship for mobile citizens could be detached from state of legal residence entirely and designated as federal citizenship without domicile. In this case there might need to be some tracking mechanism or marker to show that mobile citizens were partaking in local services at a given time in order to share out the common tax fund in a fair manner, but probably it would make more sense to just share out the fund equally between states and locales. Which would be much more respectful of privacy rights. Inevitably those places that are most frequented by mobile citizens will have their services utilized out of proportion to funds received, but tax and funding structures can be changed to compensate for this. Florida is a common vacation spot and is frequently inundated by non-residents, but funds many services primarily through sales and use taxes instead of through income taxes on state residents.

Other Concerns

There are other reasons for wanting to pin people down to permanent home locations, but I think most of these have to do with enforcement of legal and tax codes and possibly national defense matters. They do not derive from the duties of citizenship. As such there is no firm basis for imposing static living solutions on law abiding citizens. As time passes and the world becomes more interconnected electronically these concerns are also being met by various means that do not require a linked physical address. So finances and associated taxes are being tracked through the interlinked financial networks, for instance. It does not seem to be necessary now and will become less so over time to restrict people to permanent addresses for such reasons.

35.

The Last Wilderness

I wonder what happened to the enthusiasm for oceanic settlement? It strikes me as odd that there is so much excitement and drive toward the prospect of space travel and the settlement of other planets and orbital bodies, yet little or no significant effort toward settling and developing those areas of our own world that are covered by oceans. Particularly odd given the parallel congruence in required technologies, engineering capacities, and financial and social structures needed to establish viable long term settlements in both of those hostile environment types. More so as successful development of oceanic settlement patterns may serve as test bed and proof of concept for beyond earth settlement. But very few people now consider oceanic settlement to be desirable and there are no significant efforts being made toward its realization.

This was not always the case. Many people have dreamed of underwater exploration and the construction of underwater cities right alongside those dreaming of space exploration and the settlement of other planets. Prior to the end of the Cold War there was an ongoing popular conception that the technologies to make undersea living possible were just around the corner; this was often associated with the technologies of space travel in the popular imagination.

There are several parallels between the two environments in terms of what it will take for people to live in them on a permanent or semi-permanent basis. They are both hostile to human existence without artificial life support aids. They both involve great pressure variations from human norms—and though outer space environments have zero pressure and deep ocean environments have very high pressure, it is also the case that the settling of other planets may require managing high pressure environments. In all these cases we will have to develop enclosed habitat zones that are kept permanently sealed away from a hostile environment. This means total enclosure or at least control over the entire life cycle of an ecological structure and an ongoing human society, not just putting people in a box.

Which will require extensive planning but also ongoing experimentation and adaptation. It will be very expensive to get oceanic settlement going, and I think economic concerns are one of the primary reasons that it has fizzled out, but if space exploration is the goal then there may be significant long term savings in developing hostile environment technologies and paradigms here on this planet. There is a certain tyranny of distance, in that longer communication and transportation distances impose commensurately large cost increases. It will be significantly less expensive to develop habitat modules and organizational patterns and other necessities here on earth, under the sea, than it will be to do so on Luna or Mars or Titan.

Regardless of initial investment costs all human settlement must manage to become economically solvent in the long term. Money and economics are how we organize (most) human efforts and motivations, so lasting human social groups must have a positive economic balance to remain viable. Space travel promises enormous gains in resources and potential for scientific knowledge, though reaching those gains will require enormous investments. Oceanic settlement also has great potential for economic development. In the relatively short term ocean mining can alleviate the resource shortage that humans are experiencing after thousands of years of mining the continental landmasses. The profits from mining can then be reinvested into developing sustainable agricultural products, manufacturing techniques that take advantage of the specific resource environments of the oceans, and other technological and information products. Coastal ocean farming is already taking off in some places and this type of agriculture would have much greater prospects if not located directly next to the dense human settlements common to coastal regions (with corresponding pollution concerns).

Developing the bounties of the oceans will require significant changes in human waste practices. Oceans are used as convenient dumping grounds for much of the undesirable detritus of human civilization. Biological wastes, garbage, toxic chemicals, and more are all being dumped into the oceans on a daily and ongoing basis. Fertilizer wastes from field runoff into major river systems are leading to unnatural growth patterns and the spawning of large dead zones in coastal regions throughout the world. In some places this is far worse than others but every country in the world that borders the sea engages in some sort of ongoing pattern of ocean pollution.

This will need to change if humans are to be able to settle the oceans. Possibly this is a greater hurdle than the economic barrier—it will involve changing longstanding practice and will require that people all over the world alter their behavior at significant cost to themselves and for no immediate gain. Which will take some time to accomplish if it is possible at all. In the meantime I suppose oceanic settlement could be restricted to those areas of the ocean that are least effected by human pollution. There are still some clean waters, though for obvious reasons these tend to be located far from higher population densities and transport and communication costs will thus be increased. Perhaps if people do begin to settle the oceans this will increase pressure on the land-dwellers and help to reduce patterns of pollution.

Weather might be something of a problem but there are ways that it can be dealt with. Unlike the land water is always moving, so any structure which relies on water buoyancy will have to account for extreme weather conditions. The two simplest possibilities will be to move where the weather isn't or to be affixed directly to the seafloor. Free-floating settlements would be able to drift around large areas of the globe and so avoid predictable and ongoing problem zones at certain times. So they might put themselves into the southern hemisphere during hurricane season in the northern hemisphere, and vice versa. Seafloor structures will need to deal with the very high pressure environment, but they will be much less affected by water movement. Many areas of the seabed are unstable tectonic-ally but this can be taken into account before building. Tethered structures, those neither free-floating or directly attached to the seabed, will be in the most ongoing danger of damage from weather (though much less so from tectonic motion). Their primary defense will be to be built strong enough to withstand expected conditions.

Oceans settlements could be organized politically as extensions of existing nation-states, but it strikes me that doing so would waste an ideal opportunity to engage in the development of some sort of international citizenship. To surpass the ongoing barriers that serve to divide humans of one nation from those of another. To build just the type of cooperative humanistic polity that will be required for humanity to withstand the rigors and overarching dangers of space exploration and development. Oceanic settlements can surpass the land-based territorial dispute history of existing nation states. Not that I expect disputes over territory and other resources to go away, but at least there exists the opportunity for a fresh start that is not dictated by the disputes of the past.

Social structures will also need to change in order to become adapted to the very different patterns of action necessary for hostile environment living. As just one example, there will be a lot more communal property than there will be personal property. Note that this need not require a socialist or property-less organizational pattern. Though such might be feasible, it could be just as practical and perhaps more so to have something like a corporate model, where everything is organized on a shares basis. So instead of nothing being owned by individuals every individual will have a certain share, or stake, in all of the shared property of the settlement.

This section is mostly just speculation and there are very real barriers that must be overcome before permanent ocean settlement can be made viable, but I wanted to end this book with a dream, a vision. Imagine a floating community cycling through a yearly pattern of motion around the world ocean. Self-contained and self-sufficient. Its people unattached to enduring property or location, free to devote their lives to pursuits that rely more on imagination than on the material. Transcending national boundaries and divisions. Such a pattern will also be required for space settlement, but an ocean settlement in this model can be achieved now, with present technology. There will be many challenges, but without challenges to overcome we stagnate. And in pushing the boundaries of our comfort here on earth we also push back the boundaries of the human condition. So dream a dream with me of living mobile, on wheels, on the water or beneath it, or beyond the bounds of this world.

References and Resources

Books

Accetta-Scott, Ann. *The Farm Girl's Guide to Preserving the Harvest: How to Can, Freeze, Dehydrate, and Ferment your Garden's Goodness.* Lyons Press, 2019.

Alton, Joseph, MD, and Amy Alton, ARNP. *The Survival Medicine Handbook: The essential guide for when medical help is Not on the way.* 3rd Edition. Doom and Bloom, 2016

Appelhof, Mary and Joanne Olszewski. *Worms Eat My Garbage, 35th Anniversary Edition: How to Set Up and Maintain a Worm Composting System.* Storey Publishing 2017.

Auerbach, Paul S., MD. *Medicine for the Outdoors: The Essential Guide to First Aid and Medical Emergencies.* 6th Edition. Saunders, 2015.

Baggini, Julian and Peter S. Fosl. *The Philospher's Toolkit: A Compendium of Philosophical Concepts and Methods.* Chichester, West Sussex, UK: Wiley-Blackwell, 2010.

Baird, Gord and Ann Baird. *Essential Composting Toilets: A Guide to Options, design, Installation, and Use (Sustainable Building Essential Series).* New Society Publishers, 2018.

Bannerot, Scott and Wendy Bannerot. *The Cruiser's Handbook of Fishing.* Camden, ME: International Marine, 2003.

Barre, Harold. *How to Upgrade, Operate, and Troubleshoot 12V Electrical Systems.* Incline Village, NV: Summer Breeze Publishing, 2002.

Barret, Robin. *Work From Home While You Roam: The Ultimate Guide to Jobs That Can Be Done From Anywhere.* Amazon.com Services LLC, 2020.

Bartmann, Dan and Dan Fink. *Homebrew Wind Power: A Hands-On Guide to Harnessing the Wind.* Buckville Publications LLC, 2013.

Berman, Peter. *Outfitting the Offshore Cruising Sailboat.* Paradise Cay Publications, 2012.

Brewer, Ted. *Understanding Boat Design, 4th edition.* Camden, ME: International Marine, 1994.

Brown, Russell. *Epoxy Basics: Working with Epoxy Cleanly and Efficiently.* 2009.

Bryant, Jefferson. *How to Design and Install In-Car Entertainment Systems.* CarTech, Inc., 2009.

Brylske, Alex. *The Complete Diver: The History, Science and Practice of Scuba Diving.* Dive Training LLC, 2012.

Calder, Nigel. *Boatowner's Mechanical and Electrical Manual.* London: Bloomsbury, 2016.

Calder, Nigel. *Marine Diesel Engines: Maintenance, Troubleshooting, and Repair.* 3rd Edition. International Marine/Ragged Mountain Press, 2006.

Casey, Don. *Don Casey's Complete Illustrated Sailboat Maintenance Manual.* International Marine/Ragged Mountain Press, 2005.

Casey, Don. *This Old Boat, 2nd ed: Completely Revised and Expanded.* Camden, MN: International Marine, 2009.

Cohen, Michael Martin. *Healthy Boating and Sailing: Optimize Your Health and Performance on the Water.* Nautical Health Publishing, 2020.

Cunning, Terry. *Winterize Your RV: Inside and Out.* Amazon Services LLC, 2018.

Dabney, Silvia Williams. *The Boater's Cookbook: 450 Quick & Easy Galley-Tested Recipes.* Skyhorse, 2018.

Dempsey, Paul. *Home Generator Selection, Installation and Repair.* McGraw-Hill Education, 2013

Devlin, Samuel. *Devlin's Boatbuilding: How to Build Any Boat the Stitch and Glue Way.* Camden, ME: International Marine, 1996.

Doane, Charles. *The Modern Cruising Sailboat: A Complete Guide to its Design, Construction, and Outfitting.* International Marine/Ragged Mountain Press, 2009.

Drake, David. *Lt. Leary Commanding*, Baen, 2001.

Drake, David. *The Legions of Fire: The Book of the Elements, Volume One.* Tor Books, 2010.

Dunphy, Chris. *The Mobile Internet Handbook—For US Based RVers, Cruisers, and Nomads, 5th edition.* CreatSpace Independant Publishing Platform, 2018.

Elwell, Don. *The Floating Empire composting toilet book: Building your own DIY Composting Toilet with urine diverter from simple materials.* Wild Shore Press, 2019.

Emerson, Clinton. *Escape the Wolf: A Security Handbook for Traveling Professionals.* Dog Ear Publishing, 2009.

Fodor's. *The Complete Guide to the National Parks of the West.* 6th edition. Fodor's Travel, 2019.

Gerr, Dave. *The Nature of Boats.* Camden, Maine: International Marine, 1992.

Gerr, Dave. *The Elements of Boat Strength for Builders, Designers and Owners.* Camden, ME: International Marine, 2000.

Gerr, David. *Propeller Handbook: The Complete Reference for Choosing, Installing, and Understanding Boat Propellers.* International Marine/Ragged Mountain Press, 2001.

Gibilisco, Stan and Monk, Simon. *Teach Yourself Electricity and Electronics.* 6th Edition. McGraw-Hill, 2016.

Hall, Peggie. *The New Get Rid of Boat Odors, 2nd Edition: A Boat Owner's Guide to Marine Sanitation Systems and Other Sources of Aggravation and Odor.* Seaworthy Publications, 2016.

Hankinson, Ken. *Fiberglass Boatbuilding for Amateurs.* Bellflower, California: Glen-L Marine Designs, 1982.

Harless, Jesse; *Smash Your Comfort Zone with Cold Showers: How to Boost Your Energy, Defeat Your Anxiety, and Overcome Unwanted Habits.* Entrepreneurs in Recovery, 2018.

Hinz, Earl R. *The Complete Book of Anchoring and Mooring.* 2nd edition. Schiffer, 2009

Hudson, Mike. *How to Live in a Van and Travel: Live everywhere, be free and have adventures in a campervan or motorhome—your home on wheels.* Bluedog Books, 2017.

Katz, Sandor Ellix. *The Art of Fermentation: An In-Depth Exploration of Essential Concepts and Processes from Around the World.* Chelsea Green Publishing, 2012.

Kingry, Judi and Lauren Devine. *Ball Complete Book of Home Preserving.* Robert Rose, 2006.

Lang, Elliot. *Eating Insects. Eating Insects as Food. Edible insects and bugs, insect breeding, most popular insects to eat, cooking ideas, restaurants and where to buy insects all covered.* IMB Publishing, 2013.

Leitman, Seth and Bob Brant. *Build Your Own Electric Vehicle.* Third edition. McGraw-Hill Education TAB, 2013.

Ludwig, Art. *Water Storage: Tanks, Cisterns, Aquifers, and Ponds.* Oasis Design, 2009.

MacKenzie, Jennifer, Jay Nutt, and Don Mercer. *The Dehydrator Bible: Includes over 400 Recipes.* Robert Rose, 2009.

Marino, Emiliano. *The Sailmaker's Apprentice.* Camden, ME: International Marine, 2001.

Mathys, Charles. *My Electric Boats.* 2nd Edition. Netcam Publishing, 2010.

Myers, William. *Road Cash: How to make money while living on the road.* CreateSpace Independant Publishing Platform, 2017.

Modesitt, L. E., Jr. *Empire and Ecolitan.* Tor, 2001.

Nicholas, Mark. *The Essentials of Living Aboard a Boat: The Definitive Guide for Liveaboards.* 4th edition. Paradise Cay Publications, 2019.

O'Connor, Joseph. *Off-Grid Solar: A handbook for Photovoltaics with Lead-Acid or Lithium-Ion batteries.* Old Sequoia Publishing, 2019.

Olkowski, William, Sheila Daar, and Helga Olkowski. *Common-Sense Pest Control.* Taunton Press, 1991.

Rivers, Collyn. *Caravan and Motorhome Electronics: the complete guide.* RVBooks.com.au, 2019.

Rivers, Collyn. *The Caravan and Motorhome Book: the complete guide.* RVBooks, 2019.

Roberts, Lynn. *RV & Camping Cookbook — Healthy Living on a Budget: The Ultimate Guide for Recipes, Tips, and Tricks, for the Road Nomad Lifestyle - Enjoy Poultry, Seafood, Vegetarian & Vegan Full Meal Recipes.* Thames & Tower House, 2019.

Rossel, Greg. *The Boatbuilder's Apprentice.* Camden, ME: International Marine, 2007.

Rozenblatt, Lazar. *Home Generator: Selecting, Sizing and Connecting: The Complete Guide.* Createspace Independant Publishing Platform, 2015.

Sandenburgh, Roberta. *Small Space Living: Expert Tips and Techniques on Using Closets, Corners, and Every Other Space in Your Home.* Skyhorse, 2018.

Silva, Carlos. *Build Your own Hookah and Shallow Water Diving Helmet.* Amazon.com Services LLC, 2014.

Smith, Edward. *The Vegetable Gardener's Container Bible: How to Grow a Bounty of Food in Pots, Tubs, and Other Containers.* Storey Publishing, LLC, 2011.

Solomon, Robert C. and Kathleen M. Higgins. *A Short History of Philosophy.* Oxford University Press, 1996.

Steward, Robert M. and Carl Cramer. *Boatbuilding Manual, 5th edition.* Camden, ME: International Marine, 2011.

Taylor, Kathleen and Catherine Marienau. *Facilitating Learning with the Adult Brain in Mind: A Conceptual and Practical Guide.* Jossey-Bass, 2016.

Toss, Brian. *The Complete Rigger's Apprentice: Tools and Techniques for Modern and Traditional Rigging, 2nd edition.* Camden, ME: International Marine, 2016.

Ward, Jess. *The Intrepid Woman's Guide to Van Dwelling: Practical Information to Customize a Chic Home on Wheels & Successfully Transition to an Awesome Mobile Lifestyle.* Amazon.com Serrvices LLC, 2015.

Wells, Robert. *How to Live in a Car, Van or RV—And Get out of Debt, Travel and Find True Freedom.* Amazon.com Services LLC, 2012.

Wilson-Howarth, Jane. *Essential Guide to Travel Health: Don't Let Bugs, Bites and Bowels Spoil Your Trip.* 5th Edition. Cadogan Guides, 2009.

Wing, Charlie. *Boatowner's Illustrated Electrical Handbook.* Camden, MN: International Marine / MCGraw-Hill, 2006.

Wright, Don and Joyce Wright. *The Wright Guide to Free and Low-Cost Campgrounds: Includes Campgrounds $20 and Under in the United States.* 16th edition. The Wright Guide, 2018.

Video Links

Introduction

Chasing Bubbles - The Documentary.
https://youtu.be/ibP5IQxId34
Living 25 Years on the Water - Short Documentary on Boat Life.
https://youtu.be/1QRxbPSqOME
Living OFF GRID on a BUDGET Sailboat S04E24.
https://youtu.be/hRHskbdRFFs
Our RV Setup - A Tour of our Mobile Home RV after 3 Years Full-time.
https://youtu.be/tuaFGqN_UFE
STEALTH VAN TOUR // Solo Woman lives Full Time Van Life in the Urban City of Vancouver.
https://youtu.be/Cy4erT5I6dQ

The OFFICIAL Full RV Nomads Movie.
https://youtu.be/UzyWyH9r-To

VAN TOUR Veteran's AMAZING Budget Self Converted Ram ProMaster.
https://youtu.be/xdhXBYUa1UI

We Bought A Narrowboat! - Our Complete Narrowboat Tour.
https://youtu.be/AlqYKrQXh1o

WE LIVE ON A SAILBOAT WELCOME TO OUR HOME - A TRIMARAN.
https://youtu.be/mQPBZZ0Xelk

Without Bound - Perspectives on Mobile Living.
https://youtu.be/Lg37Cbx-kak

Humble Road Van Build Series 17 - Radiant Floor Heat In My Van - Done!
https://youtu.be/dxlXywAu1Cg

The Reality of #VanLife - Full Documentary Movie - 2018
https://youtu.be/A6McizBPKaE

2. Propulsion

How to Build an Electric Sailboat
https://youtu.be/bMXR1UYSMa4

Diesel to Electric Sailboat Re-Power, Part One: Installation
https://youtu.be/1Y1_TSdR2j4

Completely Solar Powered Electric Van Conversion
https://youtu.be/pcj2lQwH7N4

The reality of yachting. Yacht maintenance time lapse. Featuring Diesel Girl.
https://youtu.be/DQr4RS50v4Y

Understanding marine diesel engines: Yanmar coolant exchange
https://youtu.be/aZv4IXFPMqg

Should You Buy a Gas or Diesel Campervan? The Gas vs. Diesel Debate
https://youtu.be/9hzP133RIoE

Propane Mercury 9.9 Outboard
https://youtu.be/dRTSftUqQ9U

How to install LPG on your car
https://youtu.be/qB7h7ftdsQA

World's First Hydrogen Boat - Energy Observer
https://youtu.be/pgdXbe1in64

3. Structure

Cedar Creek RV Construction Process Built for the Years Ahead
https://youtu.be/dLdmd-Pqs84

55+ Build RV out of a U Haul with $5200 Used U Haul with an Office, Solar, all the comforts of home!
https://youtu.be/1G62JHALM5Q

Structural bridges in a Promaster van build
https://youtu.be/ezDWPijo0xU

Teardrop trailer build under $1,000!
https://youtu.be/iDVao9ZgGd8

World Amazing Motor Boat Build Process - Fastest Boats Build Factory Modern Technology
https://youtu.be/ImYd5UYukv0

How to build a boat Ep #1 - Catamaran you can live on
https://youtu.be/MrQoIqZDoOI

BoatworksToday
https://www.youtube.com/user/boatworkstoday

Steel Sailboat Build Part 1
https://youtu.be/7HlhSZWqkKk

How To Build a 27 Foot Aluminum Cabin Cruiser From a Kit
https://youtu.be/Y-MWardh9K8

4. Electricity

Boat Show 2019: How To - Design A Marine Electrical System
https://youtu.be/tdur_Ln-9cE

Camper Van Electrical System - Comprehensive Look!
https://youtu.be/NImNGe_3TYk

Off Grid Camper Electrical System Explained - Toyota Sunrader 4x4 Build Part 11
https://youtu.be/_IgSWVoa2uE

Understanding RV Electrical Systems Part I
https://youtu.be/eA7O7y5e2r4

Electricity Explained: Volts, Amps, Watts, Fuse Sizing, Wire Gauge, AC/DC, Solar Power and more!
https://youtu.be/cX4s-bxn4fs

Basic Solar Parts Needed for a DIY Camper Van or RV Solar Install
https://youtu.be/xuZg4NasCVw

Camper Solar Setup Tutorial - How to Solar Power your RV, Camper Van, & Truck Camper
https://youtu.be/Ht1kl37pJ2E

Azura Marine Aquanima 40 "Solar Eclipse" Solar Catamaran Powered by the Sun: Solar Boat
https://youtu.be/QcxFB1sVEJI

Marine Power Solar System
https://youtu.be/L4XeHDYpR_w

Wind Turbine on a Trailer Part II: The Setup
https://youtu.be/qhstBD0w2hg

Eclectic Energy D400 Wind Generator Wiring & Performance Review (Part 3)
https://youtu.be/0uArpuWHVTg

Mast-R Wind Power Turbine Installation
https://youtu.be/MsxDvm71AVg

8 Best Portable Generators (Buying Guide Updated 2020)
https://youtu.be/UaBxY-Pr_vI

Cummins Onan Marine Generator Highlights
https://youtu.be/9VVNFSH7Gjk

Electric Motor, Ocean Crossing with Regeneration | Sailing Wisdom
https://youtu.be/QWgbM9DoA7A

A Quick Look at a DIY Hydro Generator
https://youtu.be/Lj-_WMdwJSg

5. Networking

Homemade portable 1800mhz 4g LTE signal booster || even worked in no network village || AMAZING
https://youtu.be/bHWrRG_kdn8

Tips - Installing an NMEA 2000 Backbone on a Boat
https://youtu.be/jYdfH0vhBuc

How to get internet on a boat
https://youtu.be/g25yQwdtu-w

How to get SUPER FAST Internet on a sailboat - Digital Nomad Edition - Sailing Vessel Delos Ep. 260
https://youtu.be/BmNTJrdLHMc

Internet For Full Time VanLife | WeBoost Speed Test and Setup!
https://youtu.be/3bsqVPwsPwQ

The Best RV Internet Set Up - Full Time RV Living
https://youtu.be/L1EzZ6aFxPU

Marine Chartplotter PC - Open CPN on ASUS QM1

https://youtu.be/JYhsQSQOEbM

6. Applications

How to Live the Van Life and Be a Full Time Student

https://youtu.be/QzcdeFD42vU

DIY RV Office: How We Created 2 RV Work Space WITHOUT using the Dining Table | Full-Time RV Life

https://youtu.be/oE62OZ5QAww

My Morning Routine for Productivity | Minimalist VanLife

https://youtu.be/akyxfzs22hE

Creative Ways to Make Money while Cruising on a Sailboat - Sailing Miss Lone Star S5E8

https://youtu.be/caZmZs4JpxI

VAN LIFE ENTERTAINMENT - WE GOT A TV !!

https://youtu.be/iieCJk2E7dw

It's MOVIE NIGHT on Zatara! Our On-Board Entertainment System (Ep 118)

https://youtu.be/CLuESTDVZyk

7. Water

Pumped Water Systems - Camper Van Conversion Series

https://youtu.be/7gieUNuZan4

BEST WATER SYSTEM FOR VAN LIFE

https://youtu.be/9XEL-hj1F3w

PLUMBING & WATER SYSTEM In A Van Or RV (off grid plumbing for newbies) #vanlife

https://youtu.be/0kbKg3UbAXQ

How to make water on a sailboat (and how to build your own watermaker) // Ryan's tech corner #3

https://youtu.be/tETjcFKccjM

Quick Tips with Captain Frank - Water System

https://youtu.be/-Ov-24uJ8oE

Basic Sailboat Plumbing System - Pearson Triton Osprey Refit Part 11

https://youtu.be/Qq6mk2LjOzY

8. Air

Easy & Inexpensive camper Mods on a budget: DIY Electric Vent Fan

https://youtu.be/ikBuYB7S-fY

DIY $300 Dive Hookah for Boat Bottom Cleaning

https://youtu.be/nODxIJeGGyw

Life is Like Sailing - Humidity

https://youtu.be/guADtkWHRlM

Everything an Air Purifier Can and Can't Do

https://youtu.be/VidZMqmTgJQ

Moisture Is Van Life's BIGGEST Problem | VENTILATION and CONDENSATION

https://youtu.be/AiZmkcK4ufY

9. Food

Food On a Boat - Your Questions Answered

https://youtu.be/gKcVxvhb0Zk

5 Food Hacks for Living in a Van

https://youtu.be/DVwdb94G0yo

10. Heating

Best Van Heating - Which heater is best for your Camper van conversion?

https://youtu.be/ESVK57Fqi8U

22. Central Heating on my Narrowboat, Webasto Boiler

https://youtu.be/Us5dThtk2BY

Heating your boat when it's actually cold - diesel heaters compared

https://youtu.be/qV3KsQe7VPI

How to Choose a Boat Heater

https://youtu.be/d1DA4G3zUL8

11. Cooling

How to Power an RV Air Conditioner with Solar - Full Time RV Living

https://youtu.be/XHPIEy9Ciac

Return to Seasons - Boat Work and Systems - Isotherm Refridgerator Install

https://youtu.be/TEfbzXR1pPU

12. Sanitation

Laundry on a Boat: How Do We Do It?

https://youtu.be/NXYPHasQHtk

New Sailboat Laundry Room Complete with Rainman Water Maker (Sailing Satori) OTH:11

https://youtu.be/_7c7kYkT5OA

5 GREAT VANLIFE SHOWER SYSTEMS

https://youtu.be/VZkYE1K43cM

13. Wastage

Disposing of gray Water When Extended Boondocking
https://youtu.be/jipI9D72tkA
VanLife Toilet Options - What I use and some other ideas and thoughts
https://youtu.be/vN7v46Sn3Ds
Life is Like Sailing - Head Systems - Part 1
https://youtu.be/aCRFJqxga3E

14. Health

The surprisingly dramatic role of nutrition in mental health | Julia Rucklidge | TEDxChristchurch
https://youtu.be/3dqXHHCc5lA
What if I get sick on the road? Nomadic Health Care!
https://youtu.be/v6g4jefalgI
VAN LIFE SPAIN | mental health & fitness routines while traveling
https://youtu.be/DxV6qKbZrHw

15. Pests

#149 BUGS On A Boat!! What To Do??
https://youtu.be/vRO0PbCHDgA
How to check and clean your boat for marine pests - advice from an Auckland boatie
https://youtu.be/4qCyuwfuaqo
Bed Bugs in Van Life | How to Kill Bed Bugs Instantly (Save Yourself Today)
https://youtu.be/V1vcCgwuY58

16. Address

Where to Make your State Residence and How to Do it
https://youtu.be/jntFl_5FiA8
Motorhome Monday Domicile State Shootout
https://youtu.be/Z0zpGH0rXWo
How Do We Get Our Mail as RVers & Cruisers? | FAQ
https://youtu.be/-8BJDLROpnI
How to get Mail on the Road: Mail Forwarding
https://youtu.be/XylgnHXA0go

17. Stopping

HOW TO ANCHOR A SAILBOAT - TIPS & ADVICE - Sailing Q&A 20
https://youtu.be/aSLPAQGsPUk
Van Life - Top 10 Free Overnight Parking Spots
https://youtu.be/oqPiP2JYVNc
10 FREE Places to RV Park Overnight
https://youtu.be/aT_zF0OMWfA

18. Security

How We DEFEND Against PIRATES
https://youtu.be/BIZDPKRE3tk
Van Life: Solo Female Safety Tips
https://youtu.be/fHQtQWdVsh0
Internet Security While Traveling the World
https://youtu.be/jMyex5vk5yY

19. Space

Storage & Organization | Sailing Britican
https://youtu.be/aK-VdF6JXAk
TINY LIVING in our VAN with TONS of STORAGE!!! | VAN LIFE
https://youtu.be/p0pZuQIhUy8
15 amazing diy ideas for organizing your boat
https://youtu.be/VE_QnCrJb6o

20. Philosophy

The Secret of Life - Alan Watts
https://youtu.be/iZ8so-ld-l0

21. The Minivan Conversion

Fully Converted Chevy Minivan for Living the Dream - Van Tour
https://youtu.be/Z8CENn_WY6k
Minivan Conversion | Build From Start To Finish | #VanLife
https://youtu.be/eMbaenvfHNM
A Fantastic Super Cheap and Easy Van Build With Almost No Construction or Tools Required
https://youtu.be/25VBk8AOqRQ

Incredible Minivan Camper Van RV Conversion DIY Wet Bath Tour

https://youtu.be/8eP6ic-NyWs

Mini Van Camper Custom DIY Conversion Tour

https://youtu.be/s0wnLOlCaR8

VAN TOUR \\ Retired Nurse Living In a Professionally Converted Minivan

https://youtu.be/m2KkPVOvVQA

Honda Element Micro-camper

https://youtu.be/qfIWjVnueSI

Stealth MiniVan Camper conversion. Blending in with a Practical Build out in this Tiny Van Home.

https://youtu.be/PT8qOPA1zFk

22. The Van Conversion

THIS IS HOW YOU CONVERT A VAN - The Ultimate Sprinter Self-build Conversion

https://youtu.be/4hD19_0jl68

Van Tour | COUPLE design UNIQUE vanbuild, BEAUTIFUL wood work and SLIDING BED

https://youtu.be/o1Hv5MoEKV0

DIY Camper Van Build from Start to Finish | Tour and Recap

https://youtu.be/O3LUnrbhXlU

Van Life - From Cargo Van to Camper Van – Tour Our Stealth CamperVan

https://youtu.be/OigUyvSOV0Y

Dude Lives Full Time In A Van With His Dog and Cat | Shower, Solar, & Bathroom in a ProMaster!

https://youtu.be/KC2SCZL1QWc

How to Build a Home Made Camper Van - Start to Finish DIY

https://youtu.be/I-F-h8zMcJE

Our Van Build Is Done!

https://youtu.be/Plc4RKwxtvU

Chevrolet Express Camper Van - Introduction and Ceiling Build

https://youtu.be/8epCqUxFrWs

Chevy express 3500 extended cargo van tour.

https://youtu.be/3ADBOGJu_v0

Aussie VAN BUILD & CONVERSION | Van Life

https://youtu.be/8V-dPgooqMg

23. The Truck Conversion

Van Tour - Beautiful Box Van Luton Conversion
https://youtu.be/I6UsKNYpnWg

How To Convert a Luton Box Van Into an Off-Grid Camper / Tiny Home !
https://youtu.be/KOiLCGb2R20

From Box Truck to Tiny House - Full Build Time-lapse
https://youtu.be/7ohdKusa6zg

55+ Build RV out of a U Haul with $5200 Used U Haul with an Office, Solar, all the comforts of home!
https://youtu.be/1G62JHALM5Q

I'M BACK! // House truck update tour
https://youtu.be/DllYl1z1KF8

10 Impressive Truck Bed Campers Made in the Good Ole' U.S.A
https://youtu.be/vn73KzgXKgI

Off grid truck Camper build - How to Build
https://youtu.be/nMTIxlwSDIQ

Clever DIY Self-Build Tiny House Truck Camper Tour
https://youtu.be/b6UVNkP5QzI

Alaska Overland Truck Cabin Official FULL TOUR : Truck House Life Episode 4
https://youtu.be/ENZ2KjlN71A

24. The Electric Trailer Build

Making a new trailer axle #2021
https://youtu.be/PmeDIQqtYiI

Building an 18' flat trailer car carrier/hauler with dove tail project part 3
https://youtu.be/iEtZ0Ioiy24

How to Build a DIY Travel Trailer - The Frame (part 1)
https://youtu.be/bHF-qr0Z5AA

Enclosed trailer build | Episode 4 | The walls
https://youtu.be/AWbGoRzvFPg

teardrop trailer build
https://youtu.be/cxT2gcyCvvE

Cargo Trailer to Camper Conversion - How We Did It in 4 weeks
https://youtu.be/o9x3J84CrN0

Cargo trailer conversion build part 1
https://youtu.be/Xx9OmerbnS4

25. The Sailboat Refit

Catalina 30
https://youtu.be/_v9_vmKMja4
[UNAVAILABLE] Used 1982 Catalina 30 in San Pedro, California
https://youtu.be/AT1wWsXJl5Q
Bringing Matsu ll back to life. A Catalina 30 landsinker.
https://youtu.be/b3k_xiBTWNQ
1984 Catalina refit
https://youtu.be/lkXi6TC9c_w
Yacht Windora's Refit
https://youtu.be/SEkJ1SbwyrY
Buying Our Liveaboard Sailboat! - Sailing ShaggySeas Ep. 2
https://youtu.be/l63GDdzyoTI
How to buy a liveaboard sailboat - Sailing Q&A 22
https://youtu.be/PQyn02VT1jY
A Liveaboard and World Cruising Sailboat Tour - Sailing Vessel Adventurer - Season 2 Ep 12
https://youtu.be/Au6R7PLrLbo

26. The Motorboat Refit

Welcome Aboard my Vintage Chris Craft Cruiser! - Boat Tour
https://youtu.be/HOeEDIGIbXw
Nordhavn 40 Boat Tour - M/V Cassidy Ep. 14
https://youtu.be/CgUTYqZHzwQ
Moving aboard a boat - Wooden boat restoration - Boat refit - Travels With Geordie #32
https://youtu.be/16HAp_P7VQs
Turning an old boat into an adventure machine!
https://youtu.be/BBm_lPIqHfs

27. The Riverboat Build

How to Build a Small Wooden Boat #1 Not Using Marine Plywood - Electric Powered - The Keel & Stem
https://youtu.be/k0WGFmXe1-4
Bruce Roberts Voyager 388 - Boat Building Kit
https://youtu.be/ttWDy7GRHjw
Boat Building! 2 years in 22 minutes plus bilge stringer prep.
https://youtu.be/sVqIueFKfv0

28. The Sailing Catamaran Build

Antares Mast Height
https://youtu.be/adNpyoMdnf8
How to build a sailing catamaran from nothing.
https://youtu.be/EitqKNsiUOA
The Boat That Walked
https://youtu.be/u9F5xbIZbHI
Llinase Catamaran - Twelve Thousand Hours and a Two Mile Weld
https://youtu.be/5eB0VGCsOPc
Construction / Building Neos Catamaran 48 ft 1rst part
https://youtu.be/0ihuOBoL5IM

29. The Solar Trimaran Build

LEEN 56 animation
https://youtu.be/PPKX9rs5DbQ
Solar Yacht: Silent Yachts 55 Technical Tour
https://youtu.be/nVG5SMwxLYY
Building a Trimaran Part 1
https://youtu.be/duZQ6kvQNU0
BUILDING A 64' TRIMARAN FROM SCRATCH!!! THE HANSTAIGER X1
https://youtu.be/Lx4M1B3yGno

30. On Batteries

DIY 48V LiFePO4 Battery for solar system
https://youtu.be/w4Wy_dp0ad4
LiFePo4 crashtest - Lithium Ionen Crashtest
https://youtu.be/p21iZVFHEZk

31. Electric Marine Propulsion

https://www.youtube.com/channel/UC6BAWH7F1cixqeoS1XlLYww
Our Electric Motor (Electro-Beke, part 1) — Sailing Uma [Step 17]
https://youtu.be/_L1xmG5Kndw
ELECTRIC SAILBOAT | Choosing an electric motor for your sailboat (ep#29) Spoondrifters
https://youtu.be/gGO4-2SXnqY

32. Navigable Inland Waterways

Introduction to the Great Loop
https://youtu.be/hlv2RNE9eLk
America's Inland Waterways System - Part 1
https://youtu.be/rxHIk5ARHLI
The Story of British Canals - VHS - 1993 (Canal History Docu)
https://youtu.be/gDVdcTFV8Nk
Sailing through Russia's Waterways (Documentary, Discovery, History)
https://youtu.be/Cd-7riM3xzI
From Sweden to the Mediterranean Sea in 3 minutes
https://youtu.be/Jwa_1cifDss
Canal cruising hiring and buying a boat in Europe and the Canal du Midi
https://youtu.be/Gpt1zF9CrEU

33. Protecting Electronics

Electrolube Conformal Coating Vlog - Application of Conformal Coating
https://youtu.be/mtsW-aNKddQ
How to Waterproof Electronics (the clean way)
https://youtu.be/HOu5hRqSDtU
Introduction to Electronics Cooling - ATS Webinar
https://youtu.be/ucXwrU5vqVg
What is a Cold Plate and How Does it Work?
https://youtu.be/G6Ys4qQuYPw
Assembling a Raspberry Pi Based 7: Touchscreen GPS Chartplotter for $150
https://youtu.be/SZqU6Xv31ZU
Save $$$ Thousands on Boat Electronics!
https://youtu.be/ROr1j1cPkRE

Websites

2. Propulsion

https://vanclan.co/
https://evsource.com/
https://ddmotorsystems.com/
https://www.elcomotoryachts.com/
http://www.electricmotorwholesale.com/

https://www.sailinguma.com/the-motor

https://www.cloudelectric.com/default.asp

https://www.thunderstruck-ev.com/

http://motenergy.com/

https://www.hpevs.com/

https://evolveelectrics.com/

https://www.electricmotorsport.com/

https://www.cafeelectric.com/

https://www.kellycontroller.com/

https://www.curtisinstruments.com/

http://www.sevcon.com/

https://www.worldwideelectric.net/product-category/gear-reducers/

https://www.surpluscenter.com/Gear-Reducers/

http://www.evalbum.com/304

https://betamarine.co.uk/resources/Sales_Brochures/Hybrid-HE-SB/#page=1

http://bluegasmarine.com/

https://www.cruisersforum.com/forums/f48/cost-of-new-mast-and-rigging-138113.html

https://improvesailing.com/questions/cost-of-new-sails

https://www.parkermotion.com/whitepages/Comparing_AC_and_PM_motors.pdf

https://evmc2.wordpress.com/2014/12/04/basic-motor-types-pmdc-bldc-ac-induction-and-synchronous-and-series-dc/

https://plugboats.com/electric-inboard-boat-motors-guide-over-150-motors/

https://www.trailerlife.com/towing/tow-vehicles/diesel-versus-gas/

https://www.alternative-energies.net/pros-and-cons-of-biodiesel/

https://www.enginebuildermag.com/2015/05/cng-and-propane-engine-builds/

https://www.boats.com/reviews/blue-gas-marine-natural-gas-outboard-first-look-video/

https://www.sailmagazine.com/diy/fuel-consumption-tug-vs-cruiser

https://www.vicprop.com/displacement_size.php?action=calculate

3. Structure

https://www.glen-l.com/resources/lumber-suppliers.html

https://www.rvingplanet.com/blog/the-ultimate-guide-to-rv-construction-what-you-need-to-know-before-the-rv-is-yours/

http://www.jrconsumer.com/FreeRVReport.pdf

https://enrg.io/dont-buy-build-high-end-diy-rv/

https://www.synthx.com/articles/trailer-strength.html/

https://www.boats.com/resources/boat-building-construction-resin-fiberglass-cores/

http://building-strip-planked-boats.com/content/introduction

4. Electricity

https://www.gosportsart.com/status-cardio/eco-powr-line/

https://windstreampower.com/

https://www.thegreenmicrogym.com/

https://fetchinketch.net/boat-projects/battery-upgrade/

https://marinehowto.com/lifepo4-batteries-on-boats/

https://rvshare.com/blog/rv-electrical/

https://gnomadhome.com/van-build-solar-electrical-wiring/

https://faroutride.com/electrical-system/

https://marinehowto.com/

https://newwiremarine.com/how-to/wiring-a-boat/

https://www.westmarine.com/WestAdvisor/Marine-Wire-Terminal-Tech-Specs

https://www.wired2fish.com/boats-trucks-electronics/10-basic-rules-for-wiring-a-boat/

http://www.marinesurvey.com/yacht/ElectricalSystems.htm

https://www.uscgboating.org/regulations/builders-handbook-downloads.php

5. Networking

https://bareboat-necessities.github.io/

https://www.thegpsstore.com/Marine-Networking-101.aspx

https://boatprojects.blogspot.com/2012/12/beginners-guide-to-nmea-2000-nmea-0183.html

https://seabits.com/best-lte-antenna-booster-boat/

https://faroutride.com/internet-vanlife/

https://citimarinestore.com/citiguide/how-to-get-internet-on-your-boat-your-best-options/

https://www.rvmobileinternet.com/overview/

https://www.technomadia.com/2019/02/our-mobile-internet-setup-for-rv-and-boat-how-weve-kept-online-for-13-years-of-technomadic-travel/

6. Applications

https://www.mentalfloss.com/article/585137/6-benefits-reading-every-day

https://www.artofmanliness.com/articles/how-and-why-to-become-a-lifelong-learner/

https://liveyourlegend.net/self-guided-education-manifesto-teach-yourself-anything/

https://lifehacker.com/top-10-highly-desired-skills-you-can-teach-yourself-5905835

https://www.freecodecamp.org/news/a-guide-to-teaching-yourself-to-code-and-getting-a-job-db7908dfb12e/

https://lifehackmethod.com/2020/04/05/how-to-be-productive-work-at-home/

https://thisanxiousmum.com/how-to-be-productive-at-home/

https://outboundliving.com/working-making-money/

https://careerkarma.com/blog/remote-working-guide/

7. Water

https://www.cdc.gov/healthywater/drinking/travel/backcountry_water_treatment.html

https://www.msrgear.com/blog/complete-guide-to-water-treatment/

https://www.ncbi.nlm.nih.gov/books/NBK310823/

8. Air

https://www.epa.gov/sites/production/files/2018-07/documents/guide_to_air_cleaners_in_the_home_2nd_edition.pdf

https://www.deeperblue.com/beginners-guide-scuba-diving/

https://www.aircompressorsdirect.com/stories/156-How-to-Pick-the-Perfect-Air-Compressor.html

9. Food

https://theboatgalley.com/tag/boat-cooking/

www.propanesafetyfirst.com

https://www.ag.ndsu.edu/publications/food-nutrition/food-storage-guide-answers-the-question/fn579.pdf

10. Heating

https://rvshare.com/blog/rv-hvac/

https://www.sailmagazine.com/diy/warm-and-snug

11. Cooling

https://www.marinetalk.com/best-marine-refrigerators/

https://www.sailmagazine.com/diy/beat-the-heat-retrofit-an-ac-system

https://www.gonewiththewynns.com/air-conditioning-sailboat

https://rvshare.com/blog/rv-air-conditioner/

12. Sanitation

https://www.theroadisourhome.com/2018/06/18/shower-toilet-build-how-to-van-conversion/

https://outboundliving.com/hygiene/

https://www.sailorsforthesea.org/programs/green-boating-guide/non-toxic-cleaning-products

13. Wastage

https://rvshare.com/blog/rv-gray-water-tank/

https://www.boatus.org/study-guide/environment/laws/

https://www.doityourselfrv.com/rv-toilet-etiquette-tips/

https://www.boatus.org/study-guide/environment/waste/

14. Health

https://www.sailingtotem.com/2014/04/healthcare-while-cruising.html

https://winnebagolife.com/2016/01/health-insurance-challenge-coverage-for-full-time-rvers

https://matchamotovan.com/vanlife-cost-health-insurance/

https://gnomadhome.com/vanlife-anxiety/

15. Pests

https://blog.goodsam.com/creepy-crawlers-ban-bugs-from-attacking-your-rv/

https://www.tripsavvy.com/keep-your-rv-pest-free-505133

https://rvshare.com/blog/how-to-prevent-pests-and-bugs-in-your-camper/

https://insectcop.net/spider-bird-control-for-boat-dock/

https://www.godownsize.com/mice-boat-guide/

16. Address

https://www.lifesaport.com/home/2017/10/24/legally-speaking-how-the-law-can-apply-to-being-a-liveaboard

https://www.liveaboardhq.com/how-to-get-started-liveaboard

https://gnomadhome.com/vanlife-mail-and-packages-for-nomads/

https://twomeander.com/how-to-establish-a-legal-state-residency-domicile-as-a-nomad/

https://www.escapees.com

https://americasmailbox.com

17. Stopping

https://dbscweb.files.wordpress.com/2013/08/bradney-mooring-and-anchoring-leaflet.pdf

https://www.outdoorsy.com/blog/ultimate-guide-finding-best-spots-park-rv

http://mywilddreams.net/2017/10/27/vanlife-how-to-where-to-park-and-sleep-in-cities/

https://thedyrt.com/magazine/lifestyle/boondocking-guide-free-camping/

www.niche.com

www.couchsurfing.com

www.boondockerswelcome.com

www.snagaslip.com

www.dockskipper.com

piershare.com

marinas.com

find-a-mooring.com

18. Security

https://www.thefitoutpontoon.co.uk/safety-security/secuirty-onboard/

https://www.saltwatersportsman.com/fishing-boats/marine-security-systems-boats/

https://www.tripsavvy.com/installing-an-rv-security-system-2912514

https://camperreport.com/5-great-security-system-options-for-an-rv-and-what-id-pick/

https://www.wired.com/2017/12/digital-security-guide/

https://rorypecktrust.org/freelance-resources/digital-security/

19. Space

https://unclutteredsimplicity.com/storage-solutions-for-small-spaces/

https://rvshare.com/blog/rv-storage-solutions/

https://www.sailingchance.com/smart-boat-organization-hacks/

https://blueturtletrawler.com/boat-interior-storage-ideas-or-where-to-put-all-your-stuff/

20. Philosophy

https://www.philosophybasics.com/

https://newmediarockstars.com/2014/10/the-7-youtube-philosophers-you-just-cant-miss/

21. The Minivan Conversion

https://www.gettingstamped.com/diy-minivan-camper-campervan-conversion/

https://www.your-rv-lifestyle.com/how-to-live-in-a-minivan-camper-successfully/

https://www.thewaywardhome.com/san-francisco-couple-buys-used-van-converts-it-for-200-to-travel-the-us/

https://mybackpackerlife.com/canada/minivan-camper-conversion/

https://www.parkedinparadise.com/stealth-camping/

https://www.doityourselfrv.com/van-dwelling-mini-van-getting-started/

22. The Van Conversion

https://faroutride.com/build-journal/

https://outboundliving.com/van-living-diy-camper-van-conversion-guide/

https://divineontheroad.com/build-a-van/

https://meanderingexplorers.com/build/

https://www.theroadisourhome.com/2017/11/15/van-build/

https://gnomadhome.com/build-your-van/

https://thevanual.com/

https://mowgli-adventures.com/campervan-conversion-guide/

https://livelikepete.com/category/van-build/

https://www.parkedinparadise.com/how-to-live-in-van/

https://www.spintheglobeproject.com/how-to-build-a-camper-van/

https://saraandalexjames.com/van-build-layout-guide

23. The Truck Conversion

https://www.vanchitecture.com/2017/12/15/16-gorgeous-box-truck-camper-van-conversion/

https://camperism.co/2018/07/07/25-awesome-box-truck-conversion-ideas/

https://tinyhousetalk.com/box-truck-converted-into-amazing-diy-off-grid-solar-motorhome/

https://www.curbed.com/2018/7/27/17617598/camper-conversion-skoolie-diy-vanlife

https://imgur.com/a/Dmlel

https://itstillruns.com/convert-box-truck-motorhome-6308063.html

https://tinyhousetalk.com/cheap-diy-box-truck-motorhome-conversion/

https://www.doityourselfrv.com/u-haul-box-truck/

https://www.wildwewander.com/diy-truck-camper

https://campersmarts.com/truck-camper-guide

https://www.desktodirtbag.com/build-pickup-truck-bed-camper-guide/

https://outdoorfact.com/how-to-build-a-lightweight-truck-camper/

https://www.doityourselfrv.com/truck-camper-pop-top/

24. The Electric Trailer Build

https://drivinglaws.aaa.com/tag/trailer-dimensions/

https://mechanicalelements.com/trailer-axles-101/

https://www.consumerreports.org/other-motor-vehicles/beginners-guide-to-rv-trailers/

https://mechanicalelements.com/how-to-setup-a-trailer-frame/

https://rvshare.com/blog/homemade-camper/

https://rvshare.com/blog/custom-teardrop/

https://camperreport.com/travel-trailer-camping-guide-beginners/

https://newatlas.com/dethleffs-electric-coco-caravan/56056/

https://www.gorv.com.au/world-first-hybrid-drive-caravan-system/

25. The Sailboat Refit

https://sailboatdata.com/sailboat/catalina-30

https://www.thunderstruck-ev.com/sevcon-brushless-sailboat-kit-10.5kw.html

https://www.practical-sailor.com/sailboat-reviews/sailboats-21-30ft/catalina-30

https://www.practical-sailor.com/sails-rigging-deckgear/improve-your-catalina-30-upgrading-the-worlds-most-popular-30-footer

https://www.spinsheet.com/boat-reviews/catalina-30-used-boat-review

https://www.docksidereports.com/hull_to_deck_joint.htm

https://mycatalina30.wordpress.com/

https://www.catalinadirect.com/shop-by-boat/catalina-250/engine/fuel-tank-17-gal-c-250c-30-w-inspection-port/

https://refit.guide/

https://mrandmrshowe.com/lifestyle-blog/empress-sailboat-interior-refit

https://www.cruisingworld.com/classic-plastic-refit-on-budget/

https://www.cruisingworld.com/how/refit-reality-check/

26. The Motorboat Refit

https://commanderclub.com/page/42-commander

https://captainjohn.org/GL-Boat.html

https://www.pbo.co.uk/gear/pbo-great-uk-antifouling-showdown-26053/3

https://www.powerandmotoryacht.com/maintenance/refit-guide

https://yachtsurvey.com/usedboats.htm

https://www.mby.com/maintenance/refurbishing-classic-motor-yacht-16304

27. The Riverboat Build

https://carveyourcreation.com/how-to-build-a-wooden-boat

www.vicprop.com/displacement_size.php?action=calculate

28. The Sailing Catamaran Build

https://www.boatdesign.net/

https://catamaranconcepts.com/category/hull-deck-design/bridgedeck-clearance/

http://www.sail-the-difference.com/index.php?id=40

https://liveantares.com/exterior-images-antares-44-gs/

https://www.glpautogas.info/documentos/11GASOLINE%20AND%20LPG%20comparison.pdf

https://www.puremajek.com/

http://www.schionningdesigns.com.au/kit-process

https://buildacat.com/

https://thecoastalpassage.com/cheapcat.html

29. The Solar Trimaran Build

https://dmsonline.us/why-you-want-a-trimaran/

https://www.boatinternational.com/yachts/editorial-features/galaxy-of-happiness-the-trimaran-taking-yachting-to-another-world—33363

https://www.boatdesign.net/threads/round-bilge-vs-hard-chine.37594/

https://smalltridesign.com/

https://plougonver.com/home-built-trimaran-plans/

https://www.dixdesign.com/3fold6.htm

https://edhorstmanmultihulldesigns.com/triplans/index.php

30. On Batteries

https://marinehowto.com/lifepo4-batteries-on-boats/

http://nordkyndesign.com/protection-and-management-of-marine-lithium-battery-banks/

https://www.diyelectriccar.com/threads/bottom-balancing.85458/

https://kwsaki.blogspot.com/2013/01/how-to-bottom-balance.html

https://www.solarpaneltalk.com/forum/off-grid-solar/batteries-energy-storage/general-batteries/369810-what-is-wrong-with-wiring-batteries-in-parallel

http://www.smartgauge.co.uk/batt_con.html

https://batteryuniversity.com/learn/article/serial_and_parallel_battery_configurations

http://nordkyndesign.com/assembling-a-lithium-iron-phosphate-marine-house-bank/

http://nordkyndesign.com/lithium-battery-banks-fundamentals/

31. Electric Marine Propulsion

https://www.sailmagazine.com/diy/fuel-consumption-tug-vs-cruiser

https://www.passagemaker.com/technical/the-nuts-and-bolts-of-propellers-part-1

https://sailboatdata.com/sailboat/catalina-30

https://catalina30.com/TechLib/Propellers/propellers.htm

http://downeasteryachts.com/wp-content/uploads/2009/11/Universal-Diesel-Model-30-operation-and-maintenance-manual.pdf

https://www.catalinadirect.com/shop-by-boat/catalina-350/engine/props-etc/prop-shaft-46-14quot-to-58-14quot-for-c-30-c-320-c-34-and-c-36/

https://commanderclub.com/forum

https://st4.ning.com/topology/rest/1.0/file/get/2057936919?profile=original

https://sailboatdata.com/sailboat/lagoon-42-2

https://www.sailmagazine.com/boats/boat-review-lagoon-42

https://plugboats.com/electric-inboard-boat-motors-guide-over-150-motors/

32. Navigable Inland Waterways

https://www.greatloop.org/

https://captainjohn.org/

https://www.usace.army.mil/

https://en.wikipedia.org/wiki/Inland_waterways_of_the_United_States

https://canalrivertrust.org.uk/enjoy-the-waterways/canal-and-river-network

https://www.ukwaterwaysguide.co.uk/canal-maps.php

https://www.britannica.com/technology/canal-waterway/Major-inland-waterways-of-Europe

https://vagrantsoftheworld.com/russian-river-cruise-st-petersburg-to-moscow/

https://www.eurocanals.com/

http://www.unece.org/trans/main/sc3/where.html

https://www.wwinn.org/

33. Protecting Electronics

https://www.howtogeek.com/209024/htg-explains-how-water-resistance-ratings-work-for-gadgets/

https://geargadgetsandgizmos.com/what-really-is-water-resistant-waterproof-and-ipx-ratings/

https://www.w8ji.com/dielectric_grease_vs_conductive_grease.htm

https://forums.iboats.com/forum/boat-repair-and-restoration/electrical-electronics-audio-and-trolling-motors/531617-dielectric-grease-on-connections

https://www.thehulltruth.com/1309211-post1.html

https://www.dell.com/community/Desktops-General-Read-Only/Corrosion-in-computers/td-p/3679814

https://electrolube.com/knowledge_base/protecting-electronics-from-corrosive-operating-environments-to-increase-end-product-lifetime-and-reliability/

https://www.powerandmotoryacht.com/electronics/personal-computers-sea

https://www.boatdesign.net/threads/discussion-multipurpose-onboard-computers-human-inputs-human-outputs.20169/#post-169245

https://www.boatdesign.net/threads/discussion-multi-purpose-onboard-computers.19458/

https://www.boatdesign.net/threads/archive-onboard-computers.57866/#post-803490

https://www.custommarineproducts.com/marine-solar-panels.html

Lightning Source UK Ltd.
Milton Keynes UK
UKHW051513100920
369515UK00004BA/9